T0258889

Software Configuration Management

Software Configuration Management

Jessica Keyes

AUERBACH PUBLICATIONS

A CRC Press Company

Boca Raton   London   New York   Washington, D.C.

Library of Congress Cataloging-in-Publication Data

Keyes, Jessica, 1950–
    Software configuration management / Jessica Keyes.
       p. cm.
    Includes bibliographical references and index.
    ISBN 0-8493-1976-5
    1. Software configuration management. I. Title.

QA76.76.C69K49 2004
005.1′5—dc22
                                      2003062981

Visit the CRC Press Web site at www.crcpress.com

© 2004 by CRC Press LLC
Auerbach is an imprint of CRC Press LLC

No claim to original U.S. Government works
International Standard Book Number 0-8493-1976-5
Library of Congress Card Number 2003062981
2 3 4 5 6 7 8 9 0

DEDICATION

This book is most appreciatively dedicated to my friends, old and new, and particularly my family.

CONTENTS

FOREWORD

I have written more than a few books and articles about software engineering. I have also spent five years teaching this same subject to computer science graduate students. While it is easy to teach the "process" of systems development and design, it is far more difficult to implement it in such a way to produce quality-oriented systems in a productive manner.

What is needed is a framework that serves to organize the life-cycle activities that make up the software engineering process. This framework is configuration management.

Those of us in the field for more than a few years tend to think of configuration management as simple versioning or change control. It is this, but it is much more. Using configuration management, usually referred to simply as CM, the *process* of change can be managed from idea inception to product deployment, ensuring quality control as well as cost control.

CM is all things to all people. It well serves the developer, producer, supplier, and customer. Lager [2002] says that it prevents technical anarchy, avoids the embarrassment of customer dissatisfaction, and maintains the consistency between the product and the information about the product.

Computer Associates (CA) did a survey of organizations in Australia and New Zealand in 2002 [Cooper 2003]. The survey found that:

- 88 percent deploy applications on multiple platforms
- 44 percent deploy on more than four platforms
- 61 percent maintain multiple releases of software
- 52 percent require support for concurrent development
- 46 percent maintain multiple life cycles for different kinds of development
- 39 percent make frequent changes to packaged applications

Organizations are operating in an ultra-competitive global arena where change is risky. Not managing that change is even riskier. As demonstrated by the CA study, today's computer hardware and software infrastructures are complex mega-beasts that span multiple devices, platforms, and programming languages, not the least of which is Web based. Making a mistake can lead to lost customer confidence, poor quality control, wasted resources, and ultimately diminished competitive advantage.

Simply put, all organizations need CM.

Jessica Keyes

References

Cooper, Andy, "Change Management: Quality and Quantity — Does It Have to Be a Trade-Off?," White Paper, Computer Associates, May 2003.

Lager, Alan E., "The Evolution of Configuration Management Standards," Logistics Spectrum, Huntsville, AL, January–March 2002.

PREFACE

Configuration management (CM) grew up in the military. Military standard 973 (MIL-STD-973) became the "bible" for CM and to this day remains the basis for all configuration management standards, including EIA-649.

This handbook discusses CM from a standards perspective, relying on the original DoD MIL-STD-973 as well as EIA-649 to describe the elements of configuration management from a software engineering perspective.

This book has two parts. The first section is composed of 14 chapters that explain, from a practical perspective, every facet of configuration management as it relates to software engineering. The second section consists of more than 20 appendices that contain a plethora of valuable, "real-world" CM templates.

The content of the book is extensive and inclusive. In it you can find everything from CM planning to configuration identification to verification and audit. The author would like you to think of this book as a sourcebook — a compilation of techniques, templates, and best practices in the field. With it, you will have everything you need to implement and run a sound configuration management program in your organization.

This book is also vendor-neutral, which should be an important factor in your selection of a book on CM. All too often, the process of CM within an organization is wrapped around the tool that is chosen rather than the other way around, which is more appropriate. The author likes to call CM implementations based on particular toolsets "vendor-based CM" as opposed to the more robust implementation of CM, which must be vendor-neutral. So, in this book, you will not find documentation on any of the more popular CM tools on the market. What you will find, in Chapter 14, is a serious discussion of what to look for in a CM tool and then a list of some toolsets you might want to review.

Who Should Read This Book?

This book is intended for a wide audience. Those in charge of the configuration management process will find in this book everything they need to implement and run a successful CM program. However, other professionals will also benefit from this book. CIOs, project managers, and systems designers will find that this book provides a wealth of "how-to's" that correlate nicely with the software engineering tasks they must carry out on a daily basis. Quality control personnel and EDP auditors will find a close correlation between CM audit and verification and traditional testing. Finally, end-user management will find that this book provides some very useful guidance that will assist them in managing a quality and productive systems implementation effort.

Note: The author has made every attempt to acknowledge the sources of information used, including copyrighted material. If for any reason a reference has been misquoted or a source used inappropriately, please bring it to the author's attention for rectification or correction in the next edition.

1

INTRODUCTION TO SOFTWARE CONFIGURATION MANAGEMENT

Software configuration management (SCM, or just plain CM) is an organizational framework — that is, a discipline — for managing the evolution of computer systems throughout all stages of systems development. That a rigorous framework for producing quality computer systems is needed is undeniable according to the following statistics:

More than half (53 percent) of IT projects overrun their schedules and budgets, 31 percent are cancelled, and only 16 percent are completed on time.
Source: Standish Group
Publication date: 2000

Of those projects that failed in 2000, 87 percent went more than 50 percent over budget.
Source: KPMG Information Technology
Publication date: 2000

45 percent of failed projects in 2000 did not produce the expected benefits, and 88 to 92 percent went over schedule.
Source: KPMG Information Technology
Publication date: 2000

Half of new software projects in the United States will go significantly over budget.
Source: META Group
Publication date: 2000

The average cost of a development project for a large company is $2,322,000; for a medium company, it is $1,331,000; and for a small company, it is $434,000.
Source: Standish Group
Publication date: 2000

$81 billion was the estimated cost for cancelled projects in 1995.
Source: Standish Group
Publication date: 1995

More than half (52.7 percent) of projects were projected to cost over 189 percent of their original estimates.
Source: Standish Group
Publication date: 2000

Projects completed by the largest American companies have only approximately 42 percent of the originally proposed features and functions.
88 percent of all U.S. projects are over schedule, over budget, or both.
Source: Standish Group
Publication date: 2000

The average time overrun on projects is 222 percent of original estimates.
Source: Standish Group
Publication date: 2000

During the past decade, the capabilities and sheer innovativeness of software technology has far outpaced our ability to manage the complexity of problems that software development must address. Unfortunately, the ability to develop and deliver reliable, usable software within budget and schedule commitments continues to elude many software organizations.

Software configuration management (SCM) provides the means to manage software processes in a structured, orderly, and productive manner. SCM spans all areas of the software life cycle and impacts all data (see Chapter 10) and processes. Hence, maximum benefit is derived when SCM is viewed as an engineering discipline rather than an art form, which, unfortunately, many developers have a tendency to do.

As an engineering discipline, SCM provides a level of support, control, and service to the organization:

- *Support.* SCM is a support function in that it supports program engineers and developers, the program, the corporation, and, in a number of situations, the customer.
- *Control.* SCM is a control function in that it controls specifications, documents, drawings, requirements, tools, software, and other deliverables.
- *Service.* SCM is a service provider in that it supports people and controls data. The role of the SCM manager is to ensure that (1) SCM personnel are properly trained and have the necessary resources (budget and tools) to do an efficient and effective job; (2) a proper balance of control and support is tailor made to each program that is being supported; and, (3) the SCM function is flexible and can accommodate the changing needs and requirements of the developers, customers, the program, and the company.

The process of SCM has not really changed much during the past 20 to 30 years. However, the environment that SCM operates within has changed significantly and is likely to continue to change. Over the past few decades, we have migrated from centralized mainframes using just a few programming languages such as COBOL and FORTRAN to decentralized, networked, Web-based environments with thousands of devices using hundreds of software packages and dozens of programming languages.

The most significant impacts to SCM have centered on the automated tools and the library systems they operate upon. Up until the 1990s, the entire focus of SCM was on version control with very few vendors from which to choose. Today, there are literally hundreds of small to large SCM vendors promoting a variety of products from simple version control to sophisticated tools that purport to establish and monitor the entire software development and production environment.

Regardless of this amazing diversity, the process of CM is basically immutable — that is, the process does not change, only what is being managed changes. What this means is that CM is as applicable to a mainframe shop as it is to a shop running all Web-based applications in a networked, secured environment. The key is in the process.

SCM AND PROCESS IMPROVEMENT

Improvement depends upon changing current processes along with the accompanying environment. SCM, then, provides the underlying structure for change and process improvement. We refer to this as process-based configuration management.

For example, the first step to improve the product is to know how the product is currently produced. The second step for improvement is to foster an atmosphere in which change can be readily accommodated. If change does not appear possible, then improvement is also unlikely. SCM measurements of current practices and their associated metrics can help identify where processes are working and where they need to be improved. Such change efforts should lead to increased productivity, integrity, conformance, and customer satisfaction.

The Institute of Configuration Management (ICM) defines configuration management (CM) as "the process of managing the full spectrum of an organization's products, facilities, and processes by managing all requirements, including changes, and assuring that the results conform to those requirements" [ICM 1998]. By this definition, CM can also be called *process configuration management* because it includes the process of managing an organization's processes and procedures.

Many organizations can be characterized as Level 1 organizations as defined in the Software Engineering Institute's Software Capability Maturity Model® (SEI SW-CMM). These Level 1 organizations rely heavily on "heroes" to accomplish the work. The organization's processes are not documented, and few people know how the work is accomplished. "The software process is characterized as ad hoc, and occasionally even chaotic. Few processes are defined, and success depends on individual effort and heroics" [Paulk 1995].

An effective SCM program, when applied to organizational processes, identifies which processes need to be documented. Any changes to those processes are also tracked and documented. Adhering to these processes will reduce an organization's dependence on heroics for the work to be accomplished and the project to succeed. It also relieves the frustration and problems that arise if one of the "heroes" is not available to perform a task.

SCM is an essential discipline in the everyday activities of defining requirements, designing, writing, compiling, testing, and documenting the software. SCM is not simply version control or format control. It is not a clerical "after-the-fact" function. It is a technical field of expertise with formal practices.

The benefits derived from SCM are directly proportional to the extent that SCM is implemented. The primary objective is to deliver a quality product that meets the stated requirements, on schedule, and within budget. An effective SCM program supports this objective by tracking each requirement from concept through implementation to customer delivery.

MEASUREMENTS AND METRICS

The status accounting aspect of SCM provides management visibility into the state of software products. Status accounting data includes measurements (see Chapter 13) that can show the location of bottlenecks in the software development process, and can indicate the maturity of the software products.

Hermann [1998] describes the use of software changes to measure product maturity and readiness to deliver the software. He goes on to mention other metrics that may be useful, including average severity, severity level distribution, average closure time, charts for each severity level, and charts for each configuration item or sub-system.

A measure can be defined as "a standard of measurement, the extent, dimensions, capacity, etc., of anything, especially as determined by a standard, an act or process of measuring, a result of measurement" [Starrett 1998]. Examples of a measure include the number of defects found in a release or the number of source lines of code delivered. A metric can be defined as "a calculated or composite indicator based on two or more measures, or a quantified measure of the degree to which a system, component, or process possesses a given attribute. An example of a metric is defects per thousand source lines of code" [Starrett 1998].

A metric can also be "a composite of measures that yields systematic insight into the state of processes or products and drives appropriate actions" [Pitts 1997]. Measures (measurements) and metrics can be used to identify areas of the process that require attention. These areas are identified through compiling measurements into metrics. Measurements are compiled in an electronic spreadsheet, a database, or by hand. There are also several management tools that allow collection of measurements and derivation of metrics. The format is not the issue; the data is.

A metrics program should include the following fundamentals [Pitts 1997]:

- A motive that is compelling, not simply conformism
- Benchmarks that define nominal operation of the software development process
- Goals that define the purpose of the metrics program
- Strategy for achieving the goals
- An appropriate model (COCOMO, SLIM, etc.), whether it is a mathematical model or heuristic
- Collection of data that is unobtrusive
- Analysis of the data to find patterns: patterns imply consistency and consistency implies process

- Action on the analysis — change in the process to achieve better results
- Implementation ethics, including trust, value, communication, and understanding

Metrics are used to measure the progress of a project, the quality of its product, the effort necessary to complete the project, etc. One desired outcome of compiling and using these metrics to improve processes is the improvement of the product's value-to-cost ratio. If a change in a process yields an increase in production during a specific timeframe, or yields the same production in a decreased timeframe, the value-to-cost ratio is improved.

Another desired outcome is increased customer satisfaction through meeting their requirements. For example, if defects in software can be traced back to incomplete or faulty requirements definition, the requirements definition process should be reviewed to increase the clarity and completeness of the requirements. The metrics may help show that the customer needs to be more actively involved in defining the requirements clearly and precisely.

BENEFITS OF SCM

There are many benefits to be gained by an organization that practices SCM. Software developers, testers, project managers, quality assurance (QA) personnel, and the customer may benefit from SCM. Benefits include:

1. Organizes tasks and activities that maintain the integrity of the software
2. Helps manage assets
3. Provides ability to track changes made during sequential or parallel development
4. Ensures correct configurations of software (i.e., compatible configurations)
5. Ensures that engineers are implementing changes into the correct "baseline" or version of the software
6. Provides the ability to trace the process from requirement to product
7. Limits legal liability by recording all data — whether flattering to the company or not — including memos, decisions, meeting minutes, changes to requirements/code/test procedures, etc., providing a "paper trail"
8. Helps reduce the life-cycle cost of maintaining software, which can easily exceed the initial cost of development

9. Allows responsibility to be traced to the source (i.e., a requirement problem, coding problem, etc.)
10. Provides for consistent conformance to customer requirements
11. Provides a stable environment for the software development process to be defined, repeated, and improved
12. Enhances compliance with standards being applied
13. Provides an environment in which meaningful measures can be gathered and used
14. Enhances current status accounting
15. Provides data for reports that can be easily generated
16. Allows quick and easy auditing
17. Provides the ability to reproduce circumstances/conditions under which the product was produced by retaining information relative to the production process (tracks changes made to baselines, hardware, compiler versions, etc.)
18. Provides communication channels between groups (system, subsystem, test, interface, etc.)
19. Fosters an ability to improve without being punitive in nature
20. Provides an understanding of when the product is ready for release (when all changes have been processed completely)
21. Helps produce higher quality software

SCM provides visibility into the status of the evolving software product. Software developers, testers, project managers, quality assurance (QA) personnel, and the customer benefit from SCM information.

SCM COMPONENTS

SCM encompasses the everyday tasks within an organization, whether software development or maintenance. Software changes are identified, controlled, and managed throughout project life cycle.

The ten key SCM activities for most common development environments are [Platinum 1998]:

1. Accessing and retrieving software
2. Retrofitting changes across the development life cycle
3. Migrating changes across the development life cycle
4. Managing the compile and build process
5. Managing the distribution of changes
6. Obtaining approvals and sign-offs
7. Managing software change requests
8. Coordinating communication between groups

9. Obtaining project status
10. Tracking bugs and fixes

SCM is divided into the following functional areas, as shown in Figure 1.1.

CONFIGURATION IDENTIFICATION

Configuration identification (see Chapter 4) involves identifying the structure of the software system, uniquely identifying individual components, and making them accessible in some form. The goal of configuration identification is to have the ability to identify the components of a system throughout its life cycle and provide traceability between the software and related software products. Identification answers *What is the configuration of my system? What version of the file is this?* and *What are the components of the system?*

Configuration identification activities include:

- Selecting items to be placed under SCM control
- Developing the software hierarchy
- Creating an identification scheme that reflects the software hierarchy
- Identifying which version of a component can or cannot be included in a working release
- Uniquely identifying the various revisions of the software product
- Defining relationships and interfaces between the various software products
- Releasing configuration documentation
- Establishing configuration baselines

Figure 1.2 presents a typical breakdown of software into its distinct parts and presents a numbering scheme that uniquely identifies each component of a baseline release. The number to the left of the dot is the last baseline or major release. The number to the right of the dot is the version since the last baseline or minor release. Normally, after a new baseline, major release, the number to the right of the dot is zero. A hierarchical scheme is used.

Although key components to be managed are the requirements and source code, related documentation and data should be identified and placed under SCM control. It is important to store and track all environment information and support tools used throughout the software life cycle to ensure that the software can be reproduced.

Items typically put under SCM control include [Kasse 1997]:

- Source code modules

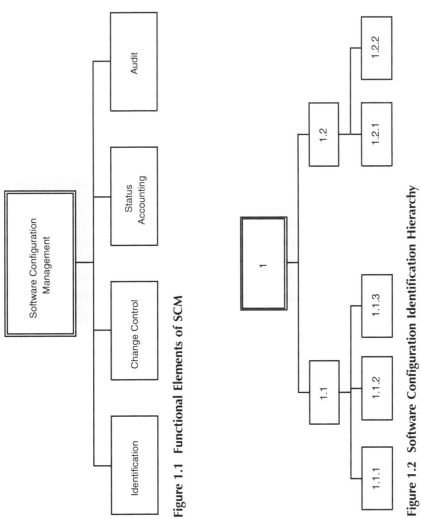

Figure 1.1 Functional Elements of SCM

Figure 1.2 Software Configuration Identification Hierarchy

- System data files
- System build files and scripts
- Requirements specifications
- Interface specifications
- Design specifications
- Software architecture specifications
- Test plans
- Test procedures
- Test data sets
- Test results
- User documentation
- Software development plan
- Quality plans
- Configuration management plans
- Compilers
- Linkers and loaders
- Debuggers
- Operating systems
- Shell scripts
- Third-party tools
- Other related support tools
- Procedure language descriptions
- Development procedures and standards

Effective configuration identification is a prerequisite for the other configuration management activities (configuration control, status accounting, and audit), which all use the products of configuration identification. If configuration items and their associated configuration documentation are not properly identified, it is impossible to control the changes to the items' configuration, to establish accurate records and reports, or to validate the configuration through audit. Inaccurate or incomplete identification of configured items and configuration documentation may result in defective products, schedule delays, and higher maintenance cost after delivery.

CONFIGURATION CHANGE CONTROL

Configuration change control involves controlling the release and changes to software products throughout the software life cycle (see Chapters 5 and 11). It is perhaps the most visible element of configuration management. It is the process to manage preparation, justification, evaluation, coordination, disposition, and implementation of proposed engineering changes and deviations to affected configuration items and baselined configuration documentation.

The goal of configuration change control is to establish mechanisms that will help ensure the production of quality software as well as ensure that each version of the software contains all necessary elements, and that all elements in a version will work correctly together. A generic change process is identified in Figure 1.3.

Configuration change control answers *What is controlled? How are the changes to the products controlled? Who controls the changes? When are the changes accepted, received, and verified?*

Configuration change control activities include:

- Defining the change process
- Establishing change control policies and procedures
- Maintaining baselines
- Processing changes
- Developing change report forms
- Controlling release of the product

Changes made to the configuration management baselines or baselined software configuration items should be done according to a documented change control process. The change control process should specify:

- Who can initiate the change requests
- What the criteria are for placing the software components under formal change control
- The "change impact" analysis expected for each requested change
- How revision history should be kept
- The check-in/check-out procedures
- The process that the Software Configuration Control Board (SCCB) follows to approve changes
- How change requests will be linked to the Trouble Reporting System
- How change requests are tracked and resolved
- The reviews and regression tests that must be performed to ensure that changes have not caused unintended effects on the baseline
- The procedure that will be followed to update all affected software life-cycle components to reflect the approved changes

To control changes made to configuration items or the system, many organizations establish a Software Configuration Control Board (SCCB). This board reviews each proposed change; approves or disapproves it; and if approved, coordinates the change with the affected groups.

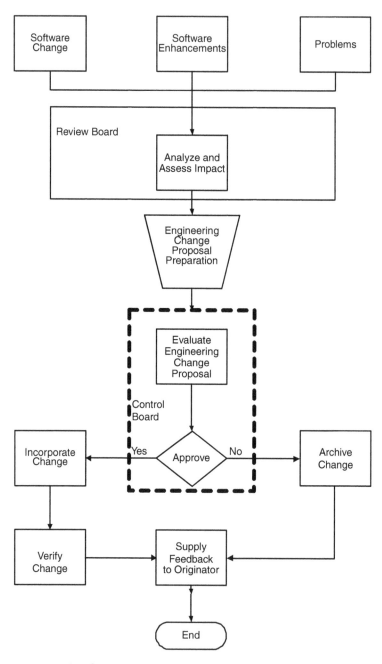

Figure 1.3 Generic Change Process [Berlack 1992]

Another key concept of change control is the use of baselines. A baseline is "a specification or product that has been formally reviewed and agreed upon, that thereafter serves as the basis for further development, and that can be changed only through formal change procedures" [IEEE 1990]. When an item is baselined, it becomes frozen and can only be changed by creating a new version.

Historically, three different types of baselines were used: functional, allocated, and product. The functional baseline is the initially approved documentation describing the functional characteristics and the verification required to demonstrate the achievement of those specified functional characteristics. The allocated baseline is the initially approved documentation describing the interface requirements, additional design constraints, and the verification required to demonstrate the achievement of those specified functional and interface characteristics. The product baseline is the initially approved documentation describing the necessary functional and physical characteristics and those designated for production acceptance testing.

Several additional but informal baselines are usually established during the software development process. The number and type of baselines depend on which life-cycle model the project is implementing. Life-cycle models, such as the spiral, incremental development, and rapid prototyping, require more flexibility in the establishment of baselines.

CONFIGURATION STATUS ACCOUNTING

Configuration status accounting (see Chapters 6, 7, and 13) involves the recording and reporting of the change process. The goal of status accounting is to maintain "a continuous record of the status and history of all baselined items and proposed changes to them. It includes reports of the traceability of all changes to the baseline throughout the software life cycle" [Kasse 1997].

Configuration status accounting answers *What changes have been made to the system?* and *How many files were affected by this problem report?*

Configuration status accounting activities include:

- Determining type of logs and reports required
- Tracking the status of SCM items
- Tracking the status of changes to the system
- Generating status reports
- Recording and reporting the activities of SCM

Questions that SCM status accounting should be able to answer include [Kasse 1997]:

1. *What is the status of an item?* A developer may want to know whether a specification has been fully approved. A developer may want to know whether a sub-system has been tested so that the developer can test the modules that interface with that sub-system. A project leader may wish to track the progress of a project as items are developed, reviewed, tested, and integrated.

2. *Which version of an item implements an approved change request?* Once a requested enhancement of a library routine is implemented, the originator and other developers will want to know which version of the routine contains the enhancement.

3. *What is different about a new version of a system?* A new version of a software system should be accompanied by a document listing the changes from the previous version. The change list should include both enhancements and fixes to faults. Any faults that have not been fixed should also be named and described.

4. *How many faults are detected each month, and how many are fixed?* Faults are continuously detected during the operational use of the system. Comparing the number of detected and fixed faults helps to assess the stability of the latest release of the system. Tracking the number of faults also helps the program manager decide when to make a new release of the system.

5. *What is the cause of the trouble report?* Trouble reports can be categorized by their causes: violation of programming standards, inadequate user interface, or invalid, incorrect, or incomplete customer requirements. Sometimes, when it is discovered that many faults have a similar cause, action can be taken to improve the process and stop such faults from recurring.

Key information about the project and configuration items can be communicated to project members through status accounting. Software engineers can see what fixes or files were included in which baseline. Project managers can track completion of problem reports and various other maintenance activities. Minimal reports to be completed include transaction log, change log, and item "delta" report. Other typically common reports include resource usage, "stock status" (status of all configuration items), changes in process, and deviations agreed upon [Ben-Menachem 1994].

CONFIGURATION AUDITING

Configuration auditing (see Chapters 8 and 9) verifies that the software product is built according to the requirements, standards (see Chapter 12), or contractual agreement. Test reports and documentation are used to verify that the software meets the stated requirements. The goal of configuration audit is to verify that all software products have been produced, correctly identified and described, and that all change requests have been resolved according to established SCM processes and procedures. Informal audits are conducted at key phases of the software life cycle. There are two types of formal audits that are conducted before the software is delivered to the customer: functional configuration audit (FCA) and physical configuration audit (PCA).

FCA verifies that the software satisfies the software requirements stated in the System Requirements Specification and the Interface Requirements Specification. That is, the FCA allows one to validate the system against the requirements. The PCA determines whether the design and reference documents represent the software that was built. Configuration audit answers *Does the system satisfy the requirements?* and *Are all changes incorporated in this version?*

Configuration audit activities include:

- Defining audit schedule and procedures
- Identifying who will perform the audits
- Performing audits on the established baselines
- Generating audit reports

IMPLEMENTING SCM IN THE ORGANIZATION

One of the first steps in successfully implementing SCM is to obtain management sponsorship. This means public endorsement for SCM, and making sure the resources needed for success are allocated to the project. Management also needs to establish SCM as a priority and help facilitate implementation.

An organization can maintain management sponsorship by identifying and resolving risks, reporting progress, managing SCM implementation details, and communicating with all members of the organization.

The next step is to assess current SCM processes. Every organization that produces software is practicing some type of SCM. This may not be a formal process or even thought of as SCM. To assess current processes, one might ask the following questions: *How are files identified? How are versions of software releases identified? How are baselines controlled? What files are included in each release? How are changes to the software identified and tracked?*

After assessing your current processes, the next step is to analyze your requirements. What is it that your organization wants to accomplish? The requirement may be a specific level SW-CMM certification, ISO 9000 certification, some other standard or certification, or simply to improve your software process. Document the requirements for your organization, how you will implement them, and how you will measure success.

Depending on the requirements of your organization, the various roles and formality of the SCM team may differ. At a minimum there should be a point-of-contact for SCM. Other recommended roles and functions include:

- A control and review board should be in place to analyze and approve changes.
- Project managers and leaders also play a role in SCM in establishing or following an SCM plan (see Appendices A and T and Chapter 2) for their project, ensuring system requirements are properly allocated, ensuring adequate tools are available to support activities, and conducting regular reviews.
- A librarian is also necessary to track baselines and versions of files included in each release. An SCM tool can assist in those activities.
- Quality assurance (QA) can be used to verify that documented SCM processes and procedures are followed. QA is also necessary for SW-CMM Level 2 certification.

MANAGE THE RISKS OF SCM

With each new software project or process, there is some amount of associated risk. The same is true when implementing SCM. Whether an organization is implementing a whole new system or just updating a few processes, there will be risks that must be addressed. Note that having risk is not bad — on the contrary, risk is a necessary part of SCM and the software development process.

Without risk, there is no opportunity for improvement. Risk-free SCM processes are typically of little use. The very nature of SCM requires risk-taking. Managing and controlling the risks associated with SCM is essential to the success of SCM processes in terms of cost, schedule, and quality.

It is always less expensive to be aware of and deal with risks than to respond to unexpected problems. A risk that has been analyzed and resolved ahead of time is much easier to deal with than one that surfaces unexpectedly [Guidelines 1996].

The Software Engineering Institute has developed a risk management program comprising six different activities, with communication being central to all of them. This program can be used when implementing SCM to effectively manage the associated risks. Risk management should be viewed as an important part of the SCM process. A brief summary of each activity follows [Paulk 1993]:

- *Identify.* Before risks can be managed, they must be identified. Identification surfaces risks before they become problems and adversely affect a project.
- *Analyze.* Analysis is the conversion of risk data into risk decision-making information.
- *Plan.* Planning turns risk information into decisions and actions (both present and future). Planning involves developing actions to address individual risk, prioritizing risk actions, and creating an integrated risk management plan.
- *Track.* Tracking consists of monitoring the status of risks and actions taken to ameliorate risks.
- *Control.* Risk control corrects for deviations from planned risk actions.
- *Communicate.* Risk communication lies at the center of the model to emphasize both its pervasiveness and its criticality. Without effective communication, no risk management approach can be viable.

As part of an organization's risk management program, a plan should be developed that integrates the above outlined activities. An SCM risk management plan may focus on addressing risks in three areas: business, people, and technology [Burrows 1996]. The *business* risks include [Burrows 1996]:

- *Cost.* The expense to incorporate SCM encompasses far more than just the licensing fee for a tool. Management must be willing to make the necessary expenditures for people and resources.
- *Culture shock.* Each organization has its own culture, to which the success of the business can be attributed. The procedures and products implemented for SCM must match that culture. The person in charge of SCM needs a broad understanding of software engineering principles and the cultural aspects of the organization.
- *Commitment.* To establish a successful SCM process, there must first be a strong commitment from management. The benefits of SCM are not always immediately recognized. "Deploying CM can be a long, costly, and sometimes painful exercise. Counter this risk by building up steam in the project. Get momentum going quickly and keep feeding it."

The risks associated with *people* include [Burrows 1996]:

- *Cheating.* Software developers may try to incorporate their code into the final product without following procedures and resist any changes to the established procedures.

- *Preferred tools.* They may have a tool they want to use that is different from that of the organization. To mitigate these risks, try to get offenders to be part of the decision-making process. Let them have input into the procedures and tools that will be used.
- *Resistance.* The greatest barrier to overcome when SCM is introduced into an organization is to change how people view SCM. People generally react negatively toward it. In many organizations, SCM has a low status, and SCM personnel are not trained or qualified to perform their duties. Many software developers perceive SCM as intrusive and have little understanding of the long-term effects of not following SCM procedures. Communication, training, and developer input to SCM processes will help ensure SCM principles are adopted by an organization.

The last area is technology. The *technology* risks include [Burrows 1996]:

- *Loss of control.* At times, it may seem that the SCM procedures and tools are at the controls. There may also be reliance on tools where previously the needed data and information were obtained manually. Again, communication will help mitigate this risk. Management will have greater control over and information about their projects after successfully implementing SCM.
- *Access.* Controlling who can have access and make changes to various baselines, data repositories, software files, or documents is also a risk that must be managed. By thorough analysis and design, the procedures implemented may restrict access to approved individuals and give up-to-date information on many aspects of the project that is current and accurate.
- *Scalability.* A project has the potential to outgrow the implemented tool. Counter this risk by selecting a tool that will adapt to the changing size of your organization over time.

The secret to SCM risk management is to identify and resolve potential risks before they surface unexpectedly or become serious problems. Develop a program for identifying and managing risks. Incorporate an SCM risk management plan that addresses risks to business, people, and technology. Central to everything is communication. Communicate as much as possible to as many people and organizations as possible.

SUMMARY

Configuration management (CM) is the framework around which software engineering processes exist. It is interesting how there is almost a one-to-one relationship between the life-cycle activities of software engineering and those of configuration management.

CM is a carefully orchestrated set of activities that provides the organization and control required to manage an idea from its inception to its deployment. This chapter serves as an introduction to the remainder of the handbook. Now that the principles of CM are a bit more well-understood, we can delve into each of the component parts in more depth.

Note: This chapter is based on the following governmental report: Software Technology Support Center, United States Air Force, Ogden Air Logistics Center, Software Configuration Management Technologies and Applications, April 1999, www.stsc.hill.af.mil.

REFERENCES

[ANSI/IEEE 1987] ANSI/IEEE Std 1042-1987, *American National Standard IEEE, Guide to Software Configuration Management,* Institute of Electrical and Electronics Engineers, Inc., New York, 1988.

[Ayer 1992] Ayer, Steve J. and Frank S. Patrinostro, *Software Configuration Management: Identification, Accounting, Control, and Management,* McGraw-Hill Software Engineering Series, McGraw-Hill, New York, 1992.

[Babich 1986] Babich, Wayne A., *Software Configuration Management: Coordination for Team Productivity,* Addison-Wesley, Reading, MA, 1986.

[Ben-Menachem 1994] Ben-Menachem, Mordechai, *Software Configuration Management Guidebook,* McGraw-Hill, New York, 1994.

[Berlack 1992] Berlack, Ronald H., *Software Configuration Management,* John Wiley & Sons, New York, 1992.

[Boehm 1981] Boehm, Barry, "Software Engineering Economics," Prentice-Hall, Englewood Cliffs, NJ, 1981.

[Bounds 1996] Bounds, Nadine M. and Susan A. Dart, *Configuration Management Plans: The Beginning to Your CM Solution,* Software Engineering Institute, Carnegie Mellon University, Pittsburgh, PA, February 1996.

[Bray 1995] Bray, Olin and Michael M. Hess, "Reengineering a Configuration Management System," *IEEE Software,* January 1995.

[Buckley 1992] Buckley, Fletcher J., *Implementing Configuration Management: Hardware, Software, and Firmware,* IEEE Computer Society Press, Los Alamitos, CA, 1993.

[Buckley 1994] Buckley, Fletcher J., "Implementing a Software Configuration Management Environment," *IEEE Computer,* 1994.

[Butler 1995] Butler, Kelley L., "The Economic Benefits of Software Process Improvement," *CrossTalk, The Defense Journal of Software Engineering,* Software Technology Support Center, July 1995.

[Burrows 96] Burrows, Clive, George W. George, and Susan Dart, *Ovum Evaluates Configuration Management,* Ovum Limited, London, U.K., 1996.

[Burrows 1998] Burrows, Clive and Ian Wesley, *Ovum Evaluates Configuration Management,* Ovum Limited, London, U.K., 1998.

[Carnegie 1998] Carnegie Mellon University and the Software Engineering Institute, "The '98 Software Engineering Symposium Preliminary Program," 1998.

[Carr 1993] Carr, M., S. Kondra, I. Monarch, F. Ulrich, and C. Walker, *Taxonomy-Based Risk Identification*, Technical Report CMU/SEI-93-TR-6, Software Engineering Institute, Carnegie Mellon University, Pittsburgh, PA, 1996.

[Conner 1982] Conner, Daryl R. and Robert W. Patterson, "Building Commitment to Organization Change," *Training and Development Journal*, 36(4), 18–30, April 1982.

[Dart 1990a] Dart, Susan A., "Issues in Configuration Management Adoption," *Proceedings of Conference on Caseware,* Software Engineering Institute Overview, Carnegie Mellon University, Pittsburgh, PA, 1990.

[Dart 1990b] Dart, Susan A., *Spectrum of Functionality in Configuration Management Systems,* Technical Report CMU/SEI-90-TR-11, ESD-90-TR-212, Software Engineering Institute, Carnegie Mellon University, Pittsburgh, PA, 1990.

[Dart 1992a] Dart, Susan A., "State-of-the-Art in Environment Support for Configuration Management," *ICSE 14 Tutorial*, Australia, Carnegie Mellon University, Pittsburgh, PA, May 1992.

[Dart 1992b] Dart, Susan A., *The Past, Present, and Future of Configuration Management*, Technical Report CMU/SEI-92-TR-8, ESC-TR-92-8, Software Engineering Institute, Carnegie Mellon University, Pittsburgh, PA, July 1992.

[Dart 1994] Dart, Susan A., "Adopting an Automated Configuration Management Solution," *Proceedings of Software Technology Conference*, April 1994.

[Dart 1996] Dart, Susan, A., "Achieving the Best Possible Configuration Management Solution," *CrossTalk, The Defense Journal of Software Engineering,* Software Technology Support Center, Hill Air Force Base, UT, September 1996.

[DeGrace 1990] DeGrace, Peter and Leslie Hulet Stahl, "Wicked Problems, Righteous Solutions," *A Catalogue of Modern Software Engineering Paradigms*, Yourdon Press, Englewood Cliffs, NJ, 1990.

[Evans 1997] Evans, Michael W. and Shawn T. O'Rourke, "CenterZone Management: The Relationship between Risk Management and Configuration Management in a Software Project," *Proceedings of Software Technology Conference*, April 1997.

[Feiler 1991] Feiler, Peter H., *Configuration Management Models in Commercial Environments,* Technical Report CMU/SEI-91-TR-7, ESD-9-TR-7, Software Engineering Institute, Carnegie Mellon University, Pittsburgh, PA, March 1991.

[Feiler 1990] Feiler, Peter H. and Grace Downey, *Transaction-Oriented Configuration Management: A Case Study*, Technical Report CMU/SEI-90-TR-23, ESD-90-TR-224, Software Engineering Institute, Carnegie Mellon University, Pittsburgh, PA, November 1990.

[Firth 1987] Firth, Robert et al., *A Guide to the Classification and Assessment of Software Engineering Tools*, Technical Report CMU/SIE-87-TR-10, ESD-TR-87-111, Software Engineering Institute, Carnegie Mellon University, Pittsburgh, PA, August 1987.

[Forte 1990] Forte, Gene, "Configuration Management Survey," *CASE Outlook*, 90(2), 1990.

[Fowler 88] Fowler, Pricilla and Stan Przybylinski, *Transferring Software Engineering Tool Technology,* IEEE Computer Society Press, Washington, D.C., 1988.

[Guidelines 1996] *Guidelines for Successful Acquisition and Management of Software-Intensive Systems: Weapon Systems, Command and Control Systems, Management Information Systems*, Software Technology Support Center, Hill Air Force Base, UT, June 1996.

[Haque 1997] Haque, Tani, "Process-Based Configuration Management: The Way to Go to Avoid Costly Product Recalls," *CrossTalk, The Defense Journal of Software Engineering*, Software Technology Support Center, Hill Air Force Base, UT, April 1997.

[Hermann 1998] Hermann, Brian and Jim Marshall, "Are You Ready to Deliver? To Ship? To Test?," *CrossTalk, The Defense Journal of Software Engineering*, Software Technology Support Center, Hill Air Force Base, UT, August 1998.

[Humphrey 1990] Humphrey, Watts S., *Managing the Software Process*, Addison-Wesley, Reading, MA, August 1990.

[ICM 1998] Institute of Configuration Management, CMII Model, Course I, "CMII-Based Business Process Infrastructure," 1998.

[IEEE 1990] IEEE Std 828-1990, IEEE Standard for Software Configuration Management Plans, 1990.

[Kasse 1997] Kasse, Tim, "Software Configuration Management for Project Leaders," *Proceedings of Software Technology Conference*, April 1997.

[Kingsbury 1996] Kingsbury, Julie, "Adopting SCM Technology," *CrossTalk, The Defense Journal of Software Engineering*, Software Technology Support Center, Hill Air Force Base, UT, March 1996.

[Marshal 1995] Marshall, A.J., "Demystifying Software Configuration Management," *CrossTalk, The Defense Journal of Software Engineering*, Software Technology Support Center, Hill Air Force Base, UT, May 1995.

[Marshal 1995] Marshall, Alexa J., "Software Configuration Management: Function or Discipline?," *CrossTalk, The Defense Journal of Software Engineering*, Software Technology Support Center, Hill Air Force Base, UT, October 1995.

[MIL-HDBK-61 1997] MIL-HDBK-61, *Military Handbook: Configuration Management Guidance*, Department of Defense, Washington, D.C., Sept. 30, 1997.

[Mosley 1995] Mosley, Vicky, "Improving Your Process for the Evaluation and Selection of Tools and Environments," *CrossTalk, The Defense Journal of Software Engineering*, Software Technology Support Center, Hill Air Force Base, UT, September 1995.

[Myers 1995] Myers, Robin J., "Configuration Management: A Prerequisite for BPR Success," Enterprise Reengineering, August 1995.

[Olson 1993] Olson, Timothy G. et al., *A Software Process Framework for the SEI Capability Maturity Model: Repeatable Level*, Technical Report CMU/SEI-93-TR-7, Software Engineering Institute, Carnegie Mellon University, Pittsburgh, PA, 1993.

[Paulk 1993] Paulk, Mark C. et al., *Key Practices of the Capability Maturity Model for Software, Version 1.1*, Technical Report CMU/SEI-93-TR-25, Software Engineering Institute, Carnegie Mellon University, Pittsburgh, PA, 1993.

[Paulk 1995] Paulk, Mark C., Charles V. Weber, Bill Curtis, and Mary Beth Chrissis, *The Capability Maturity Model: Guidelines for Improving the Software Process*, Software Engineering Institute, Carnegie Mellon University, Pittsburgh, PA, October 1995.

[Pence 1993] Pence, J.L. Pete and Samuel E. Hon, III, "Building Software Quality into Telecommunications Network Systems," *Quality Progress*, Bellcore, Piscataway, NJ, 95–97, October 1993.

[Pitts 1997] Pitts, David R., "Metrics: Problem Solved?," *CrossTalk, The Defense Journal of Software Engineering*, Software Technology Support Center, Hill Air Force Base, UT, Dec. 1997

[Platinum 1998] © 1995, 1998 PLATINUM Technology, Inc. All rights reserved. 1-800-442-6861, 630-620-5000, Fax: 630-691-0718, www.platinum.com.

[Rader 1993] Rader, Jack, Ed. J. Morris, and Alan W. Brown, *An Investigation into the State-of-the-Practice of CASE Tool Integration,* Technical Report CMU/SEI-93, Software Engineering Institute, Carnegie Mellon University, Pittsburg, PA, 1993.

[Schamp 1995] Schamp, Alan, "CM-Tool Evaluation and Selection," *IEEE Software,* 1995.

[Semiatin 1994] Semiatin, William J., "Evolution of Configuration Management," *Program Manager: Journal of the Defense Systems Management College,* November/December 1994.

[Slomer 1992] Slomer, Howard M. and Alan M. Christie, *Analysis of a Software Maintenance System: A Case Study,* Technical Report CMU/SEI-92-TR-3, ESC-TR-92-031, Software Engineering Institute, Carnegie Mellon University, Pittsburgh, PA, November 1992.

[Smith 1993] Smith, Dennis et al., *Software Engineering Environment Evaluation Issues,* Technical Report CMU/SEI-93, Software Engineering Institute, Carnegie Mellon University, Pittsburgh, PA, March 1993.

[Softool 1992] Softool Corporation, Successful Software Strategies Seminar Series: Improving Your Configuration Management Implementation Strategy, Washington, D.C., 1992.

[Starbuck 1997] Starbuck, Ronald A., "Software Configuration Management: Don't Buy a Tool First," *CrossTalk, The DefenseJournal of Software Engineering,* Software Technology Support Center, Hill Air Force Base, UT, November 1997.

[Starrett 1998] Starrett, Elizabeth C.L., "Measurement 101," *CrossTalk, The Defense Journal of Software Engineering,* Software Technology Support Center, Hill Air Force Base, UT, August 1998.

[STSC 1994] Software Technology Support Center, *Software Configuration Management Technology Report,* Software Technology Support Center, Hill Air Force Base, UT, September 1994.

[Ventimiglia 1997] Ventimiglia, Bob, *Advanced Effective Software Configuration Management,* Technology Training Corporation, 1997.

[Ventimiglia 1998] Ventimiglia, Bob, "Effective Software Configuration Management," *CrossTalk, The Defense Journal of Software Engineering,* Software Technology Support Center, Hill Air Force Base, UT, February 1998.

[Wallnau 92] Wallnau, Kurt C., *Issues and Techniques of CASE Integration with Configuration Management,* Technical Report CMU/SEI-92-TR-5, ESD-TR-92-5, Software Engineering Institute, Carnegie Mellon University, Pittsburgh, PA, March 1992.

[Whitgift 1991] Whitgift, David, *Methods and Tools for Software or Software Configuration,* John Wiley & Sons, New York, 1991.

[Wreden 1994] Wreden, Nick, "Configuration Management: Getting with the Program," *Beyond Computing,* November/December 1994.

2

PROJECT MANAGEMENT IN A CM ENVIRONMENT

Configuration management (CM) must be meticulously planned and carefully managed if the organization is to achieve an effective, predictable, repeatable CM process. This principle is consistent with the concept of a software engineering project plan and, in effect, one can say that the project plan provides a subset of the overall CM plan (see Appendix T for a detailed Software Configuration Plan). Appendix X provides software configuration management (SCM) guidance for achieving the "Repeatable" level on the Software Engineering Institute (SEI) Capability Maturity Model®.

Tasks associated with CM planning and management include:

- Identifying the scope and constraints of the project
- The creation of a written plan
- Implementation procedures
- Training
- Measurements

A typical CM plan will consist of the components shown in Table 2.1 [Bounds, 2001]. Those familiar with traditional systems development project planning will immediately see a similarity between this checklist and the contents of a typical project plan.

The remainder of this chapter ties together the principles of traditional project planning and configuration management planning and management.

Table 2.1 Typical CM Plan

1.0. Introduction
    1.1. Scope
    1.2. Definitions
    1.3. References
    1.4. Tailoring
2.0. Software Configuration Management
    2.1. SCM organization
    2.2. SCM responsibilities
    2.3. Relationship of CM to the software process life cycle
        2.3.1. Interfaces to other organizations on the project
        2.3.2. Other project organizations' CM responsibilities
3.0. Software Configuration Management Activities
    3.1. Configuration identification
        3.1.1. Specification identification
- Labeling and numbering scheme for documents and files
- How identification between documents and files relate
- Description of identification tracking scheme
- When a document/file identification number enters controlled status
- How the identification scheme addresses versions and releases
- How the identification scheme addresses hardware, application software system software, COTS products, support software (e.g., test data and files), etc.

        3.1.2. Change control form identification
- Numbering scheme for each of the forms used

        3.1.3. Project baselines
- Identify various baselines for the project
- For each baseline created, provide the following information:
- How and when it is created
- Who authorizes and who verifies it
- The purpose
- What goes into it (software and documentation)

        3.1.4. Library
- Identification and control mechanisms used
- Number of libraries and the types
- Backup and disaster plans and procedures
- Recovery process for any type of loss
- Retention policies and procedures
- What needs to be retained, for whom, and for how long
- How is the information retained (online, offline, media type and format)

    3.2. Configuration control
        3.2.1. Procedures for changing baselines (procedures may vary with each baseline)
        3.2.2. Procedures for processing change requests and approvals-change classi cation scheme

Table 2.1 Typical CM Plan (continued)

- Change reporting documentation
- Change control flow diagram

3.2.3. Organizations assigned responsibilities for change control

3.2.4. Change Control Boards (CCBs) — describe and provide the following information for each:
- Charter
- Members
- Role
- Procedures
- Approval mechanisms

3.2.5. Interfaces, overall hierarchy, and the responsibility for communication between multiple CCBs, when applicable

3.2.6. Level of control — identify how it will change throughout the life cycle, when applicable

3.2.7. Document revisions — how they will be handled

3.2.8. Automated tools used to perform change control

3.3. Configuration status accounting

3.3.1. Storage, handling, and release of project media

3.3.2. Types of information that need to be reported and the control over this information that is needed

3.3.3. Reports to be produced (e.g., management reports, QA reports, CCB reports), who the audience is for each, and the information needed to produce each report

3.3.4. Release process, to include the following information:
- What is in the release
- Who the release is being provided to and when
- The media the release is on
- Any known problems in the release
- Any known fixes in the release
- Installation instructions

3.3.5. Document status accounting and change management status accounting that needs to occur

3.4. Configuration auditing

3.4.1. Number of audits to be done and when they will be done (internal audits as well as configuration audits); for each audit, provide the following:
- Which baseline it is tied to, if applicable
- Who performs the audit
- What is audited
- What is the CM role in the audit, and what are the roles of other organizations in the audit
- How formal is the audit

3.4.2. All reviews that CM supports; for each, provide the following:
- The materials to be reviewed

Table 2.1 Typical CM Plan (continued)

> ■ CM responsibility in the review and the responsibilities of other organizations
>
> 4.0. CM Milestones
> > ■ Define all CM project milestones (e.g., baselines, reviews, audits)
> > ■ Describe how the CM milestones tie into the software development process
> > ■ Identify the criteria for reaching each milestone
>
> 5.0. Training
> > ■ Identify the kinds and amounts of training (e.g., orientation, tools)

WHO WRITES THE PROJECT PLAN

The project manager or team leader normally writes the project plan, although experienced consultants are often called in for this aspect of the project. When developing a project plan that is CM based, great care is taken to ensure that the planning process, and ultimately the developmental effort, are integrated and well-coordinated. This might seem obvious; however, integration and coordination are not things that are done well by most organizations. It has been proven that the vast majority of programming errors are due to interface problems. Similarly, the vast majority of configuration management problems are due to poor communications (i.e., interfaces) between the various departments and units that are tasked within the project plan.

In truth, there are as many ways to write a project plan as there are companies that write them. If the project is large, the proposed system might be divided into sub-systems — each with its own team. Each team leader may need to write his or her own part of the project plan. The project manager then compiles each sub-plan into a plan for the entire project.

Another alternative is divide the project plan into discrete tasks and parcel out the effort to team members. Appendix A contains a sample project plan. As one can see from its table of contents, it is easily divisible.

WHAT GOES INTO THE PROJECT PLAN

Pressman has defined the prototypical project plan [Pressman 2001]. A student implementation of this guideline can be found in Appendix A and the reader is directed there for a concrete example of how to architect a project plan.

Section 1.0 introduces the system and describes its purpose. In this section, project scope and objectives need to be defined. In EIA-649 Configuration Management parlance [EIA 1998], this is referred to as the context and the environment. This sub-section contains a formal statement of scope, a description of major functions, concerns on performance issues, and a list of management and technical constraints.

A CM value-added project plan will answer most, if not all, of the following questions:

- Who are the customers?
- What are the attributes of the customer and end-user environments that need to be addressed by the CM?
- What role will the customer play in decisions about changes?
- What is the current phase of the life cycle, and what are the anticipated future phases?
- What is the technical complexity of the product?
- Are there any product components that require separate management attention?
- Is the product, or its components, a new design, an existing design, or a modification of an existing design?
- How complex a documentation package is necessary?
- If this product is already in the operational phase, what documentation is already available and is it current?
- What level of change activity, if any, is anticipated?
- What is the operational life of the product?
- What information will users require to run and maintain the system?
- How will this system interface to other systems?

The Section 2.0 discusses project estimates and resources. Historical data used for estimates needs to be specified, as do estimation techniques. As a result of the estimation process, the estimates of effort, cost, and duration need to be reported here. Resources are required to be discussed in terms of people and minimal hardware and software requirements.

The Section 3.0 discusses risk management strategy. A risk table needs to be created first, followed by more detailed discussions on risks to be managed. Based on that, a risk mitigation, monitoring, and management (contingency) plan needs to be created for each risk that has been addressed.

Section 4.0 is an actual project schedule in terms of deliverables and milestones. A project work breakdown structure (WBS) needs to be created, followed by a task network and a timeline chart (Gantt chart). In addition, a resource table describes the demand for and availability of resources by time windows. In a WBS, the total task is broken down into series of smaller tasks. The smaller tasks are chosen based on the size and the scope to fit in the management structure of the project. Therefore, efficient planning and execution are possible.

Section 5.0 discusses staff organization. Usually, a project is carried out by a group of people and therefore a team structure needs to be defined and a management reporting relationship specified.

Section 6.0 lays out a picture on tracking and control mechanisms. It can be divided into two sub-sections: (1) Quality Assurance (i.e., verification and audit) and Control and (2) Change Management and Control.

Project plans optimized for configuration management will also provide guidance for:

- Configuration identification
- Configuration status accounting
- Configuration management of digital data
- Subcontractor configuration management

At the end of the project plan, all supporting materials that do not fit into the body of the document can be attached in the "Appendices" section.

Most project managers have a difficult time when writing a project plan because it is often required at project inception. This, unfortunately, is when information is most scarce.

The project manager must choose the process model most appropriate for the project, and then define a preliminary plan based on the set of common process framework activities.

Afterward, process decomposition (partitioning) is carried out, generating a complete plan reflecting the work tasks required to populate the framework activities.

CM-BASED PROJECT PLAN COMPONENTS

Identification

Configuration management requires that organizations develop a nomenclature for identifying all the components of a work product. Configuration identification incrementally establishes and maintains the definitive current basis for control and status accounting of a system and its configuration items (CIs) throughout their life cycle (development, production, deployment, and operational support, until demilitarization and disposal). The configuration identification process ensures that all processes have common sets of documentation as the basis for developing a new system, modifying an existing component, buying a product for operational use, and providing support for the system and its components. The configuration identification process also includes identifiers that are shorthand references to items and their documentation. Good configuration control procedures assure the continuous integrity of the configuration identification. The configuration identification process includes:

- Selecting configuration items at appropriate levels of the product structure to facilitate the documentation, control, and support of the items and their documentation
- Determining the types of configuration documentation required for each CI to define its performance, functional, and physical attributes, including internal and external interfaces (configuration documentation provides the basis to develop and procure software, parts, and material; fabricate and assemble parts; inspect and test items; and maintain systems)
- Determining the appropriate configuration control authority for each configuration document consistent with logistics support planning for the associated CI
- Issuing identifiers for the CIs and the configuration documentation
- Maintaining the configuration identification of CIs to facilitate effective logistics support of items in service
- Releasing configuration documentation and establishing configuration baselines for the configuration control of CIs

Because the project plan is one of the first documents in the long chain of systems development products, it must also adhere to the identification nomenclature developed by the organization.

Every organization has its own naming conventions. In general, the numbering system should include, at a minimum, the following information:

- System name
- Document/product type (e.g., "pp" for project plan, "srs" for systems requirement specification, etc.)
- Date
- Version number

A project plan is made up of multiple items — for example, main report, appendices, images, charts, etc. Each of these should be duly numbered.

Software Scope

Determination of software scope should be ascertained first. One establishes software scope by answering questions about context, information objectives, function, performance, and reliability. The context usually includes hardware, existing software, users, documentation, complexity, maintenance, and work procedures. Normally, a system specification developed by a systems analyst supplies the information necessary to bound the scope.

Techniques such as Question and Answer sessions and FAST (Facilitated Application Specification Techniques) can be used to gather requirements and establish project scope [Zahniser 1990]. The following constitutes the minimum that needs to be ascertained:

- *Major functions.* These are the requirements by the customers for the software as to what it should be able to do.
- *Performance issues.* This aspect is about speed, response time, and other performance-related requirements. They can seriously impact the requirement of effort and should therefore be clarified here.
- *Management and technical constraint.* These constraints should be listed as a foundation for the next section's estimation.

Project Estimates

Estimation is the one activity that lays a foundation for all other project planning activities. However, a project manager should not be overly manic in estimation. If an iterative process model is adopted, it is possible to revisit and revise the estimates when customer requirements change.

Historical data is key to a good estimation. The availability of reliable historical software metrics from previous projects assists the project planner in translating the product size estimation into effort, time, and cost estimations. Baseline productivity metrics (e.g., LOC [lines of code] or FP [function points]) should be stored by project domain for use in future estimation efforts.

Estimation Techniques

If similar projects have already been completed, estimates can be easily based on that available data. Otherwise, either a decomposition technique or an empirical model can be used. There are also software tools that automate the process using the two preceding approaches. At least two estimation methods should be used, with the final estimation being a triangulation of the two. Even so, common sense and experience should be the ultimate judge.

In the example provided in Appendix A, two estimation methodologies are used:

1. Process-based estimation, wherein the system is decomposed into discrete tasks such as analysis of the user interface and design of the user interface with an estimated amount of time allocated to each. For the Online Resource Scheduling System, the process-based estimate was 7.5 person-months.
2. LOC (or line of code) estimation is much more difficult to estimate manually. A tool such as COCOMO (an abbreviation for Cost Construction Model) makes the effort much easier. A wealth of information as well as a free version of the COCOMO automated tool can be found on the CSE (Center for Software Engineering) Web site at ⟨http://sunset.usc.edu/research/COCOMOII/index.html⟩.

COCOMO II is a model that allows one to estimate the cost, effort, and schedule when planning a software developmental activity. It is based on the original COCOMO model devised by Dr. Barry Boehm in 1981 [Boehm 1981]. The COCOMO II model is actually derived from the following original mathematical formula that is described in the second half of this book:

$$m = c_1 * KLOC^a * PROD[f_i]$$

COCOMO II permits the estimator to estimate a project cost in terms of lines of code (LOC) or function points (FP). FP calculation is quite complex. A chapter explaining function points can be found in this section.

Figure 2.1 shows the COCOMO II toolset in action. While a bit cumbersome — the non-free COCOMO tools are much more user friendly — the free version is quite functional. In this real-world example, the author used COCOMO to estimate the cost of building an Internet gaming system using the LOC option (see module size). Looking at the bottom of the screenshot, notice the three estimates: optimistic, most likely, and pessimistic. Thus, the planner needs to first estimate the size of the product to be built, and then translate that size estimate into human effort, calendar time, and dollars.

A project plan that is CM based should also fully articulate the resources that are required to be deployed by the various departments involved in the systems development effort. In addition, the estimate should include time and materials for both training and verification and audit. In addition, a reasonable "futures-based" estimate should be attempted for maintenance.

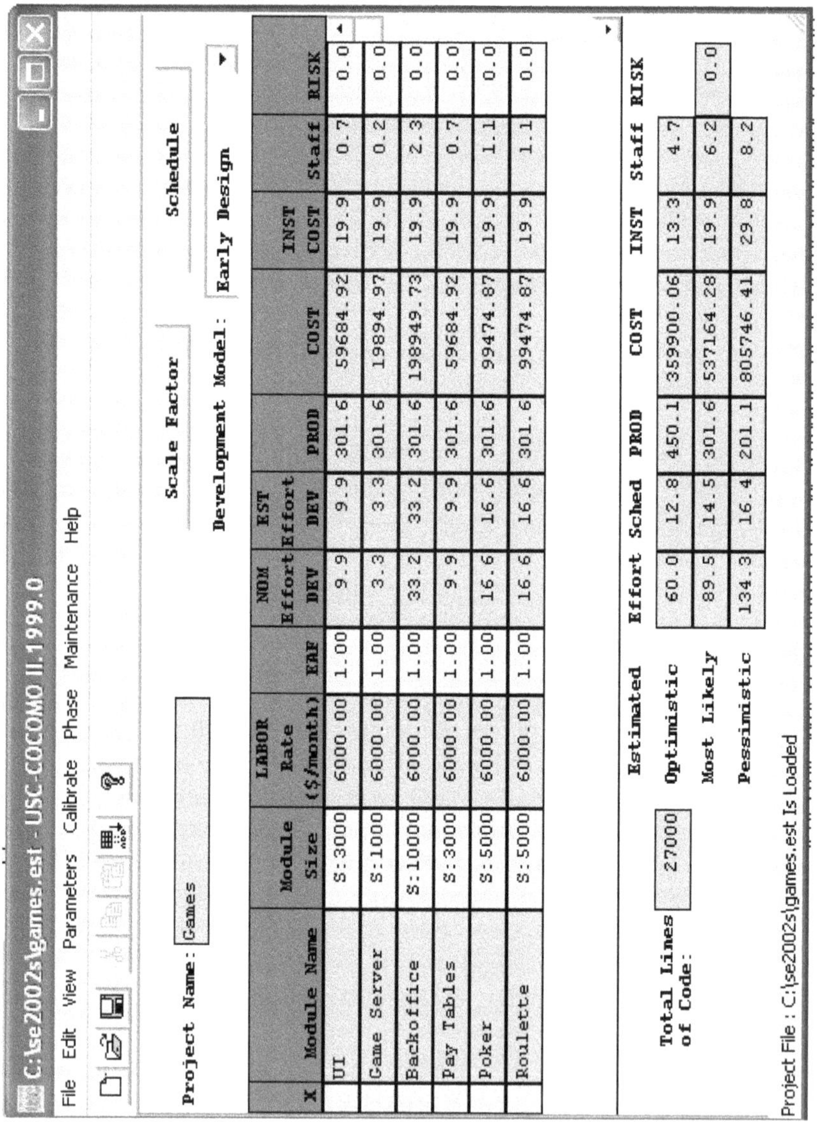

X	Module Name	Module Size	LABOR Rate ($/month)	EAF	NOM Effort DEV	EST Effort DEV	PROD	COST	INST COST	Staff	RISK
	UI	S:3000	6000.00	1.00	9.9	9.9	301.6	59684.92	19.9	0.7	0.0
	Game Server	S:1000	6000.00	1.00	3.3	3.3	301.6	19894.97	19.9	0.2	0.0
	Backoffice	S:10000	6000.00	1.00	33.2	33.2	301.6	198949.73	19.9	2.3	0.0
	Pay Tables	S:3000	6000.00	1.00	9.9	9.9	301.6	59684.92	19.9	0.7	0.0
	Poker	S:5000	6000.00	1.00	16.6	16.6	301.6	99474.87	19.9	1.1	0.0
	Roulette	S:5000	6000.00	1.00	16.6	16.6	301.6	99474.87	19.9	1.1	0.0

Estimated	Effort	Sched	PROD	COST	INST	Staff	RISK
Optimistic	60.0	12.8	450.1	359900.06	13.3	4.7	
Most Likely	89.5	14.5	301.6	537164.28	19.9	6.2	0.0
Pessimistic	134.3	16.4	201.1	805746.41	29.8	8.2	

Figure 2.1 Using COCOMO for Estimation

Decomposition Techniques

According to Putnam and Myers [1992], several approaches can be used to handle the project sizing problem, including "Fuzzy-logic" sizing, which uses the approximate reasoning technique as in the art of "guestimating;" function point sizing; standard component sizing (i.e., modules, screens, reports, etc.); and change sizing, which is used in estimating the size of an effort to modify an existing system.

Problem-based estimation techniques include FP- and LOC-based estimation, which was just discussed. They both require the project planner to decompose the software into problem functions that can each be estimated individually. Then, the project planner estimates the LOC or FP (or other estimation variable) for each function and applies the baseline productivity metrics to derive the cost or effort for the function. Finally, these function estimates are combined to produce the overall estimate for the entire project. Alternatively, a process-based estimation is commonly used. Here, the process is partitioned into a relatively small set of activities (i.e., the large project is decomposed or segmented into more manageable tasks) or tasks, and the effort required to accomplish each is estimated.

Empirical Model

There are a variety of empirical models available to calculate the effort required based on the size estimation in FP or LOC. Other than COCOMO [Boehm 1981], the most widely used model is The Software Equation [Putman and Myers 1992].

Putnam's cost estimation model is a macro-estimation model. The model recognizes the relationship between cost and the amount of time available for the development effort. The Putnam model supports the mythical man-month idea first put forth by Frederick Brooks, which states that people and time are not always interchangeable. The Software Equation is explained in the second half of this book. The results of these estimation techniques are estimates of effort, cost, and duration. They, in turn, are used in other sections of the project plan.

Risk Management Strategy

A proactive risk strategy should always be adopted. It is better to plan for possible risk than have to react to it in a crisis. Software risks include project risks, technical risks, and business risks. They can also be categorized as known, predictable, or unpredictable risks. First, risks need to be identified. One method is to create a risk item checklist. The sample project plan in Appendix A (Table A4) lists the following risks:

- Customer will change or modify requirements
- Lack of sophistication of end users
- Users will not attend training
- Delivery deadline will be tightened
- End users resist system
- Server may not be able to handle larger number of users simultaneously
- Technology will not meet expectations
- Larger number of users than planned
- Lack of training of end users
- Inexperienced project team
- System (security and firewall) will be hacked

Then, risks need to be projected in two dimensions: likelihood and consequences. This section can be a separate RMMM (Risk, Mitigation, Monitoring, and Management) Plan in itself and used as part of the overall project plan.

Risk Table

A risk table is a simple tool for risk projection. First, based on the risk item checklist, list all risks in the first column of the table. Then, in the following columns, fill in each risk's category, probability of occurrence, and assessed impact (see Table A4). Afterward, sort the table by probability and then by impact, study it, and define a cut-off line.

All risks above the cut-off line must be managed and discussed. Factors influencing their probability and impact should be specified.

RMMM Plan for Each Risk

A risk mitigation plan is a tool that can help in avoiding risks. Causes of the risks must be identified and mitigated. Risk monitoring activities take place as the project proceeds and should be planned early.

Risk management — that is, the contingency plan — consists of a list of activities that are put into action in the event a risk is realized. A plan should be created well before that.

Schedules

Before drafting a schedule, several things should be done. The project manager should first decide the type of the project from four choices: concept development, new application development, application enhance-

Table 2.2 Typical Schedule

Activities	Deliverable	From Date	To Date	Milestone
Meetings	Weekly meetings	02/04/04	05/07/04	05/07/04

ment, or reengineering project. Then, the project manager should compute a task set selector value [Pressman 2001] by: (1) grading the project for a set of adaptation criteria including its size, requirements, and constraints; (2) then assigning weighting factors to each criterion; (3) multiplying the grade by weighting factors and by the entry point multiplier for the type of the project; and (4) computing the average of all results in the previous step. Based on this average value, the project manager can choose the degree of rigor required for the project from four options: casual, structured, strict, or quick reaction. Afterward, the task set can be decided and distributed on the project timeline based on the process model choice: linear sequential, iterative, or evolutionary.

A typical schedule created contains the information displayed in Table 2.2.

Project tasks, also known as the project work breakdown structure (WBS), are now defined as shown in Figure 2.2. Alternatively, a textual WBS can be created as shown in Table 2.3.

Interdependencies among tasks are defined using a task network as shown in Figure 2.3. A task network is also known as an activity network because it shows all the activities for the project — and each activity's dependencies. In Figure 2.3, task 1.1 must be completed prior to task 1.2's initiation, and so on. A variety of automated tools implementing the Program Evaluation and Review Technique (PERT) and Critical Path Method (CPM) [Moder, Phillips, and Davis 1983] can be used for project scheduling.

DuPont developed the Critical Path Method (CPM) for use in chemical plants. The objective of CPM is to determine the trade-off between project duration and total project cost. This is done by identifying the critical path through activity network. The critical path can help management change the duration of the project. In CPM, an activity time is assumed to be known or predictable.

The Project Evaluation and Review Technique (PERT) was developed by the Navy when designing the Polaris missile. When accurate time estimates are not available, PERT is an ideal tool for project planning because it uses probability theory.

Eventually, CPM and PERT merged into a single technique. Events are shown as nodes and activities are shown as arrows that connect events.

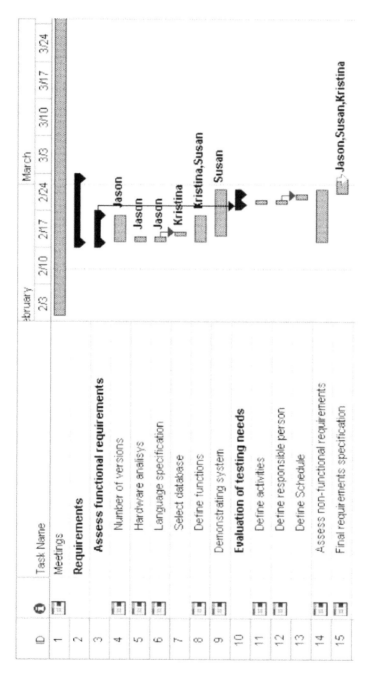

Figure 2.2 A Work Breakdown Structure (WBS)

Table 2.3   Textual WBS

Phase I: Proposal

Task	Start	Finish
Create budget	Thu 6/20/04	Fri 6/21/04
Define project team	Thu 6/20/04	Fri 6/21/04
Define material resources	Mon 6/24/04	Wed 6/26/04
Identify management team	Thu 6/27/04	Thu 6/27/04

Phase II: Planning

Task	Start	Finish
Determine performance goals	Thu 6/20/04	Thu 6/20/04
Conduct stakeholder interviews	Thu 6/20/04	Thu 6/20/04
Analyze current architecture	Thu 6/20/04	Fri 6/21/04
Produce operational metrics	Mon 6/24/04	Wed 6/26/04
Problem analysis	Thu 6/27/04	Fri 6/28/04
Problem resolution	Mon 7/1/04	Fri 7/12/04
Determine future needs	Mon 7/15/04	Tue 7/16/04

Phase III: Design

Task	Start	Finish
Produce topology maps	Wed 7/17/04	Tue 7/23/04
Determine capacity allocations	Wed 7/24/04	Thu 7/25/04
Determine backup requirements	Fri 7/26/04	Mon 7/29/04
Determine specific hardware reqs.	Tue 7/30/04	Tue 7/30/04
Determine specific software reqs.	Wed 7/31/04	Wed 7/31/04

Phase IV: Implementation

Task	Start	Finish
Install new SAN hardware	Wed 7/31/04	Tue 8/20/04
Install necessary supporting software	Thu 8/22/04	Thu 8/22/04
Verify SAN to topology maps	Fri 8/23/04	Fri 8/23/04
Perform system testing	Wed 8/21/04	Tue 8/27/04
Migrate hardware to SAN	Wed 8/28/04	Tue 9/3/04
Testing and verification	Wed 9/4/04	Tue 9/10/04
Collect operational metrics	Wed 9/11/04	Thu 9/12/04
Compare to existing system	Fri 9/13/04	Fri 9/13/04

Phase V: Support

Task	Start	Finish
Prepare training materials	Wed 7/31/04	Tue 8/13/04
Perform testing against materials	Wed 8/14/04	Wed 8/14/04
Training	Wed 8/14/04	Tue 8/20/04
Establish support needs	Mon 9/16/04	Tue 9/17/04
Implement tracking methodology	Wed 9/18/04	Thu 9/19/04
Determine additional follow-up needs	Wed 9/25/04	Wed 9/25/04

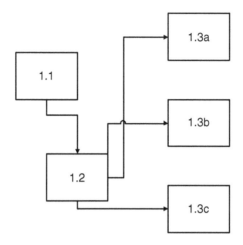

Figure 2.3   A Task Network

Arrows represents the effort required for achieving the next event. Direction specifies the order in which events must occur. There are two types of times for each event. One is the "Earliest Time," the earliest possible time at which the event can be achieved. The other is the "Latest Time," which is the latest time at which the event can occur without delaying subsequent events and completion of the project. For an event, the slack time can be obtained or calculated by the difference between the Latest and the Earliest Times.

The timeline chart (Gantt chart) is generated using automated tools after inputting the task network or task outline and each task's effort, duration, start date, and resource assignment. This chart is very visual and usually the most used part of a project plan. However, it is also possible to create a viable Gantt chart using Microsoft Excel, as shown in Figure 2.4.

Resource Table

This is another output generated by the automated tool, with a focus on the workload for and utilization of the project resources, particularly human resources.

Once a proper project schedule is developed, its tasks and milestones should be tracked and controlled as project proceeds.

Project Resources

An estimation of resources required is an important component of software planning. For each resource, the planner needs to specify the following characteristics: description, a statement of availability, and a time window.

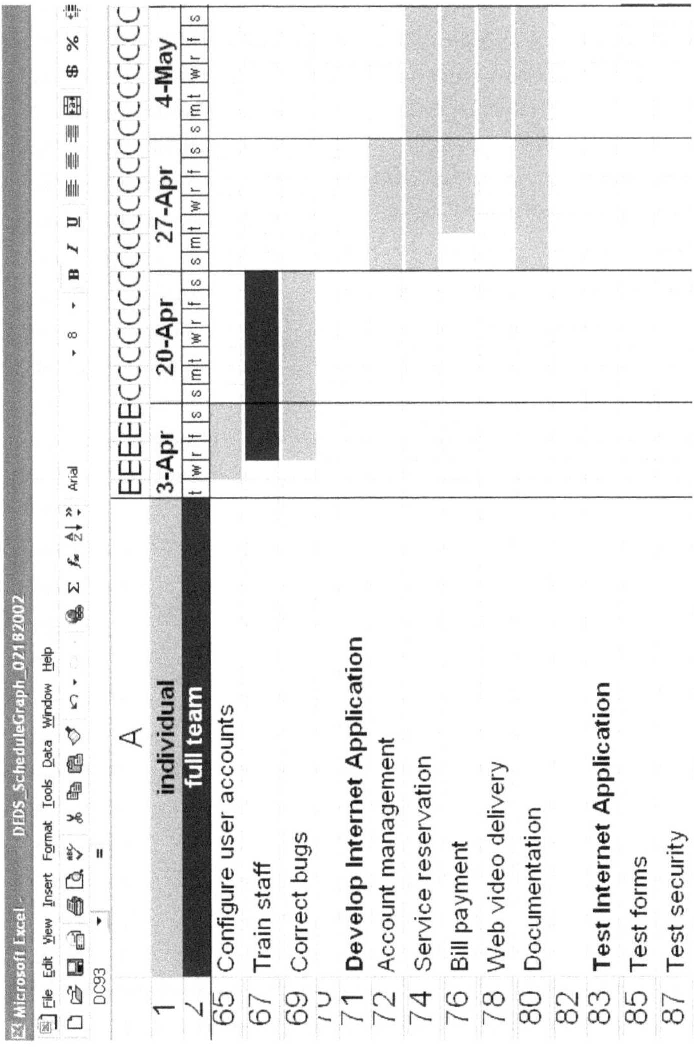

Figure 2.4 Using Excel to Draw a Gantt Chart

- *People.* The planner needs to specify the organizational position and specialty of the human resources required by the project. Only after estimating the development effort can one define the number of people required.
- *Hardware and software.* Hardware and software form the foundation of the software engineering environment [Naur and Randall 1969]. The project planner must determine its time window and verify its availability. Reusable software components should also be specified, alternatives evaluated, and acquisition be made early.
- *Training.* Special care should be taken to estimate the costs of training — both initial and ongoing.
- *Special resources.* Any other resources not covered in the previous sections should be listed here.
- *Staff organization.* People are the critical factor in a software development effort. In a typical software project, the players fall into five categories: senior managers, project (technical) managers, practitioners, customers, and end users. A good team leader should be able to motivate other players, organize the process, and innovate or encourage people to be creative.
- *Team structure (if applicable).* A project manager should decide on the organizational structure for the team. According to Mantei [1981], these three generic team organizations exist: democratic decentralized (DD), controlled decentralized (CD), and controlled centralized (CC). The factors that influence the team structure decision include difficulty of the problem, size of the resultant program(s), team lifetime, problem modularity, criticality of the solution, rigidity of timeline, and communications required. Generally speaking, a DD structure is best for difficult problems, and a CC or CD structure is best for very large projects.
- *Management reporting.* Coordination and communication issues, including management reporting relationships, should also be addressed here.

Tracking and Control Mechanisms

Errors and changes are inevitable, and one needs to plan ahead to stay prepared when they actually happen.

Quality Assurance and Control

Software quality assurance activities (SQAs) happen at each step of the software process and are carried out by both software engineers and an SQA group. Software engineers assure quality by applying rigorous technical methods and measures, and conducting formal technical reviews and, well-planned testing. The SQA group assists software engineers through a set of activities that address quality assurance planning, oversight, record keeping, analysis, and reporting. These activities must be planned in this sub-section.

In a CM-based project plan, document verification and continuing performance audit activities should also be included.

Change Management and Control

The later the changes happen in a project, the higher the cost. Change control combines human procedures and automated tools to provide a mechanism for the control of changes that, if uncontrolled, can rapidly lead a large project to chaos. The change control process begins with a change request, leads to a decision to make or reject the request, and culminates with a controlled update of the software configuration item that is to be changed. This part of such activities should be planned here.

In a CM-based system, it is critically important to provide detailed instructions for:

- Identifying changes
- Requesting changes
- Classifying changes
- Documenting requests for changes
- Change impact assessment
- Change approval

Performance Measurement

Metrics should be associated with all software development activities. They should also be associated with configuration management. The purpose of CM metrics is to measure project or program performance. It should be kept in mind that metrics should be reviewed periodically and adjusted for the environment and product life-cycle phase. Typical metrics include:

- Number of configuration documentation releases (scheduled/actual)
- Number of engineering changes (by product, phase, time period)
- Average engineering change cycle time (by product, by classification, by major process step)
- Average revisions per engineering change
- Number of changes

- Number of action items per configuration audit
- Average number of unincorporated changes

Typical software metrics include:

- Lines of code
- Pages of documentation
- Number and size of tests
- Function count
- Variable count
- Number of modules
- Depth of nesting
- Count of changes required
- Count of discovered defects
- Count of changed lines of code
- Time to design, code, test
- Defect discovery rate by phase of development
- Cost to develop
- Number of external interfaces
- Number of tools used and why
- Reusability percentage
- Variance of schedule
- Staff years of experience with team
- Staff years of experience with language
- Software years of experience with software tools
- MIPs per person
- Support-to-development personnel ratio
- Nonproject-to-project time ratio

CONFIGURATION STATUS ACCOUNTING

Configuration management is only as good as the information stored about the project or product. As a result, CM is closely tied to automated tools that correlate, store, maintain, and provide readily available views of configuration data. This includes information about the:

- Configuration documentation (e.g., document identifiers and effective dates)
- Product's configuration (e.g., part numbers)
- Product's operational and maintenance documentation
- CM process (e.g., status of change requests)

SUMMARY

Like any other software engineering task, project planning and writing a detailed project plan take time and cost money. Therefore, a natural question arises: is it worth it? The answer is yes. If one wants a system that is cost effective, does not go over budget, and actually works, then a project plan is mandatory.

More than a few people in this field use the "roadmap" metaphor to describe the role of a project plan; however, it is also a "compass." Its estimation and scheduling part can be likened to a rough roadmap (it can never be precise enough at the beginning of a project), but its risk management, organization plan, tracking, and control parts are definitely a compass. It guides the project team in handling unpredictable risks or undesired events.

A good project plan not only benefits the project itself, but also the domain as whole by its measures and metrics, which can be historical data for other, later projects.

REFERENCES

[Boehm 1981] Boehm, B., *Software Engineering Economics,* Prentice Hall, Englewood Cliffs, NJ, 1981.

[Bounds] Bounds, Nadine and Susan Dart, CM Plans: The Beginning to Your CM Solution. Retrieved from http://www.sei.cmu.edu/legacy/scm/papers/CM_Plans/CMPlans.Chapter3.html#RTFToC1, 2001.

[EIA 1998] Electronic Industries Alliance, EIA Standard: National Consensus Standard for Configuration Management. EIA-649, Arlington, VA, August 1998.

[Kerr and Hunter 1994] Kerr, J. and R. Hunter, *Inside RAD,* McGraw-Hill, New York, 1994.

[Mantei 1981] Mantei, M., "The Effect of Programming Team Structures on Programming Tasks," *Communications of the ACM,* 24(3), 106–113, March 1981.

[McDermid and Rook 1993] McDermid, J. and P. Rook, "Software Development Process Models," in *Software Engineer's Reference Book,* CRC Press, Boca Raton, FL, 1993, 15/66–15/28.

[Moder, Phillips, and Davis 1983] Moder, J.J., C.R. Phillips, and E.W. Davis, *Project Management with CPM, PERT and Precedence Diagramming,* 3rd edition, Van Nostrand Reinhold, New York, 1983.

[Naur and Randall 1969] Naur, P. and B. Randall, Eds., "Software Engineering: A Report on a Conference Sponsored by the NATO Science Committee," NATO, 1969.

[Pressman 2001] Pressman, R., *Software Engineering, A Practitioner's Approach,* 5th edition, McGraw-Hill, New York, 2001.

[Putman and Myers 1992] Putman, L. and W. Myers, *Measures for Excellence,* Yourdon Press, 1992.

[Zahniser 1990] Zahniser, R.A., "Building Software in Groups," *American Programmer,* 3(7/8), July/August 1990.

3

THE DoD CM PROCESS MODEL

The CM process, as shown in Figure 3.1, encompasses:

- Configuration items (CIs)
- Documents that define the performance, functional, and physical attributes of an item; these documents are referred to as configuration documentation
- Other documents used for training, operation, and maintenance of an item
- Associated and interfacing items used for training, operation, or maintenance of the configuration item

The CM process is embodied in rules, procedures, techniques, methodology, and resources to ensure that:

- The configuration of the system or item (its attributes) is documented.
- Changes made to the item in the course of development, production, and operation are beneficial and are effected without adverse consequences.
- Changes are managed until incorporated in all items affected.

A configuration item (CI) can be an individual item, or it can be a significant part of a system or of a higher-level CI. It is designated at an appropriate level for documenting performance attributes and managing changes to those attributes.

The CI concept has confused some people into thinking that the level at which CIs are designated is the point where configuration management

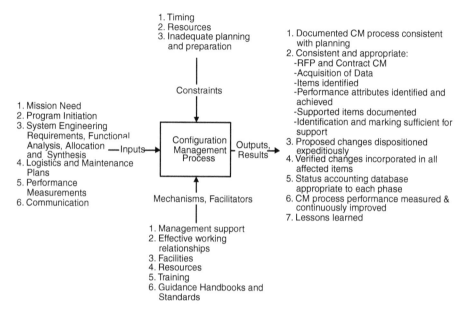

1. Timing
2. Resources
3. Inadequate planning
   and preparation

Constraints

1. Mission Need
2. Program Initiation
3. System Engineering
   Requirements, Functional
   Analysis, Allocation
   and Synthesis
4. Logistics and Maintenance
   Plans
5. Performance
   Measurements
6. Communication

— Inputs→

Configuration
Management
Process

Outputs,
Results →

↑

Mechanisms, Facilitators

1. Management support
2. Effective working
   relationships
3. Facilities
4. Resources
5. Training
6. Guidance Handbooks and
   Standards

1. Documented CM process consistent
   with planning
2. Consistent and appropriate:
   -RFP and Contract CM
   -Acquisition of Data
   -Items identified
   -Performance attributes identified and
    achieved
   -Supported items documented
   -Identification and marking sufficient for
    support
3. Proposed changes dispositioned
   expeditiously
4. Verified changes incorporated in all
   affected items
5. Status accounting database
   appropriate to each phase
6. CM process performance measured &
   continuously improved
7. Lessons learned

Figure 3.1 DoD Configuration Management Process Model Overview

stops. In reality, the CI level is where configuration management really begins; the process encompasses, to some degree, every item of hardware and software down to the lowest bolt, nut, and screw, or lowest software unit.

The attributes of CIs are defined in configuration documentation. Configuration baselines are established to identify the current approved documents. CIs are uniquely identified. They are verified to make sure they conform to, and perform as defined in, the configuration documentation.

Whenever a change to an item is contemplated, the effect of that change on other items and associated documents is evaluated. Changes are systematically processed and are approved by the appropriate change control authority.

Change implementation involves update and verification of all affected items and documentation. Information about item configuration, document identification and status, and change status is collected as activities associated with the CM process. This configuration status accounting information is correlated, maintained, and provided in usable form, as required.

CM BENEFITS, RISKS, AND COST IMPACT

Configuration management (CM) provides knowledge of the correct current configuration of assets and the relationship of those assets to associated documents. The CM process efficiently manages necessary changes, ensuring that all impacts to operation and support are addressed.

The benefits of the process should be obvious but are often overlooked. ANSI/EIA-649 summarizes the benefits of CM from an industry view, as follows:

- *Product attributes are defined.* Provides measurable performance parameters. Both buyer and seller have a common basis for acquisition and use of the product.
- *Product configuration is documented and a known basis for making changes is established.* Decisions are based on correct, current information. Production repeatability is enhanced.
- *Products are labeled and correlated with their associated requirements, design, and product information.* The applicable data (such as for procurement, design, or servicing the product) is accessible, thereby avoiding guesswork and trial and error.
- *Proposed changes are identified and evaluated for impact prior to making change decisions.* Downstream surprises are avoided. Cost and schedule savings are realized.
- *Change activity is managed using a defined process.* Costly errors of ad hoc, erratic change management are avoided.
- *Configuration information, captured during the product definition, change management, product build, distribution, operation, and disposal processes is organized for retrieval of key information and relationships, as needed.* Timely, accurate information avoids costly delays and product downtime, ensures proper replacement and repair, and decreases maintenance costs.
- *Actual product configuration is verified against the required attributes.* Incorporation of changes to the product is verified and recorded throughout the product life. A high level of confidence in the product information is established.

In the absence of CM, or where it is ineffectual, there may be:

- Equipment failures due to incorrect part installation or replacement
- Schedule delays and increased cost due to unanticipated changes
- Operational delays due to mismatches with support assets
- Maintenance problems, downtime, and increased maintenance cost due to inconsistencies between equipment and its maintenance instructions
- Numerous other circumstances that decrease operational effectiveness and add cost

The severest consequence is catastrophic loss of expensive equipment and human life. Of course, these failures can be attributed to causes other than poor CM. The point is that the intent of CM is to avoid cost increases and minimize risk.

Those who consider the small investment in the CM process a cost-driver may not be considering the compensating benefits of CM and may be ignoring or underestimating the cost, schedule, and technical risk of an inadequate or delayed CM process.

CM LIFE-CYCLE MANAGEMENT AND PLANNING

Figure 3.2 is a top-level CM activity model to be used as a reference point to plan and implement the major CM activities (functions) over the program life cycle. It provides an overview of the entire CM process and illustrates the relationships within the process. It shows the inputs (left), outputs (right), constraints (top), and implementing tools or methods (bottom) for each functional CM activity (represented by rectangular boxes).

Management and Planning

This block represents the core CM activity and its relationships to the other activities. Inputs to Management and Planning consist of the authorization to initiate the CM program, communications with all the other CM activities, and selected information and performance measurements received from the status accounting activity. The activity is facilitated by the degree of management support provided, the working relationships established with such other interfacing activities as Program Management, Engineering, and Logistics.

It is further facilitated by the resources and facilities assigned to the function, including such resources as automated tools, connectivity to a shared data environment, and other infrastructure elements. Integrated product and process development (IPPD) and the use of integrated product teams (IPTs) facilitate the interaction and communication between all parties involved in a common CM process. The training and experience of the personnel and the guidance and resources they have at their disposal are also facilitators.

The Management and Planning process may be constrained by a compressed time schedule for program execution, by a lack of needed people and tools, or by a lack of effective planning. It may also be constrained by contractual provisions that limit the CM manager's sphere of control.

The outputs from this activity consist of CM planning information and the resultant documented CM process that determine the extent of allocation

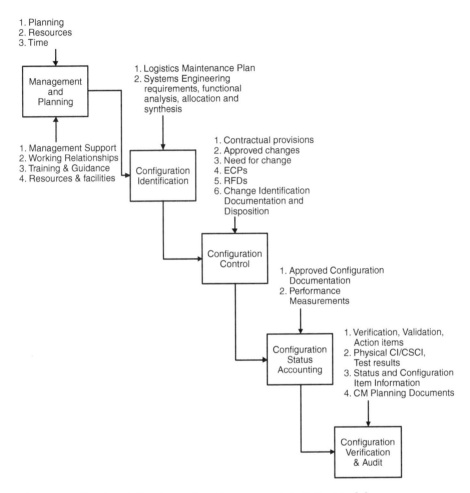

Figure 3.2 Top-Level Configuration Management Activity Model

of the CM functional activities. The need to perform the CM activities, described below, is independent of any specific organizational structure. The outputs from this activity also include statement of work language and other information to be inserted in Requests for Proposals (RFPs) and contracts.

Configuration Identification

This activity provides the foundation for all the other CM functional activities. Facilitated by the documented CM process and by open communications, this activity interacts with system engineering. It provides approved configuration documentation to document the physical and functional characteristics of the system or item, establishes baselines for configuration control, creates records in the status accounting database, and provides documentation for configuration verification and audit. In addition, product and document identifiers (nomenclature and numbering) are an important output from this activity.

Configuration Control

The Configuration Control process receives input from Configuration Identification defining the current configuration baseline. It receives and processes requests for engineering changes from technical, operational, and contracts functions, and it receives Engineering Change Proposals (ECPs) and Requests for Deviations (RFDs).

The Configuration Control activity is facilitated by communications, the documented CM process, and by information obtained from the status accounting database as needed. This information includes the current implementation status of approved changes and other pertinent information concerning the configuration of items in design, in production, and in the operational inventory.

This activity may communicate requests for documentation of engineering changes to developers. It subsequently provides for the review and approval/disapproval of proposed changes, and for the necessary authorization and direction for change implementation.

It provides input to status accounting about change identifiers, the progress of the change documentation through the steps in the configuration control decision/authorization process, and the implementation status of authorized changes.

Configuration Status Accounting (CSA)

All the other CM activities provide information to the status accounting database as a by-product of transactions that take place as the functions are performed. Limited or constrained only by contractual provisions and aided or facilitated by the documented CM process and open communications, this activity provides the visibility into status and configuration information concerning the product and its documentation.

The CSA information is maintained in a CM database. This information may include such information as the as-designed, as-built, as-delivered, or as-modified configuration of any serial-numbered unit of the product, as well as of any replaceable component within the product. Other information, such as the current status of any change, the history of any change, and the schedules for and status of configuration audits (including the status of resultant action items) can also be accessed in the database.

Metrics (performance measurements) on CM activities are generated from the information in the CSA database and provided to the Management and Planning function for use in monitoring the process and in developing continuous improvements.

Configuration Verification and Audit

Inputs to Configuration Verification and Audit (Functional and Physical Configuration Audit) include schedule information (from status accounting), configuration documentation (from configuration identification), product test results, and the physical hardware or software product or its representation, manufacturing instructions, and the software engineering environment.

Outputs include verification that the product's performance requirements have been achieved by the product design and that the product design has been accurately documented in the configuration documentation. This process is also applied to verify the incorporation of approved engineering changes. Configuration verification should be an embedded function of the process for creating and modifying the product. Process validation in lieu of physical inspection may be appropriate.

Successful completion of verification and audit activities results in a verified product and documentation set that may be confidently considered a product baseline, as well as a validated process that will maintain the continuing consistency of product to documentation.

RELATION TO SYSTEMS ENGINEERING PROCESS

Configuration management is a key element in the systems engineering process, as illustrated in Figure 3.3 because the Systems Engineering Process governs the product development and addresses all aspects of total system performance.

In general, the Systems Engineering Process is associated with operational analysis, requirements definition, and design determination. It includes defining the interfaces internal and external to the system, including hardware-to-hardware, hardware-to-software, and software-to-software interfaces. The tools of system engineering typically exercised in an integrated product team environment include:

■ *Requirements Analysis:* used to determine system technical requirements, and to provide verifiable performance-based requirements in the system utilization environments, and the top-level functional requirements that the system must meet.

■ *Functional Analysis and Allocation:* integrates the functional system architecture to the depth needed to support synthesis of solutions for people, products, processes, and management of risk. It is conducted iteratively to define successively lower-level functions; the lowest level yields a set of requirements that must be performed by components of the system to meet the top-level requirements.

■ *Synthesis:* commonly understood as preliminary and detailed design, this translates the functional and performance requirements into a description of the complete system that satisfies the requirements.

As shown in Figure 3.3, the Systems Engineering Process uses the "requirements loop" and the "design loop" in an iterative analytic approach to make operational, requirements, and design decisions at successively lower levels. As this process iterates, requirements are defined, documented, and approved within the CM process in the form of performance specifications for the functional baseline, and for the allocated baselines for specific components of the system identified as configuration items (CIs).

Outputs of the Systems Engineering Process also include the basis for drawings and data sets that are released to produce the item and, after

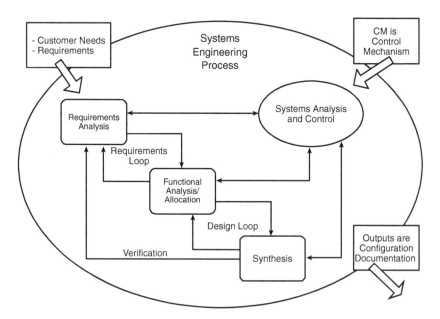

Figure 3.3 How CM relates to Systems Engineering

Table 3.1 Implementation of "Global" Government CM Management Activity

CM Management Activities

1. Prepare for next phase:
   - Perform CM planning
   - Develop/revise concept of operation
   - Determine/update CM acquisition strategy
   - Develop RFP CM requirements and goals
   - Prepare CM proposal evaluation criteria
   - Establish CM infrastructure needs/changes
   - Resources and facilities
2. Implement CM process:
   - Assign roles and responsibilities
   - Select/acquire/customize automated CM tools
   - Prepare, gain acceptance of, and implement procedures
   - Conduct training
   - Manage process
3. Measure/evaluate CM process and performance:
   - Develop/select metrics
   - Coordinate and communicate metrics
   - Establish data collection process
   - Obtain measurement data
   - Assess trends
   - Establish levels of confidence
   - Provide feedback
   - Implement appropriate corrective action
4. Effect process improvements/document lessons learned:
   - Revise process, procedures, training
   - Implement and continue measures/improvement cycle
   - Document changes, reasons, and results

verification/audit, form the product baseline. Thus, systems engineering is the process that produces the technical information for which the CM process provides technical control. As the CM process generates requirements for changes, the Systems Engineering Process is exercised to define the technical basis for the change.

Management and planning activities are common to all phases of the program life cycle, although the details upon which that management activity focuses vary from phase to phase. The global activities utilized by the federal government are illustrated in Table 3.1.

During each phase of the program life cycle, preparation for the following phase takes place. For concept exploration phases, this work

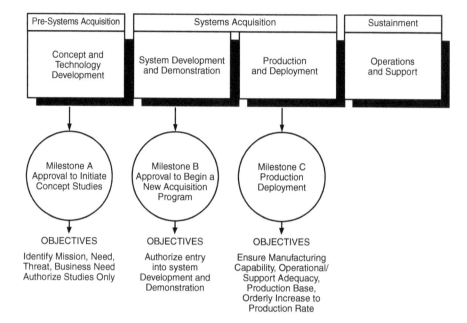

Figure 3.4 Implementation of "Global" Government CM Management Activity

takes place prior to the initiation of the conception phase, when the requirements for funded study efforts are being formulated.

CM planning is a vital part of the preparation for each phase (see Figure 3.4). CM planning consists of determining what the CM concept of operation and acquisition strategy for the forthcoming phase will be and preparing or revising the configuration management plan accordingly. Configuration managers must envision future phases and determine what information in the current phase and the immediately following phase must be captured to meet the needs of those future phases.

The CM concept of operation answers questions such as:

- What are the CM objectives for the coming phase?
- What is the rationale for these CM objectives?
- How is each CM objective related to program objectives and risks?
- What is the risk associated with not meeting the objectives?
- How can achievement of the objectives be measured?
- What information is required to support the CM goals for the next phase? Future phases?
- How can that information best be obtained?
- What are the deliverables from the next program phase?
- Which deliverables are configuration items?
- How will the final listing of CIs be officially designated?

- What is the end use of each CI?
- How are they to be supported?
- To what level are performance specifications required? CIs? Repairable components? Replaceable components?
- What level of configuration documentation (e.g., performance specifications, detail specifications, complete technical data package) will be required by the end of the next phase?
- What kinds of configuration identifiers (e.g., part numbers, serial numbers, etc.) will be required by the end of the next phase?
- Which baselines (and documents) will already be subject to configuration control at the start of the next phase?
- What baselines will be established during the next phase? Functional? Allocated? Product?
- What documents need to be included in those baselines?
- What status accounting will be needed in the next phase?

Obviously, these questions cannot and should not be answered in isolation. They require close coordination, preferably in a teaming atmosphere. Where feasible, it is desirable to work out planning for future phases within a teaming arrangement with everyone participating in the current phase. This provides an opportunity to examine all perspectives on the critical issues and goals in an open atmosphere, and to arrive at an optimum approach.

In addition to enabling the CM manager to complete his or her CM plan, the answers to these questions also provide a rational basis for developing and coordinating configuration management and data management requirements to appear in Requests for Proposal, and in formulating the criteria to be used to evaluate proposals.

IMPLEMENTING THE CM PROCESS

During each program life-cycle phase, the CM manager implements the planned CM process. Preparing procedures and coordinating them with all participants in the process completes the process definition that was initiated in the CM planning activity preceding this phase.

CM cannot be accomplished effectively without the participation and cooperation of many different functional activities. There is no single CM function that does not involve at least two or more interfaces. To accomplish the CM goals requires "team play." One of the best ways to achieve team play is to provide the vision and then solicit cooperative constructive input on the details of the implementing procedures. Each functional area must understand the particular roles and responsibilities that they have in the CM process. The tasks that they are to perform must be integrated into their workflow and given high priority. Coordinating the procedures is the initial step.

Any changes in the infrastructure necessary for the performance of CM during the phase are accomplished and tested, including the installation of appropriate automated tools and their integration with the data environment. Personnel from all disciplines and/or integrated product teams are then trained in the overall process and in the specific procedures and tools that they will use. Training pays dividends in a smooth, seamless process in which personnel, who understand their roles and the roles of others with whom they interface, work cooperatively and treat each interfacing player as a "customer."

Once a well-thought-out plan and a documented and agreed-to process are in place, the CM manager must employ modern management techniques to assess process effectiveness, ensure anticipated results, and fine-tune the process as necessary. It is also necessary to maintain the process documentation by updating plans, procedures, and training, as required.

It all starts and ends with communication:

- Articulating clear goals and objectives
- Making sure that the various players understand and cooperate
- Providing frequent feedback
- Ensuring that current status information, needed to complete process steps, is accessible
- Paying attention to the inevitable minor problems that surface

MEASURING AND EVALUATING THE CM PROCESS

The CM process is measured and evaluated using metrics and program reviews.

CM, by its very nature, is cross-functional. No important CM function is performed without interaction with other functional or team members. Therefore, CM objectives and measurements cannot and should not be divorced from the interacting systems engineering, design engineering, logistics, contracting, and other program objectives and processes. Moreover, it is not the efficiency of CM activities, per se, that add value, but their result in contributing to overall program objectives.

Improving the CM process is a venture that typically requires interaction across a broad spectrum of program activities, including technical, financial, and contractual. The process must be documented to a level of detail that is:

- Easily understood by all participants in the process

■ Focused on the key process interfaces
■ Less detailed than the procedures used to perform the process but sufficient to determine what must be measured to obtain factual information on the process

A metric involves more than a measurement; it consists of:

■ An operational definition of the metric that defines what is to be measured; why the metric is employed; and when, where, and how it is used. It can also help to determine when a metric has outlived its usefulness and should be discontinued.
■ The collection and recording of actual measurement data. In the case of the CM process, this step can often be accomplished by querying the status accounting database, which normally can provide a great deal of process flow information.
■ The reduction of the measurement data into a presentation format (e.g., run chart, control chart, cause and effect diagram, Pareto chart, histogram) to best illuminate problems or bottlenecks and lead to the determination of root cause or largest constraint.

An effective metric has the following attributes:

■ It is meaningful in terms of customer relationships (where the "customer" can be any user of information that is provided).
■ It relates to an organization's goals and objectives, and tells how well they are being met by the process, or part of the process, being measured.
■ It is timely, simple, logical, and repeatable; unambiguously defined; and economical to collect.
■ It shows a trend over time that will drive the appropriate forward-focused action and thus benefit the entire organization.

Metrics can include:

■ Average time variance from scheduled time
■ Rate of first-pass approvals
■ Volume of deviation requests by cause
■ The number of scheduled, performed, and completed configuration management audits during each phase of the life cycle
■ The rate of new changes being released and the rate that changes are being verified as completed; history compiled from successive deliveries is used to refine the slope of the expected rate

- The number of completed versus scheduled (stratified by type and priority) actions

CM BENEFITS AND RISKS BY PROGRAM LIFE-CYCLE ACTIVITY (SEE FIGURE 3.5)

Management and Planning: Concept and Technology Development Phase

This phase consists of the following steps:

1. Develop concept of operation and acquisition strategy for CM in Systems Acquisition.
2. Prepare, coordinate, and release procedures implementing the CM process; conduct training.
3. Measure and evaluate CM process.
4. Prepare and coordinate configuration management plans.
5. Define data interface and requirements.
6. Document lessons learned.
7. Develop CM requirements, information/data, and metrics.

Benefits include:

- The appropriate level of resources and the right information to efficiently and effectively conduct CM

Risks, if not done, include:

- Incompatible government and contractor CM systems
- Inadequate or excessive resources
- Inability to perform effectively due to lack of timely information

Configuration Identification: Concept and Technology Development Phase

This phase consists of the following steps:

1. Implement identification method and review process to review concept exploration studies and draft RFP material.
2. Maintain a defined document identification and release process for systems engineering products such as concept study and associated reference documentation.
3. Establish an audit trail of decisions and document iterations.

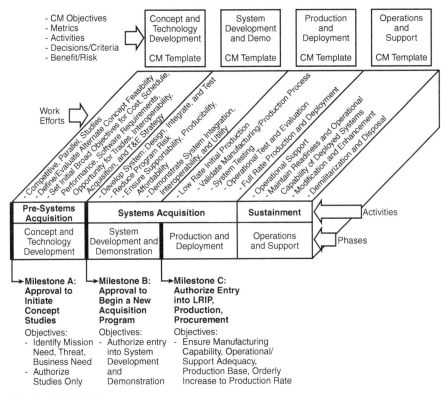

Figure 3.5 CM Objectives for Each Phase

Benefits include:

- Efficient management of information
- Access to correct, current data
- Effective information sharing

Risks, if not done, include:

- Lack of an audit trail of decisions
- Incorrect revisions used

Configuration Control: Concept and Technology Development Phase

1. Establish process for version control of concept study data files and document representations.

2. Implement common process to review and coordinate iterations of concept evaluation data.

Benefits include:

- Efficient review
- Ensures that all functional groups or integrated product teams are working to a common reference

Risks, if not done, include:

- Inconsistent, unreliable analyses, reports, and conclusions

Configuration Status Accounting: Concept and Technology Development Phase

This phase consists of the following steps:

1. Record and report status of management and technical decisions.
2. Provide traceability of all decisions to revisions in study documents and requirements documentation.
3. Record unique identifiers for the digital data files and document representations of each document and each hardware model or software package released for use on the computer.

Benefits include:

- Single information source
- Always current reference
- Common basis for decision
- Access for all with a need-to-know

Risks, if not done, include:

- Lack of decision audit trail
- Redundant document storage
- Decisions based on obsolete data

Management and Planning: System Development and Demonstration Phase

This phase consists of the following steps:

1. Develop concept of operation and acquisition strategy.
2. Prepare, coordinate, and release procedures implementing CM process; conduct training.
3. Measure and evaluate CM process.
4. Effect process improvements and document lessons learned during Engineering and Manufacturing Development and System Demonstrations.

Benefits include:

■ The appropriate level of resources and the right information to efficiently and effectively conduct CM

Risks, if not done, include:

■ Incompatible government and contractor CM systems
■ Inadequate or excessive resources
■ Inability to perform effectively due to lack of timely information
■ Loss of configuration control
■ Poor supportability
■ Excessive configuration documentation ordered that is not necessary for program management

Configuration Identification: System Development and Demonstration Phase

This phase consistes of the following steps:

1. Establish interface memoranda.
2. Implement identification method and release process for requirements and directive documentation.
3. Approve system specification establishing functional baseline.
4. Assign nomenclature, where appropriate.

Benefits include:

■ Known structure (hierarchy) of system/CI to which configuration documentation and other information is related
■ Performance, interface, and other attributes are clearly documented items and are identified and marked appropriately
■ Effective information-sharing among various groups
■ Identification of product and documentation are modified as significant changes are incorporated

- Release of configuration documents is control led, and configuration baselines are established and maintained
- Configuration documentation, and user and maintenance information correlate to product versions
- Internal control requirements for alternative solutions through a defined document release and control process
- Establish requirements traceability from top level to allocated requirements definitions
- Capture configuration definition of simulation software, prototypes, and engineering models through release and control of configuration documents
- Establish interface agreements

Risks, if not done, include:

- Poor correlation between requirements documents and test results
- Incorrect revisions used
- Not working to a common reference
- Inaccurate, incomplete interface data
- Inability to assess requirements iterations on interfaces
- Incomplete documentation

Configuration Control: System Development and Demonstration Phase

This phase consists of the following steps:

1. Establish configuration control process and procedures for development and demonstration, including change initiation, evaluation, and disposition.
2. Determine desired change effectivity.

Benefits include:

- Efficient change processing and orderly communication of change information
- Change decisions based on knowledge of change impact
- Changes limited to those necessary or beneficial
- Evaluation of cost, savings, and trade-offs facilitated
- Consistency between product and documentation
- Configuration control preserved at system interfaces
- Current baselines enable supportability
- Deviations are documented and limited

Risks, if not done, include:

- Chaotic, ad hoc change management
- Changes approved without knowledge of significant impacts
- Changes that are not necessary or offer no benefit
- Lack of confidence in cost and schedule estimates
- No assurance of product to document consistency
- Uncertainty at system interfaces
- Inconsistent basis for supportability
- No control of deviations
- Ineffective program management
- Essentially, technical anarchy

Configuration Status Accounting: System Development and Demonstration Phase

This phase consists of the following steps:

1. Select and tailor information to be provided.
2. Establish procedures and screens for interaction.
3. Test and assure the integrity of the configuration information; verify that CM business rules have been correctly applied.
4. Record and report the current performance requirements documentation.
5. Correlate definition of simulation software, prototype, and engineering model configurations to applicable test results, analyses, and trade studies.
6. Record all authorized changes to requirements documentation.
7. Provide traceability of requirements from the top-level documentation through all subordinate levels.
8. Provide controlled access to the digital data files and document representations of each document and software item released for use on the program.
9. Identify the current approved configuration documentation and configuration identifiers associated with each system.
10. Identify the digital data file(s) and document representations of all revisions and versions of each document and software delivered, or made accessible electronically.
11. Record and report the results of configuration audits, to include the status and final disposition of identified discrepancies and action items.
12. Record and report the status of proposed engineering changes from initiation to final approval to implementation.

13. Capture and report information about:
    - Product configuration status
    - Configuration documentation
    - Current baselines
    - Historic baselines
    - Change requests
    - Change proposals
    - Change notices
    - Variances
    - Warranty data and history
    - Replacements by maintenance action

Benefits include:

- Single information source providing consistency
- Always current reference
- Common basis for change decision
- Access for all with a need-to-know
- Correct, timely configuration information when needed to facilitate decision making on changes, deployment of assets, determining applicable replacements, and performing updates and upgrades

Risks, if not done, include:

- Redundant document storage and retrieval
- Costly searches for information and status
- Improper decisions made based on obsolete data
- The risk of inadequate status accounting may result in improper decisions about change effectivity, retrofit requirements, deployment of items requiring support assets that are not in place — all of which contribute to avoidable cost

Configuration Audit: System Development and Demonstration Phase

This phase consists of the following steps:

1. Assign audit co-chair for each audit.
2. Approve audit agenda(s).
3. Approve minutes.
4. Perform audit planning and pre-audit preparation.
5. Conduct formal audit when required.

6. Review performance requirements, test plans, results, and other evidence to determine that the product performs as specified, warranteed, and advertised.
7. Perform physical inspection of product and design information; ensure accuracy, consistency with, and conformance to acceptable practice.
8. Record discrepancies; review to close out or determine action; record action items.
9. Track action items to closure via status accounting.

Benefits include:

- Verified configuration and documentation consistent with operational and support requirements
- Reliable and dependable baselines

Risks, if not done, include:

- Unnecessary and avoidable support costs
- Inaccurate technical manuals
- Replacement parts that do not fit
- Loss of confidence in supplier

Management and Planning: Production and Deployment Phase

This phase consists of the following steps:

1. Prepare, coordinate, and release procedures implementing CM process; conduct training.
2. Measure and evaluate CM process.
3. Update CM planning, as required, to reflect process improvements, new deployment information, changes in support/maintenance planning, major modifications, etc.

Benefits include:

- The appropriate level of resources and the right information to efficiently and effectively conduct CM

Risks, if not done, include:

- Inadequate resources to accomplish essential tasks late in program
- Poor supportability at a time of aging assets

Configuration Identification: Production and Deployment Phase

This phase consists of the following steps:

1. Perform basic configuration identification actions for documentation, hardware, and software created or revised as a result of approved engineering changes.
2. Maintain a product baseline.
3. Assign nomenclature, where appropriate.
4. If maintenance plan is affected by a change, make sure that the level of performance specification for the new configuration remains consistent with revised maintenance planning.
5. Release engineering design data (engineering drawings, computer models, software design documents).
6. Maintain design release (release record).

Benefits include:

- Performance, interface, and other attributes are clearly documented and used as basis for configuration control
- Items are appropriately identified and marked
- Re-identification occurs as significant changes are incorporated
- Release controls and configuration baselines are maintained
- Users and maintenance personnel can locate information correlated to correct product versions

Risks, if not done, include:

- Inability to provide efficient product support after production and deployment
- Inadequate or incorrect product identification
- Inability to distinguish between product versions, resulting in deployment of assets requiring excessive supportability and assets without the functional capability needed for assigned missions
- Inadequate basis for defining changes and corrective actions
- Uncertain, wasteful, and costly configuration control decisions

Configuration Control: Production and Deployment Phase

This phase consists of the following steps:

1. Establish configuration control procedures, including change initiation and operating procedures for change evaluation and disposition.
2. Identify need for changes.
3. Document local engineering changes and ensure that they do not impact current baselines, prior to approving their implementation.
4. Communicate on status and content of changes and deviation requests contemplated and in-process.

Benefits include:

■ Efficient change processing and orderly communication of change information
■ Change decisions based on knowledge of change impact
■ Changes limited to those necessary or beneficial
■ Evaluation of cost, savings, and trade-offs facilitated
■ Consistency between product and documentation
■ Configuration control preserved at system interfaces
■ Current baselines enable supportability
■ Deviations are documented and limited

Risks, if not done, include:

■ Chaotic, ad hoc change management
■ Changes approved without knowledge of significant impacts
■ Changes that are not necessary or offer no benefit
■ Lack of confidence in accurate cost and schedule estimates
■ No assurance of product to document consistency
■ Uncertainty at system interfaces
■ Inconsistent basis for supportability
■ No control of deviations
■ Ineffective program management

Configuration Status Accounting: Production and Deployment Phase

This phase consists of the following steps:

1. Establish procedures interacting with the database(s).
2. Test the integrity of the configuration information in the database(s); verify that CM business rules have been correctly applied.

3. Identify the current approved configuration documentation and configuration identifiers associated with each system or CI.
4. Identify data file(s) and document representations of revisions and versions of each document or software delivered, or made accessible electronically.
5. Record and report the results of configuration audits, to include the status and final disposition of identified discrepancies and action items.
6. Record and report the status of proposed engineering changes, from initiation to final approval to implementation.
7. Record and report the status of all critical and major requests for deviation that affect the configuration of a system or CI.
8. Report the effectivity and installation status of configuration changes to all systems or CI(s).
9. Provide the traceability of all changes from the original released configuration documentation of each system or CI.
10. Record and report configuration changes resulting from retrofit and by replacements through maintenance action.
11. Retain information about:

   ■ Product configuration status
   ■ Configuration documentation
   ■ Current baselines
   ■ Historic baselines
   ■ Change requests
   ■ Change proposals
   ■ Change notices
   ■ Deviations
   ■ Warranty data and history
   ■ Configuration verification and audit status/action item close-out

Benefits include:

   ■ Correct, timely configuration information, when needed, to facilitate decision making on changes, deployment of assets, determining applicable replacements, and performing updates and upgrades

Risks, if not done, include:

   ■ Inadequate status accounting may result in improper decisions about change effectivity, retrofit requirements, deployment of items requiring support assets that are not in place — all of which contribute to avoidable cost

Configuration Audit: Production and Deployment Phase

This phase consists of the following steps:

1. Assign audit co-chair for each audit.
2. Approve audit agenda(s).
3. Approve minutes.
4. Certify processes for engineering.
5. Release, configuration control, and status accounting as adequate to maintain baseline control.
6. Review performance requirements, test plans, results, and other evidence to determine that the product performs as specified, warranteed, and advertised.
7. Perform physical inspection of product and design information; ensure accuracy, consistency, and conformance with acceptable practices.
8. Record discrepancies; review to close out or determine action; and record action items.
9. Track action items to closure via status accounting.

Benefits include:

- Verified configuration and documentation consistent with operational and support requirements
- Reliable and dependable baselines

Risks, if not done, include:

- Unnecessary and avoidable support costs
- Inaccurate technical manuals
- Replacement parts that do not fit
- Loss of confidence in supplier

Management and Planning: Operations and Support Phase

This phase consists of the following step:

1. Update CM planning, as required, to reflect new deployment information, changes in support and maintenance planning, major modifications, etc.

Benefits include:

- The appropriate level of resources and the right information to efficiently and effectively conduct CM

Risks, if not done, include:

- Inadequate resources to accomplish essential tasks late in the program
- Poor supportability at a time of aging assets

Configuration Identification: Operations and Support Phase

This phase consists of the following steps:

1. Perform basic configuration identification actions for documentation, hardware, and software created or revised as a result of approved engineering changes.
2. If maintenance plan is affected by a change, make sure that the level of performance specification for the new configuration remains consistent with revised maintenance planning.
3. Track traceable items via serial number or lot number.

Benefits include:

- Re-identification occurs as significant changes are incorporated
- Users and maintenance personnel can locate correct information for product versions

Risks, if not done, include:

- Inability to distinguish between product versions resulting in deployment of assets with incorrect or excessive support assets, or without the functional capability needed for assigned missions

Configuration Control: Operations and Support Phase

This phase consists of the following steps:

1. Continue configuration control procedures, including change initiation and CCB operating procedures for change evaluation and disposition.

2. Document local engineering changes and ensure they do not impact current baselines, prior to approving their implementation. Request review when necessary.
3. Communicate on status and content of changes and deviation requests contemplated and in process.
4. Process proposed changes to approved baseline configuration documentation.
5. Implement change and verify re-established consistency of product, documentation, operation, and maintenance resources.

Benefits include:

■ Consistency between product and documentation
■ Current baselines enable supportability

Risks, if not done, include:

■ No assurance of product to document consistency
■ Inconsistent basis for supportability

Configuration Status Accounting: Operations and Support Phase

This phase consists of the following steps:

1. Establish procedures for interacting with the database(s).
2. Test the integrity of the configuration information in the database(s); verify that CM business rules have been correctly applied.
3. Record and report configuration changes resulting from retrofit and by replacements through maintenance action.

Benefits include:

■ Correct, timely information for decision making on changes, deployment of assets, applicable replacements, and performing updates and upgrades

Risks, if not done, include:

■ Improper decisions about change effectivity, retrofit requirements, deployment of items requiring support assets that are not in place — all of which contribute to avoidable cost

EFFECT PROCESS IMPROVEMENT AND DOCUMENT LESSONS LEARNED

We learn from effective measurements and metrics if the process is or is not meeting objectives. We also learn which part of the process is currently the biggest contributor to detected backlogs, bottlenecks, repeat effort, or failures and errors. By focusing on that weakest link, one can isolate the problem and trace it to its root cause. Often, the cause can be corrected by streamlining the process (eliminating redundancy or non-value-adding steps, modifying sequence, performing tasks in parallel rather than in series) or improving communications. Measurements should continue as is or be altered to fit the new solution for a period of time sufficient to assess if the revised process is resulting in improved performance. This measurement/improvement cycle is an iterative process. Once a weak link is improved, the process metrics are again reviewed to determine and improve other parts of the process that stand out as contributors to deficiencies or lengthy cycle time.

The key personnel involved in the process must be participants in defining the improvements. Their "buy-in" is essential if the improvements are to be implemented effectively. Detailed procedures and effected automated systems must be modified and personnel must be retrained, as required. These "total quality management aspects" of the job are best performed as an integral part of the process of managing, rather than as isolated exercises. It is also foolish to expend effort in improving processes without clearly documenting the lessons learned to leverage the efficiency of future applications. Changes made in the process, over time, should be recorded, along with the reasons the changes were made and the measured results. A suggested place to record process changes is in the configuration management plan. Initially, the CM plan was a projection of the expected implementation of configuration management over the program life cycle. As a minimum, it is updated during each phase for application during the next. Including process change and lessons learned information makes the plan a working document that reflects the transition from anticipated action (planning) to completed action (reality). It can then serve as a better reference to use in planning for the next program phase and in the initial planning for future programs.

SUMMARY

This chapter introduces the concept of configuration management using MIL-STD-973, which has since been superseded by the EIA-649 industry standard. Where EIA-649 provides the concepts for implementing a configuration management program, the military standard (and supporting documentation) provide detailed procedural instructions for CM implementation. Because MIL-STD-973 has always been referred to as the "bible" of CM, it is worth taking the time to review the concepts and constructs of "the military way."

REFERENCES

This chapter is based on the following report: MIL-HDBK-61A(SE), February 7, 2001, *Military Handbook: Configuration Management Guidance.*

RESOURCES

The following selected specifications, standards, and handbooks form part of the DoD CM process. Many of them can be found on the Internet by typing the document name into a search engine.

MIL-PRF-28000, Digital Representation for Communication of Product Data: IGES Application Subsets and IGES Application Protocols

MIL-PRF-28001, Markup Requirements and Generic Style Specification for Exchange of Text and Its Presentation

MIL-PRF-28002, Raster Graphics Representation in Binary Format, Requirements for MIL-DTL-31000, Technical Data Packages

MIL-STD-129, Military Marking

MIL-STD-196, Joint Electronics Type Designation System

MIL-STD-787, Joint Optical Range Instrumentation Type Designation System

MIL-STD-1812, Type Designation, Assignment, and Method for Obtaining

MIL-STD-1840, Automated Interchange of Technical Information

American Society of Mechanical Engineers

ASME Y14-100M, Engineering Drawing Practices

ASME Y14.24, Types and Applications of Engineering Drawings

ASME Y14.34M, Associated Lists

(Application for copies should be addressed to the American Society of Mechanical Engineers, 345 East 47th Street, New York, NY 10017-2392.)

Electronics Industries Alliance

ANSI/EIA-649-1998, National Consensus Standard for Configuration Management (DoD adopted)
ANSI/EIA-632-1998, Processes for Engineering a System
EIA-836, Consensus Standard for CM Data Exchange and Interoperability

(Application for copies should be addressed to Global Engineering Documents, 15 Inverness Way East, Englewood, CO 80112.)

Institute of Electrical and Electronic Engineers

IEEE STD 828-1990, Software Configuration Management Plans

(Application for copies should be addressed to the IEEE Service Center, P.O. Box 1331, 445 Hoes Lane, Piscataway, NJ 08855-1331.)

International Organization for Standardization

IS0 10007, Quality Management — Guidelines for Configuration Management
ISO/IEC 12207, Information Technology — Software Life Cycle Processes

(Application for copies should be addressed to the American National Standards Institute, 11 West 42nd St., New York, NY 10036.)

4

CONFIGURATION IDENTIFICATION

Configuration identification incrementally establishes and maintains the definitive current basis for control and status accounting of a system and its configuration items (CIs) throughout their life cycle (development, production, deployment, and operational support, until demilitarization and disposal). The configuration identification process ensures that all processes have common sets of documentation as the basis for developing a new system, modifying an existing component, buying a product for operational use, and providing support for the system and its components. The configuration identification process also includes identifiers that are shorthand references to items and their documentation.

HOW CONFIGURATION IDENTIFICATION WORKS

Good configuration control procedures ensure the continuous integrity of the configuration identification. The configuration identification process includes:

- Selecting configuration items at appropriate levels of the product structure to facilitate the documentation, control, and support of the items and their documentation
- Determining the types of configuration documentation required for each CI to define its performance, functional, and physical attributes, including internal and external interfaces; configuration documentation provides the basis to develop and procure software/parts/material, fabricate and assemble parts, inspect and test items, and maintain systems

- Determining the appropriate configuration control authority for each configuration document consistent with logistics support planning for the associated CI
- Issuing identifiers for the CIs and the configuration documentation
- Maintaining the configuration identification of CIs to facilitate effective logistics support of items in service
- Releasing configuration documentation
- Establishing configuration baselines for the configuration control of CIs

Effective configuration identification is a prerequisite for the other configuration management activities (i.e., configuration control, status accounting, audit), which all use the products of configuration identification. If CIs and their associated configuration documentation are not properly identified, it is impossible to control the changes to the items' configuration, to establish accurate records and reports, or to validate the configuration through audit.

Figure 4.1 is an activity model of the configuration identification process. The boxes represent activities. The arrows entering at the left of each box are inputs; those entering the top are constraints; those entering the bottom are facilitators or mechanisms; and those leaving each box from the right are outputs.

Inaccurate or incomplete configuration documentation can result in defective products, schedule delays, and higher maintenance costs after delivery.

The basic principles of configuration identification are articulated in EIA Standard 649. It cites the following purposes and benefits of configuration identification:

- Determines the structure (hierarchy) of a product and the organization and relationships of its configuration documentation and other product information
- Documents the performance, interface, and other attributes of a product
- Determines the appropriate level of identification marking of product and documentation
- Provides unique identity to a product or to a component part of a product
- Provides unique identity to the technical documents describing a product
- Modifies identification of product and documents to reflect incorporation of major changes
- Maintains release control of documents for baseline management

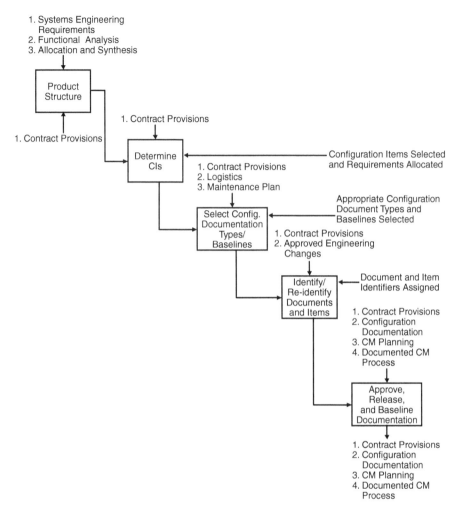

Figure 4.1 Configuration Identification Process Activity Model

- Enables a user or a service person to distinguish between product versions
- Enables a user or a service person to correlate a product to related user or maintenance instructions
- Facilitates management of information, including that in digital format
- Correlates individual product units to warranties and service life obligations
- Enables correlation of document revision level to product version or configuration
- Provides a reference point for defining changes and corrective actions

CONFIGURATION IDENTIFICATION GENERAL ACTIVITY GUIDES

A configuration identification process evaluation checklist is provided to assist in this process (see Table 4.1).

PRODUCT STRUCTURE

Product structure, also referred to as system architecture, refers to the identifiers, internal structure, and relationship of system components and associated configuration documentation. Product structure, derived from the functional analysis and allocation process of systems engineering, can be depicted graphically as a tree structure or as an indentured listing.

As a program matures through its early phases, the systems engineering process produces the optimized functional and physical composition of the system architecture to the level that it is necessary to specify and control item performance. This is the lowest level at which CIs are designated during the Engineering and Manufacturing Development phase of the life cycle. Management tools such as specification and drawing trees, and work breakdown structures are all views of the product structure that are directly relatable at the CI level.

Program and contract work breakdown structures (WBSs) are views of the product family tree structure showing the hardware, software, services (see Figure 4.2), data, and facilities against which costs are collected. The WBS relates the elements of work to be accomplished to each other and to the end product. CIs are identified as work breakdown structure elements.

CONFIGURATION ITEMS

Selected items of system hardware or software (or combinations of hardware and software) are designated as configuration items (CIs).

CIs are the basic units of configuration management. They may vary widely in complexity, size, and type, from an aircraft, ship, tank, electronic system, or software program to a test meter or a round of ammunition. Regardless of form, size, or complexity, the configuration of a CI is documented and controlled. CI selection separates system components into identifiable subsets for the purpose of managing further development.

For each CI:

■ There will be associated configuration documentation (which may range from a performance specification to a detailed drawing to a commercial item description).

Table 4.1 Configuration Identification Process Evaluation Checklist

1. Documented process:
   a. Is there a documented configuration identification process?
   b. Is the documented process followed?
   c. Are personnel from all disciplines and teams involved in the process informed and knowledgeable about the procedures they are supposed to follow?
2. Product structure:
   a. Is the product (system/CIs) structured into a rational hierarchy?
   b. Are subordinate CIs identified at a reasonable level for:
      i. Specification of and measurement of performance?
      ii. Management of the effectivity of changes?
      iii. Obtaining spare parts using performance or design documents?
   c. Can the composition of each system/CI be determined from the configuration documentation?
3. Configuration documentation:
   a. Does the configuration documentation define the performance, functional, interface, and physical attributes of each system/CI ?
   b. Do the performance requirements of the system and/or top-level configuration item specifications meet or exceed threshold performance of the acquisition program baseline?
   c. Are all configuration documents uniquely identified?
      i. Does the identification reflect the source of the preparing original design activity and current design activity, the type of document, and an alphanumeric identifier?
      ii. Can each document be easily associated with the CI configuration to which it relates and, where applicable, the range of CI serial numbers to which it applies?
4. Product identification:
   a. Are all CIs and subordinate parts down to the level of nonreparability assigned individual unique part/item identifiers?
   b. Do the assigned identifiers enable:
      i. Each part/item to be distinguished from all other parts/items?
      ii. Each configuration of an item to be distinguished from earlier and later configurations?
   c. Can the next higher assembly application of each part be determined from the design documentation (including associated lists/records)?
   d. Does the documentation indicate whether CIs are serialized (or lot controlled)?
   e. Is the common base identifier for serialization/lot numbering always a non-changing identifier?
   f. Is part/item effectivity to be defined in a manner appropriate for the product type?
   g. When an item is changed to a new configuration, is its identifier altered in both the configuration documentation and on the item itself to reflect the new configuration?

Table 4.1 Configuration Identification Process Evaluation Checklist (continued)

5. Configuration baselines:
    a. Are appropriate configuration baselines established and maintained as a basis for configuration control?
    b. Is the current configuration baseline for the system and for each CI easily determinable?
    c. Is an adequate system of release control in place and used for the release of all configuration documents?
        i. Can the as-released configuration of each CI be determined?
        ii. Can past configurations be determined? (applies to both the engineering design configuration and the product configuration)
        iii. Do release records reflect the authority for changing from one configuration to the next? Do they reference the ECP identifier and contract modification (where applicable)?
        iv. Does the release system prevent unauthorized changes to released documents?
6. Interface control:
    a. For external interfaces, are interface agreements established where necessary to document and agree to performance, functional, and physical interfaces?
    b. Do CIs being developed by different contractors for the program have well-defined interfaces?
7. Metrics:
    a. Are statistical records of document release and other measurable configuration identification actions maintained?
    b. Is the data reduced to meaningful measurement useful in maintaining and improving the process?

■ Configuration changes will be controlled.
■ Configuration status accounting records will be maintained.
■ Configuration audits will be conducted to verify performance and product configuration (unless the CI has an already established product baseline).

To define and control the performance of a system or CI does not mean that all of its hardware and software components must be designated as CIs.

Computer software items, because they typically control the functionality of a system, are almost always designated as CIs. The term "CI" encompasses both hardware and software; when a statement applies only to hardware, or only to software, the terms "HWCI" and "CSCI," respectively, are used.

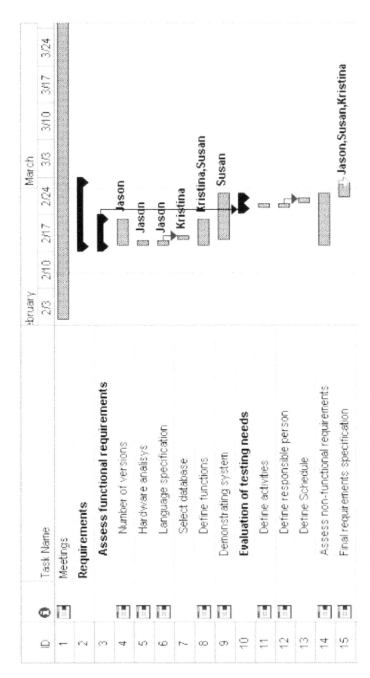

Figure 4.2 A WBS for Software Engineering Services

The determination of the need to designate items as CIs is normally simple and straightforward. However, there are many cases in which other lower-level items should also be selected based on the management needs of the program. Some of the primary reasons for designating separate CIs are:

- Critical, new, or modified design
- Independent end-use functions
- Sub-assembly factors, such as the need for separate configuration control or a separate address for the effectivity of changes
- Components common to several systems
- Interface with other systems, equipment, or software
- Level at which interchangeability must be maintained
- Separate delivery or installation requirement
- Separate definition of performance and test requirements
- High risk and critical components

Although the initial CI selection generally occurs early in the acquisition process, its consequences are lasting and affect many aspects of program management, systems engineering, acquisition logistics, and configuration management. CI selection establishes the level of configuration control throughout the system life cycle. Selecting CIs separates a system into individually identified components for the purpose of managing their development and support.

Many engineering requirements or considerations can influence the selection of CIs. Throughout development and support, the allocation of engineering effort and organization are rooted in the selection of CIs.

CONFIGURATION ITEM SELECTION CRITERIA

The process of selecting configuration items requires the exercise of good systems engineering judgment based on experience, and supported by cost trade-off considerations. No fixed rules govern CI selection or dictate the optimum number of CIs for a particular system. Rather, guidelines for making the appropriate judgments are provided in the "General Guidance," "CI Selection Checklist," and "Additional Factors" sub-sections of this section.

General Guidance

1. Designating a system component as a CI increases visibility and management control throughout the development and support

phases. For system-critical or high technical risk components, added visibility can help in meeting specified requirements and maintaining schedules.

2. For each development contract, there should be at least one CI designated.

3. For complex systems, major functional design components are usually designated as CIs. The initial selection is normally limited to the major component level of the work breakdown structure.

4. As system design evolves during development and complex items are further subdivided into their components, additional CIs may be identified.

5. Each CI should represent a separable entity that implements at least one end-use function.

6. The selection of CIs should reflect a high degree of independence among the CIs at the same level. Subordinate components of a CI, which are recommended as CIs during the detail design process, should all be functionally interrelated.

7. Operational software should always be differentiated from support software by designating each as a separate CI.

8. The complexity of CI interfaces in a system should be minimized. Complexity often results in increased risk and cost.

9. All subassemblies of a CI should have common mission, installation, and deployment requirements.

10. For systems with common components, sub-systems, or support equipment, each common item should be separately designated as a CI at an assembly level common to both systems.

11. A unique component that is peculiar to only one of multiple similar systems should be identified as a separate CI of that system.

12. Off-the-shelf, privately developed items generally should not be designated as CIs. However, commercially available items that have been modified should not necessarily be excluded from CI selection. (Factors to consider include the extent of the modification; the criticality of the modified CI to the mission of the system; and the extent of ownership, data rights, and configuration documentation required and available.)

CI Selection Checklist

If most of the answers to the following questions are "yes," the item should be considered for designation as a separate CI. If most answers are "no," it probably should not be designated as a CI. However, a single overriding "yes" may be sufficient to require an item to be separately identified as a CI.

1. Is the item's schedule critical or high risk? Would failure of the item have a significant financial impact?
2. Does the item implement critical capabilities (e.g., security protection, human safety, etc.)? Would CI designation enhance the required level of control and verification of these capabilities?
3. Will the item require development of a new design or a significant modification to an existing design?
4. Is the item computer hardware or software?
5. Does the item incorporate unproven technologies?
6. Does the item have an interface with a CI developed under another contract?
7. Can the item be readily marked to identify it as a separate, controlled item?
8. Does the item interface with a CI controlled by another design activity?
9. Will it be necessary to have an accurate record of the item's exact configuration and the status of changes to it during its life cycle?
10. Can (or must) the item be independently tested?
11. Is the item required for logistic support?
12. Is it, or does it have the potential to be, designated for separate procurement?
13. Have different activities have been identified to logistically support various parts of the system?
14. Does the item have separate mission, training, test, maintenance, and support functions, or require separately designated versions for such purposes?
15. Do all sub-assemblies of the item have common mission, installation, and deployment requirements, common testing and acceptance?

ADDITIONAL FACTORS

Many development and support planning milestones are related to CIs. Activities such as performance or design verification demonstration, system integration and testing, technical reviews and audits, and budget allocations are usually accomplished for each of the CIs selected. The number of CIs selected will determine the number of separate meetings related to the overall activity. A large number of CIs may lead to delays in completing critical milestones.

Existing CIs can be modified and designated as a separate and different configuration of that CI, thus saving time and money. Factors to be traded off include complexity, the use of new materials, processes, and the insertion of new technology.

There are no rules to dictate the optimum number of CIs for a given system. In general, however, the fewer CIs, the better. Selecting too many CIs increases development and support costs.

Each CI to be developed, especially CSCIs, comes with an associated set of technical reviews, audits, performance or design verification demonstrations, formal unit and integration tests, and documentation requirements. Each of these activities adds an increment of development cost and also adds costs for storage and upkeep of information related to the activities and the documentation.

The consequences of designating too many CIs include:

- Numerous inter-CI interfaces to be defined, and documented, which, if they are all baselined early in the EMD phase, will inhibit the freedom to evolve the design solution, solve problems expeditiously, and implement advantageous changes without contractual consequence
- CI functionality defined at too low a level or including unnecessary design constraints requiring formal test, and technical reviews, beyond what is required to achieve reasonable assurance of system performance (this is also a concern if performance specifications for the lower-level CIs are baselined too early in the EMD phase)
- Increased overall number of requirements in the documentation disproportionate to the unique technical content of the requirements
- Excessive fragmentation, which may actually decrease understanding of system performance; fragmented description of functionality increases the overall volume of requirements, is more difficult to understand, and complicates the document review, approval, and control process
- Increased cost

The consequences of having too few CIs include:

- Increased complexity of each CI, resulting in decreasing management insight and ability to assess progress
- Where the lowest-level designated CI is a complex item (implementing unrelated functions, containing both hardware and software components, etc.):
  - The potential for reuse of the CI, or portions of the CI, is diminished
  - Re-procurement of the CI and components is complicated
  - Potential re-procurement sources are limited
  - Formal testing of critical capabilities may be delayed or made more difficult

■ The inability to account for the deployment of a CI, whose component parts are disbursed to different locations
■ Difficulty in addressing the effectivity of changes and retrofit actions, particularly when there are different quantities or separately deliverable components
■ Increased complexity in managing and accounting for common assemblies and components

CONFIGURATION DOCUMENTATION

The term "configuration documentation" characterizes the information that defines the performance and functional and physical attributes of a product. As described in EIA Standard 649, all other product documentation (such as operation and maintenance manuals, illustrated parts breakdowns, test plans and procedures) are based on and relate to information in the configuration documentation. The configuration documentation associated with each CI provides the basis for configuration control, logistics support, post-deployment, and software support.

Specification Types Categorized by Object

This section describes the type of CI "objects" that a specification is intended to define. This category is part of a string of categories that comprise the specification type.

System

A system specification defines the overall performance and mission requirements for a system, allocates requirements to lower-level components of the system, and identifies system interface and interoperability constraints. It is the top-level functional requirements specification for the system. A system specification is used to establish a functional baseline for the system.

Large systems are usually decomposed; Level 2 system components are often complex enough to be called "systems" themselves (although, for configuration management purposes, they are designated as subsystems or CIs).

Item

The item specification for a CI defines the performance and interface requirements and design and interoperability constraints that have been allocated to the CI from a system or higher-level CI.

Item specifications provide the contractual basis for the development and verification of CI performance. The item performance (development) specification(s) will normally be used to establish the allocated baseline for the CI.

Software

Computer software configuration items (CSCIs) are documented with software specifications. A software detailed specification is similar to the software requirements specification plus the set of design documents describing the software, interface, and database design.

Process

Process specifications are used where a process (or service) has been developed specifically for use with a particular system/item and is critical to its performance or design. The process specification forms part of the product baseline of the CI(s).

Specification Types Categorized by Purpose

Performance

A performance specification provides requirements for a system, item, software, process, or material in terms of the required results and the criteria for verifying compliance. It defines the functional requirements, the operational environment, and interface and interchangeability requirements, but does not state how the requirements are to be achieved, require the use of specific materials or parts, or give design or construction requirements beyond those design constraints necessary to unambiguously define interface and interchangeability requirements.

The intent of a performance specification is to allow more than one design solution for the requirements specified so that interchangeable competitive products can be evaluated, and new technology can be inserted.

Detail

A detail specification may consist of all detail requirements or a blend of performance and detail requirements. The preference is for one specification to convey all the performance and detail requirements for an item.

One intent of the detail specification, as a revision of the performance specification, is to provide sufficient detail to distinguish the features of one design solution for an item from other competing design solutions.

Another intent is to specify details of the design solution, such as the use of specific parts and materials, that are essential for critical safety or economic reasons, but to state as many requirements in performance terms as possible.

What makes a stated requirement a design requirement and not a performance requirement is that it prescribes design, construction, material, or quality control solutions, rather than allow for development flexibility.

Design Solution Document Concepts

The requirements of the functional and allocated baselines are basically design constraints. The design solution evolves from the design and development process during the engineering and manufacturing development (EMD) phase of the life cycle. This process essentially converts the performance requirements of the baseline specification into a specific product definition that can be manufactured to produce a hardware item or compiled to produce a software item.

It is documented in design documentation for the hardware and the software comprising each CI. For hardware, the design documentation may be in the form of engineering drawings and associated lists, as well as the material and process documents that are referenced by the drawings. In the current information environment, the primary design documentation source may be in the form of two- or three-dimensional engineering models. In that case, a drawing is simply a two-dimensional view of a model that exists in a database file. Various models and product modeling tools can be employed. Engineering drawings may or may not exist as a central part of the product manufacturing process, depending on the product and the degree of automation technology employed.

In an automated development and production environment, an item is designed on the engineer's workstation, manufacturing instructions are added at the manufacturing planner's workstation, and the results are fed directly to automated machinery that produces the item. Commonly, items are designed using computer-aided design tools (CADAM, CATIA, AUTOCAD, etc.) and engineering drawings are plotted for human checking and review. Where engineering drawings are required as a contract deliverable, they should be delivered in place, in a CALS-compliant format.

For software, the design evolves through a software engineering process, using a variety of integrated tools, often called the software engineering environment (e.g., computer-aided software engineering [CASE]). The process results in computer-based versions of documentation, source, and executable code for every CSCI. The process employed to manage the automated software documentation (e.g., software library management and archiving) is similar to the process used to manage automated hardware documentation, although different tools can be employed. Upon close examination, it is fundamentally the same process used to manage the files, which contain software code. The same business rules apply to both software and documents in terms of their identification and relationships to other entities.

The developmental configuration management process consists of a formal process to control the documentation and repositories containing the elements of the developmental configuration. The engineering release system and engineering release records are an important part of this management process.

Each and every version of all elements of the developmental configuration released, for whatever purpose, should be maintained, along with the reasons the version was released and the rationale for superseding the previous version.

Software Documentation List

Process Implementation: Planning

- *Operational Concept Document:* proposed system; user needs
- *Software Development Plan:* development effort; process, methods, schedules, organization, resources (includes or refers to SCM and SQA plans)
- *Software Test Plan:* qualification testing; SW item; SW system; environment, tests, schedules
- *Software Installation Plan:* installing SW; user sites; preparations; training; conversion
- *Software Transition Plan:* transitioning to maintenance organization; HW; SW; resources; life-cycle support

System Requirements Analysis and Architectural Design

- *System/Sub-system Specification:* specifies system or sub-system requirements; requirement verification methods (may be supplemented with system-level IRS)
- *System/Sub-system Design Description:* system/sub-system-wide design; architectural design; basis for system development (may be supplemented with IDD, DBDD)

Software Requirements Analysis and Design

- *Software Requirements Specification:* specifies SW requirements; verification methods (may be supplemented with IRS)

- *Interface Requirements Specification:* specifies interface requirements for one or more systems, sub-systems, HW items, SW items, operations or other system components; any number of interfaces (can supplement SSS, SSDD, SRS)

Software Architectural and Detailed Design

- *Software Design Description:* SW item-wide design decisions; SW item architectural design; detailed design, basis for implementing; information for maintenance (may be supplemented by IDD, DBDD)
- *Interface Design Description:* interface characteristics; one or more systems, sub-systems, HW items, SW items, operations or other system components; any number of interfaces; detail companion to IRS; communicate and control interface design decisions
- *Database Design Description:* database design; related data, files, SW/database management system for access, basis for implementation and maintenance

Software Integration and Qualification Testing

- *Software Test Description:* test preparations; test cases; test procedures; qualification testing SW item, SW system or sub-system
- *Software Test Report:* record of test performed; assess results

As-Built Software Product Definition

- *Software Product Specification:* contains or references executable SW, source files; SW maintenance information; "as-built" design information, compilation, build, modification procedures; primary SW maintenance document
- *Software Version Description:* identifies and describes an SW version; used to release, track, and control each version

System Operation

- *Software User Manual:* hands-on software user; how to install and use SW, SW item group, SW system or sub-system
- *Software Input/Output Manual:* computer center; centralized or networked installation; how to access, input, and interpret output; batch or interactive (with SCOM as alternative to SUM)

- *Software Center Operator Manual:* computer center; centralized or networked installation; how to install and operate an SW system (with SIOM as alternative to SUM)
- *Computer Operator Manual:* information needed to operate a given computer and its peripherals

System/Software Maintenance

- *Computer Programming Manual:* information needed by programmer to program for a given computer; newly developed; special purpose; focus on computer, not on specific SW
- *Firmware Support Manual:* information to program and re-program firmware devices in a system; ROMs, PROMs, EPROMs, etc.

CONFIGURATION BASELINES

The concept of baselines is central to an effective configuration management program; it is, however, not a unique configuration management concept. The idea of using a known and defined point of reference is commonplace and is central to an effective management process. The essential idea of baselines is that in order to reach a destination, it is necessary to know one's starting point. To plan for, approve, or implement a configuration change, it is necessary to have a definition of the current configuration that is to be changed. To manage a program effectively, it is necessary to baseline the objectives for cost, schedule, and performance.

In configuration management, a configuration baseline is a fixed reference configuration established by defining and recording the approved configuration documentation for a system or CI at a milestone event or at a specified time.

Configuration baselines represent:

- Snapshots that capture the configuration or partial configuration of a CI at specific points in time
- Commitment points representing approval of a CI at a particular milestone in its development
- Control points that serve to focus management attention

Configuration Baseline Concepts

Major configuration baselines, known as the functional, allocated, and product baselines as well as the developmental configuration, are associated with milestones in the CI life cycle. Each of these major configuration baselines is designated when the given level of the CI's configuration documentation is deemed complete and correct, and needs to be formally protected from unwarranted and uncontrolled change from that point forward in its life cycle.

■ *Functional baseline:* the approved configuration documentation describing a system's or top-level configuration item's performance (functional, interoperability, and interface characteristics) and the verification required to demonstrate the achievement of those specified characteristics

■ *Allocated baseline:* the current approved performance-oriented documentation for a CI to be developed, which describes the functional and interface characteristics that are allocated from those of the higher-level CI and the verification required to demonstrate achievement of those specified characteristics

■ *Development configuration:* the design and associated technical documentation that defines the evolving design solution during development of a CI; the developmental configuration for a CI consists of internally released technical documentation for hardware and software design

■ *Product baseline:* the approved technical documentation that describes the configuration of a CI during the production, fielding/deployment, and operational support phases of its life cycle; the product baseline prescribes:
   ■ All necessary physical or form, fit, and function characteristics of a CI
   ■ The selected functional characteristics designated for production acceptance testing
   ■ The production acceptance test requirements

When used for reprocurement of a CI, the product baseline documentation also includes the allocated configuration documentation to ensure that performance requirements are not compromised.

Each configuration baseline serves as a point of departure for future CI changes. The current approved configuration documentation constitutes the current configuration baseline. Incremental configuration baselines occur sequentially over the life cycle of a CI as each new change is approved. Each change from the previous baseline to the current baseline occurs through a configuration control process.

The audit trail of the configuration control activity from the CI's original requirements documentation to the current baseline is maintained as part of configuration status accounting.

The functional baseline is established when its associated functional configuration documentation is approved. This baseline is always subject to configuration control. The functional baseline consists of the functional configuration documentation (FCD), which is the initial approved technical documentation for a system or top-level CI as set forth in a system specification prescribing:

■ All necessary functional characteristics
■ The verification required to demonstrate achievement of the specified functional characteristics
■ The necessary interface and interoperability characteristics with associated CIs, other system elements, and other systems
■ Identification of lower-level CIs, if any, and the configuration documentation for items (such as items separately developed or currently in the inventory) that are to be integrated or interfaced with the CI
■ Design constraints, such as envelope dimensions, component standardization, use of inventory items, and integrated logistics support policies

The functional baseline is usually defined as a result of the Concept and Technology Development phase, when that phase is included in the acquisition strategy. In the absence of a concept phase, the functional baseline is established during System Development and Demonstration. A functional baseline, whether formally established or not, is always in place at the inception of each phase. It is represented by whatever documentation is included or referenced by the contract to define the technical/performance requirements that the product must meet.

The allocated baseline is, in reality, a composite of a series of allocated baselines. Each allocated baseline consists of the allocated configuration documentation (ACD), which is the current approved performance-oriented documentation governing the development of a CI, in which each specification:

■ Defines the functional and interface characteristics allocated from those of the system or higher-level CI
■ Establishes the verification required to demonstrate achievement of its functional characteristics
■ Delineates necessary interface requirements with other associated CIs
■ Establishes design constraints, if any, such as component standardization, use of inventory items, and integrated logistics support requirements

The requirements in the specification are the basis for the design of the CI; the quality assurance provisions in the specification form the framework for the qualification testing program for the CI. The initial allocated baseline is established during System Development and Demonstration. The allocated baseline for each CI is documented in an item performance (or detail) specification, generally referred to as a development specification.

The product baseline is the approved documentation that completely describes the functional and physical characteristics of the CI, any required joint and combined operations interoperability characteristics of a CI (including a comprehensive summary of the other environment(s) and allied interfacing CIs or systems and equipment). It consists of the Product Configuration Documentation (PCD), which is the current approved technical documentation describing the configuration of a CI during the Production and Deployment, and Operational Support phases of its life cycle. The product baseline prescribes:

- All necessary physical or form, fit, and function characteristics of a CI
- The selected functional characteristics designated for production acceptance testing
- The production acceptance test requirements
- All allocated configuration documentation pertaining to the item, so that if the item were to be reprocured, the performance requirements for the item would also be included

The product baseline documentation includes the complete set of released and approved engineering design documents, such as the engineering models, engineering drawings, and associated lists for hardware, as well as the software, interface, and database design documents for software.

The functional, allocated, and product configuration documentation must be mutually consistent and compatible. Each succeeding level of configuration identification is a logical and detailed extension of its predecessor(s).

When viewed on a system basis, care must be exercised to ensure that all of the top-level requirements are accounted for in individual lower-level documents. This is a key function of such reviews as system, preliminary, and critical design reviews, but is greatly facilitated by the use of automated requirements allocation and traceability tools.

DOCUMENT AND ITEM IDENTIFICATION

This section describes the concepts for the assignment of identifiers to CIs, component parts, and their associated configuration documentation. Clearly identified items and documentation are essential to effective configuration management throughout the life cycle, particularly during the deployment and operational support period when the marking on a part is the key to installing a correct replacement part and finding the proper installation, operation, and maintenance instructions.

Each configuration document (as well as other documents) must have a unique identifier so that it can be associated correctly with the configuration of the item to which it relates. The DoD and all military components use the following three elements to ensure the unique identity of any document: CAGE code, document type, and document identifier. In addition, a revision identifier or date clearly specifies a specific issue of a document.

A document can have many representations, as, for example, a word processor file and a paper copy, or a CAD file and a representation of that CAD file inserted in a document. In addition to the identification assigned to each document, the digital files for each version of each representation of the document, and its component files, must be identified and managed.

It is the responsibility of each individual assigned to manage an item of configuration documentation to employ the appropriate procedures of his or her organization so as to ensure:

- The assignment of identifiers to the configuration documentation, including revision and version identifiers, when appropriate, and procedures to control the engineering release of new/revised data
- The application of applicable restrictive markings

The following principles in EIA-649 apply to the identification of configuration items:

- All products (configuration items) are assigned unique identifiers so that one product can be distinguished from other products; one configuration of a product can be distinguished from another; the source of a product can be determined; and the correct product information can be retrieved.
- Individual units of a product are assigned a unique product unit identifier (e.g., serial number) when there is a need to distinguish one unit of the product from another unit of the product.
- When a product is modified, it retains its original product unit identifier (e.g., serial number) although its part identifying number is altered to reflect a new configuration.
- A series of like units of a product is assigned a unique product group identifier (e.g., lot number or date code) when it is unnecessary or impracticable to identify individual units but, nonetheless, necessary to correlate units to a process, date, event, or test.

Items are marked or labeled with their applicable identifiers to enable correlation between the item, its configuration documentation, and other associated data, and to track maintenance and modification actions performed. Thus, serial and lot numbers are also known as tracking identifiers. For software, applicable identifiers are embedded in source code and, when required, in object code and in alterable read-only memory devices (firmware).

Part/Item Identification Numbers (PIN)

The developer assigns a discrete part/item identification number (PIN), generally referred to as a part number, to each CI and its subordinate parts and assemblies. The part number of a given part is changed whenever a noninterchangeable condition is created.

Part number format is at the developer's option and a wide variety of formats are employed. The standard constraint within the defense industry had been a limitation to no more than 15 characters including dash numbers. However, with the increasing use of commercial items that are not so limited, many current systems accommodate 52 characters. Some developers employ a mono-detail system in which one part is detailed on one drawing, and the drawing and the part number is the same. For practical reasons, some employ a multi-detailing system in which the drawing number may detail several parts and assemblies. Others use tabulated mono-detail drawings in which a drawing includes several iterations of a part. In the latter two cases, the drawing number is a base to which dash numbers are assigned for discrete parts controlled by that drawing.

The significant criteria are as expressed in the principles above: the part number must uniquely identify the specific part and unless otherwise specified, all CIs including parts, assemblies, units, sets, and other pieces of military property are marked with their identifiers.

Software Identifiers

Each CSCI shall have an identifier consisting of a name or number. It uniquely identifies the software. Each version of the software CSCI shall have a version identifier supplementing the software identifier.

- The software identifier and version identifier are embedded in the source code for the CSCI.
- Means are provided to display identifiers for installed software to user upon software initiation or upon specific command.

- In mission-critical situations, identification of the correct software version may be verified as part of system self-check, as well as during system test following equipment repair or maintenance.
- Each software medium (e.g., magnetic tape, disk) containing copies of tested and verified software entities is marked with a label containing, or providing cross-reference to, a listing of the applicable software identifiers of the entities it contains.

ENGINEERING RELEASE

Engineering release is an action that makes configuration documentation available for its intended use and subject to the developer's configuration control procedures.

All software engineering activities should follow engineering release procedures, which record the release and retain records of approved configuration documentation (engineering release records). These records provide:

- An audit trail of CI documentation status and history
- Verification that engineering documentation has been changed to reflect the incorporation of approved changes and to satisfy the requirements for traceability of deviations and engineering changes
- A means to reconcile engineering and manufacturing data to ensure that engineering changes have been accomplished and incorporated into deliverable units of the CIs

INTERFACE MANAGEMENT

Another aspect of configuration identification to be considered during development is interface management, also referred to as interface control. Systems may have interfaces with other systems.

These interfaces constitute design constraints imposed on the programs. As the system is defined, other interfaces between system components become apparent. All of the interfaces between co-functioning items should be identified and documented so that their integrity can be maintained through a disciplined configuration control process. In some cases, a formal interface management process must be employed to define and document the interface.

Interfaces are the functional and physical characteristics that exist at a common boundary with co-functioning items and allow systems, equipment, software, and data to be compatible. The purpose of all interface management activity is that:

- The detailed design of each of the co-functioning items contains the necessary information to ensure that the items, when individually designed and produced, will work together (as the 115-volt plug to the 115-volt electrical outlet).
- If either item needs to be changed for any reason, its performance, functional, or physical attributes that are involved in the interface act as constraints on the design change.

During development, part of the design effort is to arrive at and document external interface agreements, as well as to identify, define, control, and integrate all lower-level (i.e., detailed design) interfaces.

Interfaces include external interfaces with other systems, internal interfaces between CIs that comprise the system, and internal interfaces between CIs and other components of the system.

To understand how a particular interface should be defined and managed, it is necessary to categorize the interface in a number of ways:

- *Contractual relationship.* Are the items supplied by the same contractor or by different contractors? If different contractors, is there, or will there be, a contractual relationship (such as a subcontract or purchase order) between the parties to the interface?
- *Customer relationship (acquisition activity(ies)).* Is the same acquisition activity responsible for both interfacing entities, or are different activities or even services involved?
- *Hierarchical relationship.* Is the interface at the system, CI, assembly, or part level?
- *Type(s) and complexity of technical interface attribute(s) involved.* Is the interface mechanical, electrical, electronic, installation, data, language, power, hydraulic, pneumatic, space, operating range, frequency, transmission rate, capacity, etc. (to name a few)?
- *Developmental status.* Is (are) one, both, or none of the interfacing items a nondevelopmental item (NDI)? Do the interfacing items require parallel design and development?

Categorizing the interface in this manner defines the context and environment of the interface, and enables the appropriate measures to be taken to define and control it. Each interface must be defined and documented; the documentation varies from performance or detailed specifications to item, assembly, or installation drawings, to interface control documents/drawings. Some interfaces are completely managed within the design process; others require specific types of formal interface management activity. The simplest and most straightforward approach that will satisfy the above objective should always be chosen. Extravagant and complex interface management activity should only be undertaken when other methods are inappropriate.

Whether formal or informal interface management is employed, it is necessary that there be a legal responsibility on the part of the interfacing parties because even the best-intentioned technical agreements can break down in the face of fiscal pressure. If there is a contractual relationship, including a teaming arrangement, between two or more parties to an interface, there is already a vehicle for definition and control. However, where there is no contractual relationship, a separate interface agreement may be necessary to define the interface process and provide for the protection of proprietary information.

Within an organization, integrated product teams can be used to establish interfaces. Some interfaces must be defined through a formal interface management process involving interface control working groups (ICWGs). An ICWG is a specialized *integrated product team* comprised of appropriate technical representatives from the interfacing activities. Its sole purpose is to solve interface issues that surface and cannot be resolved through simple engineer-to-engineer interaction.

Once interfaces have been agreed-to by the parties concerned, they must be detailed at the appropriate level to constrain the design of each item and baseline the configuration documentation so that the normal configuration control process will maintain the integrity of the interface.

SUMMARY

If CM is the framework around which software engineering lives, then configuration identification is its foundation. One cannot control what one cannot name. By providing detailed identification information for each and every component of a system (i.e., programs, databases, forms, manuals), an infinite level of control is achievable.

REFERENCES

This chapter is based on the following report: MIL-HDBK-61A(SE), February 7, 2001, *Military Handbook: Configuration Management Guidance.*

5

CONFIGURATION CONTROL

Configuration control is perhaps the most visible element of configuration management. It is the process used to manage preparation, justification, evaluation, coordination, disposition, and implementation of proposed engineering changes and deviations to effected configuration items (CIs) and baselined configuration documentation.

The primary objective of configuration control is to establish and maintain a systematic change management process that regulates life-cycle costs, and:

- Allows optimum design and development latitude with the appropriate degree and depth of configuration change control procedures during the life cycle of a system/CI
- Provides efficient processing and implementation of configuration changes that maintain or enhance operational readiness, supportability, interchangeability, and interoperability
- Ensures complete, accurate, and timely changes to configuration documentation maintained under appropriate configuration control authority
- Eliminates unnecessary change proliferation

THE PROCESS OF CONFIGURATION CONTROL

The span of configuration control begins once the first configuration document is approved and baselined. This normally occurs when the functional configuration baseline (referred to as the requirements baseline in EIA/IS-649) is established for a system or configuration item. At that point, change management procedures are employed to systematically evaluate each proposed engineering change or requested deviation to baselined documentation; to assess the total change impact (including costs) through coordination with affected functional activities; to disposition the change or deviation and provide timely approval or disapproval; and to ensure timely implementation of approved changes by both parties. Configuration control is an essential discipline throughout the program life cycle.

Through the configuration control process, the full impact of proposed engineering changes and deviations is identified and accounted for in their implementation. The configuration control process evolves from a less formal process in the early phases of a program to a very disciplined and formal process during the System Development and Demonstration, Production and Deployment, and Operation and Support phases. In the Concept Exploration phase, the configuration control process is employed in support of systems engineering to make sure that the correct version of documents, which communicate technical decisions or definition of pertinent study parameters, is disseminated and used by all personnel. In addition, the process makes affected parties aware that a change is being developed and enables them to provide pertinent input.

In the Concept and Technology Development phase (if applicable), when the program definition documents are being developed, the configuration control process is also less formal. As part of the systems engineering control process in this phase, there may be several requirements definition baselines established for convenience to ensure that all program participants are "on the same page." A configuration control procedure is helpful in this phase for the review and coordination of changes to the evolving system-level specifications. It provides:

- The identification, documentation, dissemination, and review of changes
- Appropriate versioning of files and revision of documents
- A release process to ensure that each revision or version reflects the applicable changes

During the System Development and Demonstration, Production and Deployment, and Operation and Support phases, a formal configuration control process is essential. The informal document change control that was practiced during concept explorations is insufficient for systems acquisition and sustainment. As the product is being developed and produced, configuration control focuses on the documentation defining performance, physical and functional characteristics, and the configuration of the product.

Configuration control is a management process that uses configuration baselines as references for managing change. Within this context, however, there are several configuration control complexity levels. When viewed at the macro level, the process:

- Addresses the baseline documentation
- Determines which documents are impacted
- Proposes a change covering the impacts to all affected elements
- States when, where, and by whom the documentation will be updated and the change will be incorporated in the product and in all supporting elements

While this top-level macro view appears simple and straightforward, a micro-level view of the configuration control process can be considerably more complex. The micro view reveals the process layer dealing with what must be done to change each affected element, and thus with a wide variety of considerations such as data rights; approval authority, document custodians; design, release, production, installation, and testing organizations; and contractual and interface relationships.

ENGINEERING CHANGE PROPOSAL

An Engineering Change Proposal (ECP) is the management tool used to propose a configuration change to a CI and its baselined performance requirements and configuration documentation. See Appendix B for a sample ECP. Please note that the following discussion describes the procedure for filling out this form. The ECP consists of the items listed in Table 5.1.

Request for Deviation

A deviation is a specific written authorization to depart from a particular requirement(s) of an item's current approved configuration documentation for a specific number of units or a specified period of time. It differs from an engineering change in that a deviation does not effect a change to a configuration document.

Requests for Deviation (RFDs) are submitted if during design and development, it is determined that for a valid reason (such as long lead-time) a required performance attribute will not be met or verified before scheduled delivery of a limited number of production units.

RFDs are classified by their originators as either *minor, major,* or *critical*:

- *Critical.* The deviation consists of a departure involving safety or when the configuration documentation defining the require-ments for the item classifies defects in requirements and the deviations consist of a departure from a requirement classified as critical.
- *Major.* The deviation consists of a departure involving:
  - Performance

Table 5.1 ECP Components

ECP Justification Codes:

- *B Interface:* proposed to eliminate a deficiency consisting of an incompatibility between CIs
- *C Compatibility:* to correct a deficiency discovered during system or item functional checks or during installation and checkout, and the proposed change a necessary to make the system/item work
- *D Correction of Deficiency:* to eliminate a deficiency; code D is used if a more descriptive code (such as S, B, or C) does not apply
- *O Operational or Logistic Support:* to make a significant effectiveness or performance change in operational capability or logistic support; commonly known as an improvement change
- *P Production Stoppage:* to prevent slippage in an approved production schedule, where delivery to current configuration documentation is impractical or cannot be accomplished without delay
- *R Cost Reduction:* to provide net total life-cycle cost savings
- *S Safety Correction:* correction of a deficiency that is a hazardous condition
- *V Value Engineering:* to effect a net life-cycle cost reduction

ECP Types and Their Function:

- *Message.* Although not formally considered a type of ECP, engineering changes with an emergency priority are often submitted in a message that provides less detail than a preliminary ECP; urgent priority ECPs sometimes are also initially documented in messages, as are notifications of compatibility changes. They should be followed up by a complete ECP package within 30 days because they normally do not include sufficient detail to determine the full impact on program requirements.
- *Preliminary (Type P).* Preliminary ECPs are used to address the impact of proposed changes in general terms sufficient enough to determine if final ECPs are warranted. They are used by program managers when:
  1. The complexity of a proposed change may require extensive funding, development, or engineering.
  2. A choice of alternative proposals is appropriate, especially if a solicitation or contracting requirement is being competed between two or more contractors.
  3. Authority is required to expend resources to fully develop a change proposal.
  4. The organization wishes to restrict configuration change activity.
  5. Approval is required to proceed with software engineering development.
  6. As follow-up to a message ECP when it is impractical to submit a complete formal ECP within 30 days. This preliminary ECP would provide additional detail information supplementing the message ECP to provide a more considered analysis of the impacts and scope of the proposed change.

Table 5.1 ECP Components (continued)

■ *Formal (Type F)*. A formal ECP is the type that provides engineering information and other data sufficient to support formal CCB approval and contractual implementation.

ECP Priorities:
■ *Emergency*. An emergency priority is assigned to an ECP for any of the following reasons:
  1. To effect a change in operational characteristics which, if not accomplished without delay, may seriously compromise national security
  2. To correct a hazardous condition that may result in fatal or serious injury to personnel or in extensive damage or destruction of equipment (a hazardous condition usually will require withdrawing the item from service temporarily, or suspension of the item operation, or discontinuance of further testing or development pending resolution of the condition)
  3. To correct a system halt (abnormal termination) in the production environment
■ *Urgent*. An urgent priority is assigned to an ECP for any of the following reasons:
  1. To effect a change that, if not accomplished expeditiously, may seriously compromise the mission effectiveness of deployed equipment, software, or forces
  2. To correct a potentially hazardous condition, the uncorrected existence of which could result in injury to personnel or damage to equipment (a potentially hazardous condition compromises safety and embodies risk, but within reasonable limits, permits continued use of the affected item provided the operator has been informed of the hazard and appropriate precautions have been defined and distributed to the user)
  3. To meet significant contractual requirements (e.g., when lead-time will necessitate slipping approved production or deployment schedules if the change was not incorporated)
  4. To effect an interface change that, if delayed, would cause a schedule slippage or increased cost
  5. To effect a significant net life-cycle cost savings to the tasking activity, as defined in the contract, where expedited processing of the change will be a major factor in realizing lower costs
  6. To correct a condition causing unusable output information that is critical to mission accomplishment
  7. To correct critical CI files that are being degraded
  8. To effect a change in operational characteristics to implement a new or changed regulatory requirement with stringent completion date requirements issued by an authority higher than that of the functional proponent

Table 5.1 ECP Components (continued)

___

■ *Routine.* A routine priority is assigned to an ECP when emergency or urgent implementation is not applicable, required, or justifiable.

ECP Content:
■ ECP identification and administrative attributes:
1. *Date:* submittal date of the ECP or ECP Revision
2. *Originator name and address:* name and address of the activity submitting
3. *Model/type:* model or type designation, or identifier of the CI or CSCI for which proposal is being submitted
4. *System designation:* the system or top-level CI designation or nomenclature
5. *ECP number:* ECP identifier assigned by the originator (Once assigned, the ECP number is retained for subsequent submissions. The same ECP number can be used for a related ECP by adding a dash number to the basic identifier.)
6. *Revision:* identifier for an ECP Revision
7. *Title of change:* brief descriptive title for the engineering change proposal
8. ECP classification:
   — Name and part number of item affected
   — Name and part number of next higher assembly
   — Description of the engineering change
   — Need (reason) for making the engineering change
9. ECP justification code
10. ECP type
11. ECP priority
■ Description of proposed change:
1. Configuration item nomenclature name and type designation, CSCI name and number, or other authorized name and number of all CI(s) affected by the ECP.
2. *Is the CI in production?* If "yes," provide information as to whether deliveries have been completed on the contract(s). (This data is not always applicable to software.)
3. *Description of change:* description of the proposed change phrased in definitive language such that, if it is repeated in the contractual document authorizing the change, it will provide the authorization desired. Include the purpose and sufficient detail to describe what is to be accomplished. If the proposed change is an interim solution, it should be so stated.
4. *Need for change:* explanation of the need, identifying the benefit of the change, and as applicable:

Table 5.1 ECP Components (continued)

> — Correspondence such as a request for ECP management direction
> — Quantitative improvements in performance characteristics (range, speed, performance, endurance, striking power, and defensive or offensive capabilities)
> — Nature of a defect, failure, incident, malfunction; available failure data
> — Maintenance/logistics problems corrected
> — Identification and summary of testing accomplished
> — Supporting data as necessary
> — Consequences of disapproval

5. *Baseline affected:* indicate whether functional, allocated, or product baseline(s) is affected.

6. *Developmental requirements and status:* if proposed engineering change requires a major revision of the development program, status of current program and details of the revision. When applicable, recommendations for additional tests, trials, installations, prototypes, fit checks, etc. Include the test objective and test vehicle(s) to be used. Indicate the development status of major items to be used in and availability in terms of the estimated production incorporation point.

7. *Trade-offs and alternative solutions:* summary of the various solutions considered and reasons for adopting the solution proposed by the ECP. When analysis addresses new concepts or new technology, supporting data may be presented with the proposal to authenticate the trade-off analysis.

8. *Proposed delivery schedule:* estimated delivery schedule of items incorporating the change, either in terms of days after contractual approval, or by specific dates contingent upon contractual approval by a specified date. (Indicate if there will be no effect on the delivery schedule.)

9. *Recommendations for retrofit:* when applicable, description of recommendations for retrofit of the engineering change into accepted items (including applicable substantiating data or discussion of implications). If retrofit is not recommended, give explanation/reason for the recommendation.

10. Estimated retrofit kit delivery schedule.

■ Effects of the proposed change:

1. *Specifications affected:* identity specifications cited in the contract that are affected by the ECP

2. *Effect on performance allocations and interfaces:* the changes in performance and in functional/physical interfaces

3. Effects on employment, logistic support, training, operational effectiveness, or software:

Table 5.1 ECP Components (continued)

— Effects of the proposed change on operational employment, deployment, logistics, and/or personnel and training requirements specified in the approved system and/or CI specifications (Quantitative values shall be used whenever practicable and are required when reliability and service life are impacted.)
— Effect on interoperability
— Effect on operational software. For CSCIs, as applicable:
  a. Required changes to database parameters, values, or management procedures
  b. Anticipated effects on acceptable computer operating time and cycle-time utilization; estimate of the net effect on computer software storage
  c. Other relevant impact of the proposed change on utilization of the system
4. *Effect on acquisition logistic support elements:* the following shall be covered, as applicable:
— Effects on schedule and content of the ALS plan
— Effect on maintenance concept and plans for the levels of maintenance and procedures
— System and/or CI logistics support analysis (LSA) tasks to be accomplished and LSA data requiring update
— Extension/revision of the interim support plan
— Spares and repair parts that are changed, modified, obsolete, or added, including detailed supply data for interim support spares
— Revised or new technical manuals
— Revised or new facilities requirements and site activation plan
— New, revised, obsolete, or additional support equipment (SE), test procedures, and software
— Description of the proposed change(s) to SE and trainers and reference to related ECPs
— Effect on maintenance or training software
— Qualitative and quantitative personnel requirements data identifying additions or deletions to operator or maintenance manpower requirements in terms of personnel skill levels, knowledge, and numbers required to support the modified CI
— New operator and maintenance training requirements in terms of training equipment, trainers, and training software for operator and maintenance courses. This information should include identification of specific courses, equipment, technical manuals, personnel, etc.
— Effect on contract maintenance that increases the scope or dollar limitation established in the contract

Table 5.1 ECP Components (continued)

— Effects on packaging, handling, storage, and transportability resulting from changes in materials, dimensions, fragility, inherent environmental, or operating conditions

5. *Other considerations:* the effects of the proposed engineering change on the following shall be identified:

— Interfaces having an effect on adjacent or related items (output, input, size, mating connections, etc.)

— Physical constraints: removal or repositioning of items, structural rework, increase or decrease in overall dimensions

— Software (other than operational, maintenance, and training software) requiring a change to existing code and/or resources, or addition of new software

— Rework required on other equipment not included previously that will affect the existing operational configuration

— Additional or modified system test procedures required

— Any new or additional changes having an effect on existing warranties or guarantees

— Changes or updates to the parts control program

— Effects on life-cycle cost projections for the configuration item or program, including projections of operation and support costs/savings for the item(s) affected over the contractually defined life and projections of the costs/savings to be realized in planned future production and spares buys of the item(s) affected

6. *Lower-level items affected:* identifier of lower-level CI, CSCI, or parts affected, and the quantity and NSN of each part, where applicable

7. *Other systems/configuration items affected:* identify other systems affected by the proposed change that are outside the purview of the originator

8. *Other activities affected:* Identify other contractors or activities that will be affected by this engineering change

9. Effect on product configuration documentation

■ Estimated net total cost impact:

1. *Production costs/(savings):* estimated costs/savings applicable to production of the item resulting from the change; includes the costs of redesign of the CIs or components thereof, of factory test equipment, of special factory tooling, of scrap, of engineering design, of engineering data revision, of revision of test procedures, and of testing and verification of performance of new items

2. *Retrofit costs:* estimated costs applicable to retrofit of the item, including installation and testing costs

Table 5.1 ECP Components (continued)

3. *Logistics support costs/(savings):* estimated costs/savings of the various elements of logistics support applicable to the item; includes spares/repair parts rework, new spares and repair parts, supply/provisioning data, support equipment, retrofit kit for spares, operator training courses, maintenance training courses, revision of technical manuals, new technical manuals, training/trainers, interim support, maintenance manpower, and computer rograms/documentation

4. *Other costs/savings:* includes estimated costs of interface changes accomplished by other activities

5. *Estimated net total costs (savings):* total of all the costs (savings) under contract and from other costs (savings)

• Implementation milestones:

1. *Milestones:* ECP implementation milestones that show the time phasing of the various deliveries of items, support equipment, training equipment, and documentation incorporating the basic and related ECPs. Enter symbols and notations to show the initiation or termination of significant actions. Base all dates upon months after contractual approval of the basic ECPs.

• ECP implementation actions:

1. *CCB preparing activity:* prepares the change implementing directive/order designating specific responsibilities to associated activities in support of the change. These specific responsibilities may include:

— Obtaining, issuing, and distributing retrofit kits, including redistribution

— Obtaining, issuing, and distributing engineering and installation data packages

— Logistics, test, and evaluation activity requirements

2. Logistics manager:

a. Distributes the preliminary directive/order for review, validation, check out, and comment; revises the implementing directive/order in accordance with accepted comments; and provides the final change implementing directive/order to the ICP

b. If the change affects hardware or firmware, prepare, or have provisioning documentation prepared, and forward to the applicable Inventory Control Point (ICP)

c. Ensure that all training requirements are addressed

d. Manage ECP implementation when retrofit is involved

3. ICP:

a. Distribute the directive/order and associated documentation to the installing activities, supply storage points, repositories, training activities, and OPR, as appropriate

b. Provision the change (i.e., make sure the necessary spares are ordered)

Table 5.1 ECP Components (continued)

4. Technical data manager:
   a. Review the proposed data revision requirements, recommend or prepare necessary revisions, and forward them as directed by the preparing activity
5. *Technical manual manager:* prepare or have appropriate technical manual revisions prepared
6. Manufacturing and development activity:
   a. Prepare/revise the specifications, drawings, lists, material, process, and computer program specifications; computer programs, testing procedures, quality assurance procedures, classification of defects requirements, etc., needed for hardware or firmware manufacture or computer software change
   b. Manufacture the changed hardware and firmware, assemble the technical documentation (retrofit instructions), hardware, firmware, and computer program change into a retrofit kit to meet the delivery schedule established by the CCBD
   c. Manufacture or have the spare/support parts manufactured or modified, unless they are to be accomplished by the ICP
7. ICP:
   — Conduct initial check out/validation of the retrofit kit/retrofit instructions
   — Provide each change installing activity with a work package planning document for each approved change or block of changes; includes but is not limited to:
   a. Change implementing directive/order identification number(s)
   b. Item identification
   c. Serial numbers affected
   d. Man-hours and skill areas required to accomplish the change(s)
   e. Any prerequisite or conjunctive changes required
   f. Any special instructions (e.g., additional material, tools, equipment)
   g. Funding authority
   h. Schedule for installation
   i. Training schedules and sources required to effect the change, and operate and maintain the reconfigured item
8. Change installing activity:
   a. Based on the work package planning document, adjust work schedule to accommodate scheduled implementation, accomplish prerequisite changes, accumulate the materials, tools, equipment, etc., to implement and support the change, and implement the change as directed/ordered.
   b. Install change in accordance with the priority assigned and the dependency criteria documented in the implementing directive/order.

Table 5.1 ECP Components (continued)

---

    c. The change shall be installed in training and test items at the earliest opportunity.

    d. Changes in priority of accomplishment, addition or deletion of changes, and change substitutions shall be avoided after the actual change work has been started. However, when installation schedules cannot be met, the installing activity shall advise the appropriate OPR and CCB so that the schedules can be revised or consideration may be given to possible cancellation of the change.

    e. The installing activity shall report change implementation in accordance with the requirements of the implementing directive/order.

  9. Reporting activity:

    — All change accomplishment reports shall be initiated by the installing activity and, if different, provided to the custodian of the changed item for processing to the data repository and OPR.

    — Change accomplishment reporting shall be consistent with the applicable configuration status accounting (CSA) system, reporting the accomplishment and effectiveness of changes in the format prescribed. Accomplishment reporting shall be done promptly so that CSA and ILS can be updated. Effectiveness reporting, when required, shall be done promptly so that continued change implementation can be reevaluated.

  10. Data repository:

    — Provide for the maintenance of CSA records during the Operating and Support phase of the CI's life cycle.

- Interchangeability, reliability, survivability, maintainability, or durability of the item or its repair parts
- Health
- Effective use or operation
- Weight and size
- Appearance (when a factor)
- When the configuration documentation defining the requirements for the item classifies defects in requirements and the deviations consist of a departure from a requirement classified as major

- *Minor.* The deviation consists of a departure that does not involve any of the factors listed as critical or major, or when the configuration documentation defining the requirements for the item classifies defects in requirements and the deviations consist of a departure from a requirement classified as minor.

RFD Contents

The data content of an RFD consists of:

- Submittal date of the RFD or RFD Revision
- Originator name and address
- Identifier of the CI or CSCI for which RFD is being submitted
- The system or top-level CI designation
- RFD identifier assigned by the originator
- Brief descriptive title for the RFD
- CI(s) affected by the RFD
- Description of deviation
- Need for deviation
- Effect on integrated logistics
- Other system or configuration items affected
- Corrective action taken to prevent future recurrence of the nonconformance
- Effect on delivery schedule
- Cost/price consideration

SUMMARY

This chapter provides a close look at the elements of information required to manage the process of change using a configuration management methodology. By now it should be quite clear that anything carrying the CM "flag" must be fully documented and tracked throughout its life cycle.

REFERENCES

This chapter is based on the following report: MIL-HDBK-61A(SE), February 7, 2001, *Military Handbook: Configuration Management Guidance.*

6

CONFIGURATION STATUS ACCOUNTING

Configuration status accounting (CSA) is the process of creating and organizing the knowledge base necessary for the performance of configuration management (CM). In addition to facilitating CM, the purpose of CSA is to provide a highly reliable source of configuration information to support all program/project activities, including program management, systems engineering, manufacturing, software development and maintenance, logistic support, modification, and maintenance.

Figure 6.1 is the activity model for CSA. The inputs, outputs, facilitators, and constraints in this model are simply extracted from the overall CM activity model. CSA receives information from the other CM and related activities as the functions are performed.

In addition to the use of automated configuration management tools, the process is aided or facilitated by the documented CM process and open communications. The outputs from this activity provide visibility into CM document, activity status, and configuration information concerning the product and its documentation. They also include "metrics" developed from the information collected in the CSA system and management "prompts" resulting from analysis of the CM database.

Because the complexion of the objects about which status accounting information is collected changes during the item life cycle, as shown in Figure 6.2, the specific outputs will vary. The inputs and outputs in Figure 6.1 may be thought of as generic categories for which there are different specifics in each phase. The high-level summary of CSA tasks shown in the center of Figure 6.1 reflects the functional performance capabilities of a complete CSA process.

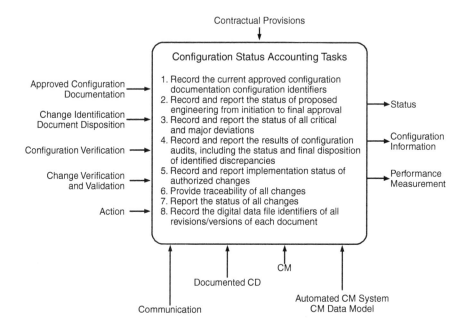

Figure 6.1 Configuration Status Accounting Activity Model

Some of these tasks also may not span the entire life cycle. The allocation of responsibilities within these functions (tailoring) must be accomplished during the CM planning activity and should take into account the degree to which the information technology infrastructure has been upgraded.

All of the information required to accomplish the complete CSA function can be captured and supplied using commercial configuration management and product data management tools.

TYPICAL CSA INFORMATION OVER THE ACQUISITION PROGRAM LIFE CYCLE

New and innovative methods of capturing the configuration of installed and spare items and software versions are becoming commonplace. These methods include bar coding and the interrogation of embedded identification via on-equipment data buses and on-board support equipment. The technology for this process is now commonplace in the commercial personal computer industry and the automotive industry.

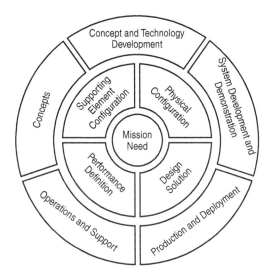

Figure 6.2 Configuration Status Accounting Evolution over the System/CI Life Cycle

The information that is loaded into CSA is considered "metadata," that is, information about the data. It provides status and cross-references actual Technical Data Package (TDP) information that is stored digitally in data repositories.

Each design activity establishes a document repository for the CIs developed, produced, or maintained by an Office of Project Responsibility (OPR) under their authority. The data repositories are normally maintained by the inventory control point responsible for the provisioning/supply support of the CI.

CSA records should be maintained in such range and depth as to be responsive to the requirements of the various support activities for access to configuration information. The data repository is the central point for the collection, storage, processing, and promulgation of this data. Configuration information should be available on a request basis, either by hard copy or online computer access. The CSA records are used as "best source" input data for purchasing data packages, design studies, and management analyses requested by the supporting/design activities. In particular, the CSA metadata records must accurately reflect the status of the configuration documents (specifications, drawings, lists, test reports, etc.) maintained in the document repositories.

Concept and Technology Development

Typical information sources include:

- Mission need statements
- Baseline performance, cost, and schedule goals
- System requirements documents for alternative configurations
- Preliminary system performance
- Specifications for selected configuration
- Engineering change proposals or contract change proposals, as applicable

Typical outputs include:

- Current revision of each document
- Current Document Change Authority (CDCA) and approval status for each document

System Development and Demonstration

Typical information sources include:

- System performance specification
- CI performance specifications
- CI detailed specifications
- Engineering drawings and associated lists
- CAD files
- Test plans and procedures, and results
- Audit plans
- Audit reports
- Audit certifications
- Engineering change proposals
- Request for deviation
- Notice of Revision (NORS)
- Engineering orders, change notices, etc.
- Installation and as-built verification
- Removal and reinstallation

Typical outputs include:

- CDCA release and approval status of each document
- Functional, allocated, and product baselines
- Baselines as of any prior date

- As-designed configuration, current, and as of any prior date
- As-built configuration, current up to time of delivery, and any prior date
- As-delivered configuration
- Status of ECPs and RFDs in process
- Effectivity and incorporation status of approved
- ECPs and RFDs, including retrofit effectivity
- Test and certification requirements to be completed prior to milestones, such as reviews, demonstrations, tests, trials, and delivery
- Verification and audit status and action items

Production and Deployment

Typical information sources include:

- All development phase items
- System CI location by serial number (S/N)
- Support equipment and software
- Spares
- Trainers
- Training material
- Operating and maintenance manuals
- CI delivery dates and warranty data
- Shelf life or operating limits on components with limited life or limited activations, etc.
- Operational history (e.g., for aircraft — takeoffs and landings)
- Verification/validation of retrofit instructions, retrofit kits
- Incorporation of retrofit kits
- Installation of spares, replacements by maintenance action

Typical outputs include:

- All development phase items
- Current configuration of all systems/CIs in all locations (as-modified/as-maintained)
- Required and on-board configuration of all support equipment, spares, trainers, training, manuals, software, facilities needed to operate and maintain all systems/CIs at all sites
- Status of all requested, in-process, and approved changes and deviation requests
- Authorization and ordering actions required to implement approved changes, including recurring retrofit
- Warranty status of all CIs

- Predicted replacement date for critical components
- Retrofit actions necessary to bring any serial-numbered CI to the current or any prior configuration

Operational Support

Typical information sources include:

- All production and deployment phase items

Typical outputs include:

- All production and deployment phase items

CONFIGURATION STATUS ACCOUNTING PROCESS EVALUATION CHECKLIST

Documented process:

- Is there a documented configuration status accounting (CSA) process?
- Is the documented process followed?
- Are personnel from all disciplines involved in the process informed and knowledgeable about the procedures they are supposed to follow?

CSA information:

- Has an accurate, timely information base concerning the product and its associated product information, appropriate to the applicable phase(s) of the life cycle, been established?
- Is configuration information appropriate to the product systematically recorded and disseminated?
- Is applicable CSA information captured as CM tasks are performed, and is it available for display or retrieval in a timely fashion?

CSA system:

- Is the data collection and information processing system based on, and consistent with, the configuration status accounting information needs of the organization?
- Are the data relationships in the system based on a sound set of business rules?

Metrics:

- Does the status accounting data being collected and the information system enable meaningful metrics to be developed and used to maintain and improve the CM process?

SUMMARY

Configuration management is based on rules. These rules must be codified and deployed to the various members of the development, support, and administrative staffs. This is done through configuration status accounting (CSA) via a knowledge base that is generally automated through the use of a CM toolset.

REFERENCES

This chapter is based on the following report: MIL-HDBK-61A(SE), February 7, 2001, *Military Handbook: Configuration Management Guidance.*

7

A PRACTICAL APPROACH TO DOCUMENTATION AND CONFIGURATION STATUS ACCOUNTING

Without adequate documentation, the system can neither be utilized efficiently nor maintained properly. IT departments have been notoriously lax about developing and then maintaining documentation.

Documentation within the context of configuration management has the following attributes:

- All documents are defined, verified, managed, and controlled through use of the configuration identification of each document.
- An information base is maintained that contains information about the product and its associated documentation. Configuration status accounting (CSA) provides the ability to review this collection of information, usually through automated means.

This chapter discusses the relationship between proper documentation techniques and related configuration status accounting procedures.

CONFIGURATION IDENTIFICATION

Configuration identification provides a unique identity to a product and its associated documentation. This uniqueness enables users and systems people to:

- Distinguish between product versions
- Match product to documentation
- Easily ascertain a reference point for maintenance
- Maintain release control of the product and associated documents

Configuration documentation consists of, but is not limited to:

- Feasibility study
- Project plan
- Requirements specification
- Design specification
- Test plan
- End-user manuals
- Help-desk manuals
- Administrative manuals (e.g., operating procedures)
- Interface manuals
- Reports
- Letters
- Forms

As one can see, configuration documentation is consistent with the documentation produced throughout the life cycle of a typical systems development effort.

Configuration identification requires an organization to develop a nomenclature for naming or numbering systems. The nomenclature should adhere to the following rules:

Product Structure

The structure is the hierarchy of a product from the highest level to the lowest. Often represented using a tree structure, each level references associated configuration documentation.

Product Identifiers

There are two levels of product and, thus, two levels of product identifier. End users require a product identifier to possess the ability to order or discuss a particular product or part of that product. The developer, on the other hand, will be privy to internal documentation such as test plans and system specifications. These will not be seen by the end user.

Every industry and many companies develop their own nomenclature. The scheme might consist of:

- *Company identifier.* This is only necessary if the company is one of a group of companies using a common configuration management system (i.e., subsidiaries).
- *System identifier.* For example, PAY for payroll.
- *Program identifier.* This is the root number for the program; for example, PAY00001.
- *Version identifier:* The version number is typically added to the root program identifier. It is attached using a dot or a dash. For example, PAY00001.01 or PAY00001.Y0312, where .01 indicates version one and .Y0312 suggests the version for December 2003.
- *Part identifier.* Software has corresponding documentation such as requirements specifications and design specifications. The part number identifies the specific documentation and associates it with the software. For example, the program specification for the PAY00001.Y0312 program might be PAY00001.Y0312.PSPEC.

An effective configuration identification methodology will enable:

- Someone to figure out the product composition from its configuration documentation
- One product to be distinguished from another
- Systems people to easily track the source for the product
- Operations staff to run the system as per the correct administrative manual
- End users to use the most up-to-date version of the manuals
- Systems people to locate the documentation that corresponds to the product to be maintained

Baselines

Configuration management enforces the stability of product releases. All maintenance and modifications are usually variations of an agreed-upon baseline. Therefore, it is important to establish and then document the baseline of a system prior to any system modification. A baseline is established by agreeing to the stated definition of a product's attributes. Any deviation from this baseline is managed through the configuration management change process.

CONFIGURATION STATUS ACCOUNTING

It is obvious that enforcing configuration management within a company requires the use of automated systems to keep track of the various configuration information about the product.

Configuration status accounting (CSA) enables appropriate users to review this information quickly and effectively to:

- Get information on change decisions
- Assist future planning efforts
- Review the complete configuration of a product or any of its component parts
- Review maintenance information
- Review documentation
- Review source code

Table 7.1 shows typical status accounting information across a product life cycle as per EIA-649.

THE EFFECTIVE DOCUMENTATION OF SYSTEMS

Documentation promotes software quality. There are numerous, well-documented reasons for this. David Tufflye, a consultant who specializes in producing high-quality documentation to a predefined standard, says that consistent, accurate project documentation is known to be a major factor contributing to information systems quality. He goes on to say that document production, version control, and filing are often not performed, thus contributing to a higher number of software defects that impact the real and perceived quality of the software, as well as leading to time and expense being spent on rework and higher maintenance costs [Tufflye 2002].

Marcello Alfredo Visconti [1993], in an article that proposes a Software System Documentation Process Maturity Model, argues that one of the major goals of software engineering is to produce the best possible working software along with the best possible supporting documentation.

Decades worth of empirical data shows that software documentation process and products are key components of software quality. These studies show that poor-quality, out-of-date, or missing documentation is a major cause of errors in future software development and maintenance. For example, the majority of defects discovered during integration testing are design and requirements defects (e.g., defects in documentation that were introduced before any code was written).

Visconti's four-level documentation maturity model provides the basis for an assessment of an organization's current documentation process and identifies key practices and challenges to improve the process. The four-level enhanced model appears in Table 7.2. Key practices, as defined by Cook and Visconti [2000], are listed in Table 7.3.

Table 7.1 Typical Status Accounting Information across Product Life Cycle

Typical CSA Information (select, where applicable and appropriate)	Conception	Definition	Build	Distribution	Operation	Disposal
			Life-Cycle Phases			
Requirements documentation	•	•	•	•	•	•
Product structure information		•	•	•	•	•
Configuration documentation		•	•	•	•	•
Configuration documentation change notice		•	•	•	•	
Change request and proposal	•	•	•	•	•	
Engineering change effectivity		•	•	•	•	
Variance documentation		•	•	•	•	•
Verification and audit action item status		•	•	•	•	•
Event date entries		•	•	•	•	•
Product as-built record			•	•	•	
Product as-delivered record				•	•	
Product warranty information				•	•	•
Product as maintained, modified					•	•
Limited use, shelf-life restrictions, etc.			•	•	•	•
Product operation and maintenance information revision status					•	•
Product information change requests and change notices					•	•
Online information access directory or index					•	•
Restrictions due to facility/product performance degradation					•	•
Product replacement information						•
Environmental impact information (when applicable)	•	•	•	•	•	•
Product or parts salvage information						•

Table 7.2 Visconti's Four-Level Documentation Maturity Model

	Level 1 Ad hoc	Level 2 Inconsistent	Level 3 Defined	Level 4 Controlled
Keywords	Chaos, variability	Standards Check-off list Inconsistency	Product assessment Process definition	Process assessment Measurement Control feedback Improvement
Succinct description	Documentation not a high priority	Documentation recognized as important and must be done	Documentation recognized as important and must be done well	Documentation recognized as important and must be done well consistently
Key practices	Ad hoc process Documentation not important	Inconsistent application of standards	Documentation quality assessment Documentation usefulness assurance Process definition	Process quality assessment and measures
Key indicators	Documentation missing or out-of-date	Standards established and use of check-off list	SQA-like practices	Data analysis and improvement mechanisms
Key challenges	Establish documentation standards	Exercise quality control over content Assess documentation usefulness Specify process	Establish process measurement Incorporate control over process	Automate data collection and analysis Continually striving for optimization

Table 7.3 Key Practices and Sub-practices

1. Creation of basic software documents:
   - Consistent creation of basic software development documents
   - Consistent creation of basic software quality documents
2. Management recognition of importance of documentation:
   - Documentation generally recognized as important
3. Existence of documentation policy or standards:
   - Written statement or policy about importance of documentation
   - Written statement or policy indicating what documents must be created for each development phase
   - Written statement or policy describing the contents of documents that must be created for each development phase
4. Monitor implementation of policy or standards:
   - Use of a mechanism, such as a check-off list, to verify that required documentation is done
   - Monitor adherence to documentation policy or standards
5. Existence of a defined process for creation of documents:
   - Written statement to prescribe process for creation of documents
   - Mechanism to monitor adherence to prescribed process
   - Adequate time to carry out the prescribed process
   - Training material or classes about the prescribed process
6. Methods to assure quality of documentation:
   - Mechanism to monitor quality of documentation
   - Mechanism to update documentation
   - Documentation is traceable to previous documents
7. Assessments of usability of documentation:
   - Person/group perception of usability of documents created
   - Mechanism to obtain user feedback about usability of created documentation
8. Definition of software documentation quality and usability measures:
   - Definition of measures of documentation quality
   - Definition of measures of documentation usability
9. Collection and analysis of documentation quality measures:
   - Collection of measures about quality of documentation
   - Analysis of documentation quality measures
   - Recording of documentation error data
   - Tracking of documentation errors and problem reports to solutions
   - Analysis of documentation error data and root causes
   - Generation of recommendations based on analysis of quality measurements and error data
10. Collection and analysis of documentation usability measures:
    - Collection of measures about usability of documentation
    - Analysis of documentation usability measurement
    - Generation of recommendations based on analysis of usability measurements
    - Generation of documentation usage profile

Table 7.3 Key Practices and Sub-practices (continued)

11. Process improvement feedback loop:
    - Mechanism to feedback improvements to documentation process
    - Mechanism to incorporate feedback on quality of documentation
    - Mechanism to incorporate feedback on usability of documentation

An assessment procedure was developed to determine where an organization's documentation process stands relative to the model. This enables a mapping from an organization's past performance to a documentation maturity level and ultimately generates a documentation process profile. The profile indicates key practices for that level and identifies areas of improvement and challenges to move to the next-higher level.

Application of the model has a definite financial benefit. The software documentation maturity model and assessment procedure have been used to assess a number of software organizations and projects, and a cost/benefit analysis of achieving documentation maturity levels has been performed using COCOMO, yielding an estimated return on investment of about 6:1 when moving from the least mature level to the next. According to Visconti [1993], these results support the main claim of this research: software organizations that are at a higher documentation process maturity level also produce higher-quality software, resulting in reduced software testing and maintenance effort.

METHODS AND STANDARDS

Although the majority of software documentation is produced manually — that is, done with word processing programs or with tools such as Microsoft Visio — there are also some systems designed to ease the process, that will produce "automatic" documentation. Some of the automatic documentation capabilities are subset systems of a wider range of capabilities; such is the case with many computer-aided software engineering (CASE) tools. These products are designed to support development efforts throughout the software development life cycle (SDLC), with documentation being just one small part.

An example of one such tool is Hamilton Technologies 001 (http://world.std.com/~hti/), a CASE tool (now usually called an application development tool in lieu of the term CASE) that surrounds itself with an intriguing methodology called "Development before the Fact" (DBTF). The premise behind 001 and DBTF is that developing systems in a quality manner begets quality and error-reduced systems. One of the intriguing features of the 001 toolset is that not only does 001 generate programming source code from maps (i.e., models) of a business problem, but it also actually generates the documentation for said system.

On one end of the documentation spectrum, one will find that many companies utilize no tools other than a word processor and some drawing tool to extract documentation out of their reluctant programmers. On the other end of the documentation spectrum, forward-thinking companies make significant investments in their software development departments by outfitting them with tool suites such as 001. The vast majority of organizations lie somewhere in between these two extremes.

The world of client/server has afforded the developer new opportunities and decisions to make in terms of which toolset to use. When Microsoft Office was first introduced, it was primarily utilized for word processing. Today, Microsoft Access, the database component of the MS Office product set, has become a significant player in corporations with a requirement for a robust but less-complex database than the powerhouse computers that run their back offices (e.g., Sybase, Oracle, and Microsoft SQL Server).

Microsoft Access enables the automated production of several kinds of documents related to the datasets that are implemented with the program. The documents describe schemas, queries, and entity relationship diagrams (ERDs) as shown in Figure 7.1.

Some products are dedicated to producing documentation. One such product is Doc-o-Matic by toolsfactory.com. It is designed to work with the Borland Delphi software development environment. The product works with Delphi's internal structures, which may consist of Author, Bugs, Conditions, Examples, Exceptions, History, Ignore, Internal, Notes, Parameters, Remarks, Return Value, See Also, Todo, and Version [Leahy 2002]. Doc-o-Matic has been compared to a gigantic parsing routine.

As software systems grow in size and sophistication, it becomes increasingly difficult for humans to understand them and anticipate their behavior, says Charles Robert Wallace [2000] in his dissertation, "Formal Specification of Software Using Abstract State Machines." This method essentially enables walk-through before code is written. Wallace argues that normal specification techniques aim to foster understanding and increase reliability

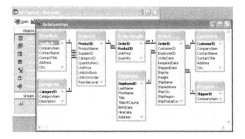

Figure 7.1 An Access Entity Relationship Diagram (ERD)

by providing a mathematical foundation to software documentation. His technique calls for layering information onto a model through a series of refinements.

Generating Documentation the Right Way

At present, many organizations are practicing a "hit-or-miss" form of software documentation. These are usually the companies that follow no or few policies and procedures, and loosely follow standards.

Good software development is standards based and, thus, documentation must also be standards based.

At a minimum, software documentation should consist of the following items.

1. All Documentation Produced prior to the Start of Code Development

Most projects go through a systems development life cycle. The life cycle often starts with a feasibility study, goes on to create a project plan, and then enters into the requirements analysis and system design phases. Each of these phases produces one or more deliverables, schedules, and artifacts. In sum, the beginnings of a systems documentation effort should include the feasibility study, project plan, requirements specification, and design specification, where available.

2. Program Flowcharts

Programmers usually, although not always, initiate their programming assignment by drawing one or more flowcharts that diagram the "nuts and bolts" of the actual program. Where systems analysts utilize diagrammatic tools such as dataflow diagrams (DFDs) or UML-based (Unified Modeling Language) class diagrams (Figures 7.2 and 7.3, respectively) to depict the entire system from a physical design level, the programmer is often required to utilize flowcharts (Figure 7.4) to depict the flow of a particular component of the DFD or UML class diagram.

3. Use or Business Cases

Item 1 above (all documentation produced prior to the start of code development) recommends including in your documentation all documentation created during the analysis and design component of the systems development effort. Use cases may or may not be a part of these documents — although they should be. Use cases, an example of which is

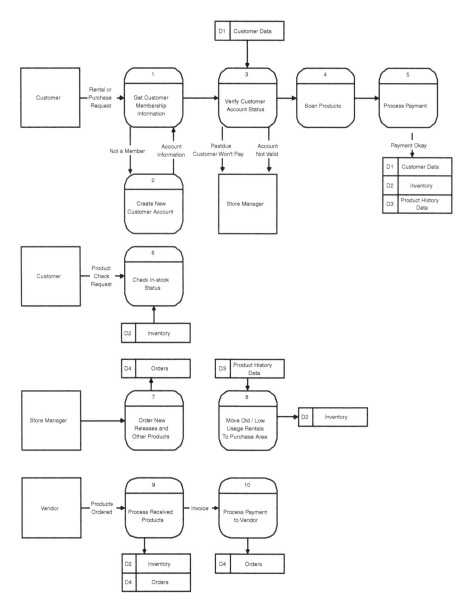

Figure 7.2 A Dataflow Diagram (DFD)

shown in Figure 7.5, provide a series of end-user procedures that make use of the system in question. For example, in a system that handles student registration, typical use cases might include student log-in, student registering for the first time, and a student request for financial aid. Use cases are valuable in all phases of systems development: (1) during systems

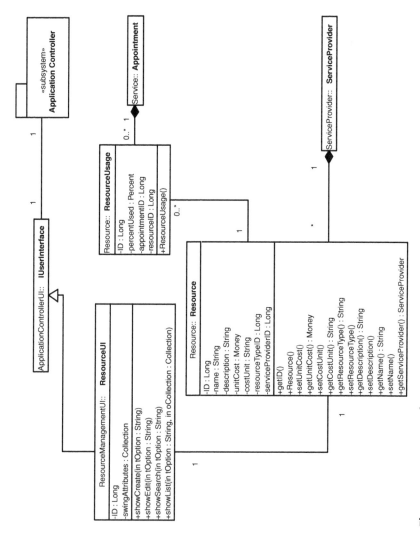

Figure 7.3 A UML Class Diagram

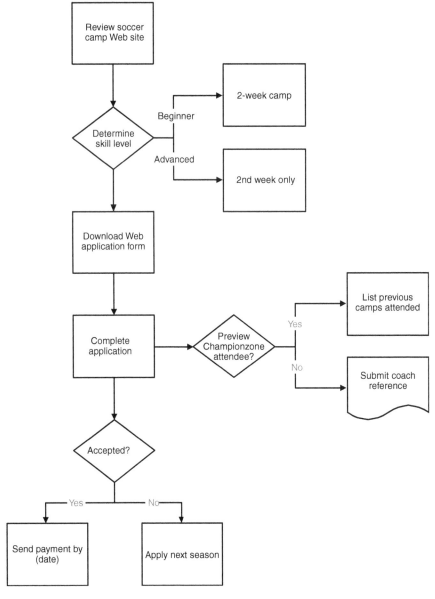

Figure 7.4 A Flowchart

analysis, use cases enable analysts to understand what the end user wants out of the new system; (2) during programming, use cases assist the programmer in understanding the logic flow of the system; and (3) during testing, use cases can form the basis of the preliminary test scripts.

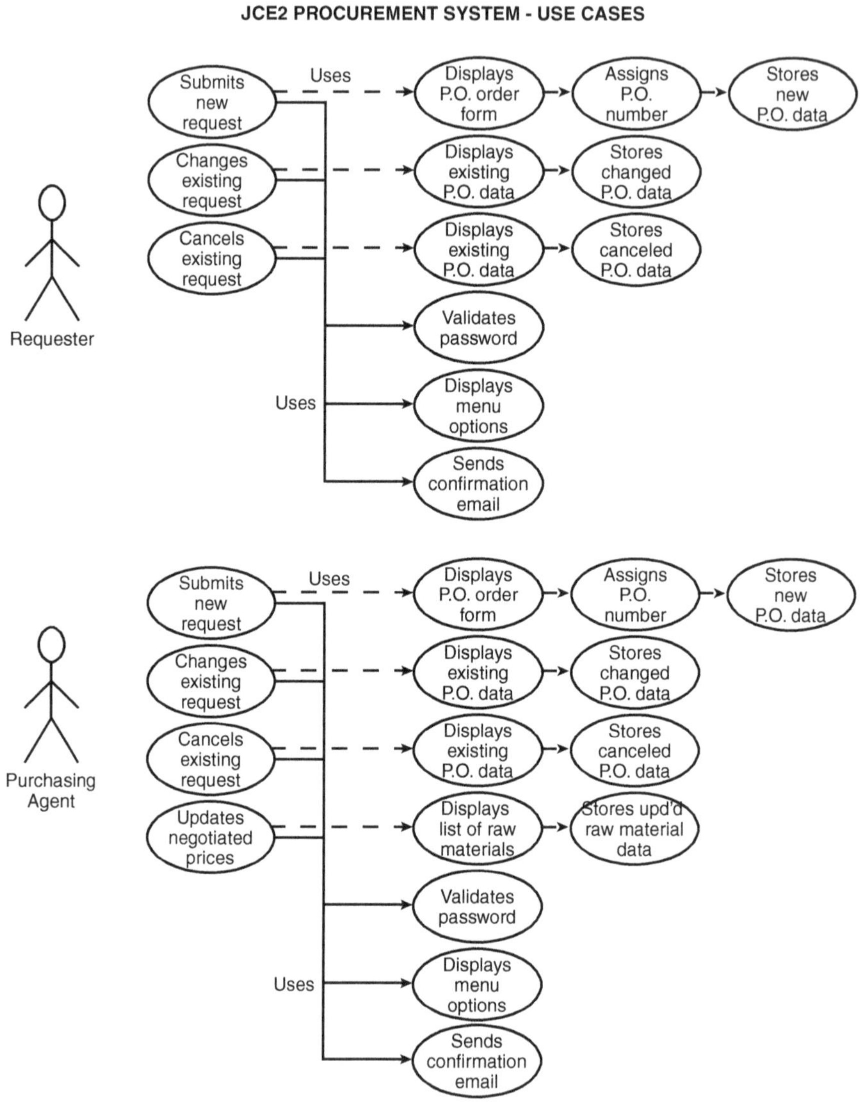

JCE2 PROCUREMENT SYSTEM - USE CASES

Figure 7.5 A Sample Use Case

4. Terms of Reference

Every organization is unique, in that it has its own vocabulary. Systems people are also unique, in that they often use a lingo incoherent to most end users. A "dictionary" of terms used is beneficial in clearing up any misunderstandings.

Table 7.4 A Sample Use Case

Requester Logs into the System to Submit a New Request

1. Requester keys in log-on ID and a six- to eight-digit password. The log-on ID and password are verified against the valid IDs and valid passwords in the procurement database. If the ID and/or password do not match, an error message is displayed on the screen. The requester is prompted to re-key his ID and/or password. The requester is allowed three log-in attempts. If unsuccessful, his password is flagged and a message is displayed for him to call Data Security for resolution. If successful, the procurement menu is displayed.
2. The requester selects the menu option ENTER PURCHASE REQUEST by pressing the radio button next to that option.
3. The system displays the Purchase Request Order Form on the screen. The requester keys his Department Name, Number, and Cost Center in the appropriate fields. The requester also keys the product number(s), product selections, and quantities. The requester presses the radio button for SUBMIT ORDER.
4. A purchase order number is automatically assigned by the system and is displayed on the screen as confirmation of the order taken.
5. An e-mail is also sent to the requester confirming the order.

5. Data Dictionary

While a data dictionary (DD) is usually included in a System Design Specification (SDS), if it is not included, it should be included here. An excerpt of a DD is provided in Table 7.5 and in Appendix C. A data dictionary consits of the "terms of reference" for the data that is used in the system. It describes database, tables, records, fields, and all attributes such as length and type (i.e., alphabetic, numeric). The DD should also describe all edit criteria, such as the fact that a social security number must be numeric and must contain nine characters.

6. Program/Component/Object Documentation

Aside from flowcharts, unless the programmer is using an automated CASE tool that generates documentation, the programmer should provide the following documentation: (1) control sheet (see Appendix D); (2) comments within the program (Figure 7.6); (3) textual description of what the program is doing, including pseudocode, as shown in Table 7.6.

Table 7.5 Data Dictionary Excerpt

Name: CI:	Membership Database/mem001
Aliases:	None
Where Used/How Used	Used by the database management system to process requests and return results to the Inquiry and Administration sub-systems
Content Description:	Attributes associated with each asset, including: Membership Number = 10 numeric digits Member Since Date = Date Last Name = 16 alphanumeric characters First Name = 16 alphanumeric characters Address = 64 alphanumeric characters Phone Number = 11 numeric digits (1, area code, phone number) Assets on Loan = array containing 10 strings, each containing 64 alphanumeric characters Assets Overdue = array containing 10 strings, each containing 64 alphanumeric characters Late Fees Due = 10 numeric digits Maximum Allowed Loans = 2 numeric digits
Name:	**Member Data**
Aliases:	None
Where Used/How Used	A file used to validate username and passwords for members, librarians, and administrator when attempting to access the system. The username and password entered are compared with the username and password in this file. Access is granted only if a match is found.
Content Description:	Attributes associated with each asset, including: Member Username = 16 alphanumeric digits Member Password = 16 alphanumeric digits

7. All Presentation Material

It is likely that, at some point, the system team will be asked to make a presentation about the system. All presentation paraphernalia, such as slides, notes, etc., should be included in the system documentation.

8. Test Cases (Appendix E) and Test Plan

While use cases form the basis of the initial set of test cases, they are but a small subset of test cases. An entire chapter has been dedicated to

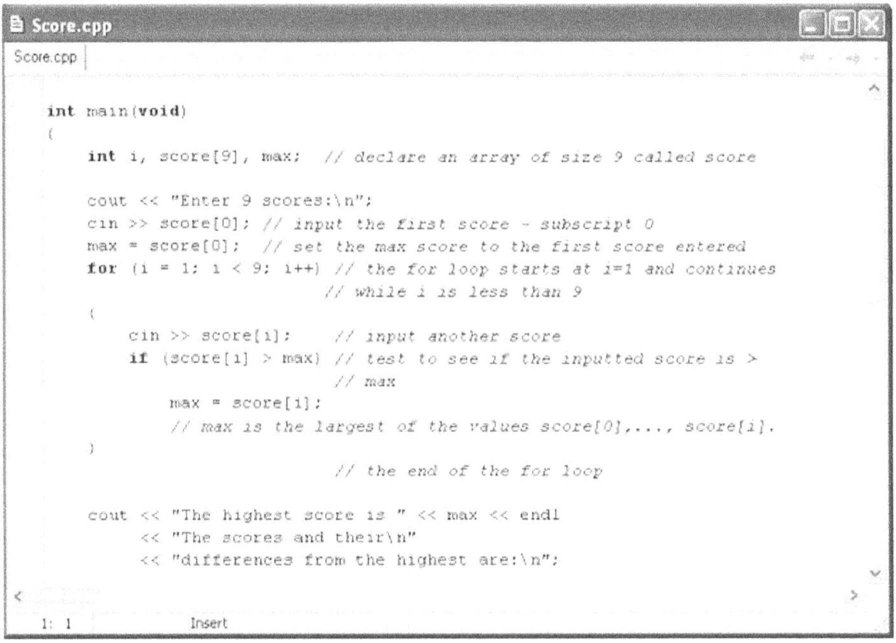

```
int main(void)
{
    int i, score[9], max;   // declare an array of size 9 called score

    cout << "Enter 9 scores:\n";
    cin >> score[0]; // input the first score - subscript 0
    max = score[0];  // set the max score to the first score entered
    for (i = 1; i < 9; i++) // the for loop starts at i=1 and continues
                            // while i is less than 9
    {
        cin >> score[i];    // input another score
        if (score[i] > max) // test to see if the inputted score is >
                            // max
            max = score[i];
            // max is the largest of the values score[0],..., score[i].
    }
                            // the end of the for loop

    cout << "The highest score is " << max << endl
         << "The scores and their\n"
         << "differences from the highest are:\n";
```

Score.cpp   1: 1   Insert

Figure 7.6 Sample Program Comments

software testing, so we will not prolong the discussion here. Suffice it to say that any and all test cases used in conjunction with the system — along with the results of those test cases — should be included in the system documentation.

9. Metrics

It is sad to say that most organizations do not measure the effectiveness of their programmers. Those that do should add this information to the system documentation. This includes a listing of all metrics (formulae) used and the results of those measurements. At a minimum, the weekly status reports and management reports generated from toolsets such as Microsoft Project should be included in the system documentation.

10. Operations Instructions

Once the system is implemented, aside from the end users that the system was developed for, there might be some computer support operations personnel who are required to support this system in some way. Precise instructions for these support personnel are mandatory and must be included in the documentation for the system.

Table 7.6 Sample Program Comments

//Get cost of equipment
rsEquipment = Select * from Equipment Utilized Where Pothole ID =
NewPotholeID
Loop through rsEquipment and keep running total of cost by equipment *
rsRepairCrew("Repair Time")
Total Cost = Total Employee Cost + Total Equipment Cost + Material Cost
Update Employee Set Total Cost Where Pothole ID = NewPotholeID

11. End-User Help Files

Most systems are built using a client/server metaphor that is quite inter-active. Most systems, therefore, provide end users with online help. A copy of each help file should be saved as documentation. Most corporate systems are Windows based. Hence, a Windows-style format in creating help files (Figure 7.7) has become the *de facto* standard. Microsoft Help Workshop is often used to assist in developing these help files, which are compiled from RTF (rich-text format) files.

12. User Documentation

Aside from the built-in help file, there must be a user manual included in what is provided to the end user. Increasingly, this user manual is being supplied right on the CD rather than on paper. There are two different types of end-user manuals. One is more of an encyclopedia that explains the terms and workings of the system when the end user has a specific question. The second type of end-user documentation is more of a tutorial.

User tutorials are easy to develop; it is important to approach the task in a step-by-step manner, going through all the motions of using the software exactly like a user would. Simply record every button you push and every key you press. A table format works well, as seen in Table 7.7, documenting the use of the SecureCRT program, which is a product of New Mexico-based Van Dyke Software.

Another advantage is that the user documentation development process serves double duty as a functional test. As the analyst or tech writer is developing the tutorial, he or she might just uncover some bugs.

MAINTAINING DOCUMENTATION

In his discussion of system documentation for the article "Tools and Evidence," Ambler [2002] suggests that modeling and documentation are

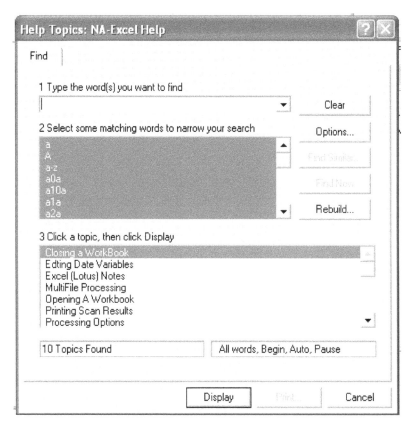

Figure 7.7 A Typical Help File

effective when employed with sense and restraint, thus enhancing system functionality. He makes a case that there is a need for restraint, that models should be discarded once they have fulfilled their purpose. As a project progresses, models are superseded by other artifacts such as other models, source code, or test cases that represent the information more effectively. Ambler takes a fresh approach: while it is important to know what to keep, it is also important to know what to throw away.

Documentation is particularly critical for maintenance work. Code can be mysterious to maintenance programmers who must maintain the system for years after the original system was written and the original programmers have moved on to other jobs [Graham et al. 2000].

Documentation is critically important. Kalakota [1996] wrote about organizing practices in his dissertation entitled "Organizing for Electronic Commerce." Echoing the concept of configuration management, Kalakota stressed that organizing has three distinct dimensions:

1. Organizing large amounts of data and digital documents

Table 7.7 User Tutorial in Table Format

Steps	Screen
1. When you first start the program, you will see a screen similar to the screen at the right. The default Protocol selected is telnet.	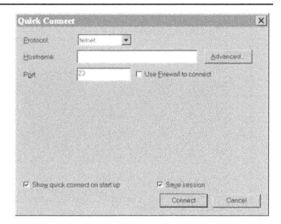
2. Pick the down arrow on the drop-down box, and select the ssh1 option.	
3. With the ssh1 option selected, notice that the fields change, now different from those available on the telnet screen. Enter the appropriate Hostname and Username. Leave the Port, Cipher, and Authentication options populated with the default settings.	

2. Organizing business processes and workflows
3. Organizing computing and processing

Distributed documents must be organized such that users and programs are able to locate, track, and use online documents. The growth of networking brings with it a corresponding increase in the number of documents to be organized. Current document organization techniques are derived from techniques used in file systems and are not sufficient for organizing the large number of heterogeneous documents that are becoming available for various purposes.

Kalakota suggests that:

■ New computing forms must be developed to process, filter, and customize online documents.
■ The traditional notion of client/server computing is not sufficient to deal with the complexity and needs of electronic commerce.
■ Workflows must be structured to take advantage of the online documents. Workflows often dictate organization structure but are difficult to study because they are essentially complex patterns of interaction between agents. One can easily characterize the variable properties of sequential actions, but not real-time patterns for tasks occurring in parallel.

SUMMARY

Documentation is an often-neglected but very necessary component of the software development life cycle (SDLC). There are numerous approaches and methods available to software development teams to assist with the task. Most important are a commitment to documenting software, setting standards for the organization, and making them stick — that is, adhering to the standards.

Configuration management (CM) enhances documentation by providing a framework of standardization through configuration identification and configuration status accounting.

REFERENCES

[AISI 1996] Applied Information Science International, "Entity Relationship Diagram," 1996; available online at http://www.aisintl.com/case/olais/pb96/er_model.htm

[Cook and Visconti 2000] Cook, Curtis R. and Marcello Visconti, "Software System Documentation Process Maturity Model," available online at http://www.cs.orst.edu/~cook/doc/Model.htm

[Graham et al. 2000] Graham, C., J.A. Hoffer, J.F. George, and J.S. Valacich, *Introduction to Business Systems Analysis,* Pearson Custom Publishing, Boston, MA, 2000.

[Kalakota 1996] Kalakota, Ravi Shankar, "Organizing for Electronic Commerce," *DAI-A,* 57/02, 1996, from University of Phoenix Online Collection [ProQuest Digital Dissertations], publication number AAT 9617262, Available online at http://www.apollolibrary.com:2118/dissertations/fullcit/9617262

[Leahey 2002] Leahey, Robert, *Doc-O-Matic 1.0: Generates Docs in WinHelp, RTF, HTML or HTML Help,* Delphi Informant, http://www.delphizine.com/productreviews/2001/07/di200107rl_p/di200107rl_p.asp

[Liebhaber 2002] Liebhaber, Karen Powers, "Documentation for a Technical Audience," *Intercom,* 49(2), February 2002.

[Scott 2002] Ambler, Scott W., "Tools and Evidence," *Software Development*, available online at http://www.sdmagazine.com/documents/s=7134/sdm0205i/0205i.htm

[Tufflye 2002] Tufflye, David, "How to Write, Version & File Software Development Documentation," 2002, available online at http://tuffley.hispeed.com/tcs20006.htm

[Visconti 1993] Visconti, Marcello Alfredo, Software System Documentation Process Maturity Model, *DAI-B*, 55/03, 1993, from University of Phoenix Online Collection [ProQuest Digital Dissertations], publication number AAT 9422184, available online at http://www.apollolibrary.com:2118/dissertations/fullcit/9422184

[Wallace 2000] Wallace, Charles Robert, Formal Specification of Software Using Abstract State Machines, *DAI-B*, 61/02, 2000, from University of Phoenix Online Collection [ProQuest Digital Dissertations], IBSN: 0-599-63514-2, Available online at http://www.apollolibrary.com:2118/dissertations/fullcit/9959880

8

CONFIGURATION VERIFICATION AND AUDIT

A variety of things can go wrong with the CM (configuration management) process. Brown et al. [1999] list a set of "antipatterns" — commonly repeated flawed practices:

- Reliance on a software configuration tool to implement an SCM program.
- The CM manager becomes a controlling force beyond his or her planned role. This leads to the CM manager dictating the delivery sequence and dominating all other processes.
- Delegating CM functions to whoever happens to be available. Project managers, often strapped for resources, frequently parcel out the CM function to developers. CM really needs to be process that stands apart from development. Brown says that their role as a developer compromises their role as software configuration manager, because their primary responsibility is for the development of software. Developers use this as the "product." From a CM perspective, the product is not just the software, but also the documentation.
- Use of decentralized repositories. The key behind CM is shared information. This requires a shared repository. Many organizations utilize a decentralized mode of operation. Decentralization negates shared information.
- Object-oriented development poses granularity problems. CM must happen at a detailed level of the interaction of a few objects and at a higher level where component interfaces are deployed.

The configuration verification and audit process includes:

■ Configuration verification of the initial configuration of a CI, and the incorporation of approved engineering changes, to assure that the CI meets its required performance and documented configuration requirements
■ Configuration audit of configuration verification records and physical product to validate that a development program has achieved its performance requirements and configuration documentation or the system/CI being audited is consistent with the product meeting the requirements

The common objective is to establish a high level of confidence in the configuration documentation used as the basis for configuration control and support of the product throughout its life cycle. Configuration verification should be an imbedded function of the process for creating and modifying the CI or CSCI.

As shown in Figure 8.1, inputs to the configuration verification and audit activity include:

■ Configuration, status, and schedule information from status accounting
■ Approved configuration documentation (which is a product of the configuration identification process)
■ The results of testing and verification
■ The physical hardware CI or software CSCI and its representation
■ Manufacturing
■ Manufacturing/build instructions and engineering tools, including the software engineering environment, used to develop, produce, test, and verify the product

Successful completion of verification and audit activities results in a verified system/CI(s) and a documentation set that can be confidently considered a product baseline. It also results in a validated process to maintain the continuing consistency of product to documentation. Appendices V and W provide sample checklists for performing both a functional configuration and physical configuration audit.

CONFIGURATION VERIFICATION AND AUDIT CONCEPTS AND PRINCIPLES

There is a functional and a physical attribute to both configuration verification and configuration audit. Configuration verification is an ongoing

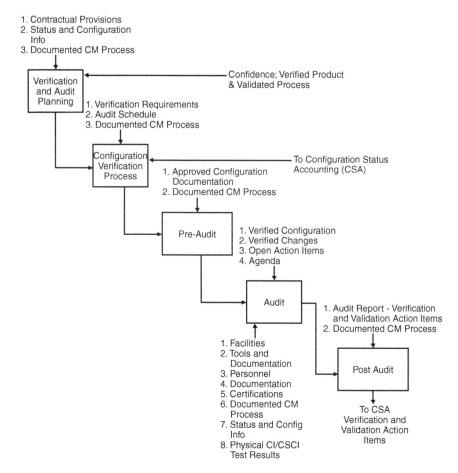

Figure 8.1 Configuration Verification and Audit Activity Model

process. The reward for effective release, baselining, and configuration/change verification is delivery of a known configuration that is consistent with its documentation and meets its performance requirements. These are precisely the attributes needed to satisfy the ISO 9000 series requirements for design verification and design validation as well as the ISO 10007 requirement for configuration audit.

Configuration Verification

Configuration verification is a process that is common to configuration management, systems engineering, design engineering, manufacturing, and quality assurance. It is the means by which a developer verifies his or her design solution.

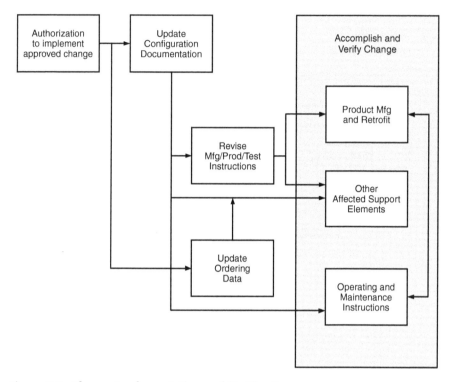

Figure 8.2 Change Implementation and Verification

The functional aspect of configuration verification encompasses all of the test and demonstrations performed to meet the quality assurance sections of the applicable performance specifications. The tests include verification/qualification tests performed on a selected unit or units of the CI, and repetitive acceptance testing performed on each deliverable CI, or on a sampling from each lot of CIs, as applicable. The physical aspect of configuration verification establishes that the as-built configuration conforms to the as-designed configuration. The developer accomplishes this verification by physical inspection, process control, or a combination of the two.

Once the initial configuration has been verified, approved changes to the configuration must also be verified. Figure 8.2 illustrates the elements in the process of implementing an approved change.

Change verification may involve a detailed audit, a series of tests, a validation of operation, maintenance, installation, or modification instructions, or a simple inspection. The choice of the appropriate method depends on the nature of the CI, the complexity of the change, and the support commodities that the change impacts.

Configuration Audit

The dictionary definition of the word "audit" as a final accounting gives some insight into the value of conducting configuration audits. Configuration management is used to define and control the configuration baselines for the CIs and the system. In general, a performance specification is used to define the essential performance requirements and constraints that the CI must meet.

For complex systems and CIs, a "performance" audit is necessary to make this determination. Also, because development of an item involves the generation of product documentation, it is prudent to ascertain that the documentation is an accurate representation of the design being delivered.

Configuration audits provide the framework, and the detailed requirements, for verifying that the development effort has successfully achieved all the requirements specified in the configuration baselines. If there are any problems, it is the auditing activity's responsibility to ensure that all action items are identified, addressed, and closed out before the design activity can be deemed to have successfully fulfilled the requirements.

There are three phases to the audit process, and each is very important. The pre-audit part of the process sets the schedule, agenda, facilities, and rules of conduct and identifies the participants for the audit. The actual audit itself is the second phase; and the third phase is the post-audit phase, in which diligent follow-up of the audit action items must take place. For complex products, the configuration audit process may be a series of sequential/parallel audits of various CIs conducted over a period of time to verify all relevant elements in the system product structure. Audit of a CI can include incremental audits of lower-level items to assess the degree of achievement of requirements defined in specifications/documentation.

Functional Configuration Audit

The functional configuration audit (FCA) is used to verify that the actual performance of the CI meets the requirements stated in its performance specification and to certify that the CI has met those requirements. For systems, the FCA is used to verify that the actual performance of the system meets the requirements stated in the system performance specification. In some cases, especially for very large, complex CIs and systems, the audits can be accomplished in increments. Each increment can address a specific functional area of the system/CI and will document any discrepancies found in the performance capabilities of that increment. After all the increments have been completed, a final (summary) FCA can be held to address the status of all the action items that have been identified by the incremental meetings and to document the status of the FCA for the system or CI in the minutes and certifications. In this way, the audit is effectively accomplished with minimal complications.

Physical Configuration Audit

The physical configuration audit (PCA) is used to examine the actual configuration of the CI that is representative of the product configuration in order to verify that the related design documentation matches the design of the deliverable CI. It is also used to validate many of the supporting processes that were used in the production of the CI. The PCA is also used to verify that any elements of the CI that were redesigned after the completion of the FCA also meet the requirements of the CI's performance specification.

Application of Audits during Life Cycle

It is extremely unlikely that FCAs or PCAs will be accomplished during the Concept Exploration and Definition phase or the Program Definition and Risk Reduction phase of the life cycle. Audits are intended to address the acceptability of a final, production-ready design and that is hardly the case for any design developed this early in the life cycle.

It is during the Engineering and Manufacturing Development (EMD) phase that the final, production, operationally ready design is developed. Thus, this phase is normally the focus for the auditing activity. A PCA will be preformed for each HW CI that has completed the FCA process to "lock down" the detail design by establishing a product baseline. Hardware CIs built during this phase are sometimes "pre-production prototypes" and are not necessarily representative of the production hardware. Therefore, it is very common for the PCAs to be delayed until early in the Production phase of the program.

Requirements to accomplish FCAs for systems and CIs are included in the Statement of Work (SOW) tasking. The FCA is accomplished to verify that the requirements in the system and CI performance specifications have been achieved in the design. It does not focus on the results of the operational testing that is often accomplished by operational testing organizations in the services, although some of the findings from the operational testing may highlight performance requirements in the baselined specification that have not been achieved. Deficiencies in performance capability, as defined in the baselined specification, result in FCA action items requiring correction without a change to the contract. Deficiencies in the operational capability, as defined in user-prepared need documents, usually result in Engineering Change Proposals (ECPs) to incorporate revised requirements into the baselined specifications or to fund the development of new or revised designs to achieve the operational capability.

Because the final tested software design verified at the FCA normally becomes the production design, the PCAs for CSCIs are normally included as a part of the SOW tasking for the EMD phase. CSCI FCAs and PCAs can be conducted simultaneously to conserve resources and to shorten schedules.

During a PCA, the deliverable item (hardware or software) is compared to the product configuration documentation to ensure that the documentation matches the design. This ensures that the exact design that will require support is documented. The intent is that an exact record of the configuration will be maintained as various repair and modification actions are completed. The basic goal is sometimes compromised in the actual operation and maintenance environment. Expediency, unauthorized changes, cannibalization, overwork, failure to complete paperwork, and carelessness can cause the record of the configuration of operational software or hardware to become inaccurate. In some situations, a unit cannot be maintained or modified until its configuration is determined. In these kinds of circumstances, it is often necessary to inspect the unit against approved product configuration documentation, as in a PCA, to determine where differences exist. Then the unit can be brought back into conformance with the documentation, or the records corrected to reflect the actual unit configuration.

As discussed, configuration audits address two major concerns:

1. The ability of the developed design to meet the specified performance requirements (the FCA addresses this concern)
2. The accuracy of the documentation reflecting the production design (the PCA addresses this concern)

Audit checklists are provided in Table 8.1.

SUMMARY

Testing is a critical component of software engineering. It is the final step taken prior to deploying the system. Configuration Verification and Audit organizes this process to ensure that the deployed system is as expected by the end users.

Table 8.1 Audit Checklists

Audit Planning Checklist:
1. Global plan and schedule for all FCAs/PCAs expanding on CM PLAN
2. CIs/CSCIs to be audited; specific units to be audited
3. Scope: contract requirements, SOW, specification, approved plans
4. Location and dates for each audit
5. Composition of audit team and their functions in the audit
6. Documentation to be audited and reference material
7. Administrative requirements; security requirements

Audit Agenda Checklist:
1. Covering a specific audit, targeted 60 days before audit
2. Date, time, location, duration — unless otherwise specified, configuration audits will be conducted at the contractor or a designated sub-contractor facility
3. Chairpersons
4. Specific CIs or CSCIs
5. Documentation to be available for review
6. Chronological schedule for conduct of the audit
7. Detailed information pertinent to the audit (e.g., team requirements, facility requirements, administrative information, security requirements)

Audit Teams Checklist:
1. Assign a co-chair for each audit in audit plan
2. For FCA: base specific personnel needs on the type and complexity of the CIs to be audited, their technical documentation, and the logistics, training, human factors, safety, producibility, deployability, and other requirements of the governing specification
3. For PCA: experts in engineering design, computer-aided design, engineering release, computer-aided manufacturing, manufacturing, assembly, and acceptance test processes are needed
4. Task DCMC plant representatives to review and certify engineering release, configuration control, and verification processes
5. Prior to each audit, provide organization and security clearance of each participating individual on the audit team

Conducting Configuration Audits
Introductory Briefings Checklist:
1. All participants
2. Purpose of the audit
3. Specific items to be audited; pertinent information/characteristics of the system/CIs
4. Basic criteria for problem identification and documentation
5. Schedule and location of audit events
6. Teams, team leaders, and location of teams

Table 8.1   Audit Checklists (continued)

7. Administrative procedures for the audit (e.g., problem input format, processing flow, audit logistics)
8. Location of necessary facilities

Conduct Reviews. Prepare Audit Findings (problem write-ups) Checklist:
Sub-teams facilitate the conduct of the audit by enabling parallel effort; auditors assigned to work in area of expertise.

1. Review specification, verification processes, and results:
   a. Test plans/procedures comply with specification requirements
   b. Test results, analyses, simulations, etc.; verify CI requirements as required by specification
   c. ECPs are incorporated and verified
   d. Interface requirements verified
   e. Configuration documentation reflects configuration of item for which test data is verified
   f. Data for items to be provisioned are sampled to ensure that they reference applicable performance and test requirements
   g. For CSCIs:
      i. Database, storage allocation, timing, and sequencing are in compliance with speci ed requirements
      ii. Software system operation and maintenance documentation is complete
      iii. Test results and documentation re ect correct softw are version
      iv. Internal QA audits are satis ed
2. Temporary departures documented by approved Deviation Request
3. Product baseline:
   a. Formal examination of the as-built configuration of a CI or CSCI against the specifications and design documentation constituting its product baseline
   b. Ensure proper parts as reflected in the engineering drawings (see below) are actually installed and correctly marked
   c. Determine that the configuration being produced accurately reflects released engineering data
4. Engineering drawing or CAD representations (design detail) review:
   a. Representative number of drawings (or CAD representations) and associated manufacturing instructions reviewed for accuracy and to ensure that the manufacturing instructions (from which the hardware is built) reflect all design details and include authorized engineering changes
      i. Drawing number and revision on manufacturing instructions matches correct released drawing or
      ii. CAD representation
      iii. Drawing and revisions are correctly represented in release records; drawings do not have more than five unincorporated changes

Table 8.1 Audit Checklists (continued)

    iv. List of materials on manufacturing instructions matches drawing parts list

    v. Nomenclature, part number, and serial number markings are correct

    vi. All approved changes have been incorporated

    vii. There is a continuity of part references and other characteristics for a major assembly from the top drawing down to the piece part

    viii. Required approvals are present

  b. Sampling of parts reflected on drawing reviewed to ensure compatibility with program parts selection list (or criteria)

5. Acceptance test procedures and results:

  a. CI acceptance test data and procedures comply with item specification

  b. Acceptance test requirements prescribed by the documentation are adequate for acceptance of production units of a CI

  c. CIs being audited pass acceptance tests as reflected in test results

6. Engineering release and configuration control:

  a. System is adequate to properly control the processing and release of engineering changes on a continuing basis

  b. Software changes are accurately identified, controlled, and tracked to the software and documentation affected

7. Logistics support plan for pre-operational support:

  a. Spares and repair parts provisioned prior to PCA are the correct configuration

8. For CSCIs:

  a. Documentation is complete and meets applicable conventions, protocols, coding standards, etc.

  b. Software listings reflect design descriptions

  c. Delivery media is appropriately marked and in agreement with specification requirements for packaging and delivery

  d. Documentation of the correct relationship to the components to which the software is to be loaded; for firmware, it contains complete installation and verification requirements

  e. Demonstrate that each CSCI can be compiled from library-based source code

  f. Review operational and support manuals for completeness, correctness, and incorporation of comments made at prior reviews (FCA, test readiness, QA audits, etc.)

Problem Write-up Checklist:

1. Originator:

  a. Identify contract or configuration document

  b. Item being audited

  c. Requirement

Table 8.1 Audit Checklists (continued)

    d. Narrative description of the problem/discrepancy

    e. Recommendation

2. Sub-team leader preliminary review:

    a. Preliminary control number assigned

    b. Approved and signed

    c. Disapproved

    d. Returned to originator for revision or further analysis

3. If approved, forwarded to Executive Panel

Disposition Audit Findings Checklist:

1. Executive panel:

    a. Final review of problem write-ups

    b. Assign control numbers and enter selected problems into official record of the audit

    c. Submit to developer with suspense time (typically a period of hours) for responding to the problem

2. Developer response:

    a. Concur with problem and recommend action

    b. Offer additional information that resolves or clarifies the problem

    c. Disagree with problem finding or obligation

3. Review response:

    a. Determine if it appears to provide satisfactory resolution

    b. Provide to Executive Panel

4. Disposition all problem write-ups that were submitted

5. Make final decision as to further action:

    a. Close item

    b. Agree on further actions to close out problem

6. Officially record all dispositions, action assignments, and suspense dates in audit minutes

7. Co-chairs sign all problem write-ups

Documenting Audit Results Checklist:

1. Prepare official audit minutes, to include:

    a. Typical meeting minutes: time, place, purpose, participants, etc.

    b. Action item lists reflecting all actions and suspense dates agreed to

    c. Applicable audit certifications documenting key audit review activities

    d. Specific items, systems, documents, or processes reviewed

    e. Summary of discrepancies/deficiencies in each area referenced to control number of applicable audit problem write-ups (action items)

    f. Definitive statements about acceptability or non-acceptability

    g. Final status of the developer's effort in the area being certified

REFERENCES

This chapter is based on the following report: MIL-HDBK-61A(SE), February 7, 2001, *Military Handbook: Configuration Management Guidance.*

[Brown 1999] Brown, William, Hays McCormick, and Scott Thomas, *AntiPatterns and Patterns in Software Configuration Management,* John Wiley & Sons, New York, 1999.

9

A PRACTICAL APPROACH TO CONFIGURATION VERIFICATION AND AUDIT

EIA-649, the standard for configuration management, requires the organization to verify that a product's stated requirements have been met. Verification can be accomplished by a systematic comparison of requirements with the results of test, analyses, and inspections.

There are three components to establishing a rigorous configuration verification and audit methodology:

1. Establishing and implementing a standard design and document verification methodology
2. Establishing and implementing a standard configuration audit methodology
3. Establishing and implementing a standard testing methodology

This chapter correlates the CM process of verification and audit with traditional software engineering testing methodology.

COMPONENTS OF A DESIGN AND DOCUMENT VERIFICATION METHODOLOGY

The basis of configuration management is the rigorous control and verification of all system artifacts. These artifacts include:

- The feasibility study
- The project plan

- The requirements specification
- The design specification
- The database schemas
- The test plan

EIA-649 states that the documentation must be accurate and sufficiently complete to permit the reproduction of the product without further design effort. What this means is that if the set of documents described in the list above was given to a different set of programmers, the same exact system would be produced.

Activities that can accomplish this end include:

- Rigorous review of all documentation by inspection teams.
- Continuous maintenance of documentation through using an automated library of documentation with check-in and check-out facilities.
- Maintenance of the product's baseline.
- Implementation of requirements traceability review. All requirements were originally stated needs by a person or persons. Traceability back to this person or persons is critical if the product is to be accurately verified.
- Implementation of data dictionary and/or repository functionality to manage digital data.

COMPONENTS OF A CONFIGURATION AUDIT METHODOLOGY

Configuration audit requires the following resources:

- Appropriately assigned staff, to include a team leader as well as representatives of the systems and end-user groups
- A detailed audit plan
- Availability of all documentation discussed in the prior section (it is presumed that this documentation is readily available in a controlled, digitized format)

Audits can be performed upon implementation of a new system or the maintenance of an existing one. Prior to conducting the audit, the audit plan, which details the scope of the effort, is created and approved by all appropriate personnel.

The audit process itself is not unlike the testing process described in the first part of this chapter. An audit plan, therefore, is very similar to a test plan. During the audit, auditors:

- Compare the specification to the product and record discrepancies and anomalies.
- Review the output of the testing cycle and record discrepancies and anomalies.
- Review all documentation and record discrepancies and anomalies. In a CM (configuration management) environment, the following should be verified for each document:
  - A documentation library control system is being utilized.
  - The product identifier is unique.
  - All interfaces are valid.
  - Internal audit records of CM processes are maintained.
- Record questions, if any, about what was observed. Obtain answers to these questions.
- Make recommendations as to action items to correct any discovered discrepancies and anomalies.
- Present formal findings.

Audit minutes provide a detailed record of the findings, recommendations, and conclusions of the audit committee. The committee follows up until all required action items are complete.

COMPONENTS OF A TESTING METHODOLOGY

The goal of testing is to uncover and correct errors. Because software is so complex, it is reasonable to assume that software testing is a labor- and resource-intensive process. Automated software testing helps to improve testers' productivity and reduce the resources that may be required. By its very nature, automated software testing increases test coverage levels, speeds up test turn-around time, and cuts costs of testing.

The classic software development life-cycle model suggests a systematic, sequential approach to software development that progresses through software requirements analysis, design, code generation, and testing. That is, once the source code has been generated, program testing begins with the goal of finding differences between the expected behavior specified by system models and the observed behavior of the system.

The process of creating software applications that are error-free requires technical sophistication in the analysis, design, and implementation of that software, proper test planning, as well as robust automated testing tools. When planning and executing tests, software testers must consider the software and the function it performs, the inputs and how they can be combined, and the environment in which the software will eventually operate.

There are a variety of software testing activities that can be implemented, as discusses below.

Inspections

Software development is, for the most part, a team effort, although the programs themselves are coded individually. Periodically throughout the coding of a program, the project leader or project manager will schedule inspections of a program (see Appendices F and G). An inspection is the process of manually examining the code in search of common errors.

Each programming language has it own set of common errors. It is therefore worthwhile to spend a bit of time in search of these errors.

An example of what an inspection team would look for follows:

```
int i;
for (i = 0; i < 10; i++)
{
  cout << "Enter velocity for "
  << i << "numbered data point: "
  cin >> data_point[i].velocity;
  cout << "Enter direction for that data point"
  << " (N, S, E or W): ";
  cin >> data_point[i].direction;
}
```

The C++ code displayed above looks correct. However, the semicolon was missing from the fifth line of code:

```
int i;
for (i = 0; i < 10; i++)
{
  cout << "Enter velocity for "
  << i << "numbered data point: ";//the ; was missing
  cin >> data_point[i].velocity;
  cout << "Enter direction for that data point"
  << " (N, S, E or W): ";
  cin >> data_point[i].direction;
}
```

Walk-Throughs

A walk-through is a manual testing procedure that examines the logic of the code. This is somewhat different from an inspection, where the goal is to find syntax errors. The walk-through procedure attempts to answer the following questions:

- Does the program conform to the specification for that program?
- Is the input being handled properly?
- Is the output being handled properly?
- Is the logic correct?

The best way to handle a walk-through is:

- Appoint a chairperson who schedules the meeting, invites appropriate staff, and sets the agenda.
- The programmer presents his or her code.
- The code is discussed.
- Test cases can be used to "walk through" the logic of the program for specific circumstances.
- Disagreements are resolved by the chairperson.
- The programmer goes back and fixes any problems.
- A follow-up walk-through is scheduled.

Unit Testing

During the early stages of the testing process, the programmer usually performs all tests. This stage of testing is referred to as unit testing. Here, the programmer usually works with the debugger that accompanies the compiler. For example, Visual Basic, as shown in Figure 9.1, enables the programmer to "step through" a program's (or object's) logic one line of code at a time, viewing the value of any and all variables as the program proceeds.

Daily Build and Smoke Test

McConnell [1996] describes a testing methodology commonly used at companies such as Microsoft that sell shrink-wrapped software. The "daily build and smoke" test is a process whereby every file is compiled, linked, and combined into an executable program on a daily basis. The executable is then put through a "smoke" test, a relatively simple check, to see if the product "smokes" when it runs.

According to McConnell [1996], this simple process has some significant benefits, including:

- It minimizes integration risk by ensuring that disparate code, usually developed by different programmers, is well integrated.

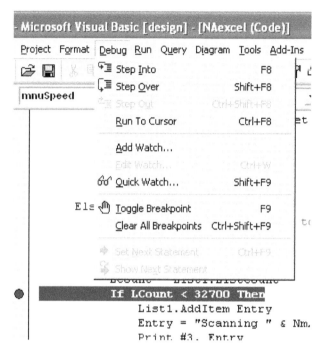

Figure 9.1 Visual Basic, along with Other Programming Toolsets, Provides Unit Testing Capabilities to Programmers

■ It reduces the risk of low quality by forcing the system to a minimally acceptable standard of quality.
■ It supports easier defect diagnosis by requiring the programmers to solve problems as they occur rather than waiting until the problem is too large to solve.

For this to be a successful effort, the build part of this task should:

■ Compile all files, libraries, and other components successfully
■ Link successfully all files, libraries, and components
■ Not contain any "show-stopper bugs" that prevent the program from operating properly

The "smoke" part of this task should:

■ Exercise the entire system from end to end with a goal of exposing major problems
■ Evolve as the system evolves: as the system becomes more complex, the smoke test should become more complex

Integration Testing

A particular program is usually made up of many modules. An OO (object-oriented) system is composed of many objects. Programmers usually architect their programs in a top-down, modular fashion. Integration testing proves that the module interfaces are working properly. For example, in Figure 9.2, a programmer doing integration testing would ensure that the Module2 (the Process module) correctly interfaces with its subordinate, Module2.1 (the Calculate process).

If Module2.1 had not yet been written, it would have been referred to as a *stub*. It would still be possible to perform integration testing if the programmer inserts two or three lines of code in the stub, which would act to prove that it is well integrated to Module2.

On occasion, a programmer will code all the subordinate modules first and leave the higher-order modules for last. This is known as bottom-up programming. In this case, Module2 would be empty, save for a few lines of code to prove that it is integrating correctly with Module2.1, etc. In this case, Module2 would be referred to as a *driver*.

System Testing

Where integration testing is performed on the discrete programs or objects with a master program, system testing refers to testing the interfaces between programs within a system. Because a system can be composed of hundreds of programs, this is a vast undertaking.

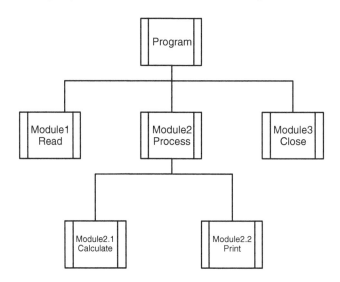

Figure 9.2   Integration Testing Proves that Module Interfaces Are Working Properly

Parallel Testing

It is quite possible that the system being developed is a replacement for an existing system. In this case, parallel testing is performed. The goal here is to compare outputs generated by each of the systems (old versus new) and determine why there are differences, if any.

Parallel testing requires that the end user(s) be part of the testing team. If the end user determines that the system is working correctly, one can see that the customer "has accepted" the system. This, then, is a form of *customer acceptance* testing.

THE QA PROCESS

As the testing progresses, testing specialists may become involved (see Appendix H for a sample QA Handover Document). Within the vernacular of IT, staff members who are dedicated to performing testing are referred to as *quality assurance (QA) engineers* and reside within the *quality assurance department*. QA testers must have a good understanding of the program being tested, as well as the programming language in which the program was coded. In addition, the QA engineer must be methodical and able to grasp complex logic. Generally speaking, technical people with these attributes are hard to come by and even harder to keep as most of them aspire to become programmers themselves.

Even simple software can present testers with obstacles. Couple this complexity with the difficulty of attracting and keeping QA staff and one has the main reason why many organizations now automate parts of the testing process.

THE TEST PLAN

Software testing is one critical element of software quality assurance (SQA) that aims to determine the quality of the system and its related models. In such a process, a software system will be executed to determine whether it matches its specification and executes in its intended environment. To be more precise, the testing process focuses on both the logical internals of the software, ensuring that all statements have been tested, and on the functional externals by conducting tests to uncover errors and ensure that defined input will produce actual results that agree with required results.

To ensure that the testing process is complete and thorough, it is necessary to create a test plan (Appendix E).

A thorough test plan consists of the items listed in Table 9.1. A sample test plan, done by this author's students for an OO dog grooming system,

Table 9.1   Thorough Test Plan

1. Revision History
2. System Introduction
    2.1 Goals and Objectives
    2.2 Statement of Scope
    2.3 Major Constraints
3. Test Plan
    3.1 System Description
    3.2 Testing Strategy
    3.3 Testing Resources
    3.4 Testing Metrics
    3.5 Testing Artifacts
    3.6 Testing Schedule
4. Test Procedures
    4.1 Class Testing
    4.2 Integration Testing
5. Appendix 1: Class Testing Test Cases
    5.1 Application Controller Sub-system
    5.2 User Management Sub-system
    5.3 Resource Management Sub-system
    5.4 Order Sub-system
    5.5 Accounting Sub-system
    5.6 Customer Relationship Management Sub-system
    5.7 Persistence Sub-system
6. Appendix 2: Integration Testing Test Cases
    6.1 Customer Registration
    6.2 Reallocate Resources
    6.3 Search for Service Provider and Initiate Order
    6.4 Place Order
    6.5 Pay for Service
7. Appendix: Project Schedule

can be found in Appendix E. While all components of this test plan are important, one notes that the test plan really focuses on three things:

1. The test cases
2. Metrics that will determine whether there has been testing success or failure
3. The schedule

The test cases are the heart of the test plan. A test case specifies the exact steps the tester must take to test a particular function of the system. A sample test case appears in Table 9.2.

Test plans must be carefully created. A good test plan contains a test case for every facet of the system to be tested.

Some organizations purchase automated testing tools that assist the developer in testing the system. These are particularly useful for:

- *Automatically creating test cases.* Testing tools can "watch" what a person does at the keyboard and then translate what it records into a testing script. For example, a loan application transaction consists of logging into a system, calling up a particular screen, and then entering some data. Automatic testing tools can "watch" someone keyboard this transaction and create a script that details the steps that person took to complete the transaction.
- *Simulating large numbers of end users.* If a system will ultimately have dozens, hundreds, or even thousands of end users, then testing the system with a handful of testers will be insufficient. An automatic testing tool has the capability to simulate any number of end users. This is referred to as testing the "load" of a system.

Success must be measured. The test plan should contain metrics that assess the success or failure of the system's components. Examples of viable metrics include:

- For each class, indicators of test failure (as identified in the test cases)
- Number of failure indicators per class
- Number of failure indicators per sub-system
- A categorization of failure indicators by severity
- Number of repeat failures (not resolved in the previous iteration)
- Hours spent by test team in test process
- Hours spent by development team in correcting failures

TEST AUTOMATION

The usual practice in software development is that the software is written as quickly as possible, and once the application is done, it is tested and debugged. However, this is a costly and ineffective way because the software testing process is difficult, time consuming, and resource intensive. With manual test strategies, this can be even more complicated and cumbersome. A better alternative is to perform unit testing that is inde-

Table 9.2   Sample Test Case

C1. Log-in Page (based on case A1)

Description/Purpose:

Test the proper display of the login, user verification, and that the user is redirected to the correct screen.

Stubs Required:

- Data Interface — The data interface stub/driver is required to verify log-in data as the user enters it through the Web page.
- Database Interface — The database interface stub/driver is required to check the database for log-in data.

Steps:

1. Go to the main log-in screen.
2. Enter the username and password, both including special characters. This should be the login of a customer.
3. Execute Data Interface stub within the test framework to confirm that ID and password are a valid pair.
4. Select Veterinary Services link.
5. Confirm that the list of dogs that appear are dogs that only belong to that customer.
6. Go to the main log-in screen.
7. Enter the username and password, both including special characters. This should be the login of an employee/administrator.
8. Execute Data Interface stub within the test framework to confirm that ID and password are a valid pair.
9. Select Veterinary Services link.
10. Confirm that the list of dogs is a list of all dogs in the database.
11. Go to the main log-in screen.
12. Enter a bad user name and password.
13. Execute Data Interface stub within the test framework to confirm that ID and password are not a valid pair.
14. Confirm that the log-in screen presented an error message and stayed at the log-in screen.

Expected Results:

- Successful login with username and matching password.
- Able to log in with passwords with special characters.
- Veterinary display screen presents the correct list of dogs in the database, from zero to many. This list of dogs is a list of dogs for a customer if the user is a customer; otherwise, the user is a staff member and has access to all the dogs in the database.

pendent of the rest of the code. During unit testing, developers compare the object design model with each object and sub-system. Errors detected at the unit level are much easier to fix; one only has to debug the code in that small unit. Unit testing is widely recognized as one of the most effective ways to ensure application quality. It is a laborious and tedious task, however. The workload for unit testing is tremendous, so that to manually perform unit testing is practically impossible — and hence the need for automatic unit testing. Another good reason to automate unit testing is that when performing manual unit testing, one runs the risk of making mistakes [Aivazis 2000].

In addition to saving time and preventing human errors, automatic unit testing helps facilitate integration testing. After unit testing has removed errors in each sub-system, combinations of sub-systems are integrated into larger sub-systems and tested. When tests do not reveal new errors, additional sub-systems are added to the group, and another iteration of integration testing is performed. The re-execution of some subset of tests that have already been conducted is regression testing. This ensures that no errors are introduced as a result of adding new modules or modification in the software [Kolawa 2001].

As integration testing proceeds, the number of regression tests can grow very large. Therefore, it is inefficient and impractical to re-execute every test manually once a change has occurred. The use of automated capture/playback tools may prove useful in this case. Such tools enable the software engineer to capture test cases and results for subsequent playback and comparison.

Test automation can improve testers' productivity. Testers can apply one of several types of testing tools and techniques at various points of code integration. Some examples of automatic testing tools in the marketplace include:

- C++Test for automatic C/C++ unit testing by ParaSoft
- Cantata++ for dynamic testing of C++ by IPL
- WinRunner for unit and system tests by Mercury Interactive

WinRunner is probably one of the more popular tools in use today because it automates much of the painful process of testing. Used in conjunction with a series of test cases (see Appendix E, Section 5), a big chunk of the manual processes that constitute the bulk of testing can be automated. The WinRunner product actually records a particular business process by recording the keystrokes a user makes (e.g., emulates the user actions of placing an order). The QA person can then directly edit the test script that WinRunner generates and add checkpoints and other validation criteria.

When done correctly, and with appropriate testing tools and strategies, automated software testing provides worthwhile benefits such as repeatability and significant time savings. This is true especially when the system moves into system test. Higher quality is also a result because less time is spent in tracking down test environmental variables and rewriting poorly written test cases [Raynor 1999].

Pettichord [2001] describes several principles that testers should adhere to in order to succeed with test automation. These principles include:

- Taking testing seriously
- Being careful who you choose to perform these tests
- Choosing what parts of the testing process to automate
- Being able to build maintainable and reliable test scripts
- Using error recovery

Testers must realize that test automation itself is a software development activity and thus it needs to adhere to standard software development practices. That is, test automation systems themselves must be tested and subjected to frequent review and improvement to make sure that they are indeed addressing the testing needs of the organization.

Because automating test scripts is part of the testing effort, good judgment is required in selecting appropriate tests to automate. Not everything can or should be automated. For example, overly complex tests are not worth automating. Manual testing is still necessary for this situation. Zambelich [2002] provides a guideline to make automated testing cost-effective. He says that automated testing is expensive and does not replace the need for manual testing or enable one to "down-size" a testing department. Automated testing is an addition to the testing process. Some pundits claim that it can take between three and ten times as long (or longer) to develop, verify, and document an automated test case than to create and execute a manual test case. Zambelich indicates that this is especially true if one elects to use the "record/playback" feature (contained in most test tools) as the primary automated testing methodology. In fact, Zambelich says that record/playback is the *least* cost-effective method of automating test cases.

Automated testing can be made cost-effective, according to Zambelich, if some common sense is applied to the process:

- Choose a test tool that best fits the testing requirements of your organization or company. An "Automated Testing Handbook" is available from the Software Testing Institute (http://www.soft waretestinginstitute.com).

■ Understand that it does not make sense to automate everything. Overly complex tests are often more trouble than they are worth to automate. Concentrate on automating the majority of tests, which are probably fairly straightforward. Leave the overly complex tests for manual testing.

■ Only automate tests that are going to be repeated; one-time tests are not worth automating.

Isenberg [1994] explains the requirements for success in automated software testing. To succeed, the following four interrelated components must work together and support one another:

1. *Automated testing system.* It must be flexible and easy to update.
2. *Testing infrastructure.* This includes a good bug tracking system, standard test case format, baseline test data, and comprehensive test plans.
3. *Software testing life cycle.* This defines a set of phases outlining what test activities to do and when to do them. These phases are planning, analysis, design, construction, testing (initial test cycles, bug fixes, and retesting), final testing and implementation, and post implementation.
4. *Corporate support.* Automation cannot succeed without the corporation's commitment to adopting and supporting repeatable processes.

Automated testing systems should have the ability to adjust and respond to unexpected changes to the software under test, which means that the testing systems will stay useful over time. Some of the practical features of automated software testing systems suggested by Isenberg [1994] include:

■ Run all day and night in unattended mode
■ Continue running even if a test case fails
■ Write out meaningful logs
■ Keep test environment up-to-date
■ Track tests that pass, as well as tests that fail

When automated testing tools are introduced, there may be some difficulties that test engineers must face. Project management should be used to plan the implementation of testing tools. Without proper management and selection of the right tool for the job, automated test implementation will fail [Hendrickson 1998]. Dustin [1999] has accumulated a list of "Automated Testing Lessons Learned" from his experiences with real projects and test engineer feedback. Some include:

- The various tools used throughout the development life cycle do not integrate easily if they are from different vendors.
- An automated testing tool can speed up the testing effort; however, it should be introduced early in the testing life cycle to gain benefits.
- Duplicate information may be kept in multiple repositories and difficult to maintain. As a matter of fact, in many instances, the implementation of more tools can result in decreased productivity.
- The automated testing tool drives the testing effort. When a new tool is used for the first time, more time is often spent on installation, training, initial test case development, and automating test scripts than on actual testing.
- It is not necessary for everyone on the testing staff to spend his or her time automating scripts.
- Sometimes, elaborate test scripts are developed through overuse of the testing tool's programming language, which duplicates the development effort. That is, too much time is spent on automating scripts without much additional value gained. Therefore, it is important to conduct an automation analysis and to determine the best approach to automation by estimating the highest return.
- Automated test script creation is cumbersome. It does not happen automatically.
- Tool training needs to be initiated early in the project so that test engineers have the knowledge to use the tool.
- Testers often resist new tools. When first introducing a new tool to the testing program, mentors and advocates of the tool are very important.
- There are expectations of early payback. When a new tool is introduced to a project, project members anticipate that the tool will narrow down the testing scope right away. In reality, it is the opposite — that is, initially the tool will increase the testing scope.

SUMMARY

Test engineers can enjoy productivity increases as the testing task becomes automated and a thorough test plan is implemented. Creating a good and comprehensive automated test system requires an additional investment of time and consideration, but it is cost-effective in the long run. More tests can be executed while the amount of tedious work on construction and validation of test cases is reduced.

Automated software testing is by no means a complete substitute for manual testing. That is, manual testing cannot be totally eliminated; it should always precede automated testing. In this way, the time and effort that will be saved from the use of automated testing can now be focused on more important testing areas.

Configuration management insists that we create and follow procedures for verification of a product's adherence to the specification from which it was derived. A combination of rigorously defined testing, documentation, and audit methodologies fulfills this requirement.

REFERENCES

Aivazis, M., "Automatic Unit Testing," *Computer,* 33(5), back cover, May 2000.

Bruegge, B. and A.H. Dutoit, *Object-Oriented Software Engineering: Conquering Complex and Changing Systems,* Prentice Hall, Upper Saddle River, NJ, 2000.

Dustin, E., "Lessons in Test Automation," *STQE Magazine,* September/October 1999, and from the World Wide Web: http://www.stickyminds.com/pop_print.asp?ObjectId=1802&ObjectType=ARTCO

Hendrickson, E., *The Difference between Test Automation Failure and Success,* Quality Tree Software, August, 1998, retrieved from http://www.qualitytree.com/feature/dbtasaf.pdf

Isenberg, H.M., "The Practical Organization of Automated Software Testing," *Multi Level Verification Conference 95,* December 1994, retrieved from http://www.automated-testing.com/PATfinal.htm

Kolawa, A., "Regression Testing at the Unit Level?," *Computer,* 34(2), back cover, February 2001.

McConnell, Steve, "Daily Build and Smoke Test," *IEEE Software,* 13(4), July 1996.

Pettichord, B., "Success with Test Automation," June 2001, retrieved from http://www.io.com/~wazmo/succpap.htm

Pressman, R.S., *Software Engineering: A Practitioner's Approach,* 5th ed., McGraw-Hill, Boston, MA, 2001.

Raynor, D.A., "Automated Software Testing," retrieved from http://www.trainersdirect.com/resources/articles/ProjectManagement/AutomatedSoftwareTestingRaynor.html

Whittaker, J.A., "What Is Software Testing? And Why Is It So Hard?," *IEEE Software,* January/February 2000, 70–79.

Zallar, K., "Automated Software Testing – A Perspective," retrieved from http://www.testingstuff.com/autotest.html

Zambelich, K., "Totally Data-Driven Automated Testing," 2002, retrieved from http://www.sqa-test.com/w_paper1.html

10

CONFIGURATION MANAGEMENT AND DATA MANAGEMENT

In this age of rapidly developing information technology, data management and particularly the management of digital data constitute an essential prerequisite to the performance of configuration management. Digital data is information prepared by electronic means and made available to users by electronic data access, interchange, transfer, or on electronic/magnetic media. There is virtually no data today, short of handwritten notes, that does not fall into this category. Configuration management (CM) of data is therefore part of data management activity; and management of the configuration of a product configuration cannot be accomplished without it.

Figure 10.1 is an activity model for configuration management of data. All the activities shown apply to configuration documentation. Most of the activities apply to all data. The model illustrates that the process is driven by business rules established based on the concept of operations for the processing of digital data, and specific data requirements.

When the data process is initiated to create or revise an item of data, or to perform any of the actions necessary to bring it from one status level to the next, the various rule sets illustrated in Figure 10.1 are triggered to facilitate the workflow. The result is a data product with:

- Appropriate document, document representation, and data file identification
- Version control
- Clear and unambiguous relationships to the product configuration with which it is associated, and to the changes that delineate each configuration of the product

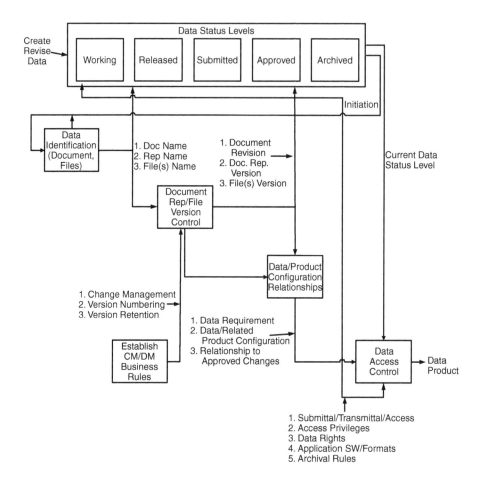

Figure 10.1 CM-Related Data Management Activity Model

In addition, the data is available for access in accordance with contractually agreed-to rules for submittal, transmission, or online access (as appropriate), in the prescribed format (document representation) that can be used by the application software available to the authorized user.

CM-RELATED DATA MANAGEMENT CONCEPTS AND PRINCIPLES

Configuration management principles ensure the integrity of digital representations of product information and other data, and enhance good data management practice. The concepts are described, as follows, based on elements and principles expressed in EIA Standard 649 (EIA-649):

- Document identification
- Data status level management
- Data and product configuration relationships
- Data version control and management of review, comment, annotation, and disposition
- Digital data transmittal
- Data access control

Document Identification

Each document reflecting performance, functional, or physical requirements or other product-related information must be given a unique identifier so that it can be:

- Correctly associated with the applicable configuration (product identifier and revision) of the associated item
- Referred to precisely
- Retrieved when necessary

Document identifier formats include all or most of the following parameters:

- Date
- Assigned numeric or alphanumeric identifier unique to the document
- Revision indicator
- Type of document
- Title or subject
- Originator/organization

A document is digitally represented by one or more electronic data files. Each document representation is the complete set of all the individual digital data files (e.g., word processor, CAD/CAM, graphics, database, spreadsheet, software) constituting one document.

As shown in Figure 10.2, the same document can have several different, equally valid representations, such as different word processing or standard neutral formats (IGES, ASCII, SGML-tagged ASCII). Any individual file (such as a raster graphics file, an ASCII file, or a spreadsheet file) may be part of several document representations of the same document/same revision; same document/different revision; or different document. The business rules relating documents, documentation representations, and files are as follows:

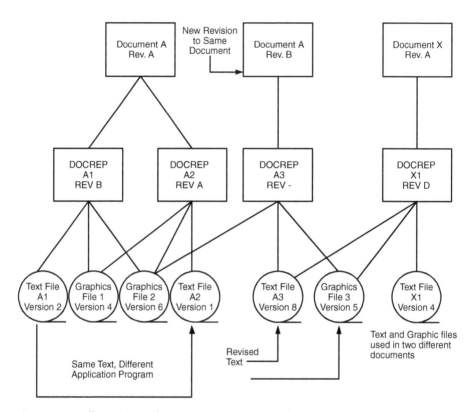

Figure 10.2 Illustration of Document Representation Concepts

1. Each document iteration exists as one or more document representations, identified by:
   a. Document identifier
   b. Document representation identifier
   c. Document representation revision identifier
2. Each document representation is comprised of zero or more files. To facilitate the proper relationships, apply the following digital data identification rules to maintain document, document representation, and file version relationships:
   a. Assign a unique identifier to each file
   b. Assign a unique identifier to each document representation
   c. Assign a version identifier to each file
   d. Maintain, in a database, the relationship between:
      ■ Document identifier and its revision level
      ■ Associated document representation(s)
      ■ File identifiers and versions

■ Retain multiple versions of files as necessary to recreate prior document revisions and provide a traceable history of each document

3. Identify the tool and version of the tool (e.g., MSWord 2000) used to generate the document when the document is not in neutral format

Data Status Level Management

Document status level is important as a foundation for the business rules defining access, change management, and archiving of digital data documents. It is the basis for establishing data workflow management and enhances data integrity. The standard data life-cycle model shows the data status levels (also referred to as states) that a specific document or document revision is processed through in its life cycle.

■ *Working* is the status used to identify data (document representations or document revisions) that is in preparation — a work in progress that is subject to unilateral change by the originator. Each design activity can define any number of subordinate states within the working category, to define the unique processes that different document types go through before release in their organization.

■ *Released* is the status of document representations, and revisions thereto, that have been reviewed and authorized for use (such as for manufacture, or for submittal to, or access by a customer or supplier). Released data is under originating organization (for example, a contractor) change management rules, which prohibit a new revision of the document representation from replacing a released revision of a document representation until it has also been reviewed and authorized by the appropriate authority. The content of a document representation revision is fixed once it is in the released state. It is only changed by release of a superseding document representation revision. Once a document (or document revision) is in the approved state, changes are made only by release of a new document representation related to the next document revision.

■ *Submitted* data is a proposed or approved document revision in the form of a released document representation that has been made available for customer review. This status applies only to data that requires submittal to or access by a customer (usually the government). If a submitted document revision that has not been approved is commented to or disapproved, a new working revision of the related document representation can be started and eventually submitted to replace the original document representation without affecting the identifier proposed for the new document revision. If a submitted document revision that has been approved is commented to, or disapproved by the customer, a new working representation of the next document revision can be started and eventually replace the original document revision.

■ *Approved* is the status of documents and document revisions signifying that the data (document revision) has been approved by the Current Document Change Authority (CDCA) of the document. The content of a document revision is fixed once it is in the approved state. It is only changed by approval of a superseding document revision.

■ Some tools include *Archived* as a data status for document representations and documents. This status is independent of the approval status (released, submitted, and approved) and merely means that the data has been removed from an active access storage mode.

No changes are allowed in the document representations that progress to the released state, or in document revisions that progress to the approved state. If there are changes to be made, they are accomplished by the generation and release or approval of a new revision. Documents must have at least one released document representation in order to be approved by the CDCA or submitted to a non-CDCA customer for review and adoption. Some data will exist only at the working level.

Business rules related to document or data status apply to each document type by defining requirements such as the following:

■ Is submittal to (or access by) customer(s) required?
■ In which application software and data format is submittal or access required?
■ Who will be granted access privileges to the data in each of the applicable states?
■ What are the approval requirements (reviewers/approvers) and method of approval (e.g., electronic signature) to promote a document to the released state?; the approved state?
■ What are the archiving rules for this document type (e.g., all released versions upon release of a superseding version, all released versions, 90 days after release of a superseding version, etc.)?

Data and Product Configuration Relationships

A product data management system must provide an effective system to maintain the key relationships between digital data, data requirements, and the related product configuration so that the correct revision of an item of data can be accessed or retrieved when needed. Data files are related to documents via document representations.

Each product document, with a specific source, document type, document identifier (title, name, and number), and document revision identifier, may have the following relationships:

- Program/project or contractual agreement
- Contract data item identifiers
- Document revision/change authorization
- Associated product (hardware or software) name
- Associated product (end item), part, or software identifying number and revision/version identifier, where applicable
- The effectivity in terms of end item serial numbers for the associated product, part, or software item
- Status (working, released, submitted, approved, archived) of the data
- Associated data (document name, document title, document revision number, and date)
- Associated correspondence: document number, subject, date, references

The business rules for document retrieval should use these key relationships within a database to assure the integrity of the data that users can extract. Thus, information concerning a given product or part is associated with the configuration and effectivity (serial number) of the end item that uses the part.

This capability is particularly significant during the operation and support phase, when data is needed to support maintenance activity and to determine the appropriate replacement parts for a specific end item.

Data Version Control

Disciplined version control of data files is the prerequisite to effective electronic management of digital documentation and must be encompassed within the product data management software. Version occurs whenever a file is changed. The simplest form of version management is the file save feature incorporated in application software, which advances the file date and time identification each time a file is saved.

However, to retain the superseded version, it must be renamed. True version control business rules require automatic version identifier advance whenever a file is revised and not when the file is saved without change. Furthermore, they require all versions to be retained, subject to archiving guidelines and special rules pertinent to specific document types.

Because a single document representation can consist of many files, a very disciplined process is necessary to manage a document review process electronically. Version control rules facilitate the establishment of an audit trail of comments and annotations by reviewers, and the disposition of each comment. Each version of each document representation provided to, or received from, each reviewer is uniquely identified and associated with the source of the comment. Essentially, this means that a reviewer's version of a set of files (document representation) constituting a document being reviewed is renamed to enable the annotated comment copy to be distinguished from the official current version of the document.

Digital Data Transmittal

Part of the obligation of the sender of any document, regardless of transmission method, is to make sure that the document is in a format (document representation) that can be read by the receiver and converted to human-readable form. Appropriate identification is affixed to physical media such as floppy disks or tapes to clearly identify its contents. If all the file identifications cannot be included on the label, a directory, a reference to an accompanying listing or to a read-me file is used.

EIA-STD-649 lists the following common-sense guidelines for information to be provided to the user (via such means as "read-me" files, reference to standard protocols, online help), where applicable:

- Identification of the files included in the transfer by file name, description, version, data status level, application/file type, and application version
- Applicable references to associate the data with the basis (requirement) for its transmittal, approval, and payment, where applicable
- If there are multiple files, such as separate text and graphics, how to assemble each included data item for reading, review, or annotation, as applicable
- The naming convention for file versions and data status level distinguishes altered (for example, annotated or red-line/strike-out) file versions from unaltered files
- If and how changes from previous versions are indicated
- How to acknowledge receipt of the data, provide comments, and/or indicate disposition of the data digitally
- Time constraints, if any, relating to review and disposition

Data Access Control

Access to digital data involves retrieving the appropriate files necessary to compile the correct version of each digital data document, view it, and perform the prescribed processing. Seeking digital data access should be as user-friendly as possible. Users should be provided with data/documents they are entitled to in the correct revision/version. Before this can be accomplished, there are a number of pertinent parameters concerning access privileges, security, and protection of data rights that must be set up.

Access privileges limit access to applicable users. Access privileges vary according to the individual's credentials (security clearance, need-to-know, organizational affiliation, etc.), data status level, the document type, program milestones, and user need. Users of accessed data must respect all contractual and legal requirements for data rights, security, licenses, copyrights, and other distribution restrictions that apply to the data. The applicable distribution code, which represents the type of distribution statement, must be affixed to a document or viewable file to indicate the authorized circulation or dissemination of the information contained in the item.

Typically, working data should be made available only to the originating individual, group, or team (such as an integrated product development team); or to other designated reviewers of the data.

EIA-STD-649 provides us with the following checklist of ground rules to be preestablished prior to initiating interactive access (i.e., predefined query and extraction of data):

- How data is to be accessed
- Request for access and logging of access for read-only or annotation
- Naming of temporary working version of the file(s) for purpose of annotation/mark-up
- Means of indicating whether a comment/annotation is essential/suggested
- Re-identification of marked-up versions, as required
- Method of indicating acceptance, approval, or rejection, as applicable
- Time constraints, if any, on data acceptance
- Tracking of disposition of required actions
- Re-identification of changed files

SUMMARY

Software engineering methodology requires developers to carefully plan data requirements for all systems. This usually entails the development of a data dictionary for the databases and file structures required by the system. In companies where formal data dictionaries and repositories are in use, data management migrates easily to configuration data management. In companies where no formal data management processes are in place, the control of the flow of data through the organization must be rigorously addressed. This chapter serves that purpose by providing a very detailed structural framework for managing organizational data.

REFERENCES

This chapter is based on the following report: MIL-HDBK-61A(SE), February 7, 2001, *Military Handbook: Configuration Management Guidance.*

11

CONFIGURATION CHANGE MANAGEMENT

Maintenance is the most expensive component of the software life cycle. IT departments often spend from 75 to 80 percent of their budgets [Guimaraes 1983] and time on the maintenance process of system development. In addition, the cost of fixing an error rises dramatically as the software progresses through the life cycle. Maintaining systems in a nonsystematic, measurable way is counterproductive. Changes made but not properly documented can be detrimental to the system and to the people using that system. This chapter discusses the concept of *configuration change management.*

WHAT IS CONFIGURATION CHANGE MANAGEMENT?

Configuration change management is an organized process that provides a standardized framework for managing change. The EIA-649 standard defines the purpose and benefits of the change management process as follows:

- Change decisions should be based on detailed knowledge of the impact of that change.
- Changes should be limited to those that are necessary or that offer significant benefit.
- Ensure that customer perspectives and interests are considered.
- Enable orderly communication of change information.
- Preserve configuration control at product interfaces.
- Maintain consistency between the product and its documentation.
- Maintain the configuration baseline for the product.

THE MAINTENANCE PROCESS

Once a new system is implemented, the real work begins for most IT departments. As users utilize the system, errors are discovered and changes are requested. As systems have become more widely used within critical departments of the organization, the maintenance process has taken on a more important role. The management of systems maintenance has perhaps become the most critical phase of systems development because change is now considered an opportunity for improvement. Change can be initiated for a wide variety of reasons, including:

- Add new capabilities
- Enhance product support
- Replace worn technology with more modern technology
- Fix bugs
- Implement preplanned product improvement
- Reduce costs

Just as in the development of a new system, maintenance requires that steps be carefully taken in making changes or fixing errors. In the event of an error, this can be even more critical. Each step of the maintenance process is similar to steps in the systems development life cycle [Curtis et al. 2000], as seen in Figure 11.1. This is a logical extension of the development process as changes being made to the system can affect the whole system and therefore need to be carefully controlled.

Configuration management depends on orderly record keeping. From the moment a system is proposed, a paper trail — that is, configuration status accounting — needs to be initiated and maintained (see Appendix T for a sample Software Configuration Management Plan and Appendix S for a sample Maintenance Plan). All systems eventually wind up in maintenance mode. It is critically important to capture proper documen-

SDLC					
Project Identification and Selection	Project Initiation and Planning	Analysis	Logical Design	Physical Design	Implementation
Obtain Maintenance Requests	Requests into Changes		Design Changes		Implementing Changes
Maintenance Process					

Figure 11.1 The Maintenance Life Cycle Compared to the Development Life Cycle

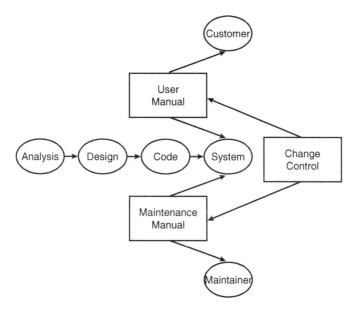

Figure 11.2 An Overview of System Maintenance

tation for all requests for changes as well as for the change itself. Maintenance can come in many forms — for example, the software requires change for new functionality, end users notice problems, and even the documentation might require modification. The first step in the process is to obtain a maintenance request from a user. Appendices B, and I through R are examples of a wide variety of change request forms, trouble reports, library baseline change requests, and specification change requests. Once the request has been received, the requests can be transformed into changes that can then be used to make design changes. Once the changes are designed and tested, they can be implemented.

Figure 11.2 is an overview of system maintenance. Both the customer and maintainer are interacting with their own documentation (i.e., user manual and maintainer manual). The customer poses questions, problems, and suggestions to the maintainer, and the maintainer, in turn, gives the answers and they are filtered through a change control process and back into the system.

The maintenance process should provide for documenting:

■ The need for the change
■ Documentation of the impact of the proposed change
■ Evaluation of the proposed change
■ Coordinating the change process, including whether it has been approved or not approved

- Making the change to the product
- Making the change to appropriate documentation, including user manuals
- Maintaining the product's configuration baseline; any change that modifies the baseline from that which the customer expects needs to be approved by the customer
- Verifying the change

THE PRODUCT BASELINE

To accomplish the change systematically, the configuration baseline of the product must be known. The baseline usually consists, at a minimum, of the approved detail design specification. As the product is modified by approved changes, the configuration baseline must also be changed. Configuration management cannot be accomplished if the product baseline is not continually kept up-to-date.

TYPES OF MAINTENANCE

Categorizing the types of maintenance required is helpful in organizing and prioritizing user requests. Software maintenance is more than fixing mistakes. Maintenance activities can be broken down into four sub-activities.

1. Corrective maintenance
2. Adaptive maintenance
3. Perfective maintenance or enhancement
4. Preventive maintenance or reengineering

Corrective Maintenance

Corrective maintenance involves fixing bugs or errors in the system as they are discovered. Corrective maintenance is the type most users are familiar with because they are the most aggravating to users. These usually receive top priority as they can be paralyzing to the organization if not identified and fixed. Corrective maintenance consumes approximately 17 percent of the maintainer's time [Lientz and Swanson 1978].

The major skills required for corrective maintenance include:

- Good diagnostic skills
- Good testing skills
- Good documentation skills

Adaptive Maintenance

Adaptive software maintenance is performed to make a computer program usable in a changed environment. For example, the computer on which the software runs is going to use a new operating system; thus, the system requires some adaptive tweaking. Adaptive maintenance is typically part of a new release of the code or part of a larger development effort. Approximately 18 percent of software maintenance is adaptive [Lientz and Swanson 1978].

Perfective Maintenance

Perfective maintenance is the act of improving the software's functionality as a result of end-user requests to improve product effectiveness. It includes:

■ Adding additional functionality
■ Making the product run faster
■ Improving maintainability

   This is the biggest maintenance time consumer. Approximately 60 percent of software maintenance time is spent on perfective maintenance [Lientz and Swanson 1978].

Preventive Maintenance

Preventive maintenance refers to performing "pre-maintenance" in order to prevent system problems. This is different from corrective maintenance, which is performed to correct an existing problem. This is similar to maintaining a car in which you change the oil and air filter not in response to some problem, but to prevent a problem from occurring in the first place.

MAINTENANCE COSTS

As computers and their systems become more widely used, the need for maintenance grows. As these same systems age, maintenance becomes more critical and time consuming. Since the early 1980s it is estimated that maintenance costs have skyrocketed from 40 percent of the IT budget to 75 to 80 percent (see Figure 11.1). The reason for these increases stems from the once newly designed systems aging. This shift from development to maintenance is a natural occurrence as organizations avoid the high cost of new systems and struggle to maintain their current systems.

Many factors affect the cost in time and money expended on system maintenance. One of the most costly is design defects. The more defects in a system, the more time is spent identifying them and fixing them. If a system is designed and tested properly, most defects should have been eliminated; but in the case of poor design or limited testing, defects can cause system downtimes, and downtimes cost the organization in terms of lost efficiency and perhaps lost sales.

The number of users can also affect the cost of system maintenance. The more users, the more time will be spent on changes to the system. More importantly, the greater the number of platforms the system is installed on, the higher the cost of maintenance. If a single system needs a change, then the time it takes to change the system is limited; but if that system resides on platforms across the country, such as is the case in many branch offices of corporations, then the cost increases significantly.

The quality of the documentation can also affect the overall cost of maintenance. Poor documentation can result in many lost hours searching for an answer that should have been explained in the documentation. Managing change using a configuration change management approach ensures that the documentation will be consistent with the current version of the product.

The quality of the people and their skill level can also cost an IT department many wasted hours. Inexperienced or overloaded programmers can increase the cost of maintenance in two ways. First, they can waste hours learning on the job at the IT department's expense. Second, if the programmers are overwhelmed with projects, they may skip steps in the maintenance process and, in turn, make mistakes that cost time and money to fix.

The tools available to maintenance personnel can save many hours of work. Using automation tools, such as CASE tools, debuggers, and other automation tools, can help programmers pinpoint problems faster or make changes more easily.

The structure of the software can also contribute to maintenance costs [Gibson and Senn 1989]. If software is built in a rational and easy-to-follow manner, making changes will be much easier and thus much faster, thereby saving time and resources. Software maintenance costs can be reduced significantly if the software architecture is well-defined, clearly documented, and creates an environment that promotes design consistency through the use of guidelines and design patterns [Hulse et al. 1999].

A MODEL FOR MAINTENANCE

Harrison and Cook [not dated] have developed a software maintenance model based on an objective decision rule that determines whether a given software module can be effectively modified, or if it should instead be rewritten. Their take is that completely rewriting a module can be expensive. However, it can be even more expensive if the module's structure has been severely degraded over successive maintenance activities. A module that is likely to experience significant maintenance activity is called change-prone. Their paper suggests that early identification of change-prone modules through the use of change measures across release cycles can be an effective technique in efficiently allocating maintenance resources.

In maintenance requests for non-change-prone modules, the process flow is as follows:

> Analyze code and identify change → Implement change and update documentation → Apply metric analysis → Compare with baseline → Check to see if it exceeds the threshold → If yes, then declare module to be "change-prone"; otherwise, declare module to be "non-change-prone"

The process for maintenance requests for a change-prone module is as follows:

> Identify the highest-level artifact affected by the request → Regenerate artifact → Identify artifacts that can be reused → Iterate through "development" → Declare module to be "non-change-prone"

CONFIGURATION MANAGEMENT STEPS

The generic change management model consists of the following steps:

1. *Change identification process.* The change is visualized, described, assessed, classified, and approved.
2. *Evaluation and coordination process.* The cost, scope, and effects are evaluated.
3. *Incorporation and verification process.* Change is planned, scheduled, implemented, documented, and verified.

Change Identification

Each and every change needs to be uniquely identified. The premise behind configuration management is that every component of every system carries with it a unique identification number.

Rather than using a random numbering scheme, it is best to create a nomenclature system that is meaningful. An important component of the identification number is its classification. Most configuration management systems classify changes as "major" or "minor." A change is considered major if it has one or more of the following attributes:

- Affects baseline
- Affects one or more of the following: how the product behaves, safety, interface with other products, instructions, user skills, training
- Requires a retrofit or recall of products out in the field
- Affects cost, guarantees, or warranties

Minor changes do not impact customer requirements but usually affect configuration documentation or system processes not considered major, as itemized above.

Documentation of proposed major changes should include the following information so that an informed decision can be made as to whether or not to make the change:

- Change identifier
- Change effectivity (e.g., this is commonly done using a serial number and date of manufacture)
- Individual requesting change
- Class of change
- Products affected
- Interfaces affected
- Documents affected
- Description of change
- Effects of change (i.e., performance, training, etc.)
- Justification for change
- What would happen if change were not done
- Requested approval date
- Schedule
- Costs and savings
- Alternatives

Minor changes require, at minimum, the following information:

- Change identifier
- Change effectivity (e.g., this is commonly done using a serial number and date of manufacture)
- Individual requesting change

- Class of change
- Products affected
- Documents affected
- Description of change
- Justification for change

Evaluation and Coordination

The vast majority of organizations launch into their maintenance efforts without first ascertaining the effect of the desired change on the system as well as on the organization.

The proper methodology is to consider the cost, schedules, and impacts of all requested changes, garner approval, and then implement the change. But how can this be done effectively?

Traditional change requests filter up through the company via many sources. In general, however, changes are requested by end users who work on discrete systems. Change requests are then sent to the IT department for prioritization and implementation.

As problems arise or the need for change is discovered, the flow of these requests must be handled in a methodical way. Because each request is not equal to any other and they arrive at the project manager's desk at various times, a system has been developed by most IT departments. This system provides a logical path for the approval of requests, and prioritizes and organizes those that are approved. The project manager has the job of categorizing the requests and passing them on to the "priority board," which decides if the request is within the business model and what, if any, priority should be given to the change request. As decisions are made by the board, they are passed back to the project manager for action. It is the project manager who then reports back to the user regarding the decision and acts on the change based on the priority given.

The type of change and severity help decide what priority to give the change. If the change is important enough, it can be placed at the top of the queue for immediate action. If several changes occur in a single module, a batch change can be requested. A batch change involves making changes to an entire module at once to avoid working on the same module several times. This also allows users to view the changes as a single update that may change the use of a module through screen changes or functionality.

The queue of changes (see Figure 11.3) is a valuable tool in controlling the work that needs to be done. Items high in the queue receive the immediate attention they deserve, and those of lesser importance may

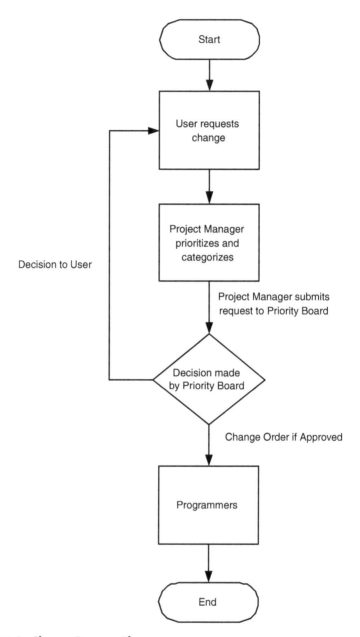

Figure 11.3 Change Request Flow

never be acted on due to a change in needs or a new system that solves the problem.

Configuration management "change evaluation and coordination" adds a level of standardization to this process. The priority board should:

- Have as its chairperson someone with signatory authority (i.e., this person should be able to sign off on the requested change)
- Have a diversity of board members representing the major functional areas of the organization
- Be provided with an agenda of what will be discussed prior to each board meeting
- Be provided with all documentation (e.g., costs, schedules, alternatives, etc.) prior to each board meeting. The board needs to be fully informed as to all cost factors involved in the decision-making process. This should include cost of development, cost of implementation, and expected future costs.
- Document all decisions and then disseminate them to all affected departmental units

The change priority board should be provided with full documentation that includes a discussion of the lead-times associated with changing the product as well as whatever changes need to be made to affected associated areas. One of the problems with maintenance is that it often fails to assess the impact of change on peripheral but associated departments (e.g., is the sales department ready to sell the product; is the training department ready to train on the new product; are the required interfaces ready?) Effectivity is used to provide a clear and precise designation of what is going to be changed. Effectivity can be designated by serial number, date code, product group, version number, lot number, batch number, etc. Effectivity is a critical component of configuration management because it clearly distinguishes one product from another. For example, if a piece of software has both version 2 and version 3 implementations being used by end users, then a change to version 2 needs to be clearly distinguished from version 3.

A variation of the priority board discussed above is a series of tiered boards or committees. In this variation, priority boards are appointed at the unit level. Once changes have been approved at this level, they are passed to a priority board at the departmental level, and then finally to the organization-wide priority board.

Change Implementation and Verification

Change must be carefully planned. Planning should be done prior to making any changes. Implementation of a change requires the release of the following documentation:

- Requirements information
- Design information

- Operation instructions
- Build and test information
- Sales and marketing change information

The usual method of disseminating document changes is through a document change request (DCR) (see Appendix J).

Once the change has been proposed, approved, implemented, and documented, it is important that it be verified. Appendix E contains a sample test plan. Test plans should be created prior to the development of the original product. When the product is maintained, the test plan must be updated to reflect any changes to system functionality.

Handling Variances

There are always exceptions. In the case of change management, it is important that a product, whose change varies from the system requirements, not be delivered to the end user unless the variance has been fully documented and fully authorized.

MANAGING MAINTENANCE PERSONNEL

As systems age and demand increases for maintenance personnel, there has been loud debate over just who should be doing the maintaining. Should it be the original developers? Or should it be a separate maintenance department? Many have argued that the people who developed the system should maintain it. The logic here is that they will best understand the system and be better able to change the system [Swanson 1990]. This logic is correct but difficult to fulfill because developers want to keep building new stuff and consider maintenance a less desirable function. IT professionals view maintenance as fixing someone else's mistakes. One solution to this problem has been tried recently; it involves rotating IT personnel from development to maintenance and back to allow everyone to share in the desirable as well as undesirable functions of the department.

MEASURING EFFECTIVENESS

An important part of configuration management is to understand and measure the effectiveness of the maintenance process. As a system is implemented, service requests may be quite high as bugs are still being worked out and needs for change are discovered. If the maintenance process is operating properly, an immediate decrease in failures should be seen (Figure 11.4). Good management of maintenance should include

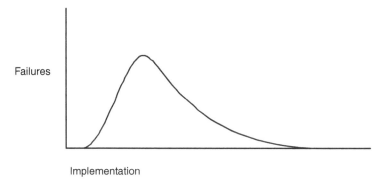

Failures

Implementation

Figure 11.4 Normal Distribution of Failures Following Implementation

the recording of failures over time and analyzing these for effectiveness. If a decrease is not noticed, the problem should be identified and resolved.

Another measure of the success of the maintenance process is the time between failures. The longer the time between failures, the more time can be spent on improving the system and not just fixing the existing system [Lientz 1983]. Failures will happen, but more costly is the time taken to fix even the simplest failure.

Recording the type of failure is important in understanding how the failure happened and can assist in avoiding failures in the future. As this information is recorded and maintained as a permanent record of the system, solutions can be developed that fix the root cause of a variety of failures.

SUMMARY

Managing system maintenance requires that steps be taken similar to the development of new systems. System maintenance is, in many ways, an extension of the system development life cycle and involves similar steps to ensure that the system is properly maintained. As a new system is implemented, system maintenance is required to fix the inevitable errors and track them for future use. As a system ages and changes are requested, system maintenance has the job of categorizing, prioritizing, and implementing changes to the system. A configuration management approach ensures systematic, organized changes.

The proper management of system maintenance is vital to the continued success of the system. A well-managed systems maintenance department can save time and money by providing an error-free system that meets the needs of the users it serves.

REFERENCES

Curtis, G., J. Hoffer, J. George, and S. Valacich, *Introduction to Business Systems Analysis,* Pearson Custom Publishing, Boston, MA, 2000.

Electronic Industries Alliance, EIA-649, National Consensus Standard for Configuration Management, 1998.

Gibson, V. and J. Senn, "System Structure and Software Maintenance Performance," ACM Press, New York, 1989.

Guimaraes, T., "Managing Application Program Maintenance Expenditures," ACM Press, New York, 1983.

Harrison, W. and C. Cook, "Insights on Improving the Maintenance Process through Software Measurement," no data http://www.cs.pdx.edu/~warren/Papers/CSM.htm

Hulse, C., S. Edgerton, M. Ubnoske, and L. Vazquez, "Reducing Maintenance Costs through the Application of Modern Software Architecture Principles," ACM Press, New York, 1999.

Lientz, B., "Issues in Software Maintenance," ACM Press, New York, 1983.

Lientz, B.P. and E.B. Swanson, "Characteristics of Application Software Maintenance," *Communications of the ACM*, 21(6), 466–481, June 1978.

Lientz, B.P. and E.B. Swanson, "Problems in Application Software Maintenance," ACM Press, New York, 1981.

Swanson, E.B., "Departmentalization in Software Development and Maintenance," ACM Press, New York, 1990.

Unknown, "How to Increase Uptime," Cognizant Applications Maintenance Solution Series, Cognizant Technology Solutions Corporation, 2000.

Unknown, "16 Critical Software Practices for Performance-Based Management," QSM, Inc., 1999, http://www.techrepublic.com

12

CONFIGURATION MANAGEMENT AND SOFTWARE ENGINEERING STANDARDS REFERENCE

Software engineering (i.e., development) consists of many components: definitions, documentation, testing, quality assurance, metrics, and configuration management (CM). Standards bodies have crafted standards for many of these.

Standards enable software developers to develop quality-oriented, cost-effective, and maintainable software in an efficient, cost-productive manner. The goal of each standard is to provide the software developer with a set of benchmarks, enabling him or her to complete the task and be assured that it meets at least a minimum level of quality. Indeed, the dictionary definition of standard is "*an acknowledged measure of comparison for quantitative or qualitative value; a criterion.*" Thus, standards provide the developer with the criteria necessary to build a system.

The Software Engineering Institute's (http://www.sei.cmu.edu/cmm/cmms/cmms.html) Capability Maturity Model (CMM), although not usually considered a standard in the strict definition of the word, is still a valid benchmark that organizations use to ensure that they are adhering to a robust quality software engineering set of processes. Configuration management (CM) is very much a factor in the CMM.

Paulk et al. [1995] have correlated CM and CMM. From a CMM perspective, software configuration management (SCM) should consist of the following goals, commitments, abilities, activities, measurements, and verifications:

1. SCM activities are planned.
2. Selected software work products are identified, controlled, and available.
3. Changes to identified software work products are controlled.
4. Affected groups and individuals are informed of the status and content of software baselines.

The *commitment* is that the project follows a written organizational policy for implementing SCM. The abilities consist of:

1. A board having the authority for managing the project's software baselines exists or is established.
2. A group that is responsible for coordinating and implementing SCM for the project exists.
3. Adequate resources and funding are provided for performing the SCM activities.
4. Members of the SCM group are trained in the objectives, procedures, and methods for performing their SCM activities.

The *activities* include:

1. An SCM plan is prepared for each software project according to a documented procedure.
2. A documented and approved SCM plan is used as the basis for performing the SCM activities.
3. A configuration management library system is established as a repository for the software baselines.
4. The software work products to be placed under configuration management are identified.
5. Change requests and problem reports for all configuration items/units are initiated, recorded, reviewed, approved, and tracked according to a documented procedure.
6. Changes to baselines are controlled according to a documented procedure.
7. Products from the software baseline library are created, and their release is controlled according to a documented procedure.
8. The status of configuration items/units is recorded according to a documented procedure.
9. Standard reports documenting the SCM activities and the contents of the software baseline are developed and made available to affected groups and individuals.
10. Software baseline audits are conducted according to a documented procedure.

Measurements are made and used to determine the status of the SCM activities. The *verifications* include:

1. SCM activities are reviewed with senior management on a periodic basis.
2. SCM activities are reviewed with the project manager on both a periodic and event-driven basis.
3. The SCM group periodically audits software baselines to verify that they conform to the documentation that defines them.
4. The software quality assurance group reviews and/or audits the activities and work products for SCM and reports the results.

THE STANDARDS BODIES

The three most significant industry standards bodies are ANSI, IEEE, and ISO. The EIA (Electronic Industries Alliance) has also played a significant role by creating EIA-649, the National Consensus Standard for Configuration Management. Most recently, EIA-836 has come to the forefront of CM standards. Essentially, EIA-836 is an extension of EIA-649. It provides a fundamental reference vocabulary for the access, sharing, and exchange of CM data (including product configuration information), and for developing, mapping, and using CM-enabled tools, systems, and databases using XML (eXtensible Markup Language). Figure 12.1 shows the relationship between these two standards.

As one can see, the primary focus of EIA-836 is on data element definitions, relationships, and business objects for information exchange. The body of EIA-836 essentially consists of CM Business Objects, the CM Data Dictionary, and CM Reference Schemas. The Business Objects and Reference Schemas are annotated with data element definitions. Annexes to the standard contain user guidance and several informative cross-reference tables.

The EIA-836 standard (version 1.0) is comprised of six parts, each contained in a Zip file:

1. EIA836-1.0 Standard Body Zip file
2. EIA836-1.0 Data Dictionary Zip file
3. EIA836-1.0 Reference Schema Zip file
4. EIA836-1.0 Live DTD Zip file
5. EIA836-1.0 Schema Diagrams Zip file
6. EIA836-1.0 User Views Zip file

and can be downloaded from http://www.dcnicn.com/cm/index.cfm.

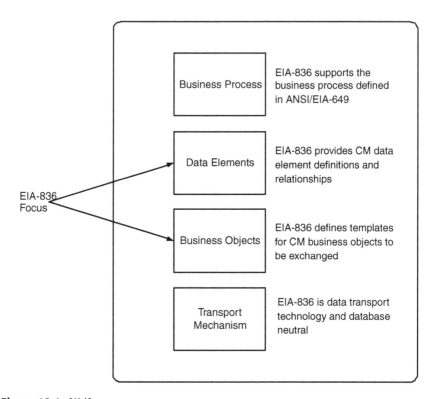

Figure 12.1 XML

MIL-STD-2549, Configuration Management Data Interface (http://wwwedms.redstone.army.mil/edrd/ms2549.pdf), might also be of interest to the reader.

A SUMMARY OF THE EIA STANDARD (EIA-649)

EIA-649 [EIA 1998] was developed in 1994 and rapidly became the pivotal standard around which most other standards bodies rallied. EAI-649 is addressed more comprehensively in other sections of this book; however, its principles are summarized here:

Configuration Management Planning and Management

1. Plan CM processes for the context and environment in which they are to be preformed and manage in accordance with the planning: assign responsibilities, train personnel, measure performance, and assess measurements/trends to effect process improvements.

2. To determine the specific CM value-adding functions and levels of emphasis for a particular product, identify the context and environment in which to implement CM.

3. A configuration management plan describes how CM is accomplished and how consistency between the product definition, the product's configuration, and the configuration management records is achieved and maintained throughout the applicable phases of the product's life cycle.

4. Prepare procedures to define how each configuration management process will be accomplished.

5. Conduct training so that all responsible individuals understand their roles and responsibilities as well as the procedures for implementing configuration management processes.

6. Assess the effectiveness of CM plan implementation and performance of the configuration management discipline with defined metrics (performance indicators).

7. Performing configuration management includes responsibility for the configuration management subordinate activities (e.g., subcontractors, suppliers).

Configuration Identification

1. Configuration identification is the basis on which the configuration of products are defined and verified; products and documents are labeled; changes are managed; and accountability is maintained.

2. Configuration documentation defines the functional, performance, and physical attributes of a product. Other product information is derived from configuration documentation.

3. The product composition (i.e., relationship and quantity of parts that comprise the product) is determined from its configuration documentation.

4. All products are assigned unique identifiers so that one product can be distinguished from other products; one configuration of a product can be distinguished from other; the source of a product can be determined; and the correct product information can be retrieved.

5. Individual units of a product are assigned unique product identifiers when there is a need to distinguish one unit of a product from another unit of the product.

6. When a product is modified, it retains its original product unit identifier although its part identifying number is altered to reflect a new configuration.

7. A series of like units of a product is assigned a unique product group identifier when it is unnecessary or impractical to identify individual units but nonetheless necessary to correlate units to a process, date, event, or test.
8. All documents reflecting product performance, functional, or physical requirements and other product information are uniquely identified so that they can be correctly associated with the applicable configuration of the product.
9. A baseline identifies an agreed-to description of the attributes of a product at a point in time and provides a known configuration to which changes are addressed.
10. Baselines are established by agreeing to the stated definition of a product's attributes.
11. The configuration of any product, or any document, plus the approved changes to be incorporated constitute the current baseline.
12. Maintaining product information is important because time-consuming and expensive recovery may be necessary if records of operational units of a product do not match the actual units (as reported by maintenance activities) or such records do not exist.
13. For product interfaces external to the enterprise, establish an interface agreement and mutually agreed-to documentation of common attributes.
14. Changes to a product are accomplished using a systematic, measurable change process.

Configuration Change Management

1. Each change is uniquely identified.
2. Changes represent opportunities for improvement.
3. Classify requested changes to aid in determining the appropriate levels of review and approval.
4. Change requests must be clearly documented.
5. Consider the technical, support, schedule, and cost impacts of a requested change before making a judgment as to whether the change should be approved for implementation and incorporation in the product and its documentation.
6. Determine all potential effects of a change and coordinate potential impacts with the impacted areas of responsibility.
7. Change documentation delineates which unit(s) of the product are to be changed. Change effectivity includes both production break-in and retrofit/recall, as applicable.

8. A changed product should not be distributed until support and service areas are able to support it.
9. The decision maker is aware of all cost factors in making the decision.
10. Change approval decisions are made by an appropriate authority who can commit resources to implement the change.
11. Implement an approved change in accordance with documented direction approved by the appropriate level of authority.
12. Verify implementation of a change to ensure consistency between the product, its documentation, and its support elements.
13. If it is considered necessary to temporarily depart from specified baseline requirements, a variance is documented and authorized by the appropriate level of authority.

Configuration Status Accounting

1. An accurate, timely information base concerning a product and its associated product information is important throughout the product life cycle.
2. Configuration information, appropriate to the product, is systematically recorded, safeguarded, validated, and disseminated.
3. Configuration information content evolves and is captured over the product life cycle as tasks occur.
4. Data collection and information processing system requirements are determined by the need for configuration information.

Configuration Verification and Audit

1. Verification that a product's requirement attributes have been met and that the product design meeting those attributes has been accurately documented are required to baseline the product configuration.
2. Verification that a design achieves its goals is accomplished by a systematic comparison of requirements with the results of tests, analyses, or inspections.
3. Documentation of a product's definition must be complete and accurate enough to permit reproduction of the product without further design effort.
4. Where necessary, verification is accomplished by configuration audit.

5. Periodic reviews verify continued achievement of requirements, identify and document changes in performance, and ensure consistency with documentation.

Management of Digital Data

1. Apply configuration management principles to ensure the integrity of digital representations of product information and other data.
2. Apply digital data identification rules to maintain document, document representation, and file version relationships.
3. Apply business rules using data status levels for access, change management, and archiving of digital data documents.
4. Maintain relationships between digital data, data requirements, and the related product configuration to ensure accurate data access.
5. Apply disciplined version control to manage document review electronically.
6. Ensure that a transmitted digital data product is usable.
7. Effective digital data access fulfills requirements, preserves rights, and provides users with data they are entitled to in the correct version

ANSI

The American National Standards Institute (ANSI; http://www.ansi.org), founded in 1918, is one of the oldest and most prestigious of standards bodies. ANSI is the final arbiter of national standards within the United States and is also a key member of international standards bodies such as the ISO. For the most part, ANSI focuses on standards used by the software and hardware vendors that make the products that the software engineer uses. These standards pertain to programming languages, telecommunications, and even the physical properties of devices such as diskettes, cartridges, and magnetic tapes. ANSI will often work in conjunction with cooperating standards bodies such as the IEEE. In effect, ANSI will "join forces" with another standards body to endorse a particular standard.

The acronym "ANSI" is quite familiar to most software developers, even if they know nothing about standards. The ANSI character set is used by programmers everywhere. It consists of 256 characters, the first 128 of which are ASCII (**A**merican **S**tandard **C**ode for **I**nformation **I**nterchange). The remaining 128 characters are math and foreign language symbols.

IEEE

The IEEE (Institute of Electrical and Electronics Engineers; http://www.ieee.org) is a professional trade organization with close to 400,000 members in over 150 countries. More than a few computer science students join this organization for its publications, meetings, and networking opportunities. One branch of the IEEE is its standards governing body (http://standards.ieee.org/index.html).

Currently, the IEEE has more than 900 active standards, with hundreds more in development. Many of these are related to software development.

IEEE Software Engineering Standards Summary

The standards listed in Table 12.1, which include configuration standards, are outlined. **Boldfaced** titles indicate applicability to configuration management.

ISO

In 1946, the International Organization for Standardization (ISO; www.iso.ch) was founded in Geneva, Switzerland. More than 75 countries, including the United States through ANSI, have member organizations. The ISO has over 160 technical committees and 2300 sub-committees working on a variety of standards. Indeed, the ISO has developed more than 13,000 standards in such esoteric disciplines as clothing, road vehicles, railway engineering, and information technology.

ISO 9000 is the most recognizable of ISO standards. It defines the criteria for quality in the manufacturing and service industries. It was first popularized in Europe but its popularity has spread worldwide as more and more companies deem "ISO certification" to be a competitive advantage.

ISO 9000 is actually a "family" of standards (see Table 12.2).

ISO Software Engineering Standards Summary

The ISO standards listed in Table 12.3, including configuration management standards, are summarized. Boldfaced titles indicate applicability to configuration management.

Table 12.1 IEEE Software Engineering Standards Summary

ANSI/IEEE STD 1002-1987	IEEE Standard Taxonomy for Software Engineering Standards
ANSI/IEEE STD 1008-1987	IEEE Standard for Software Unit Testing
IEEE STD 1012-1986	IEEE Standard for Software Verification and Validation Plans
IEEE STD 1016-1987	IEEE Recommended Practice for Software Design Descriptions
IEEE STD 1016.1-1993	IEEE Guide to Software Design Descriptions
IEEE STD 1028-1988	IEEE Standard for Software Reviews and Audits
ANSI/IEEE STD 1042-1987	IEEE Guide to Software Configuration Management
IEEE STD 1044-1993	IEEE Standard Classification for Software Anomalies
IEEE STD 1045-1992	IEEE Standard for Software Productivity Metrics
IEEE STD 1058.1-1987	IEEE Standard for Software Project Management Plans
IEEE STD 1059-1993	IEEE Guide for Software Verification and Validation Plans
IEEE STD 1061-1992	IEEE Standard for a Software Quality Metrics Methodology
IEEE STD 1062-1993	IEEE Recommended Practice for Software Acquisition
IEEE STD 1063-1987	IEEE Standard for Software User Documentation
IEEE STD 1074-1991	IEEE Standard for Developing Software Life-Cycle Processes
IEEE STD 1074.1-1995	IEEE Guide for Developing Software Life-Cycle Processes
IEEE STD 1175-1992	IEEE Trial-Use Standard Reference Model for Computing System Tool Interconnections
IEEE STD 1220-1994	IEEE Trial-Use Standard for Application and Management of the Systems Engineering Process
IEEE/EIA 12207.0-1996	Industry Implementation of International Standard ISO/IEC: ISO/IEC12207 Standard for Information Technology Software Life-Cycle Processes
IEEE STD 1228-1994	IEEE Standard for Software Safety Plans
IEEE STD 1298-1992	Software Quality Management System Part 1: Requirements
IEEE STD 1362-1998	IEEE Guide for Information Technology — System Definition — Concept of Operations (ConOps) Document
IEEE STD 610.12-1990	IEEE Standard Glossary of Software Engineering Terminology
IEEE STD 730-1989	IEEE Standard for Software Quality Assurance Plans
IEEE STD 828-1990	IEEE Standard for Software Configuration Management Plans
ANSI/IEEE STD 829-1983	IEEE Standard for Software Test Documentation
IEEE STD 830-1993	IEEE Recommended Practice for Software Requirements Specifications
IEEE STD 982.1-1988	IEEE Standard Dictionary of Measures to Produce Reliable Software

Table 12.1 IEEE Software Engineering Standards Summary (continued)

IEEE STD 982.2-1988	IEEE Guide for the Use of IEEE Standard Dictionary of Measures to Produce Reliable Software
IEEE STD 990-1987	IEEE Recommended Practice for Ada as a Program Design Language
J-STD-016-1995 30 September 1995	Trial Use Standard Standard for Information Technology Software Life-Cycle Processes Software Development Acquirer–Supplier Agreement

ANSI/IEEE STD 1002-1987 IEEE Standard Taxonomy for Software Engineering Standards
Contents
1. Introduction
    1.1 Scope
    1.2 Terminology
    1.3 References
2. Definitions
3. Taxonomy of Software Engineering Standards
    3.1 Standards Partition
    3.2 Software Engineering Partition
    3.3 Taxonomy Framework

ANSI/IEEE STD 1008-1987 IEEE Standard for Software Unit Testing
Contents
1. Scope and References
    1.1 Inside the Scope
    1.2 Outside the Scope
    1.3 References
2. Definitions
3. Unit Testing Activities
    3.1 Plan the General Approach, Resources, and Schedule
    3.2 Determine Features to Be Tested
    3.3 Refine the General Plan
    3.4 Design the Set of Tests
    3.5 Implement the Refined Plan and Design
    3.6 Execute the Test Procedures
    3.7 Check for Termination
    3.8 Evaluate the Test Effort and Unit

IEEE STD 1012-1986 IEEE Standard for Software Verification and Validation Plans
Contents
1. Scope and References
    1.1 Scope
    1.2 References
2. Conventions, Definitions, and Acronyms
    2.1 Conventions
    2.2 Definitions
3. Software Verification and Validation Plan
    3.1 Purpose.
    3.2 Referenced Documents
    3.3 Definitions

Table 12.1 IEEE Software Engineering Standards Summary (continued)

3.4 Verification and Validation Overview
3.5 Life-Cycle Verification and Validation
3.6 Software Verification and Validation Reporting
3.7 Verification and Validation Administrative Procedures

IEEE STD 1016-1987 IEEE Recommended Practice for Software Design
 Descriptions
Contents
1. Scope
2. References
3. Definitions
4. Considerations for Producing a Software Design Description (SDD)
    4.1 Software Life Cycle
    4.2 Software Design Description (SDD) within the Life Cycle
    4.3 Purpose of a Software Design Description (SDD)
5. Design Description Information Content
    5.1 Introduction
    5.2 Design Entities
    5.3 Design Entity Attributes
6. Design Description Organization
    6.1 Introduction
    6.2 Design Views

IEEE STD 1016.1-1993 IEEE Guide to Software Design Descriptions
Abstract: The application of design methods and design documentation
 recommended in IEEE STD 1016-1987 is described. Several common design
 methods are used to illustrate the application of IEEE STD 1016-1987, thus
 making the concepts of that standard more concrete. The information in this
 guide may be applied to commercial, scientific, or military software that runs
 on any computer. Applicability is not restricted by the size, complexity, or
 criticality of the software.
Keywords: design entity, design method, design view, software design process
Contents
1. Overview
    1.1 Purpose
    1.2 Scope
2. References
3. Definitions
4. Description of IEEE STD 1016-1987
5. Design Description Organization
    5.1 Design Views
    5.2 Recommended Design Views
    5.3 Design Description Media
6. Considerations
    6.1 Selecting Representative Design Methods
    6.2 Representative Design Method Descriptions
    6.3 Design Document Sections
    6.4 Method-Oriented Design Documents
7. Design Methods
    7.1 Function-Oriented Design Methods
    7.2 Data-Oriented Design Methods
    7.3 Real-Time Control-Oriented Design Methods
    7.4 Object-Oriented Design Methods

Table 12.1 IEEE Software Engineering Standards Summary (continued)

7.5 Formal Language-Oriented Design Methods
8. Bibliography

IEEE STD 1028-1988 — Revision of Corrected Edition June 30, 1989, IEEE Standard for Software Reviews and Audits
Contents
1. Scope and References
    1.1 Scope
    1.2 References
2. Definitions
3. Introduction
    3.1 Review Process Prerequisites
    3.2 Audit Process Prerequisites
    3.3 Procedural Description Template
4. The Management Review Process
    4.1 Objective
    4.2 Abstract
    4.3 Special Responsibilities
    4.4 Input
    4.5 Entry Criteria
    4.6 Procedures
    4.7 Exit Criteria
    4.8 Output
    4.9 Auditability
5. The Technical Review Process
    5.1 Objective
    5.2 Abstract
    5.3 Special Responsibilities
    5.4 Input
    5.5 Entry Criteria
    5.6 Procedures
    5.7 Exit Criteria
    5.8 Output
    5.9 Auditability
6. The Software Inspection Process
    6.1 Objective
    6.2 Abstract
    6.3 Special Responsibilities
    6.4 Input
    6.5 Entry Criteria
    6.6 Procedures
    6.7 Exit Criteria
    6.8 Output
    6.9 Auditability
   6.10 Data Collection Requirements
7. The Walk-Through Process
    7.1 Objective
    7.2 Abstract
    7.3 Special Responsibilities
    7.4 Input
    7.5 Entry Criteria
    7.6 Procedures
    7.7 Exit Criteria

Table 12.1 IEEE Software Engineering Standards Summary (continued)

7.8 Output
7.9 Auditability
8. The Audit Process
   8.1 Objective
   8.2 Abstract
   8.3 Special Responsibilities
   8.4 Input
   8.5 Entry Criteria
   8.6 Procedures
   8.7 Exit Criteria
   8.8 Output
   8.9 Auditability

ANSI/IEEE STD 1042-1987 IEEE Guide to Software Configuration Management
Contents
1. Introduction
   1.1 Scope
   1.2 References
   1.3 Mnemonics
   1.4 Terms
2. SCM Disciplines in Software Management
   2.1 The Context of SCM
   2.2 The Process of SCM
   2.3 The Implementation of SCM
   2.4 The Tools of SCM
   2.5 The Planning of SCM
3. Software Configuration Management Plans
   3.1 Introduction
   3.2 Management
   3.3 SCM Activities
   3.4 Tools, Techniques, and Methodologies
   3.5 Supplier Control
   3.6 Records Collection and Retention

IEEE STD 1044-1993 IEEE Standard Classification for Software Anomalies
Abstract: A uniform approach to the classification of anomalies found in software
and its documentation is provided. The processing of anomalies discovered
during any software life-cycle phase are described, and comprehensive lists of
software anomaly classifications and related data items that are helpful to
identify and track anomalies are provided. This standard is not intended to
define procedural or format requirements for using the classification scheme.
It does identify some classification measures but does not attempt to define
all the data supporting the analysis of an anomaly.
Keywords: anomaly, category, classification, classification process, supporting
data item
Contents
1. Overview
   1.1 Background
   1.2 Scope
2. References
3. Definitions

Table 12.1 IEEE Software Engineering Standards Summary (continued)

4. Classification Standard
    4.1 Classification Process
    4.2 Standard Classification Scheme

IEEE STD 1045-1992 IEEE Standard for Software Productivity Metrics
Abstract: A consistent way to measure the elements that go into computing software productivity is defined. Software productivity metrics and terminology are given to ensure an understanding of measurement data for both source code and document production. Although this standard prescribes measurements to characterize the software process, it neither establishes software productivity norms, nor does it recommend productivity measurements as a method to evaluate software projects or software developers. This standard does not measure the quality of software. This standard does not claim to improve productivity, only to measure it. The goal of this standard is to provide a better understanding of the software process, which may lend insight to improving it.
Keywords: attribute, primitive, productivity ratio, source statement, staff-hour
Contents
1. Overview
    1.1 Scope
    1.2 Terminology
    1.3 Audience
2. References
3. Definitions
4. Software Productivity Metrics
5. Output Primitives
    5.1 Source Statement Output Primitives
    5.2 Function Point Output Primitive
    5.3 Document Output Primitives
6. Input Primitive
    6.1 Staff-Hour Input Primitive
    6.2 Staff-Hour Attribute
    6.3 Activities
7. Relationships
    7.1 Productivity Ratios
    7.2 Output-to-Output Ratios
    7.3 Input-to-Input Ratios
8. Characteristics
    8.1 Project Characteristics
    8.2 Management Characteristics
    8.3 Product Characteristics

IEEE STD 1058.1-1987 IEEE Standard for Software Project Management Plans
Contents
1. Scope and References
    1.1 Scope
    1.2 References
2. Definitions
3. Software Project Management Plans
    3.1 Introduction (Section 1 of the SPMP)

Table 12.1 IEEE Software Engineering Standards Summary (continued)

3.2 Project Organization (Section 2 of the SPMP)
3.3 Managerial Process (Section 3 of the SPMP)
3.4 Technical Process (Section 4 of the SPMP)
3.5 Work Packages, Schedule, and Budget (Section 5 of the SPMP)
3.6 Additional Components

IEEE STD 1059-1993 IEEE Guide for Software Verification and Validation Plans
Abstract: Guidance in preparing Software Verification and Validation Plans
(SVVPs) that comply with IEEE STD 1012-1986 are provided. IEEE STD 1012-1986
specifies the required content for an SVVP. This guide recommends approaches
to Verification and Validation (V&V) planning. This guide does not present
requirements beyond those stated in IEEE STD 1012-1986.
Keywords: baseline change assessment, life-cycle phases, master schedule, V&V
tasks
Contents
1. Overview
    1.1 Scope
2 References
3. Conventions, Definitions, and Acronyms and Abbreviations
    3.1 Conventions
    3.2 Definitions
    3.3 Acronyms and Abbreviations
4. Software Verification and Validation
    4.1 Software V&V Planning Guidance
    4.2 Integrating and Continuing V&V Tasks
5. SVVP Guidance
    5.1 Purpose
    5.2 Referenced Documents
    5.3 Definitions
    5.4 Verification and Validation Overview
    5.5 Life-Cycle Verification and Validation
    5.6 Reporting
    5.7 Verification and Validation Administrative Procedures

IEEE STD 1061-1992 IEEE Standard for a Software Quality Metrics Methodology
Abstract: A methodology for establishing quality requirements and identifying,
implementing, analyzing, and validating the process and product of software
quality metrics is defined. The methodology spans the entire software life cycle.
Although this standard includes examples of metrics, it does not prescribe
specific metrics.
Keywords: direct metric, factor, metrics framework, software quality metric,
subfactor
Contents
1. Overview
    1.1 Scope
    1.2 Audience
2. Definitions
3. Purpose of Software Quality Metrics
4. Software Quality Metrics Framework
5. The Software Quality Metrics Methodology
    5.1 Establish Software Quality Requirements
    5.2 Identify Software Quality Metrics

Table 12.1 IEEE Software Engineering Standards Summary (continued)

5.3 Implement the Software Quality Metrics
5.4 Analyze the Software Metrics Results
5.5 Validate the Software Quality Metrics

IEEE STD 1062-1993 IEEE Recommended Practice for Software Acquisition
Abstract: A set of useful quality practices that can be selected and applied during one or more steps in a software acquisition process is described. This recommended practice can be applied to software that runs on any computer system, regardless of the size, complexity, or criticality of the software, but is more suited for use on modified-off-the-shelf software and fully developed software.
Keywords: acquirer, modified-off-the-shelf software, software acquisition life cycle, software acquisition process, supplier
Contents
1. Overview
    1.1 Scope
    1.2 Terminology
2. References
3. Definitions
4. Introducing the Software Acquisition Process
    4.1 Software Acquisition Life Cycle
    4.2 Nine Steps in Acquiring Quality Software
5. Software Acquisition Process
    5.1 Planning Organizational Strategy
    5.2 Implementing Organization's Process
    5.3 Defining the Software Requirements
    5.4 Identifying Potential Suppliers
    5.5 Preparing Contract Requirements
    5.6 Evaluating Proposals and Selecting Supplier
    5.7 Managing for Supplier Performance
    5.8 Accepting the Software
    5.9 Using the Software
6. Summary

IEEE STD 1063-1987 IEEE Standard for Software User Documentation
Contents
1. Scope
    1.1 Applicability
    1.2 Organization
2. Definitions
3. Identifying Required User Documents
    3.1 Identifying the Software
    3.2 Determining the Document Audience
    3.3 Determining the Document Set
    3.4 Determining Document Usage Modes
4. User Document Inclusion Requirements
5. User Document Content Requirements
    5.1 Title Page
    5.2 Restrictions
    5.3 Warranties and Contractual Obligations
    5.4 Table of Contents
    5.5 List of Illustrations

Table 12.1 IEEE Software Engineering Standards Summary (continued)

5.6 Introduction
5.7 Body of Document
5.8 Error Messages, Known Problems, and Error Recovery
5.9 Appendices
5.10 Bibliography
5.11 Glossary
5.12 Index
6. User Document Presentation Requirements
    6.1 Highlighting
    6.2 Consistency
    6.3 Terminology
    6.4 Referencing Related Material
7. Bibliography

IEEE STD 1074-1991 IEEE Standard for Developing Software Life-Cycle Processes
Abstract: The set of activities that constitute the processes that are mandatory for the development and maintenance of software, whether stand-alone or part of a system, is set forth. The management and support processes that continue throughout the entire life cycle, as well as all aspects of the software life cycle from concept exploration through retirement, are covered. Associated input and output information is also provided. Utilization of the processes and their component activities maximizes the benefits to the user when the use of this standard is initiated early in the software life cycle. This standard requires definition of a user's software life cycle and shows its mapping into typical software life cycles; it is not intended to define or imply a software life cycle of its own.
Keywords: project management processed, project monitoring and control process, software development process, software implementation process, software installation process, software life cycle, software life-cycle model process, software life-cycle process, software maintenance process, software operation and support process, software post-development process, software pre-development process, software quality management process, software requirements process, software retirement process, software system allocation process
Contents
1. Introduction
    1.1 Scope
    1.2 References
    1.3 Definitions and Acronyms
    1.4 Organization of This Document
    1.5 Use of This Standard
2. Software Life-Cycle Model Process
    2.1 Overview
    2.2 Activities List
    2.3 Identify Candidate Software Life-Cycle Models
    2.4 Select Project Model
3. Project Management Processes
    3.1 Project Initiation Process
    3.2 Project Monitoring and Control Process
    3.3 Software Quality Management Process

Table 12.1 IEEE Software Engineering Standards Summary (continued)

4. Pre-Development Process
    4.1 Concept Exploration Process
    4.2 System Allocation Process
5. Development Processes
    5.1 Requirements Process
    5.2 Design Process
    5.3 Implementation Process
6. Post-Development Processes
    6.1 Installation Process
    6.2 Operation and Support Process
    6.3 Maintenance Process
    6.4 Retirement Process
7. Integral Processes
    7.1 Verification and Validation Process
    7.2 Software Configuration Management Process
    7.3 Documentation Development Process
    7.4 Training Process
8. Bibliography

IEEE STD 1074.1-1995 IEEE Guide for Developing Software Life-Cycle Processes
Abstract: Selected topics covered in IEEE STD 1074-1995, IEEE Standard for
  Developing Software Life-Cycle Processes, are addressed in this guide. The
  guide provides assistance with Software Life-Cycle Model (SLCM) selection,
  activity mapping, and management of a software life cycle (SLC).
Keywords: software life cycle, processes, software life-cycle model, software life-
  cycle process, activities, mapping
Contents
1. Overview
    1.1 Scope
    1.2 Purpose
    1.3 Prerequisites
    1.4 References
    1.5 Definitions and Acronyms
2. General Concepts of the Standard
    2.1 Process Standard
    2.2 Compliance
        2.2.1 Upward Adaptation
        2.2.2 Downward Adaptation
    2.3 Applicability
    2.4 Intended Audience
    2.5 How to Start Using the Standard
        2.5.1 SLCM
        2.5.2 Project Type
    2.6 SLC, SLCM, and Methodology
    2.7 Organizational Concerns
3. Mapping Guidelines
    3.1 An Approach to Mapping
    3.2 SLCM + Activities = SLC
    3.3 Information Tracing
    3.4 Hidden Information and Tasks
    3.5 Information Mapping
    3.6 Mapping Constraints

Table 12.1 IEEE Software Engineering Standards Summary (continued)

4. Concepts of the Standard Used in Mapping
    4.1 Time Ordering
    4.2 Iterations and Instances
    4.3 Ownership
    4.4 Integral Processes
    4.5 Management Processes
    4.6 Risk Management
    4.7 Maintenance
    4.8 Retirement
    4.9 Reuse and the SLC

IEEE STD 1175-1992 IEEE Trial-Use Standard Reference Model for Computing System Tool Interconnections

Abstract: Reference models for tool-to-organization interconnections, tool-to-platform interconnections, and information transfer among tools are provided. The purpose is to establish agreements for information transfer among tools in the contexts of human organization, a computer system platform, and a software development application. To make the transfer of semantic information among tools easier, a semantic transfer language (STL) is also provided. Interconnections that must be considered when buying, building, testing, or using computing system tools for specifying behavioral descriptions or requirements of system and software products are described.
Keywords: information transfer, reference model, semantic transfer language (STL), tool-to-organization interconnections, tool-to-platform interconnections

Contents
■ Part 1 Description of this Standard
1. Introduction
    1.1 Purpose
    1.2 Scope
    1.3 Audience
    1.4 Organization of this Document
    1.5 Definitions
    1.6 Conformance
■ Part 2 Context for Tool Interconnections
2. Reference Model for Tool-to-Organization Interconnections
    2.1 Organizational Context for Tools
    2.2 Role or Job Function View of a Tool
    2.3 Life-Cycle View of a Tool
    2.4 Support View of a Tool
    2.5 Tool-to-Organization Interconnection Standard Profile
3. Reference Model for Tool-to-Platform Interconnections
    3.1 Hardware-Software Platform Context for Tools
    3.2 Platforms
    3.3 Hardware Platforms
    3.4 Software Platforms
    3.5 Tool-to-Platform Interconnection Standard Profile
4. Reference Model for Information Transfer among Tools
    4.1 Information Transfer Context
    4.2 Mechanisms for Information Transfer among Tools
    4.3 Processes of Information Transfer: Services for Information Transfer
    4.4 Descriptions of Information Being Transferred

Table 12.1 IEEE Software Engineering Standards Summary (continued)

4.5 Information Transferred
4.6 Tool Interconnection Standard Profile
■   Part 3 Interconnection Language
5. Semantic Transfer Language (STL) Overview and Syntax
  5.1 STL Goals
  5.2 STL Sentence Form
  5.3 STL Notation
  5.4 STL Information Packet
  5.5 STL Sentences
  5.6 STL Language Elements
  5.7 Language Integrity
  5.8 STL Syntax Summary
6. STL Concepts and Meanings
  6.1 STL Concept Organization
  6.2 Concept Definition Conventions
  6.3 Concept Definition Sentence Templates
  6.4 STL Summary
7. STL Conformance and Extensibility
  7.1 STL Interconnection Profile
  7.2 STL Extensibility
8. Bibliography

IEEE STD 1220-1994 IEEE Trial-Use Standard for Application and Management of the Systems Engineering Process

Abstract: The interdisciplinary tasks that are required throughout a system's life cycle to transform customer needs, requirements, and constraints into a system solution are defined. This standard applies to a performing activity within an enterprise that is responsible for developing a product design and establishing the life-cycle infrastructure needed to provide for life-cycle sustainment. It specifies the requirements for the systems engineering process and its application throughout the product life cycle. The requirements of this standard are applicable to new products as well as incremental enhancements to existing products.

Keywords: enterprise, Systems Engineering Detailed Schedule (SEDS), Systems Engineering Management Plan (SEMP), Systems Engineering Master Schedule (SEMS), systems engineering process

Contents
1. Overview
  1.1 Scope
  1.2 Purpose
  1.3 Understanding This Standard
  1.4 Organization of This Standard
2. References
3. Definitions and Acronyms
  3.1 Definitions
4. General Requirements
  4.1 Systems Engineering Process
  4.2 Policies and Procedures for Systems Engineering
  4.3 Planning the Technical Effort
  4.4 Evolutionary Development Strategies
  4.5 Modeling and Prototyping

Table 12.1 IEEE Software Engineering Standards Summary (continued)

4.6 Integrated Database
4.7 Product and Process Data Package
4.8 Specification Tree
4.9 Drawing Tree
4.10 System Breakdown Structure (SBS)
4.11 Integration of the Systems Engineering Effort
4.12 Technical Reviews
4.13 Quality Management
4.14 Continuing Product and Process Improvement
5. Application of Systems Engineering throughout the System Life Cycle
  5.1 System Definition Stage
  5.2 Preliminary Design Stage
  5.3 Detailed Design Stage
  5.4 Fabrication, Assembly, Integration, and Test (FAIT) Stage
  5.5 Production and Customer Support Stages
  5.6 Simultaneous Engineering of Products and Services of Life Cycle Processes
6. The Systems Engineering Process
  6.1 Requirements Analysis
  6.2 Requirements Validation
  6.3 Functional Analysis
  6.4 Functional Verification
  6.5 Synthesis
  6.6 Physical Verification
  6.7 Systems Analysis
  6.8 Control

IEEE/EIA 12207.0-1996 Industry Implementation of International Standard ISO/IEC: ISO/IEC12207 Standard for Information Technology Software Life-Cycle Processes
Abstract: ISO/IEC 12207 provides a common framework for developing and managing software. IEEE/EIA 12207.0 consists of the clarifications, additions, and changes accepted by the Institute of Electrical and Electronics Engineers (IEEE) and the Electronic Industries Association (EIA) formulated by a joint project of the two organizations. IEEE/EIA 12207.0 contains concepts and guidelines to foster a better understanding and application of the standard. Thus, this standard provides industry with a basis for software practices that would be usable for both national and international business.

IEEE STD 1228-1994 IEEE Standard for Software Safety Plans
Abstract: The minimum acceptable requirements for the content of a software safety plan are established. This standard applies to the software safety plan used for the development, procurement, maintenance, and retirement of safety-critical software. This standard requires that the plan be prepared within the context of the system safety program. Only the safety aspects of the software are included. This standard does not contain special provisions required for software used in distributed systems or in parallel processors.
Keywords: safety-critical software, software safety plan, software safety program, safety requirements
Contents
1. Overview
  1.1 Purpose
  1.2 Scope

Table 12.1 IEEE Software Engineering Standards Summary (continued)

1.3 Application
1.4 Disclaimer
2. References
3. Definitions and Abbreviations
    3.1 Definitions
    3.2 Abbreviations
4. Contents of a Software Safety Plan
    4.1 Purpose (Section 1 of the Plan)
4.2 Definitions, Acronyms and Abbreviations, and References (Section 2 of the
    Plan)
4.3 Software Safety Management (Section 3 of the Plan)
4.4 Software Safety Analyses (Section 4 of the Plan)
4.5 Post Development (Section 5 of the Plan)
4.6 Plan Approval (Section 6 of the Plan)

IEEE STD 1298-1992 Software Quality Management System Part 1: Requirements
Abstract: Requirements for a software developer's quality management system
are established. Each of the elements of a quality management system to be
designed, developed, and maintained by the developer are identified, with the
objective of ensuring that the software will meet the requirements of a contract,
purchase order, or other agreement (collectively referred to as a "contract").
Keywords: software development, software quality, software quality management
Contents
1. Scope and Field of Application
    1.1 Scope
    1.2 Application
2. Referenced Documents
3. Definitions
4. Quality System Requirements
    4.1 Management Responsibility
    4.2 Quality System
    4.3 Contract Review, Planning, and Requirements Control
    4.4 Design, Programming, and User Documentation Control
    4.5 Quality System Document Control
    4.6 Purchasing
    4.7 Customer-Supplied Information and Material
    4.8 Configuration Management (including product identification and traceability)
    4.9 Process Control
    4.10 Inspection and Testing
    4.11 Inspection, Measuring, and Test Equipment
    4.12 Inspection and Test Status
    4.13 Control of Non-Conforming Product
    4.14 Corrective Action
    4.15 Handling, Storage, Packaging, and Delivery
    4.16 Quality Records
    4.17 Internal Quality Audits
    4.18 Training
    4.19 Software Maintenance
    4.20 Statistical techniques
    4.21 Control of Development Environment

IEEE STD 1362-1998 (Incorporates IEEE STD 1362a-1998) IEEE Guide for
Information Technology — System Definition — Concept of Operations
(ConOps) Document

Table 12.1 IEEE Software Engineering Standards Summary (continued)

Abstract: The format and contents of a concept of operations (ConOps) document are described. A ConOps is a user-oriented document that describes system characteristics for a proposed system from the users' viewpoint. The ConOps document is used to communicate overall quantitative and qualitative system characteristics to the user, buyer, developer, and other organizational elements (for example, training, facilities, staffing, and maintenance). It is used to describe the user organization(s), mission(s), and organizational objectives from an integrated systems point of view.
Keywords: buyer, characteristics, concept of operation, concepts of operations document, ConOps, developer, operational requirements, scenario, software-intensive system, software system, system, user, user requirements, viewpoint
Contents
1. Scope
2. References
3. Definitions
4. Elements of a ConOps Document
    4.1 Scope (Clause 1 of the ConOps document)
    4.2 Referenced Documents (Clause 2 of the ConOps document)
    4.3 Current System or Situation (Clause 3 of the ConOps document)
    4.4 Justification for and Nature of Changes (Clause 4 of the ConOps document)
    4.5 Concepts for the Proposed System (Clause 5 of the ConOps document)
    4.6 Operational Scenarios (Clause 6 of the ConOps document)
    4.7 Summary of Impacts (Clause 7 of the ConOps document)
    4.8 Analysis of the Proposed System (Clause 8 of the ConOps document)
    4.9 Notes (Clause 9 of the ConOps document)
    4.10 Appendices (Appendices of the ConOps document)
    4.11 Glossary (Glossary of the ConOps document)
    ■ Annex A IEEE: EIA 12207.1-1997 Compliance Statement

IEEE STD 610.12-1990 IEEE Standard Glossary of Software Engineering Terminology
Abstract: IEEE STD 610.12-1990, IEEE Standard Glossary of Software Engineering Terminology, identifies terms currently in use in the field of software engineering. Standard definitions for those terms are established.
Keywords: software engineering, glossary, terminology, definitions, dictionary
Contents
1. Scope
2. Glossary Structure
3. Definitions for Software Engineering Terms
4. Bibliography

IEEE STD 730-1989 IEEE Standard for Software Quality Assurance Plans
Contents
1. Scope and References
    1.1 Scope
    1.2 References
2. Definitions and Acronyms
    2.1 Definitions
3. Software Quality Assurance Plan
    3.1 Purpose (Section 1 of the SQAP)
    3.2 Reference Documents (Section 2 of the SQAP)
    3.3 Management (Section 3 of the SQAP)
    3.4 Documentation (Section 4 of the SQAP)
    3.5 Standards, Practices, Conventions, and Metrics (Section 5 of the SQAP)

Table 12.1 IEEE Software Engineering Standards Summary (continued)

3.6 Reviews and Audits (Section 6 of the SQAP)
3.7 Test (Section 7 of the SQAP)
3.8 Problem Reporting and Corrective Action (Section 8 of the SQAP)
3.9 Tools, Techniques, and Methodologies (Section 9 of the SQAP)
3.10 Code Control (Section 10 of the SQAP)
3.11 Media Control (Section 11 of the SQAP)
3.12 Supplier Control (Section 12 of the SQAP)
3.13 Records Collection, Maintenance, and Retention (Section 13 of the SQAP)
3.14 Training (Section 14 of the SQAP)
3.15 Risk Management (Section 15 of the SQAP)

IEEE STD 828-1990 IEEE Standard for Software Configuration Management Plans
Abstract: IEEE STD 828-1990, IEEE Standard for Software Configuration
Management Plans, establishes the minimum required contents of a Software
Configuration Management Plan and defines the specific activities to be
addressed and their requirements for any portion of a software product's life
cycle.
Keywords: configuration control board, configuration items, software
configuration management, software configuration management activities
Contents
1. Introduction to the Standard
    1.1 Scope
    1.2 References
    1.3 Definitions and Acronyms
2. The Software Configuration Management Plan
    2.1 Introduction
    2.2 SCM Management
    2.3 SCM Activities
    2.4 SCM Schedules
    2.5 SCM Resources
    2.6 SCM Plan Maintenance
3. Tailoring of the Plan
    3.1 Upward Tailoring
    3.2 Downward Tailoring
    3.3 Format
4. Conformance to the Standard
    4.1 Minimum Information
    4.2 Presentation Format
    4.3 Consistency Criteria
    4.4 Conformance Declaration

ANSI/IEEE STD 829-1983 IEEE Standard for Software Test Documentation
Contents
1. Scope
2. Definitions
3. Test Plan
    3.1 Purpose
    3.2 Outline
4. Test-Design Specification
    4.1 Purpose
    4.2 Outline
5. Test-Case Specification
    5.1 Purpose
    5.2 Outline
6. Test-Procedure Specification

Table 12.1 IEEE Software Engineering Standards Summary (continued)

6.1 Purpose
6.2 Outline
7. Test-Item Transmittal Report
    7.1 Purpose
    7.2 Outline
8. Test Log
    8.1 Purpose
    8.2 Outline
9. Test-Incident Report
    9.1 Purpose
    9.2 Outline
10. Test-Summary Report
    10.1 Purpose
    10.2 Outline

IEEE STD 830-1993 IEEE Recommended Practice for Software Requirements
  Specifications
Abstract: The content and qualities of a good software requirements
  specification (SRS) are described and several sample SRS outlines are
  presented. This recommended practice is aimed at specifying requirements of
  software to be developed but also can be applied to assist in the selection of
  in-house and commercial software products.
Keywords: contract, customer, prototyping, software requirements specification,
  supplier, system requirements specifications
Contents
1. Overview
    1.1 Scope
2. References
3. Definitions
4. Considerations for Producing a Good SRS
    4.1 Nature of the SRS
    4.2 Environment of the SRS
    4.3 Characteristics of a Good SRS
    4.4 Joint Preparation of the SRS
    4.5 SRS Evolution
    4.6 Prototyping
    4.7 Embedding Design in the SRS
    4.8 Embedding Project Requirements in the SRS
5. The Parts of an SRS
    5.1 Introduction (Section 1 of the SRS)
    5.2 Overall Description (Section 2 of the SRS)
    5.3 Specific Requirements (Section 3 of the SRS)
    5.4 Supporting Information

IEEE STD 982.1-1988 IEEE Standard Dictionary of Measures to Produce Reliable
  Software
Contents
1. Introduction
    1.1 Scope
    1.2 References
2. Definitions
3. Functional Classification of Measures
    3.1 Product Measures

Table 12.1 IEEE Software Engineering Standards Summary (continued)

3.2 Process Measures
4. Measures for Reliable Software
    4.1 Fault Density
    4.2 Defect Density
    4.3 Cumulative Failure Profile
    4.4 Fault-Days Number
    4.5 Functional or Modular Test Coverage
    4.6 Cause and Effect Graphing
    4.7 Requirements Traceability
    4.8 Defect Indices
    4.9 Error Distribution(s)
    4.10 Software Maturity Index
    4.11 Man-Hhours per Major Defect Detected
    4.12 Number of Conflicting Requirements
    4.13 Number of Entries and Exits per Module
    4.14 Software Science Measures
    4.15 Graph-Theoretic Complexity for Architecture
    4.16 Cyclomatic Complexity
    4.17 Minimal Unit Test Case Determination
    4.18 Run Reliability
    4.19 Design Structure
    4.20 Mean Time to Discover the Next K Faults
    4.21 Software Purity Level
    4.22 Estimated Number of Faults Remaining (by Seeding)
    4.23 Requirements Compliance
    4.24 Test Coverage
    4.25 Data or Information Flow Complexity
    4.26 Reliability Growth Function
    4.27 Residual Fault Count
    4.28 Failure Analysis Using Elapsed Time
    4.29 Testing Sufficiency
    4.30 Mean-Time-to-Failure
    4.31 Failure Rate
    4.32 Software Documentation and Source Listings
    4.33 RELY (Required Software Reliability)
    4.34 Software Release Readiness
    4.35 Completeness
    4.36 Test Accuracy
    4.37 System Performance Reliability
    4.38 Independent Process Reliability
    4.39 Combined Hardware and Software (System) Operational Availability

IEEE STD 982.2-1988 IEEE Guide for the Use of IEEE Standard Dictionary of Measures to Produce Reliable Software
Contents
1. Scope and References
    1.1 Scope
    1.2 References
2. Definitions
3. Measures to Produce Reliable Software
    3.1 Constructive Approach to Reliable Software
    3.2 Measurement Environment
    3.3 Measurement Selection Criteria
4. Measure Organization and Classification

Table 12.1 IEEE Software Engineering Standards Summary (continued)

4.1 Functional Classification
4.2 Life-Cycle Classification
4.3 Indicators and Predictors
5. Framework for Measures
    5.1 Measurement Process
    5.2 Stages of a Measurement Process
6. Errors, Faults, and Failure Analysis for Reliability Improvement
    6.1 Dynamics of Errors, Faults, and Failures
    6.2 Analysis of Error, Fault, Failure Events
    6.3 Minimizing Failure Events
    6.4 Summary
IEEE STD 990-1987 IEEE Recommended Practice for Ada as a Program Design
  Language
Contents
1. Introduction
    1.1 Scope
    1.2 Scope Restrictions
    1.3 Terminology
    1.4 Cautions
    1.5 Examples
2. Definitions and References
    2.1 Definitions
    2.2 References
3. Characteristics
    3.1 General Methodology Support
    3.2 Specific Design Support
    3.3 Other Support
    3.4 Ada Relationships

J-STD-016-1995 30 September 1995 Trial Use Standard for Information
  Technology Software Life-Cycle Processes Software Development
  Acquirer–Supplier Agreement
Keywords: builds/incremental development, database, joint
  technical/management reviews, operational concept, reusable software, risk
  management, security/privacy protection, software, software configuration
  management, software development, software documentation, software
  implementation, software management indicators, software product
  evaluation, software quality assurance, software requirements definition,
  software safety, software maintenance, software testing, software unit, tailoring
Contents
1. Scope
    1.1 Purpose
    1.2 Application
2. Referenced Documents
3. Definitions
    3.1 Terms
    3.2 Abbreviations and Acronyms
4. General Requirements
    4.1 Software Development Process
    4.2 General Requirements for Software Development
5. Detailed Requirements
    5.1 Project Planning and Oversight

Table 12.1 IEEE Software Engineering Standards Summary (continued)

5.2 Establishing a Software Development Environment
5.3 System Requirements Definition
5.4 System Design
5.5 Software Requirements Definition
5.6 Software Design
5.7 Software Implementation and Unit Testing
5.8 Unit Integration and Testing
5.9 Software Item Qualification Testing
5.10 Software/Hardware Item Integration and Testing
5.11 System Qualification Testing
5.12 Preparing for Software Use
5.13 Preparing for Software Transition
5.14 Software Configuration Management
5.15 Software Product Evaluation
5.16 Software Quality Assurance
5.17 Corrective Action
5.18 Joint Technical and Management Reviews
5.19 Risk Management
5.20 Software Management Indicators
5.21 Administrative Security and Privacy Protection
5.22 Managing Subcontractors
5.23 Interfacing with Software IV&V Agents
5.24 Coordinating with Associate Developers
5.25 Project Process Improvement
6. Notes
6.1 Cross Reference of Standard Subclauses to Annex Subclauses
6.2 Delivery of Tool Contents

Table 12.2 ISO 9000 Family of Standards

1. *ISO 9000* — is the actual standard. ISO 9001, ISO 9002, and ISO 9003 are the three quality assurance models against which organizations can be certified.

2. *ISO 9001* — is the standard of interest for companies that perform the entire range of activities, from design and development to testing. ISO 9001 is of most interest to the software developer. It is this standard that provides the all-important checklist of quality initiatives such as:

   a. Develop your quality management system:
      i. Identify the processes that make up your quality system.
      ii. Describe your quality management processes.

   b. Implement your quality management system:
      i. Use quality system processes.
      ii. Manage process performance

   c. Improve your quality management system:
      i. Monitor process performance.
      ii. Improve process performance

   ISO 9001 is directly applicable to configuration management as it specifies that change requests be maintained and tracked.

3. *ISO 9002* — is the standard for companies that do not engage in design and development. This standard focuses on production, installation, and service.

4. *ISO 9003* — is the appropriate standard for companies whose business processes do not include design control, process control, purchasing, or servicing. This standard focuses on testing and inspection.

Table 12.3 ISO Software Engineering Standards Summary

ISO/IEC 2382-20:1990	Information technology — vocabulary — Part 20: System development
ISO 3535:1977	Forms DESIGN SHEET and LAYOUT CHART
ISO 5806:1984	Information processing — specification of single-hit decision tables
ISO 5807:1985	Information processing — documentation symbols and conventions for data, program, and system flowcharts, program network charts, and system resources charts
ISO/IEC 6592:2000	Information technology — guidelines for the documentation of computer-based application systems. No abstract.
ISO 6593:1985	Information processing — program flow for processing sequential files in terms of record groups
ISO/IEC 8211:1994	Information technology — specification for a data descriptive file for information interchange
ISO/IEC 8631:1989	Information technology — program constructs and conventions for their representation
ISO 8790:1987	Information processing systems — computer system configuration diagram symbols and conventions
ISO 9000-3:1997	Quality management and quality assurance standards — Part 3: Guidelines for the application of ISO 9001:1994 to the development, supply, installation, and maintenance of computer software. No abstract.
ISO/IEC 9126-1:2001	Software engineering — product quality — Part 1: Quality model. No abstract.
ISO 9127:1988	Information processing systems — user documentation and cover information for consumer software packages
ISO/IEC TR 9294:1990	Information technology — guidelines for the management of software documentation
ISO 10007:2003	Quality management systems — guidelines for configuration management

Table 12.3 ISO Software Engineering Standards Summary (continued)

ISO/IEC 10746-1:1998	Information technology — Open Distributed Processing — Reference Model: Overview. No abstract.
ISO/IEC 10746-2:1996	Information technology — Open Distributed Processing — Reference Model: Foundations
ISO/IEC 10746-3:1996	Information technology — Open Distributed Processing — Reference Model: Architecture
ISO/IEC 10746-4:1998	Information technology — Open Distributed Processing — Reference Model: Architectural semantics. No abstract.
ISO/IEC 10746-4:1998/Amd 1:2001	Computational formalization. No abstract.
ISO/IEC 11411:1995	Information technology — representation for human communication of state transition of software
ISO/IEC 12119:1994	Information technology — Software packages — quality requirements and testing
ISO/IEC TR 12182:1998	Information technology — Categorization of software. No abstract.
ISO/IEC 12207:1995	Information technology — Software life-cycle processes
ISO/IEC 12207:1995/Amd 1:2002	
ISO/IEC 13235-1:1998	Information technology — Open Distributed Processing — Trading function: Specification. No abstract.
ISO/IEC 13235-3:1998	Information technology — Open Distributed Processing — Trading Function — Part 3: Provision of Trading Function using OSI Directory Service. No abstract.
ISO/IEC 13244:1998	Information technology — Open Distributed Management Architecture. No abstract.
ISO/IEC 13244:1998/Amd 1:1999	Support using Common Object Request Broker Architecture (CORBA). No abstract.
ISO/IEC 13800:1996	Information technology — procedure for the registration of identifiers and attributes for volume and file structure. No abstract.

Table 12.3 ISO Software Engineering Standards Summary (continued)

ISO/IEC 14102:1995	Information technology — guideline for the evaluation and selection of CASE tools. No abstract.
ISO/IEC 14143-1:1998	Information technology — Software measurement — functional size measurement — Part 1: Definition of concepts
ISO/IEC 14143-2:2002	Information technology — Software measurement — functional size measurement — Part 2: Conformity evaluation of software size measurement methods to ISO/IEC 14143-1:1998. No abstract.
ISO/IEC TR 14143-3:2003	Information technology — Software measurement — functional size measurement — Part 3: Verification of functional size measurement methods
ISO/IEC TR 14143-4:2002	Information technology — Software measurement — functional size measurement — Part 4: Reference model. No abstract.
ISO/IEC TR 14471:1999	Information technology — Software engineering — guidelines for the adoption of CASE tools. No abstract.
ISO/IEC 14598-1:1999	Information technology — Software product evaluation — Part 1: General overview. No abstract.
ISO/IEC 14598-2:2000	Software engineering — Product evaluation — Part 2: Planning and management. No abstract.
ISO/IEC 14598-3:2000	Software engineering — Product evaluation — Part 3: Process for developers. No abstract.
ISO/IEC 14598-4:1999	Software engineering — Product evaluation — Part 4: Process for acquirers. No abstract.
ISO/IEC 14598-5:1998	Information technology — Software product evaluation — Part 5: Process for evaluators. No abstract.
ISO/IEC 14598-6:2001	Software engineering — Product evaluation — Part 6: Documentation of evaluation modules. No abstract.

Table 12.3 ISO Software Engineering Standards Summary (continued)

ISO/IEC 14750:1999	Information technology — Open Distributed Processing — Interface Definition Language. No abstract.
ISO/IEC 14752:2000	Information technology — Open Distributed Processing — protocol support for computational interactions. No abstract.
ISO/IEC 14753:1999	Information technology — Open Distributed Processing — interface references and binding. No abstract.
ISO/IEC 14756:1999	Information technology — measurement and rating of performance of computer-based software systems. No abstract.
ISO/IEC TR 14759:1999	Software engineering — Mock-up and prototype — a categorization of software mock-up and prototype models and their use. No abstract.
ISO/IEC 14764:1999	Information technology — Software maintenance. No abstract.
ISO/IEC 14769:2001	Information technology — Open Distributed Processing — Type Repository Function. No abstract.
ISO/IEC 14771:1999	Information technology — Open Distributed Processing — naming framework. No abstract.
ISO/IEC 14834:1996	Information technology — Distributed Transaction Processing — the XA Specification
ISO/IEC 14863:1996	Information technology — System-Independent Data Format (SIDF). No abstract.
ISO/IEC 15026:1998	Information technology — System and software integrity levels. No abstract.
ISO/IEC TR 15271:1998	Information technology — Guide for ISO/IEC 12207 (Software Life-Cycle Processes). No abstract.
ISO/IEC 15288:2002	Systems engineering — System life-cycle processes. No abstract.
ISO/IEC 15414:2002	Information technology — Open distributed processing — Reference model — Enterprise language. No abstract.
ISO/IEC 15437:2001	Information technology — Enhancements to LOTOS (E-LOTOS). No abstract.

Table 12.3 ISO Software Engineering Standards Summary (continued)

ISO/IEC 15474-1:2002	Information technology — CDIF framework — Part 1: Overview. No abstract.
ISO/IEC 15474-2:2002	Information technology — CDIF framework — Part 2: Modeling and extensibility. No abstract.
ISO/IEC 15475-1:2002	Information technology — CDIF transfer format — Part 1: General rules for syntaxes and encodings. No abstract.
ISO/IEC 15475-2:2002	Information technology — CDIF transfer format — Part 2: Syntax SYNTAX.1. No abstract.
ISO/IEC 15475-3:2002	Information technology — CDIF transfer format — Part 3: Encoding ENCODING.1. No abstract.
ISO/IEC 15476-1:2002	Information technology — CDIF semantic metamodel — Part 1: Foundation. No abstract.
ISO/IEC 15476-2:2002	Information technology — CDIF semantic metamodel — Part 2: Common. No abstract.
ISO/IEC TR 15504-1:1998	Information technology — Software process assessment — Part 1: Concepts and introductory guide. No abstract.
ISO/IEC TR 15504-2:1998	Information technology — Software process assessment — Part 2: A reference model for processes and process capability. No abstract.
ISO/IEC TR 15504-3:1998	Information technology — Software process assessment — Part 3: Performing an assessment. No abstract.
ISO/IEC TR 15504-4:1998	Information technology — Software process assessment — Part 4: Guide to performing assessments. No abstract.
ISO/IEC TR 15504-5:1999	Information technology — Software process assessment — Part 5: An assessment model and indicator guidance. No abstract.
ISO/IEC TR 15504-6:1998	Information technology — Software process assessment — Part 6: Guide to competency of assessors. No abstract.
ISO/IEC TR 15504-7:1998	Information technology — Software process assessment — Part 7: Guide for use in process improvement. No abstract.

Table 12.3 ISO Software Engineering Standards Summary (continued)

ISO/IEC TR 15504-8:1998	Information technology — Software process assessment — Part 8: Guide for use in determining supplier process capability. No abstract.
ISO/IEC TR 15504-9:1998	Information technology — Software process assessment — Part 9: Vocabulary. No abstract.
ISO/IEC TR 15846:1998	Information technology — Software life-cycle processes — Configuration Management. No abstract.
ISO/IEC 15910:1999	Information technology — Software user documentation process. No abstract.
ISO/IEC 15939:2002	Software engineering — Software measurement process. No abstract.
ISO/IEC TR 16326:1999	Software engineering — Guide for the application of ISO/IEC 12207 to project management. No abstract.
ISO/IEC 19500-2:2003	Information technology — Open Distributed Processing — Part 2: General Inter-ORB Protocol (GIOP)/Internet Inter-ORB Protocol (IIOP)
ISO/IEC 19761:2003	Software engineering — COSMIC-FFP — a functional size measurement method
ISO/IEC 20968:2002	Software engineering — Mk II Function Point Analysis — counting practices manual

ISO/IEC 2382-20:1990 Information technology — Vocabulary — Part 20: System development

Serves to facilitate international communication in information processing. Presents English and French terms and definitions of selected concepts as regards the field of information processing and defines relationships between the entries. The provided concepts concern a system life cycle ranging from the requirements analysis to the implementation, including system design and quality assurance.

ISO 3535:1977 Forms design sheet and layout chart

Abstract: Lays down the basic principles for the design of forms, whether discrete forms or continuous forms, and establishes a forms design sheet and a layout chart based on these principles. Applies to the design of forms for administrative, commercial, and technical use, whether for completion in handwriting or by mechanical means such as typewriters and automatic printers.

Table 12.3 ISO Software Engineering Standards Summary (continued)

ISO 5806:1984 Information processing — Specification of single-hit decision tables
Abstract: The basic format of single-hit decision tables and relevant definitions are described, together with recommended conventions for preparation and use. Is concerned with the use of decision tables in the context of documentation of computer-based information systems.

ISO 5807:1985 Information processing — Documentation symbols and conventions for data, program, and system flowcharts; program network charts; and system resources charts
Abstract: Defines symbols to be used in information processing documentation and gives guidance on conventions for their use in data flowcharts, program flowcharts, system flowcharts, program network charts, and system resources charts. Applicable in conjunction with ISO 2382/1.

ISO 6593:1985 Information processing — Program flow for processing sequential files in terms of record groups
Abstract: Describes two alternative general procedures for any program for processing sequential files logically organized in groups of records: Method A — checking of control head conditions after termination of appropriate level; Method B — checking of control head conditions before initiation of appropriate level.

ISO/IEC 8211:1994 Information technology — Specification for a data descriptive file for information interchange
Abstract: Cancels and replaces the first edition (1985). Specifies an interchange format to facilitate the moving of files or parts of files containing data records between computer systems. Specifies: media-independent file and data record descriptions for information interchange; the description of data elements, vectors, arrays, and hierarchies containing character strings, bit strings, and numeric forms; a data descriptive file; a data descriptive record; three levels of complexity of file and record structure; FTAM unstructured and structured document types.

ISO/IEC 8631:1989 Information technology — Program constructs and conventions for their representation
Abstract: Is concerned with the expression of procedure-oriented algorithms. Defines: (1) the nature of program constructs; (2) the manner in which constructs can be combined; (3) specifications for a set of constructs; a variety of subsets of the defined constructs.

ISO 8790:1987 Information processing systems — Computer system configuration diagram symbols and conventions
Abstract: Defines graphical symbols and their conventions for use in configuration diagrams for computer systems, including automatic data processing systems.

Table 12.3 ISO Software Engineering Standards Summary (continued)

ISO 9127:1988 Information processing systems — User documentation and cover information for consumer software packages

Abstract: Describes user documentation and cover information supplied with software packages. Is applicable to software packages sold off-the-shelf to consumers for business, scientific, educational, and home use. References: ISO 6592; ISO 7185.

ISO/IEC TR 9294:1990 Information technology — Guidelines for the management of software documentation

Abstract: Addresses the policies, standards, procedures, resources, and plans to produce effective software. Applicable to all types of software, from the simplest program to the most complex software system and to all stages of the software life cycle. Detailed advice on the content and layout of software documentation is not provided. Annex A contains checklists of the policies, standards, procedures, and project planning on the software production.

ISO 10007:2003 Quality management systems — Guidelines for configuration management

Abstract: ISO 10007:2003 gives guidance on the use of configuration management within an organization. It is applicable to the support of products from concept to disposal.

> It first outlines the responsibilities and authorities before describing the configuration management process that includes configuration management planning, configuration identification, change control, configuration status accounting, and configuration audit.
>
> Since ISO 10007:2003 is a guidance document, it is not intended to be used for certification/registration purposes.

ISO/IEC 10746-2:1996 Information technology — Open Distributed Processing — Reference Model: Foundations

Abstract: Contains the concepts needed to perform the modeling of ODP systems, and the principles of conformance to ODP systems.

ISO/IEC 10746-3:1996 Information technology — Open Distributed Processing — Reference Model: Architecture

Abstract: Defines how ODP systems are specified, making use of concepts in ITU-T Recommendation X.902 (ISO/IEC 10746-2); identifies the characteristics that qualify systems as ODP systems.

ISO/IEC 11411:1995 Information technology — Representation for human communication of state transition of software

Abstract: Defines diagrams and symbols for representing software functions and transitions, and in improving human communication. Covers development, communication, and review of software requirement analysis and design. Effective in interactive software, data communication software, and language/command.

Table 12.3 ISO Software Engineering Standards Summary (continued)

ISO/IEC 12119:1994 Information technology — Software packages — quality requirements and testing

Abstract: Applicable to software packages. Establishes requirements for software packages and instructions on how to test a software package against these requirements. Deals only with software packages as offered and delivered; does not deal with their production process. The quality system of a supplier is outside the scope of this standard.

ISO/IEC 12207:1995 Information technology — Software life-cycle processes

Abstract: Establishes a system for software life-cycle processes with well-defined terminology. Contains processes, activities, and tasks that are to be applied during the acquisition of a system that contains software, a stand-alone software product, and software services.

ISO/IEC TR 14143-3:2003 Information technology — Software measurement — functional size measurement — Part 3: Verification of functional size measurement methods

Abstract: ISO/IEC TR 14143-3:2003 establishes a framework for verifying the statements of an FSM method and/or for conducting tests requested by the verification sponsor, relative to the following performance properties:

1. Repeatability and reproducibility
2. Accuracy
3. Convertibility
4. Discrimination threshold
5. Applicability to functional domains

Note: Statements and test requests relative to other performance properties are outside the scope of ISO/IEC TR 14143-3:2003.

ISO/IEC TR 14143-3:2003 aims to ensure that the output from the verification is objective, impartial, consistent, and repeatable.

The verification report, produced as a result of applying ISO/IEC TR 14143-3:2003, will enable prospective users to select the FSM method that best meets their needs.

ISO/IEC 14834:1996 Information technology — Distributed Transaction Processing — the XA specification

Abstract: Specifies the bi-directional interface between a transaction manager and a resource manager (the XA interface) in an X/Open Distributed Transaction Processing (DTP) environment. Technically identical to X/Open CAE specification. Also contains the text of the X/Open DTP Reference Model Version 3.

ISO/IEC 19500-2:2003 Information technology — Open Distributed Processing — Part 2: General Inter-ORB Protocol (GIOP)/Internet Inter-ORB Protocol (IIOP)

Table 12.3 ISO Software Engineering Standards Summary (continued)

Abstract: ISO/IEC 19500-2:2003 specifies the General Inter-ORB Protocol (GIOP) for Object Request Broker (ORB) interoperability. GIOP can be mapped onto any connection-oriented transport protocol that meets a minimal set of assumptions defined by this standard.

ISO/IEC 19500-2:2003 also de nes the Internet Inter -ORB Protocol (IIOP), a speci c mapping of the GIOP that runs directly o ver connections that use the Internet Protocol and the Transmission Control Protocol (TCP/IP connections).

ISO/IEC 19500-2:2003 provides a widely implemented and used particularization of ITU-T Rec. X.931 | ISO/IEC 14752. It supports interoperability and location transparency in ODP systems.

ISO/IEC 19761:2003 Software engineering — COSMIC-FFP — a functional size measurement method

Abstract: ISO/IEC 19761:2003 specifies the set of definitions, conventions, and activities of the COSMIC-FFP Functional Size Measurement Method. It is applicable to software from the following functional domains:

1. Application software that is needed to support business administration
2. Real-time software, the task of which is to keep up with or control events happening in the real world
3. Hybrids of the above

ISO/IEC 19761:2003 has not been designed to measure the functional size of a piece of software, or its parts, which:

1. Are characterized by complex mathematical algorithms or other specialized and complex rules, such as may be found in expert systems, simulation software, self-learning software, and weather forecasting systems, or
2. Process continuous variables such as audio sounds or video images, such as may be found, for example, in computer game software, musical instruments, and the like.

However, within the local environment of an organization using the COSMIC-FFP Functional Size Measurement Method, it might be possible to measure these FUR (Functional User Requirement) in a way that is meaningful as a local standard. ISO/IEC 19761:2003 contains provision for the local customization of the method for this purpose.

ISO/IEC 20968:2002 Software engineering — Mk II Function Point Analysis — Counting Practices Manual

Abstract: ISO/IEC 20968:2002 specifies the set of definitions, conventions, and activities of the MkII FPA Functional Size Measurement Method.

Table 12.3 ISO Software Engineering Standards Summary (continued)

The method can be used to measure the functional size of any software application that can be described in terms of logical transactions, each comprising an input, process, and output component. The sizing rules were designed to apply to application software from the domain of business information systems, where the processing component of each transaction tends to be dominated by considerations of the storage or retrieval of data.

The method may be applicable to software from other domains, but the user should note that the sizing rules do not take into account contributions to size such as from complex algorithms as typically found in scientific and engineering software, nor do the rules specifically take into account real-time requirements.

Mk II FPA is independent of the project management method to be used and of the development method employed. It is a measure of the logical business requirements, but is independent of how they are implemented.

SUMMARY

This chapter provides a reference listing of the pertinent industry CM standards.

REFERENCES

[EIA 1998] Electronic Industries Alliance, EIA Standard: National Consensus Standard for Configuration Management, EIA-649, Arlington, VA, August 1998.

[Paulk et al. 1995] Paulk, Mark C., Charles V. Weber, Bill Curtis, and Mary Beth Chrissis, *The Capability Maturity Model: Guidelines for Improving the Software Process,* Software Engineering Institute, Carnegie Mellon University, Pittsburgh, PA, October 1995.

13

METRICS AND CONFIGURATION MANAGEMENT REFERENCE

If configuration management (CM) provides the framework for the management of all systems engineering activities, then metrics provide the framework for measuring whether or not configuration management has been effective.

That metrics are an absolute requirement is proven by the following dismal statistics:

- Over half (53 percent) of IT projects overrun their schedules and budgets, 31 percent are cancelled, and only 16 percent are completed on time. *Source:* Standish Group, publication date: 2000.
- Of those projects that failed in 2000, 87 percent went more than 50 percent over budget. *Source:* KPMG Information Technology, publication date: 2000.
- In 2000, 45 percent of failed projects did not produce the expected benefits, and 88 to 92 percent went over schedule. *Source:* KPMG Information Technology, publication date: 2000.
- Half of new software projects in the United States will go significantly over budget. *Source:* META Group, publication date: 2000.
- The average cost of a development project for a large company is $2,322,000; for a medium-sized company, it is $1,331,000; and for a small company, it is $434,000. *Source:* Standish Group, publication date: 2000.
- In 1995, $81 billion was the estimated cost for cancelled projects. *Source:* Standish Group, publication date: 1995.

- Over half (52.7 percent) of projects were projected to cost more than 189 percent of their original estimates. *Source:* Standish Group, publication date: 2000.
- Some 88 percent of all U.S. projects are over schedule, over budget, or both. *Source:* Standish Group, publication date: 2000.
- The average time overrun on projects is 222 percent of original estimates. *Source:* Standish Group, publication date: 2000.

While configuration management is not a panacea for all problems, practicing sound CM methodologies can assist in effectively controlling the systems engineering effort. This chapter surveys a wide variety of metrics that can be deployed to measure the developmental process. Not all metrics are applicable to all situations. The organization must carefully consider which of the following metrics are a best fit.

WHAT METRICS ARE AND WHY THEY ARE IMPORTANT

Why should anyone care about productivity and quality? There are several reasons for this. The first and foremost reason is that our customers and end users require a working, quality product. Measuring the process as well as the product tells us whether we have achieved our goal. However, there are other, more subtle reasons why one needs to measure productivity and quality, including:

- The development of systems is becoming increasing complex. Unless one measures, one will never know whether or not one's efforts have been successful.
- On occasion, technology is used just for the sake of using a new technology. This is not an effective use of a technology. Measuring the effectiveness of an implementation ensures that one's decision has been cost-effective.

One measures productivity and quality to quantify the project's progress as well as to quantify the attributes of the product. A metric enables one to understand and manage the process as well as to measure the impact of change to the process — that is, new methods, training, etc. The use of metrics also enables one to know when one has met his goals — that is, usability, performance, test coverage, etc.

In measuring software systems, one can create metrics based on the different parts of a system — for example, requirements, specifications, code, documentation, tests, and training. For each of these components, one can measure its attributes, which include usability, maintainability, extendibility, size, defect level, performance, and completeness.

While the majority of organizations will use metrics found in books such as this one, it is possible to generate metrics specific to a particular task. Characteristics of metrics dictate that they should be:

- Collectable
- Reproducible
- Pertinent
- System independent

Sample product metrics include:

- *Size:* lines of code, pages of documentation, number and size of test, token count, function count
- *Complexity:* decision count, variable count, number of modules, size/volume, depth of nesting
- *Reliability:* count of changes required by phase, count of discovered defects, defect density = number of defects/size, count of changed lines of code

Sample process metrics include:

- *Complexity:* time to design, code, and test, defect discovery rate by phase, cost to develop, number of external interfaces, defect fix rate
- *Methods and tool use:* number of tools used and why, project infrastructure tools, tools not used and why
- *Resource metrics:* years of experience with team, years of experience with language, years of experience with type of software, MIPS per person, support personnel to engineering personnel ratio, non-project time to project time ratio
- *Productivity:* percent time to redesign, percent time to redo, variance of schedule, variance of effort

Once the organization determines the slate of metrics to be implemented, it must develop a methodology for reviewing the results of the metrics program. Metrics are useless if they do not result in improved quality or productivity. At a minimum, the organization should:

1. Determine the metric and measuring technique.
2. Measure to understand where you are.
3. Establish worst, best, planned cases.
4. Modify the process or product, depending on results of measurement.

5. Remeasure to see what has changed.
6. Reiterate.

TRADITIONAL CM METRICS

The following metrics are typically used by those measuring the CM process:

- Average rate of variance from scheduled time
- Rate of first-pass approvals
- Volume of deviation requests by cause
- The number of scheduled, performed, and completed configuration management audits by each phase of the life cycle
- The rate of new changes being released and the rate that changes are being verified as completed; the history compiled from successive deliveries is used to refine the scope of the expected rate
- The number of completed versus scheduled (stratified by type and priority) actions
- Man-hours per project
- Schedule variances
- Tests per requirement
- Change category count
- Changes by source
- Cost variances
- Errors per thousand source lines of code (KSLOC)
- Requirements volatility

IEEE PROCESS FOR MEASUREMENT

Using the IEEE methodology [IEEE 1989], the measurement process can be described in nine stages. These stages may overlap or occur in different sequences, depending on organization needs. Each of these stages in the measurement process influences the production of a delivered product with the potential for high reliability. Other factors influencing the measurement process include:

- A firm management commitment to continually assess product and process maturity, or stability, or both during the project
- The use of trained personnel in applying measures to the project in a useful way
- Software support tools

■ A clear understanding of the distinctions among errors, faults, and failures

Product measures include:

■ *Errors, faults, and failures:* the count of defects with respect to human cause, program bugs, and observed system malfunctions
■ *Mean-time-to-failure, failure rate:* a derivative measure of defect occurrence and time
■ *Reliability growth and projection:* the assessment of change in failure-freeness of the product under testing or operation
■ *Remaining product faults:* the assessment of fault-freeness of the product in development, test, or maintenance
■ *Completeness and consistency:* the assessment of the presence and agreement of all necessary software system parts
■ *Complexity:* the assessment of complicating factors in a system

Process measures include:

■ *Management control measures* address the quantity and distribution of error and faults and the trend of cost necessary for defect removal.
■ *Coverage measures* allow one to monitor the ability of developers and managers to guarantee the required completeness in all the activities of the life cycle and support the definition of correction actions.
■ *Risk, benefit, and cost evaluation measures* support delivery decisions based both on technical and cost criteria. Risk can be assessed based on residual faults present in the product at delivery and the cost with the resulting support activity.

The nine stages consist of the following.

Stage 1: Plan Organizational Strategy

Initiate a planning process. Form a planning group and review reliability constraints and objectives, giving consideration to user needs and requirements. Identify the reliability characteristics of a software product necessary to achieve these objectives. Establish a strategy for measuring and managing software reliability. Document practices for conducting measurements.

Stage 2: Determine Software Reliability Goals

Define the reliability goals for the software being developed to optimize reliability in light of realistic assessments of project constraints, including size scope, cost, and schedule.

Review the requirements for the specific development effort to determine the desired characteristics of the delivered software. For each characteristic, identify specific reliability goals that can be demonstrated by the software or measured against a particular value or condition. Establish an acceptable range of values. Consideration should be given to user needs and requirements.

Establish intermediate reliability goals at various points in the development effort.

Stage 3: Implement Measurement Process

Establish a software reliability measurement process that best fits the organization's needs. Review the rest of the process and select those stages that best lead to optimum reliability.

Add to or enhance these stages as needed. Consider the following suggestions:

- Select appropriate data collection and measurement practices designed to optimize software reliability.
- Document the measures required, the intermediate and final milestones when measurements are taken, the data collection requirements, and the acceptable values for each measure.
- Assign responsibilities for performing and monitoring measurements, and provide the necessary support for these activities from across the internal organization.
- Initiate a measure selection and evaluation process.
- Prepare educational material for training personnel in concepts, principles, and practices of software reliability and reliability measures.

Stage 4: Select Potential Measures

Identify potential measures that would be helpful in achieving the reliability goals established in Stage 2.

Stage 5: Prepare Data Collection and Measurement Plan

Prepare a data collection and measurement plan for the development and support effort. For each potential measure, determine the primitives needed to perform the measurement. Data should be organized so that information related to events during the development effort can be properly recorded in a database and retained for historical purposes.

For each intermediate reliability goal identified in Stage 2, identify the measures needed to achieve this goal. Identify the points during development when the measurements are to be taken. Establish acceptable values or a range of values to assess whether the intermediate reliability goals are achieved.

Include in the plan an approach for monitoring the measurement effort itself. The responsibility for collecting and reporting data, verifying its accuracy, computing measures, and interpreting the results should be described.

Stage 6: Monitor the Measurements

Monitor measurements. Once the data collection and reporting begin, monitor the measurements and the progress made during development, so as to manage the reliability and thereby achieve the goals for the delivered product. The measurements assist in determining whether the intermediate reliability goals are achieved and whether the final goal is achievable. Analyze the measure and determine if the results are sufficient to satisfy the reliability goals. Decide whether a measure's results assist in affirming the reliability of the product or process being measured. Take corrective action.

Stage 7: Assess Reliability

Analyze measurements to ensure that reliability of the delivered software satisfies the reliability objectives and that the reliability, as measured, is acceptable.

Identify assessment steps that are consistent with the reliability objectives documented in the data collection and measurement plan. Check the consistency of acceptance criteria and the sufficiency of tests to satisfactorily demonstrate that the reliability objectives have been achieved. Identify the organization responsible for determining final acceptance of the reliability of the software. Document the steps in assessing the reliability of the software.

Stage 8: Use Software

Assess the effectiveness of the measurement effort and perform the necessary corrective action. Conduct a follow-up analysis of the measurement effort to evaluate the reliability assessment and development practices, record lessons learned, and evaluate user satisfaction with the software's reliability.

Stage 9: Retain Software Measurement Data

Retain measurement data on the software throughout the development and operation phases for use in future projects. This data provides a baseline for reliability improvement and an opportunity to compare the same measures across completed projects. This information can assist in developing future guidelines and standards.

METRICS AS A COMPONENT OF THE PROCESS MATURITY FRAMEWORK

The Contel Technology Center's Software Engineering lab has as one of its prime goals the improvement of software engineering productivity. As a result of work in this area, Pfleeger and McGowan [1990] have suggested a set of metrics for which data is to be collected and analyzed. This set of metrics is based on a process maturity framework developed at the Software Engineering Institute (SEI) at Carnegie Mellon University. The SEI framework divides organizations into five levels based on how mature (i.e., organized, professional, aligned to software tenets) the organization is. The five levels range from initial, or ad hoc, to an optimizing environment. Contel recommends that metrics be divided into five levels as well. Each level is based on the amount of information made available to the development process. As the development process matures and improves, additional metrics can be collected and analyzed.

Level 1: Initial Process

This level is characterized by an ad hoc approach to software development. Inputs to the process are not well-defined but the outputs are as expected. Preliminary baseline project metrics should be gathered at this level to form a basis for comparison as improvements are made and maturity increases. This can be accomplished by comparing new project measurements with the baseline ones.

Level 2: Repeatable Process

At this level, the process is repeatable in much the same way that a subroutine is repeatable. The requirements act as input, the code as output, and constraints are such things as budget and schedule. Although proper inputs produce proper outputs, there is no means to easily discern how the outputs are actually produced. Only project-related metrics make sense at this level because the activities within the actual transitions from input to output are not available to be measured. Measures are this level can include:

- Amount of effort needed to develop the system
- Overall project cost
- Software size: non-commented lines of code, function points, object, and method count
- Personnel effort: actual person-months of effort, report person-months of effort
- Requirements volatility: requirements changes

Level 3: Defined Process

At this level, the activities of the process are clearly defined. This means that the input to and output from each well-defined functional activity can be examined, which permits a measurement of the intermediate products. Measures include:

- *Requirements complexity:* number of distinct objects and actions addressed in requirements
- *Design complexity:* number of design modules, Cyclomatic complexity, McCabe design complexity
- *Code complexity:* number of code modules, Cyclomatic complexity
- *Test complexity:* number of paths to test, of object-oriented development, and then number of object interfaces to test
- *Quality metrics:* defects discovered, defects discovered per unit size (defect density), requirements faults discovered, design faults discovered, fault density for each product
- Pages of documentation

Level 4: Managed Process

At this level, feedback from early project activities is used to set priorities for later project activities. At this level, activities are readily compared and contrasted; the effects of changes in one activity can be tracked in the others. At this level, measurements can be made across activities and are used to control and stabilize the process so that productivity and quality can match expectation. The following types of data are recommended to be collected. Metrics at this stage, although derived from the following data, are tailored to the individual organization.

- *Process type.* What process model is used, and how is it correlating to positive or negative consequences?
- *Amount of producer reuse.* How much of the system is designed for reuse? This includes reuse of requirements, design modules, test plans, and code.
- *Amount of consumer reuse.* How much does the project reuse components from other projects? This includes reuse of requirements, design modules, test plans, and code. (By reusing tested, proven components effort can be minimized and quality can be improved.)
- *Defect identification.* How and when are defects discovered? Knowing this will indicate whether those process activities are effective.
- *Use of defect density model for testing.* To what extent does the number of defects determine when testing is complete? This controls and focuses testing as well as increases the quality of the final product.
- *Use of configuration management.* Is a configuration management scheme imposed on the development process? This permits traceability, which can be used to assess the impact of alterations.
- *Module completion over time.* At what rates are modules being completed? This reflects the degree to which the process and development environment facilitate implementation and testing.

Level 5: Optimizing Process

At this level, measures from activities are used to change and improve the process. This process change can affect the organization as well as the project. Studies by the SEI report that 85 percent of organizations are at level 1, 14 percent at level 2, and 1 percent at level 3. None of the firms surveyed had reached Levels 4 or 5. Therefore, the authors have not recommended a set of metrics for Level 5.

STEPS TO TAKE IN USING METRICS

1. Assess the process: determine the level of process maturity.
2. Determine the appropriate metrics to collect.
3. Recommend metrics, tools, and techniques.
4. Estimate project cost and schedule.
5. Collect appropriate level of metrics.
6. Construct project database of metrics data, which can be used for analysis and to track the value of metrics over time.
7. Cost and schedule evaluation: when the project is complete, evaluate the initial estimates of cost and schedule for accuracy. Determine which of the factors might account for discrepancies between predicted and actual values.
8. Form a basis for future estimates.

IEEE Defined Metrics

The IEEE standards [1988] were written with the objective of providing the software community with defined measures currently used as indicators of reliability. By emphasizing early reliability assessment, this standard supports methods through measurement to improve product reliability.

This section presents a sub-set of the IEEE standard that is easily adaptable by the general IT community.

1. Fault Density

This measure can be used to predict remaining faults by comparison with expected fault density, determine if sufficient testing has been completed, and establish standard fault densities for comparison and prediction.

$$F_d = F/KSLOC$$

Where:

F = total number of unique faults found in a given interval and resulting in failures of a specified severity level

KSLOC = number of source lines of executable code and nonexecutable data declarations, in thousands

2. Defect Density

This measure can be used after design and code inspections of new development or large block modifications. If the defect density is outside the norm after several inspections, it is an indication of a problem.

$$DD = \frac{\sum_{i=1}^{I} D_i}{KSLOD}$$

Where:

D_i = total number of unique defects detected during the ith design or code inspection process

I = total number of inspections

KSLOD = in the design phase, this is the number of source lines of executable code and nonexecutable data declarations, in thousands

3. Cumulative Failure Profile

This is a graphical method used to predict reliability, estimate additional testing time to reach an acceptable reliable system, and identify modules and sub-systems that require additional testing. A plot is drawn of cumulative failures versus a suitable time base.

4. Fault-Days Number

This measure represents the number of days that faults spend in the system, from their creation to their removal. For each fault detected and removed, during any phase, the number of days from its creation to its removal is determined (fault-days). The fault-days are then summed for all faults detected and removed, to get the fault-days number at system level, including all faults detected and removed up to the delivery date. In those cases where the creation date of the fault is not known, the fault is assumed to have been created at the middle of the phase in which it was introduced.

5. Functional or Modular Test Coverage

This measure is used to quantify a software test coverage index for a software delivery. From the system's functional requirements, a cross-reference listing of associated modules must first be created.

$$\text{Functional (Modular) Test Coverage Index} = \frac{FE}{FT}$$

Where:
FE = number of the software functional (modular) requirements for which all test cases have been satisfactorily completed
FT = total number of software functional (modular) requirements

6. Requirements Traceability

This measure aids in identifying requirements that are either missing from, or in addition to, the original requirements.

$$TM = \frac{R1}{R2} \times 100\%$$

Where:

R1 = number of requirements met by the architecture

R2 = number of original requirements

7. Software Maturity Index

This measure is used to quantify the readiness of a software product. Changes from previous baselines to the current baselines are an indication of the current product stability.

$$SMI = \frac{M_T - \left(F_a + F_c + F_{del}\right)}{M_T}$$

Where:

SMI = software maturity index

M_T = number of software functions (modules) in the current delivery

F_a = number of software functions (modules) in the current delivery that are additions to the previous delivery

F_c = number of software functions (modules) in the current delivery that include internal changes from a previous delivery

F_{del} = number of software functions (modules) in the previous delivery that are deleted in the current delivery

SMI can be *estimated* as:

$$SMI = \frac{M_T - F_c}{M_T}$$

8. Number of Conflicting Requirements

This measure is used to determine the reliability of a software system resulting from the software architecture under consideration, as represented by a specification based on the entity-relationship-attributed model. What is required is a list of the system's inputs, its outputs, and a list of the functions performed by each program. The mappings from the software architecture to the requirements are identified. Mappings from the same specification item to more than one differing requirement are examined for requirements inconsistency. Additionally, mappings from more than one specification item to a single requirement are examined for specification inconsistency.

9. Cyclomatic Complexity

This measure is used to determine the structured complexity of a coded module. The use of this measure is designed to limit the complexity of the module, thereby promoting understandability of the module.

$$C = E - N + 1$$

Where:
C = complexity
N = number of nodes (sequential groups of program statements)
E = number of edges (program flows between nodes)

10. Design Structure

This measure is used to determine the simplicity of the detailed design of a software program. The values determined can be used to identify problem areas within the software design.

$$DSM = \sum_{i=1}^{6} W_i D_i$$

Where:
DSM = design structure measure
P1 = total number of modules in program
P2 = number of modules dependent on input or output
P3 = number of modules dependent on prior processing (state)
P4 = number of database elements
P5 = number of nonunique database elements
P6 = number of database segments
P7 = number of modules not single entrance/single exit

The design structure is the weighted sum of six derivatives determined using the primitives given above.

D_1 = designed organized top-down
D_2 = module dependence (P2/P1)
D_3 = module dependent on prior processing (P3/P1)
D_4 = database size (P5/P4)
D_5 = database compartmentalization (P6/P4)
D_6 = module single entrance/exit (P7/P1)

The weights (W_i) are assigned by the user based on the priority of each associated derivative. Each W_i has a value between 0 and 1.

11. Test Coverage

This is a measure of the completeness of the testing process, from both a developer's and user's perspective. The measure relates directly to the development, integration, and operational test stages of product development.

$$TC(\%) = \frac{(\text{Implemented capabilities})}{(\text{Required capabilities})}$$

$$\times \frac{(\text{Program primitives tested})}{(\text{Total program primitives})} \times 100\%$$

Where:
Program functional primitives are either modules, segments, statements, branches, or paths
Data functional primitives are classes of data
Requirement primitives are test cases or functional capabilities

12. Data or Information Flow Complexity

This is a structural complexity or procedural complexity measure that can be used to evaluate the information flow structure of large-scale systems, the procedure and module information flow structure, the complexity of the interconnections between modules, and the degree of simplicity of relationships between sub-systems, and to correlate total observed failures and software reliability with data complexity.

$$\text{Weighted IFC} = \text{Length} \times (\text{Fan-in} \times \text{Fan-out})^2$$

Where:
IFC = information flow complexity
Fan-in = local flows into a procedure + number of data structures from which the procedures retrieves data
Fan-out = local flows from a procedure + number of data structures that the procedure updates
Length = number of source statements in a procedure (excluding comments)

The flow of information between modules or sub-systems needs to be determined either through the use of automated techniques or charting mechanisms. A local flow from module A to B exists if one of the following occurs:

1. A calls B.
2. B calls A, and A returns a value to B that is passed by B.
3. Both A and B are called by another module that passes a value from A to B.

13. Mean-Time-to-Failure

This measure is the basic parameter required by most software reliability models. Detailed record keeping of failure occurrences that accurately track time (calendar or execution) at which the faults manifest themselves is essential.

14. Software Documentation and Source Listings

The objective of this measure is to collect information to identify the parts of the software maintenance products that may be inadequate for use in a software maintenance environment. Questionnaires are used to examine the format and content of the documentation and source code attributes from a maintainability perspective.

The questionnaires examine the following product characteristics:

1. Modularity
2. Descriptiveness
3. Consistency
4. Simplicity
5. Expandability
6. Testability

Two questionnaires — the Software Documentation Questionnaire and the Software Source Listing Questionnaire — are used to evaluate the software products in a desk audit.

For the software documentation evaluation, the resource documents should include those that contain the program design specifications, program testing information and procedures, program maintenance information, and guidelines used in the preparation of the documentation. Typical questions from the questionnaire include:

1. The documentation indicates that data storage locations are not used for more than one type of data structure.
2. Parameter inputs and outputs for each module are explained in the documentation.
3. Programming conventions for I/O processing have been established and followed.

4. The documentation indicates the resource (storage, timing, tape drives, disks, etc.) allocation is fixed throughout program execution.
5. The documentation indicates that there is a reasonable time margin for each major time-critical program function.
6. The documentation indicates that the program has been designed to accommodate software test probes to aid in identifying processing performance.

The software source listing evaluation reviews either high-order language or assembler source code. Multiple evaluations using the questionnaire are conducted for the unit level of the program (module). The modules selected should represent a sample size of at least 10 percent of the total source code. Typical questions include:

1. Each function of this module is an easily recognizable block of code.
2. The quantity of comments does not detract from the legibility of the source listings.
3. Mathematical models as described and derived in the documentation correspond to the mathematical equations used in the source listing.
4. Esoteric (clever) programming is avoided in this module.
5. The size of any data structure that affects the processing logic of this module is parameterized.
6. Intermediate results within this module can be selectively collected for display without code modification.

IT DEVELOPER'S LIST OF METRICS

McCabe's Complexity Metric

McCabe's [1976] proposal for a cyclomatic complexity number was the first attempt to objectively quantify the "flow of control" complexity of software.

The metric is computed by decomposing the program into a directed graph that represents its flow of control. The cyclomatic complexity number is then calculated using the following:

$$V(g) = Edges - Nodes + 2$$

In its shortened form, the cyclomatic complexity number is a count of decision points within a program with a single entry and a single exit plus one.

Halstead's Effort Metric

In the 1970s, Halstead [1976] developed a theory regarding the behavior of software. Some of his findings evolved into software metrics. One of these is referred to as "Effort" or just "E," and is a well-known complexity metric.

The Effort measure is calculated as:

$$E = Volume/Level$$

where Volume is a measure of the size of a piece of code and Level is a measure of how "abstract" the program is. The level of abstracting varies from almost zero (0) for programs with low abstraction, to almost one (1) for programs that are highly abstract.

SUMMARY

This chapter provides a detailed reference listing for pertinent CM and software engineering metrics.

REFERENCES

[Halstead 1977] Halstead, M., Elements of Software Science, Elsevier, New York, 1977.

[IEEE 1989] IEEE Guide for the Use of IEEE Standard Dictionary of Measures to Produce Reliable Software, Standard 982.2-1988, June 12, 1989, IEEE Standards Department, Piscatawy, NJ.

[IEEE 1988] IEEE Standard of Measures to Produce Reliable Software, Standard 982.1-1988, IEEE Standards Department, Piscataway, NJ.

[McCabe 1976] McCabe, T., "A Complexity Measure," *IEEE Transactions on Software Engineering,* 308–320, December 1976.

[Pfleeger and McGowan 1990] Pfleeger, S.L. and C. McGowan, "Software Metrics in the Process Maturity Framework," *Journal of Systems Software,* 12, 255–261, 1990.

Note: The information contained within the IEEE standards metrics section is copyrighted information of the IEEE, extracted from IEEE Std. 982.1-1988, IEEE Standard Dictionary of Measures to Produce Reliable Software. This information was written within the context of IEEE Std 982.1-1988 and the IEEE takes no responsibility for or liability for damages resulting from the reader's misinterpretation of said information resulting from the placement and context of this publication. Information is reproduced with the permission of the IEEE.

14

CM AUTOMATION

Automating software configuration management (CM) consists of all the steps involved in introducing a CM tool into an organization and ensuring that it is routinely used on all projects. Implementing an automated CM system is a complex process. It affects all levels of the organization; therefore, an in-depth evaluation of the organization is required to determine how the processes and people will be affected.

Failure to understand the issues involved in the automation of CM technology is the main reason why organizations do not successfully deploy the CM tool. A defined strategy that addresses these complex issues becomes a necessity. Before beginning the automation effort, organizations must consider complex technical issues that may affect the effort. These issues include:

- The size and intricacy of the software system
- Client/server and Web-based systems support
- Heterogeneous hardware and software platforms
- Tool integration
- Legacy systems
- Interfaces to external systems

AUTOMATING CM

Many organizations thought that purchasing an CM tool would solve their problems, but soon discovered that there was no "silver-bullet" CM tool. To attempt to automate an immature CM process will not raise an organization's level of maturity as defined by the SW-CMM. In all likelihood, such attempts would only further amplify any process shortcomings and inadequacies. "Automating a money-losing process allows you to lose more money faster and with greater accuracy" [Ventimiglia 1997]. A tool alone will not solve an organization's CM problems and, in fact, Brown et al. [1999] have referred to the impractical reliance on a software configuration management tool as the "silver-bullet antipattern." Choosing the right tool to satisfy an organization's CM requirements will in itself fail if other issues are not addressed. To ensure an effective CM solution, an organization must address the complexities that it faces when implementing a change. These complexities include:

- *Technical.* These issues relate to how the tool operates, how it will be installed to maximize performance, and how it will be customized. For example, how will the tool be installed over the company's network in the client/server architecture given the different platforms, and how can it be used to suit the parallel development activities of the various teams?
- *Managerial.* These issues relate to the necessary planning, monitoring, setting of priorities, making of schedules, and resource management. For example, who will be allocated to fulfill the automation activities, how will the product schedules be affected, and who will implement the tool first?
- *Process related.* These issues relate to the way the company does its business. For example, what is the current flow throughout the company, and how do the developers, testers, QA personnel, build managers, document writers, etc. work together to ensure this flow?
- *Organizational.* These issues relate to the infrastructure in the company. For example, how will the tool affect the responsibilities of each department and their intercommunication?
- *Cultural.* These issues relate to the way people operate and achieve their goals. For example, what kind of culture exists at the company, and what is the best way to invoke change in that culture?
- *Political.* These issues relate to "who is stepping on whose toes." For example, how will the organizational boundaries change, who will be responsible for what, and how will people be rewarded based on making the change?
- *People related.* These issues relate to people's comfort level. For example, how will resistance be managed, and will people lose their jobs because of this tool? This complexity is closely tied to the cultural issue.
- *Risk related.* These issues relate to unknown information and tricky problems. For example, how will the effect of making concurrent changes, such as a new operating system and new hardware, as well as reengineering the legacy code, impact the new CM system [Dart 1994]?

The CM automation effort must be treated as a project with realistic goals and a defined schedule. CM automation can be successfully carried out using the phases listed below developed by Susan Dart, a former member of the environment team at the Software Engineering Institute (SEI). The phases provide structured guidance, identify tasks, and address the complexities involved with automating CM. Key activities are carried out during each phase of the implementation. At all phases, it is important to reinforce management's commitment to the automation effort and to provide training.

The phases are as follows:

Phase 1: Preparation and Planning
Phase 2: Process Definition
Phase 3: Tool Evaluation
Phase 4: Pilot Project Implementation
Phase 5: Roll-out to Other Projects
Phase 6: Capture and Communicate Improvements

Phase 1: Preparation and Planning

This is the stage most organizations fail to perform, thereby resulting in the unsuccessful automation of CM. The purpose of this phase is to plan for the automation activities, to establish management support, and to assess the status of current CM activities.

First, a CM automation team is created. The automation team is responsible for implementing the automation strategy and plays an important role in the implementation effort. The team monitors and participates in all phases of the automation effort. Members of the automation team typically include:

- A leader who is responsible for the automation effort
- A sponsor who has the authority to empower the team and provide the support required to tackle difficult CM problems
- A champion or technical expert who understands the technology
- Representatives from the user community

The automation team begins by developing the CM automation plan. The plan details the benefits of CM, outlines the automation schedule and resources required, defines the policies and procedures involved in the automation effort, establishes success criteria, and establishes the roles of the automation team.

Next, the requirements are defined and prioritized. Developing a clear understanding of the organization's strategic goals is required to evaluate the CM requirements. The evaluation of CM requirements should not be conducted in a vacuum. All members of the organization who will be affected by CM must be surveyed to identify their CM requirements and to determine their roles in the CM process. Careful attention must be paid to the training requirements of all people affected by the CM tool, process, and procedures.

In addition, all levels of management must be aware of the benefits of CM. Many times, this involves showing financial and scheduling benefits, that is, increase in programmer productivity by automating CM tasks.

Next, an inventory of present hardware and software platforms is conducted and future hardware and software platforms are identified. And, finally, a risk management plan is developed. This plan identifies risks that could affect the outcome of the automation effort. The automation team is responsible for identifying and addressing risks throughout the project.

Phase 2: Process Definition

The goals of this phase are to define the current CM process, evaluate the process, and define a new, improved process if required. The process is then analyzed to identify which areas would benefit from automation. A defined software change process is pertinent to the successful implementation of CM. Without a defined process, the organization will make little progress in the adoption. A variety of methods exist to define the process. Additional information on process definition can be obtained from the SEI, IEEE, or the Software Technology Support Center. During this phase, process-related requirements will be identified. These should be added to the requirements developed in phase 1, as appropriate.

Phase 3: Tool Evaluation

This phase consists of matching the organization's requirement to CM tools. Before the evaluation begins, tool requirements identified in phase 1 are refined and prioritized. The evaluation method is chosen, and test scenarios required to test the capabilities of the tools are developed. It is important to include representatives from all users' groups in the evaluation to gain a better understanding of how different groups will use the tool. Results of a study conducted by the Gartner Group determined that the cost of the software tool represents only 10 percent of the total cost of implementing a solution. Lost productivity accounts for 50 percent, and the remaining 40 percent of the solution is derived from the cost of manpower [Softool 1992].

Many tool vendors are expanding the functionality of their tools to meet the requirements of today's software development organizations. Several companies sell their products as a series of components. For example, the case product handles version control and process control, whereas the problem reporting function may be purchased separately. State-of-the-art CM tools may contain the following features:

- Version control
- Configuration support
- Process support
- Change control
- Team support
- Library and repository support
- Security and protection
- Reporting and query
- Tool integration
- Build support
- Release management
- Customization support
- Graphical user interfaces
- Distributed development
- Client-server development support
- Web support

The CM process should first be defined before tool selection. The tool should implement or automate the defined processes. The tool alone should not be used to define a project's CM process or procedures. It may take as long as six months to completely understand the functionality of a CM tool.

When evaluating CM tools, it is important to assess not just the functionality and robustness of the tool, but the *CM-readiness* of the tool vendor as well. Appendix Y provides a "Supplier SM Market Analysis Questionnaire" that should be filled out by each potential CM vendor. The key question is: Does the CM tool vendor practice configuration management, or do we have a typical case of the "shoemaker's children?"

Phase 4: Pilot Project Implementation

The purpose of this phase is to determine how well the CM tool, processes, and procedures satisfy the organization's requirements. A pilot project allows testing of the tool's functionality on a real project with real data. In addition, the pilot allows for the prototyping of processes and procedures and provides feedback on how users respond to the tool.

It is important to select a pilot that will address all areas of CM but not affect the project's critical path. The automation team develops standards, policies, and procedures, as well as ensures users are trained to perform their CM duties. Successes and failures are documented and compared to the success criteria identified in the automation plan.

Phase 5: Rollout to Other Projects

This phase involves incremental migration of the tool into other projects. Training and dealing with resistance to change are key activities of this phase. The CM tool, process, procedures, and training needs are examined and adapted for each project. The automation team implements, evaluates, and monitors roll-out activities. This stage is complete when CM is routinely used on all projects.

Phase 6: Capture and Communicate Improvements

This phase involves evaluation of automation activities, capturing strategies that worked, and making recommendations for process improvements. The use of measurements and metrics can be very beneficial during this phase. More details on CM automation can be found in "Adopting an Automated Configuration Management Solution," by Susan Dart in *Proceedings of the Software Technology Conference,* April 1994.

A SELECTION OF CM TOOLS

A variety of Web sites are dedicated to listing CM tools, including:

- Free or public domain tools: http://www.cmtoday.com/yp/free.html
- Tools FAQ from the *comp.software.config-mgmt* newsgroup: http://www.daveeaton.com/scm/CMTools.html
- Open directory project CM tools list: http://dmoz.org/Computers/Software/Configuration_Management/Tools
- CM Today Yellow Pages: http://www.cmtoday.com/yp/commercial.html
- Omniseek CM tools: http://www.omniseek.com/srch/{23049}

Table 14.1 contains a listing of CM tools compiled by the author's students.

Table 14.1 CM Tools Compiled by Students

1. Teamcenter solution for Pro/ENGINEER
Company: EDS, Electronic Data Systems Corporation
Company address: EDS Headquarters
                5400 Legacy Drive
                Plano, Texas 75024-3199
Company phone: 1-800-566-9337
Company Web site: http://www.eds.com/
Company e-mail: info@eds.com
Product description: The Teamcenter Engineering's Pro/ENGINEER solution
  authorizes the user to create, modify, browse, search, and access
  Pro/ENGINEER's parts, assemblies, and attributes.

2. Teamcenter Aerospace and Defense
Company: EDS, Electronic Data Systems Corporation
Company address: EDS Headquarters
                5400 Legacy Drive
                Plano, Texas 75024-3199
Company phone: 1-800-566-9337
Company Web site: http://www.eds.com/
Company e-mail: info@eds.com
Product description: It provides product management life-cycle capabilities,
  which are obtained from the best services, practices, and experience that
  deliver a fast solution to the customers, which are basically contractors and
  suppliers.

3. Teamcenter Engineering Management solution for AutoCAD
Company: EDS, Electronic Data Systems Corporation
Company address: EDS Headquarters
                5400 Legacy Drive
                Plano, Texas 75024-3199
Company phone: 1-800-566-9337
Company Web site: http://www.eds.com/
Company e-mail: info@eds.com
Product description: The Teamcenter Engineering's AutoCAD solution
  authorizes the user to create, modify, browse, search, and access AutoCAD
  parts, assemblies, and attributes.

4. Teamcenter Engineering Management solution for CATIA
Company: EDS, Electronic Data Systems Corporation
Company address: EDS Headquarters
                5400 Legacy Drive
                Plano, Texas 75024-3199
Company phone: 1-800-566-9337
Company Web site: http://www.eds.com/
Company e-mail: info@eds.com
Product description: The Teamcenter Engineering's CATIA solution authorizes
  the user to create, modify, browse, search, and access CATIA parts,
  assemblies, and attributes.

5. Unigraphics NX-Data Exchange
Company: EDS, Electronic Data Systems Corporation

Table 14.1   CM Tools Compiled by Students (continued)

Company address: EDS Headquarters

5400 Legacy Drive

Plano, Texas 75024-3199

Company phone: 1-800-566-9337

Company Web site: http://www.eds.com/

Company e-mail: info@eds.com

Product description: They enable Virtual Product Development across internal

AU: "they ensure" or "it ensures"? and extended customer and supplier programs. While maintaining simplicity, they ensure   totality and quality.

6. Femap

Company: EDS, Electronic Data Systems Corporation

Company address: EDS Headquarters

5400 Legacy Drive

Plano, Texas 75024-3199

Company phone: 1-800-566-9337

Company Web site: http://www.eds.com/

Company e-mail: info@eds.com

Product description: It has the ability to import, create, and edit CAD geometry, provides support for physical material and structural properties, and has the ability to apply loads and boundary conditions.

7. E-factory

Company: EDS, Electronic Data Systems Corporation

Company address: EDS Headquarters

5400 Legacy Drive

Plano, Texas 75024-3199

Company phone: 1-800-566-9337

Company Web site: http://www.eds.com/

Company e-mail: info@eds.com

Product description: E-factory is an open system designed to manage data from a variety of manufacturing applications.

8. AXALANT2000 SERVICE PACK 3

Company: EIGNER

Company address: EIGNER Corporate Headquarters

200 Fifth Avenue

Waltham, Massachusetts 02451

Company phone: 781-472-6300

Company Web site: http://www.eigner.com/

Company e-mail: info@eigner.com

Product description: It provides solutions for the entire management of a product, from initial to final post-manufacturing support.

9. Requirements Management and MRO Capabilities

Company: EIGNER

Company address: EIGNER Corporate Headquarters

200 Fifth Avenue

Waltham, Massachusetts 02451

Company phone: 781-472-6300

Company Web site: http://www.eigner.com/

Table 14.1 CM Tools Compiled by Students (continued)

Company e-mail: info@eigner.com
Product description: These solutions enable the company to manage even the most complex product projects.

10. Program Central
Company: MatrixOne
Company address: **MatrixOne, Inc.**
210 Littleton Road
Westford, Massachusetts 01886
Company phone: 978-589-4000
Company Web site: www.matrixone.com
Company e-mail: IR@matrixone.com
Product description: MatrixOne Program Central is a unified environment for coordinating multiple, large-scale programs to provide globally distributed collaborative participants with real-time visibility into all project information and status, from both MatrixOne solutions and other systems.

11. Engineering Central
Company: MatrixOne
Company address: **MatrixOne, Inc.**
210 Littleton Road
Westford, Massachusetts 01886
Company phone: 978-589-4000
Company Web site: www.matrixone.com
Company e-mail: IR@matrixone.com
Product description: It provides a safe environment for its complex projects and ensures quality.

12. MCad Integrations
Company: MatrixOne
Company address: **MatrixOne, Inc.**
210 Littleton Road
Westford, Massachusetts 01886
Company phone: 978-589-4000
Company Web site: www.matrixone.com
Company e-mail: IR@matrixone.com
Product description: It brings product developments and integrations right to the developer's disposal.

13. Collaborative Product Development solution
Company: MatrixOne
Company address: **MatrixOne, Inc.**
210 Littleton Road
Westford, Massachusetts 01886
Company phone: 978-589-4000
Company Web site: www.matrixone.com
Company e-mail: IR@matrixone.com
Product description: It coordinates and manages the complex outsourcing of organizational information, responsibilities, schedules, deliverables, product information, and business processes.

Table 14.1   CM Tools Compiled by Students (continued)

14. PVCS Version Manager
Company: Merant
Company address: **Corporate Headquarters**
             3445 NW 211th Terrace
             Hillsboro, Oregon 97124
Company phone: 503-645-1150
Company Web site: www.merant.com
Company e-mail: info@merant.com
Product description: It is used for source code control, software configuration
  management (CM), and protection of digital assets during any kind of change
  process.

15. PVCS Tracker
Company: Merant
Company address: **Corporate Headquarters**
             3445 NW 211th Terrace
             Hillsboro, Oregon 97124
Company phone: 503-645-1150
Company Web site: www.merant.com
Company e-mail: info@merant.com
Product description: It helps establish priorities, assign ownerships, manage
  hand-offs, and track issues from emergence to resolution.

16. PVCS Professional
Company: Merant
Company address: **Corporate Headquarters**
             3445 NW 211th Terrace
             Hillsboro, Oregon 97124
Company phone: 503-645-1150
Company Web site: www.merant.com
Company e-Mail: info@merant.com
Product description: It is used for version control, bug tracking, change
  management, and build capability in a single integrated suite.

17. KONFIG CM
Company: Auto-trol Technology
Company address: Auto-trol Technology Corporation
             12500 North Washington Street
             Denver, Colorado 80241-2400
Company phone: 303-452-4919
Company Web site: www.auto-trol.com
Company e-mail: info@auto-trol.com
Product description: With this tool, one can access the company database
  through a GUI, and maintain the security and integrity of product
  information.

18. Tech Illustrator
Company: Auto-trol Technology
Company address: Auto-trol Technology Corporation
             12500 North Washington Street
             Denver, Colorado 80241-2400

Table 14.1   CM Tools Compiled by Students (continued)

Company phone: 303-452-4919
Company Web site: www.auto-trol.com
Company e-mail: info@auto-trol.com
Product description: It captures the power of graphical knowledge for communication. It facilitates the creation of complex, composite artwork.

19. KONFIG NM
Company: Auto-trol Technology
Company address: Auto-trol Technology Corporation
12500 North Washington Street
Denver, Colorado 80241-2400
Company phone: 303-452-4919
Company Web site: www.auto-trol.com
Company e-mail: info@auto-trol.com
Product description: It provides a graphical application for data input, network design, and drawing output.

20. Asset Management System
Company: Auto-trol Technology
Company address: Auto-trol Technology Corporation
12500 North Washington Street
Denver, Colorado 80241-2400
Company phone: 303-452-4919
Company Web site: www.auto-trol.com
Company e-mail: info@auto-trol.com
Product description: It is an Oracle-form based application for managing asset information.

21. Graphic Report Builder
Company: Auto-trol Technology
Company address: Auto-trol Technology Corporation
12500 North Washington Street
Denver, Colorado 80241-2400
Company phone: 303-452-4919
Company Web site: www.auto-trol.com
Company e-Mail: info@auto-trol.com
Product description: It creates drawings that are directly related to the data in the KONFIG database.

22. Pathfinder
Company: Auto-trol Technology
Company address: Auto-trol Technology Corporation
12500 North Washington Street
Denver, Colorado 80241-2400
Company phone: 303-452-4919
Company Web site: www.auto-trol.com
Company e-mail: info@auto-trol.com
Product description: It has full update capability.

23. eB Doc Controller
Company: Spescom Software

Table 14.1 CM Tools Compiled by Students (continued)

Company address: Spescom Software
9339 Carroll Park Drive
San Diego, California 92121
Company phone: 858-625-3000, 800-992-6784
Company Web site: http://www.spescomsoftware.com/
Company e-mail: info-us@spescom.com
Product description: It enables users to categorize and question documents and related document data and performs document change management and allocation.

24. eB Item Controller
Company: Spescom Software
Company address: Spescom Software
9339 Carroll Park Drive
San Diego, California 92121
Company phone: 858-625-3000, 800-992-6784
Company Web site: http://www.spescomsoftware.com/
Company e-mail: info-us@spescom.com
Product description: It has the competence of separately identifying objective and efficient items and allows the connecting of documents, objective and efficient items in multidimensional structures.

25. eB Action Explorer
Company: Spescom Software
Company address: Spescom Software
9339 Carroll Park Drive
San Diego, California 92121
Company phone: 858-625-3000, 800-992-6784
Company Web site: http://www.spescomsoftware.com/
Company e-mail: info-us@spescom.com
Product description: eB Action Controller enables the contemporaneous administration and control of work involved in the design, release, and modifying/updating of data, documents, processes, and assets within an enterprise.

26. eB Explorer
Company: Spescom Software
Company address: Spescom Software
9339 Carroll Park Drive
San Diego, California 92121
Company phone: 858-625-3000, 800-992-6784
Company Web site: http://www.spescomsoftware.com/
Company e-mail: info-us@spescom.com
Product description: It provides a convenient and speedy search/view/print tool, which is implanted into Microsoft Windows Explorer and Internet Explorer (version 5 or above). Utilizing this perceptive and recognizable environment, users can generate and save various document or objective item queries as well as view and interpret associated electronic file(s) for the preferred document record in the search result list.

Table 14.1 CM Tools Compiled by Students (continued)

27. Windchill
Company: PTC
Company address: PTC
          140 Kendrick Street
          Needham, Massachusetts 02494
Company phone: 781-370-5000
Company Web site: www.ptc.com
Company e-mail: cs_ptc@ptc.com
Product description: It supports key product development processes,
  including configuration, release, and change management.

28. Pro/ENGINEER Wildfire
Company: PTC
Company address: PTC
          140 Kendrick Street
          Needham, Massachusetts 02494
Company Phone: 781-370-5000
Company Web site: www.ptc.com
Company e-mail: cs_ptc@ptc.com
Product description: It provides an enhanced user interface in addition to a
  perceptive workflow.

29. Agile Program Execution
Company: Agile
Company address: Agile Software Corporation
         One Almaden Blvd.
         San Jose, California 95113-2253
Company phone: 408-975-3900
Company Web site: www.agile.com
Company e-mail: info@agilesoft.com
Product description: Agile Program Execution is the foremost program
  management solution, enabling companies to convey and advance products,
  generate additional revenue, and continue spirited advantage.

30. Agile Configurator
Company: Agile
Company address: Agile Software Corporation
         One Almaden Blvd.
         San Jose, California 95113-2253
Company phone: 408-975-3900
Company Web site: www.agile.com
Company e-mail: info@agilesoft.com
Product description: Agile Configurator automates ISO 9000 compliance,
  saving time and money.

31. TeamTrack
Company: Teamshare, Inc.

Table 14.1 CM Tools Compiled by Students (continued)

Company address: TeamShare, Inc.
1975 Research Parkway, Suite 200
Colorado Springs, Colorado 80920
Company phone: 1-888-TEAMSHARE (888-832-6742)
Company Web site: www.teamshare.com
Company e-mail: inquiries@teamshare.com
Product description: TeamTrack helps you speedily mechanize your business
processes, handle issues throughout the complete life cycle of your projects,
and aid collaboration with all stakeholders across the venture and beyond
— apart from those of your industry. TeamTrack integrates to your other
enterprise applications, allowing you to force your investment and boost
work efficiency between teams.

32. Bk/Pro
Company: BitMover
Company address: BitMover, Inc.
550 Valley St.
San Francisco, California 94131
Company phone: 415-401-8808
Company Web site: www.bitkeeper.com
Company e-mail: support@bitmover.com
Product description: BK/Pro is a scalable configuration management system,
sustaining globally distributed expansion, detached operation, condensed
repositories, adjust sets, and repositories as branches.

33. Breeze
Company: Chicago Interface Group
Company address: Chicago Interface Group, Inc.
368 W. Huron, Ste. 2N
Chicago, Illinois 60610
Company phone: 312-337-3709
Company Web site: www.cigi.net
Company e-mail: cigi_sales@cigi.net
Product description: Breeze allows remote approvers to vote on packages of
changed source from any Web-ready workstation.

34. Cloud 9
Company: Chicago Interface Group
Company Address: Chicago Interface Group, Inc.
368 W. Huron, Ste. 2N
Chicago, Illinois 60610
Company phone: 312-337-3709
Company Web site: www.cigi.net
Company e-mail: cigi_sales@cigi.net
Product description: With Cloud 9, organizations can accomplish real
enterprise change management, considering legacy systems as well as strewn
elements. Cloud 9 allows organizations to leverage their savings in either
CA-Endeavor or IBM's SCLM to work for enterprise change control.

Table 14.1 CM Tools Compiled by Students (continued)

35. Source Integrity
Company: Mortice Kern Systems (MKS)
Company address: Mortice Kern Systems
                                185 Columbia Street West
                                Waterloo, Ontario, Canada N2L 5Z5
Company phone: 519-884-2251
Company Web site: www.mks.com
Company e-mail: info@mks.com
Product description: Available for use on small to medium-sized projects
  operating over a LAN, where it offers good, all-around capability.

36. TRUEchange
Company: TRUE Software
Company address: TRUE Software
                                300 Fifth Avenue
                                Waltham, Massachusetts 02451
Company phone: 781-890-4450
Company Web site: www.truesoft.com
Company e-mail: info@truesoft.com
Product description: TRUEchange is ideally suited for managing the ongoing
  flow of changes to production applications, particularly in large IT
  organizations moving mission-critical systems to the distributed world.

37. TeamConnection
Company: IBM Direct Sales
Company address: IBM
                                7100 Highlands Parkway
                                Smyrna, Georgia 30081
Company phone: 800-426-2255 x 31825
Company Web site: www.software.ibm.com/ad/teamcom
Company e-mail: n/a
Product description: A good CM tool with good all-around capability for most
   development team requirements, but not suited to remote development with
   closed repositories.

38. Endevor for MVS
Company: Computer Associates
Company address: Computer Associates
                                One Computer Associates Plaza
                                Islandia, New York 11788
Company phone: 1-800-225-5224
Company Wesite: www.cai.com
Company e-mail: info@cai.com
Product description: This is a good CM product for those already using
  Endevor for MVS.

39. Razor
Company: Tower Concepts, Inc.

Table 14.1 CM Tools Compiled by Students (continued)

Company address: Tower Concepts, Inc.
248 Main Street
Oneida, New York 13421
Company phone: 315-363-8000
Company Web site: www.tower.com
Company e-mail: info@tower.com
Product description: Razor is a tool best suited for projects using a single repository with well defined development and maintenance processes, or where problem tracking and change management are important requirements.

40. CCC/Harvest
Company: Chicago Interface Group
Company address: Chicago Interface Group, Inc.
368 W. Huron, Ste. 2N
Chicago, Illinois 60610
Company phone: 312-337-3709
Company Web site: www.cigi.net
Company e-mail: cigi_sales@cigi.net
Product description: With Cloud 9, organizations can accomplish real enterprise change management, considering legacy systems as well as strewn elements. Cloud 9 allows organizations to leverage their savings in either CA-Endeavor or IBM's SCLM to work for enterprise change control.

41. ChangeMan
Company: Serena Software
Company address: Serena Software
500 Airport Blvd.
Burlingame, California 94010
Company phone: 650-696-1800
Company Web site: www.serena.com
Company e-mail: info@serena.com
Product description: A strong contender for many mainframe sites, particularly those with distributed mainframe operations, or those requiring a high degree of integrity for software changes to the production environment.

42. ClearCase
Company: Rational Software/IBM
Company address: Rational Software
18880 Homestead Road
Cupertino, California 95014
Company phone: 408-863-9900
Company Web site: www.rational.com
Company e-mail: info@rational.com
Product description: ClearCase is suited to medium-to-large-scale Windows or UNIX development projects, or for organizations migrating from UNIX to NT development environments.

SUMMARY

Configuration management, given the level of detail required, is not possible without the use of an automated tool. This chapter discusses an approach to automation as well as provides a list of CM tools.

*Note:*The introduction to this chapter was adapted from the following report: Software Technology Support Center, United States Air Force, Ogden Air Logistics Center, Software Configuration Management Technologies and Applications, April 1999, www.stsc.hill.af.mil.

REFERENCES

[Brown et al. 1999] Brown, William, Hays McCormick, and Scott Thomas, *AntiPatterns and Patterns in Software Configuration Management,* John Wiley & Sons, New York, April 1999.

[Dart 1994] Dart, Susan A., "Adopting an Automated Configuration Management Solution," *Proceedings of Software Technology Conference*, April 1994.

[Softool 1992] Softool Corporation, Successful Software Strategies Seminar Series: Improving Your Configuration Management Implementation Strategy, Washington, D.C., 1992.

[Ventimiglia 1997] Ventimiglia, Bob, *Advanced Effective Software Configuration Management*, Technology Training Corporation, 1997.

Appendix A

PROJECT PLAN

ORSS SOFTWARE PROJECT PLAN

I. TABLE OF CONTENTS

1.0 GOALS AND OBJECTIVES

The Online Resource Scheduling System is a Web-based scheduling system. It is designed for colleges, universities, and schools. The purpose of this system is to provide an online service for the faculty to reserve any type of resource such as computer systems, VCRs, projectors, and videotapes. This scheduling system can accept the requestors' orders, make a schedule for the orders, and do some critical checks. It will enable faculty members to make their orders at anytime and from anyplace. The system will be able to create new orders and update old orders.

Configuration Identification: ORSS-01.

1.1 System Statement of Scope

General Requirements

The following general requirements were specified for our project titled ORSS:

- A Web-based application allowing users easy access and use
- The ability to originate or update resource reservations
- The ability to link to the faculty database to verify "authorized users"
- A method to maintain and update a resource database
- The ability to limit simultaneous reservations against total resources available
- A way to search for resources available
- A method to disallow duplication of "special" classrooms
- The ability to disallow duplicate orders from the same user
- A method to print a confirmation from the Web site
- The ability to send e-mail confirmations to the user
- The ability to print a daily list
- *Database administration interface.* There will be a need for the Resource Center office to maintain the database of the resources. There will also be a need to link to the faculty database to verify "authorized users." If neither of these databases exists, Global Associates will need to create them and train personnel in the maintenance and administration of both.
- *Online help.* We will need to develop an online help program for this system, which will include a detailed help menu and "online" telephone assistance.
- *Training.* We will need to conduct training for the Resource Center staff as well as all full-time faculty members. We may consider a training manual for the adjunct faculty, or conduct training sessions at times when they are available.

1.2 System Context

Multiple users will be using the product simultaneously and from many different locations. The only requirement is access to the Internet.

1.3 Major Constraints

Security

This project will be uploaded to a server and this server will be exposed to the outside world, so we need to research and develop security protection. We will need to know how to configure a firewall and how to restrict access to only "authorized users." We will need to know how to deal with load balance if the number of visits to the site is very large at one time.

Database

We will need to know how to maintain the database in order to make it more efficient, and what type of database we should use. We will also have a link to the faculty database to verify the users.

2.0 PROJECT ESTIMATES

This portion of the document provides cost, effort, and time estimates for the project using two estimation techniques: Process-Based and Lines of Code (COCOMO II model).

2.1 Historical Data Used for Estimates

We obtained the following data according to "2001 Computer Industry Salary Survey" from EDP Staffing Service Inc. for Northeast area.

Job Function: Web Developer (Java/ASP)
　　Low $U.S.79,500
　　Median $U.S.92,500
　　High $U.S.105,500
Job Function: Sr. Database Analyst/Admin.
　　Low $U.S.78,100
　　Median $U.S.87,200
　　High $U.S.105,900

Low is the salary paid at the 25th percentile of all respondents in this data set; median is the 50th percentile; high is the 75th percentile. Data: *2001 Computer Industry Salary Survey* (EDP Staffing Service Inc.) http://www.edpstaffing.com/salary.html

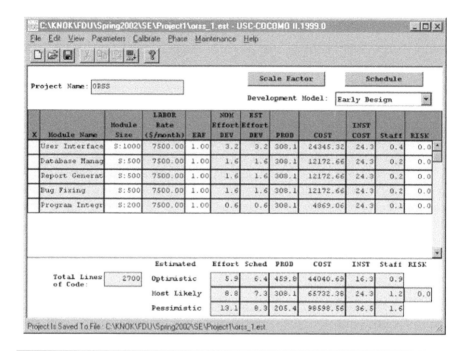

Figure A1 COCOMO II Model

We estimate labor cost per month for two Web programmers and one database analyst using the low salary level. (The low salary level is used due to the slowdown in the U.S. economy.) Note that 15 percent overhead is added in the average labor cost per month.

$$\$(((79,500/12)*2 + (78,100/12)*1)/3) * 1.15 \approx \$7,500$$

Note: Members' roles will be discussed in Section 5.0: Project Team Organization.

2.2 Estimation Techniques Applied and Results

Two estimation techniques have been used to generate two independent results for higher accuracy.

- Process based
- Lines of code (LOC) (COCOMO II Model) (Figure A1)

2.2.1 Process-Based Estimation

The process is divided into smaller tasks, for process-based estimation purposes (see Table A1). We estimated, in person-months, the effort required to perform each task. We defined the following software functions:

- User interface (UI)
- Database management (DB)
- Report generation (RG)
- Bug fixing (BF)
- Program integration (PI)

Based on the historical data we obtained, the estimated effort is approximately **7.5 person-months,** and the estimated project cost is $7500 × 7.5 ≈ **$56,250**.

2.2.2 LOC-Based Estimation

The estimates in Table A2 are based on "best-effort" estimation from previous programming experiences and existing software size.

The estimates for LOC are plugged into the COCOMO II formula for effort and duration estimation. The basic COCOMO II model is used in Table A3.

Results in Table A3 indicate that the total effort is 8.8 person-months to finish the project. Because we have three team members, we will finish the project in approximately **three months**. Based on that calculation, the estimated project cost will be $7500 × 3 × 3 ≈ **$67,500**.

2.3 Project Resources

2.3.1 People

This project requires two Web developers and one database analyst in order to be finished in time. The developers must have adequate experience in Web design and have knowledge of HTML, JavaScript, Photoshop, ASP (VB Script), and Access. Experience in how to set up a Web server is preferred. The database analyst should be able to analyze, design, and maintain an efficient and secure database. The candidates must also have good personal communication skills.

Table A1 Process-Based Estimation Table

| | Activity/Task | | | | | | | | |
| | | | | Engineering | | Construction Release | | | |
Function	Cust. Comm.	Planning	Risk Analysis	Analysis	Design	Code	Test	Cust. Eval.	Totals
UI	0.50	0.20	0.05	0.10	0.30	0.50	0.80	0.10	2.55
DB	—	0.30	0.10	0.20	0.30	0.20	0.20	—	1.30
RG	0.20	0.20	0.02	0.05	0.40	0.40	0.10	0.05	1.42
BF	0.20	0.10	0.02	0.10	0.10	0.30	0.10	0.05	0.97
PI	0.02	0.10	0.05	0.20	0.10	0.30	0.50	—	1.27
Total	0.92	0.90	0.24	0.65	1.20	1.70	1.70	0.20	7.51
% Effort	12.25	11.98	3.20	8.66	15.98	22.64	22.64	2.66	100.0

Table A2 LOC-Based Estimation

Functions		Estimated LOC
User interface	UI	1000
Database management	DB	500
Report generation	RG	500
Bug fixing	BF	500
Program integration	PI	200
Total estimated lines of codes		2700

Table A3 COCOMO II Formula

Project Name ORSS
Total Size 2700
Total Effort 8.764317

Overall	Schedule (%)	Schedule (Months)	Effort (%)	Effort	Staff
Plans and requirements	16.23	1.187959	7.00	0.6135	0.516434
Product design	24.12	1.764864	17.00	1.4899	0.84422
Programming	55.53	4.063943	63.65	5.5785	1.372679
Integration and test	20.35	1.489218	19.35	1.6959	1.138782

2.3.2 Minimal Hardware Requirements

Development

Three IBM PC or compatibles with the following configurations:

- Intel Pentium III 700 MHz processor
- 512 MB SDRAM
- 40G hard disk space
- Internet connection

User Server-Side

IBM PC or compatible with the following configurations:

- Intel Pentium IV 1.7 GHz processor
- 512 MB SDRAM
- 80G hard disk space
- Internet connection

User Client-Side

IBM PC or compatible with the following configurations:

- Intel Pentium III 450 MHz processor
- 128 MB SDRAM
- 20 GMB hard disk space
- Internet connection

2.3.3 Minimal Software Requirements

Development

- Windows 2000 Professional Version
- FrontPage 2000 or DreamWeaver 4.0
- Microsoft Access 2000

User Server-Side

- Windows 2000 Server Version with Internet Information Server (IIS)
- Microsoft Access 2000

User Client-Side

- Windows 98 or higher operating system
- Internet Explorer browser 4.0 or Netscape Navigator 4.0

3.0 RISK MANAGEMENT

3.1 Scope and Intent of RMMM Activities

This project will be uploaded to a server and this server will be exposed to the outside world, so we need to develop security protection. We will need to configure a firewall and restrict access to only "authorized users" through the linked faculty database. We will have to know how to deal with load balance if the number of visits to the site is very large at one time.

We will need to know how to maintain the database in order to make it more efficient, what type of database we should use, who should have the responsibility to maintain it, and who should be the administrator. Proper training of the aforementioned personnel is very important so that the database and the system contain accurate information.

3.2 Risk Management Organizational Role

The software project manager must maintain a track record of the efforts and schedules of the team. They must anticipate any "unwelcome" events that might occur during the development or maintenance stages and establish plans to avoid these events or minimize their consequences.

It is the responsibility of everyone on the project team with the regular input of the customer to assess potential risks throughout the project. Communication among everyone involved is very important to the success of the project. In this way, it is possible to mitigate and eliminate possible risks before they occur. This is known as a proactive approach or strategy for risk management.

3.3 Risk Description

This section describes the risks that may occur during this project.

3.3.1 Description of Risks

- *Business impact risk.* This risk would entail that the software produced does not meet the needs of the client who requested the product. It would also have a business impact if the product no longer fits into the overall business strategy for the company.
- *Customer characteristics risk.* This risk is the customer's lack of involvement in the project and their non-availability to meet with the developers in a timely manner. Also, the customer's sophistication as to the product being developed and ability to use it are part of this risk.
- *Development risk.* Pressman describes this as "risks associated with the availability and quality of the tools to be used to build the product." The equipment and software provided by the client on which to run the product must be compatible with the software project being developed.
- *Process definition risk.* Does the software being developed meet the requirements as originally defined by the developer and client? Did the development team follow the correct design throughout the project? The above are examples of process risks.
- *Product size risk.* The product size risk involves the overall size of the software being built or modified. Risks involved would include the customer not providing the proper size of the product to be developed, and if the software development team misjudges the size or scope of the project. The latter problem could create a product that is too small (rarely) or too large for the client, and could result

in a loss of money to the development team because the cost of developing a larger product cannot be recouped from the client.

■ *Staff size and experience risk.* This would include appropriate and knowledgeable programmers to code the product as well as the cooperation of the entire software project team. It would also mean that the team has enough team members who are competent and able to complete the project.

■ *Technology risk.* Technology risk could occur if the product being developed is obsolete by the time it is ready to be sold. The opposite effect could also be a factor: if the product is so "new" that the end users would have problems using the system and resisting the changes made. A "new" technological product could also be so new that there may be problems using it. It would also include the complexity of the design of the system being developed.

3.4 Risk Table

The risk table provides a simple technique to view and analyze the risks associated with the project. The risks were listed and then categorized using the description of risks listed in section 3.3.1. The probability of each risk was then estimated and its impact on the development process was then assessed. A key to the impact values and categories appears at the end of the table.

Probability and Impact for Risk

Table A4 is the sorted version of Table A3 by probability and impact.

4.0 PROJECT SCHEDULE

Following is the master schedule and deliverables planned for each stage of the project development life cycle, and their respective planned completion dates.

4.1 Deliverables and Milestones

Table A5 lists deliverables and milestones.

4.2 Work Breakdown Structure

Figure A2 shows a work breakdown structure.

Table A4 Risks Table (sorted)

Risks	Category	Probability (%)	Impact
Customer will change or modify requirements	PS	70	2
Lack of sophistication of end users	CU	60	3
Users will not attend training	CU	50	2
Delivery deadline will be tightened	BU	50	2
End users resist system	BU	40	3
Server may not be able to handle larger number of users simultaneously	PS	30	1
Technology will not meet expectations	TE	30	1
Larger number of users than planned	PS	30	3
Lack of training of end users	CU	30	3
Inexperienced project team	ST	20	2
System (security and firewall) will be hacked	BU	15	2

Impact values:

1 – catastrophic
2 – critical
3 – marginal
4 – negligible

Category abbreviations:

BU – business impact risk
CU – customer characteristics risk
PS – process definition risk
ST – staff size and experience risk
TE – technology risk

The above table was sorted first by probability and then by impact value.

5.0 PROJECT TEAM ORGANIZATION

The structure of the team and the roles of the team members are defined in this section. The project team organization is divided into four parts. First is the conceptual planning phase. Second is the software design and development part. The third section is editing/master testing and maintenance. The final phase of the project is training and user documentation.

Table A5 Deliverables and Milestones

Activities	Deliverable	From Date	To Date	Milestone
Meetings	Weekly meetings	02/04/02	05/07/02	05/07/02
Requirements	Assess functional requirements	02/18/02	02/22/02	03/01/02
	Demonstrate system	02/19/02	02/27/02	
	Evaluation of testing needs	02/25/02	02/27/02	
	Assess nonfunctional requirements	02/18/02	02/27/02	
	Final requirements specification	02/27/02	03/01/02	
Documentation	Quality assurance plan	02/04/02	02/06/02	05/03/02
	Project plan	02/07/02	02/15/02	
	Requirements document	02/18/02	03/01/02	
	Design document	03/04/02	03/15/02	
	User guide	04/30/02	05/02/02	
	Final project notebook	04/29/02	05/03/02	
	Maintenance plan	04/29/02	05/03/02	
Programmer training	Web design training	03/01/02	03/07/02	03/12/02
	Database design training	03/08/02	03/12/02	

Phase	Task			
Preliminary design	Brainstorming	03/13/02	03/14/02	03/20/02
Detailed design	Architectural layout	03/15/02	03/20/02	
	Design user interface	03/21/02	04/01/02	04/01/02
	Database design	03/21/02	04/01/02	
Coding	Build database	04/02/02	04/04/02	04/19/02
	User interface of campus version	04/05/02	04/19/02	
	User interface of in-house version	04/05/02	04/19/02	
Integration testing	In-house testing	04/22/02	04/26/02	04/26/02
Post-test	Necessary modifications	04/23/02	04/26/02	
	On-campus testing	04/29/02	05/03/02	05/03/02
	Necessary modifications	04/30/02	05/03/02	
Modification	"Clean-up" and finalized for delivery, additional "perks"	05/06/02	05/07/02	05/07/02
Faculty training	In-house training	05/08/02	05/08/02	05/10/02
	Campus training	05/09/02	05/10/02	

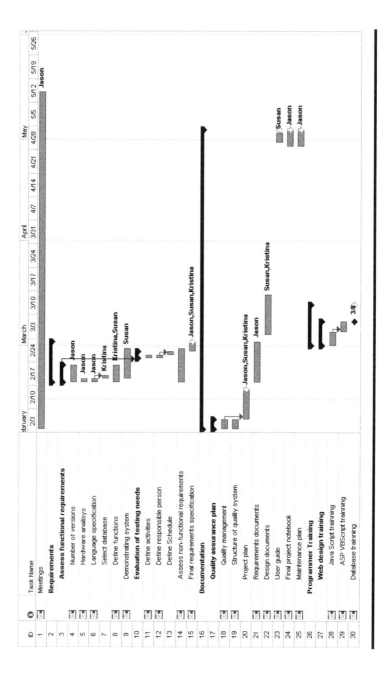

Figure A2a Work Breakdown Structure

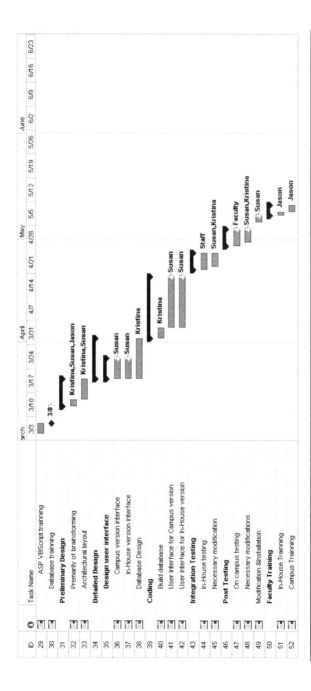

Figure A2b Work Breakdown Structure (cont'd)

5.1 Team Structure

We separate part of the team project by following the responsibilities of the team members and dividing the functions of the system.

Conceptual Planning

- Interview and specify software scope
- Database reengineering
- Overall process specifications
- Draft documentation

Software Design and Development

- Database design and development
- User interface and control facilities
- Function development
- Report generation
- Draft documentation

Editing/Master Testing and Maintenance

- Maintenance system
- Integration testing
- Report software errors
- System documentation

Training and User Documentation

- Training sessions
- User documentation

This organization of the project team allows the project planner to know the area of responsibility for each team member and all of the functions of the team project.

6.0 TRACKING AND CONTROL MECHANISMS

6.1 Quality Assurance Mechanisms

- Careful monitoring of the project

- Maintaining close contact with the client using weekly meetings and regular e-mail contacts to communicate
- Having periodic status meetings in which each team member reports on his or her progress and problems
- Careful monitoring of each phase as it relates to the milestone dates listed in Chapter 4
- Paying careful attention to all of the testing results, and making changes as needed as quickly as reasonably possible and then retesting the changes

6.2 Change Management and Control

- A change request is submitted and evaluated to assess technical merit, potential side effects, overall impact on other configuration objects and system functions, and the projected cost of the change.
- An engineering change order is generated for each approved change.
- Access control and synchronization control are implemented.
- The change is made, and appropriate software quality assurance (SQA) activities are applied.
- Appropriate version control mechanisms are used to create the next version of the software.

Appendix B

DOD ENGINEERING CHANGE PROPOSAL

ENGINEERING CHANGE PROPOSAL, PAGE 1

		1. DATE(YYMMDD)	2. PROCURING ACTIVITY NO.

3. ORIGINATOR NAME AND ADDRESS

4. DODAAC	5. CLASS OF ECP

6. JUST. CODE	7. PRIORITY

8. ECP DESIGNATION

a. MODEL/TYPE	b. CAGE CODE	c. SYSTEM DESIGNATION

d. ECP No.	e. TYPE	f. REV.

9. BASELINE AFFECTED
☐ FUNCTIONAL ☐ ALLOCATED ☐ PRODUCT

10. OTHER SYS/CONFIG ITEM AFFECTED
☐ YES ☐ NO

11. SPECIFICATIONS AFFECTED - TEST PLAN

	CAGE CODE	SPEC/DOC NO	REV.	SCN/NOR
a. SYSTEM				
b. DEVELOPMENT				
c. PRODUCT				

12. DRAWINGS AFFECTED

CAGE CODE	NUMBER	REV.	NOR

13. TITLE OF CHANGE

14. CONTRACT NO & LINE ITEM

15. PROCURING CONTRACTING OFFICER

16. CONFIGURATION ITEM NOMENCLATURE

17. IN PRODUCTION
YES NO

18. LOWEST ASSEMBLY AFFECTED

a. NOMENCLATURE	b. PART NO.	c. NSN

19. DESCRIPTION OF CHANGE

20. NEED FOR CHANGE

21. PRODUCTION EFFECTIVITY BY SERIAL NUMBER

22. EFFECT ON PRODUCTION DELIVERY SCHEDULE

23. RETROFIT

a. RECOMMENDED ITEM EFFECTIVITY

c. PLATFORMS AFFECTED

b. ESTIMATED KIT DELIVERY SCHEDULE

d. LOCATIONS OF SHIPS/VEHICLE NUMBERS AFFECTED

24. ESTIMATED COSTS/SAVINGS UNDER CONTRACT

25. ESTIMATED NET TOTAL COST/SAVINGS

26. SUBMITTING ACTIVITY AUTHORIZING SIGNATURE

26a. TITLE

27. APPROVAL/DISAPPROVAL

a. CLASS I

☐ APPROVAL RECOMMENDED ☐ DISAPPROVAL RECOMMENDED

b. CLASS II

☐ APPROVED ☐ DISAPPROVED

c. CLASS II

☐ CONCUR WITH CLASSIFICATION OF CHANGE ☐ DO NOT CONCUR IN CLASSIFICATION OF CHANGE

d. GOVERNMENT ACTIVITY

e. SIGNATURE

f. DATE SIGNED (YYMMDD)

g. APPROVAL

☐ APPROVED

☐ DISAPPROVED

h. GOVERNMENT ACTIVITY

I. SIGNATURE

j. DATE SIGNED (YYMMDD)

DD Form 1692-5

ENGINEERING CHANGE PROPOSAL, PAGE 2

ORIGINATOR NAME AND ADDRESS		ECP NUMBER
EFFECT ON FUNCTIONAL/ALLOCATED CONFIGURATION IDENTIFICATION		
28. OTHER SYSTEMS AFFECTED	29. OTHER CONTRACTORS/ACTIVITIES AFFECTED	
30. CONFIGURATION ITEMS AFFECTED		
31. EFFECTS ON PERFORMANCE ALLOCATIONS AND INTERFACES IN SYSTEM SPECIFICATION		
32. EFFECTS ON EMPLOYMENT, INTEGRATED LOGISTICS SUPPORT, TRAINING, OPERATIONAL, EFFECTIVENESS, OR SOFTWARE		

33. EFFECTS ON CONFIGURATION ITEM SPECIFICATIONS

34. DEVELOPMENTAL REQUIREMENTS AND STATUS

35. TRADE-OFFS AND ALTERNATIVE SOLUTIONS

36. DATE BY WHICH CONTRACTUAL AUTHORITY IS NEEDED

DD Form 1692-5

ENGINEERING CHANGE PROPOSAL, PAGE 3

ORIGINATOR NAME AND ADDRESS

ECP NUMBER

EFFECTS ON PRODUCT CONFIGURATION IDENTIFICATION, LOGISTICS, AND OPERATIONS

(X)	FACTOR	ENCL.	PAR.	(X)	FACTOR	ENCL.	PAR.
	37. EFFECT ON PRODUCT CONFIGURATION IDENTIFICATION OR CONTRACT				39. EFFECT ON OPERATIONAL EMPLOYMENT		
—	a. PERFORMANCE	—	—	—	a. SAFETY	—	—
—	b. WEIGHT-BALANCE STABILITY (Aircraft)	—	—	—	b. SURVIVABILITY	—	—
—	c. WEIGHT-MOMENT (Other equipment)	—	—	—	c. RELIABILITY	—	—
—	d. CDRL, TECHNICAL DATA	—	—	—	d. MAINTAINABILITY	—	—
—	e. NOMENCLATURE	—	—	—	e. SERVICE LIFE	—	—
				—	f. OPERATING PROCEDURES	—	—
	38. EFFECT ON INTEGRATED LOGISTICS SUPPORT (ILS) ELEMENTS			—	g. ELECTROMAGNETIC INTERFERENCE	—	—
				—	h. ACTIVATION SCHEDULE	—	—
—	a. ILS PLANS	—	—	—	I. CRITICAL SINGLE POINT FAILURE ITEMS	—	—
—	b. MAINTENANCE CONCEPT, PLANS, PROCEDURES	—	—	—	j. INTEROPERABILITY	—	—
—	c. LOGISTICS SUPPORT ANALYSIS	—	—				
—	d. INTERIM SUPPORT PROGRAMS	—	—		40. OTHER CONSIDERATIONS		
—	e. SPARES AND REPAIR PARTS	—	—	—	a. INTERFACE	—	—
—	f. TECH MANUALS/PROGRAMMING TAPES	—	—	—	b. OTHER AFFECTED EQUIPMENT/GFE/GFP	—	—
—	g. FACILITIES	—	—	—	c. PHYSICAL CONSTRAINTS	—	—
—	h. SUPPORT EQUIPMENT	—	—	—	d. COMPUTER PROGRAMS AND RESOURCES	—	—
—	I. OPERATOR TRAINING	—	—				

j. OPERATING TRAINING EQUIPMENT	—	—	e. REWORK OF OTHER EQUIPMENT	—
k. MAINTENANCE TRAINING	—	—	f. SYSTEM TEST PROCEDURES	—
l. MAINTENANCE TRAINING EQUIPMENT	—	—	g. WARRANTY/GUARANTEE	—
m. CONTRACT MAINTENANCE	—	—	h. PARTS CONTROL	—
n. PACKAGING, HANDLING, STORAGE, AND TRANSPORTABILITY	—	—	i. LIFE CYCLE COSTS	—

41. ALTERNATE SOLUTIONS

42. DEVELOPMENTAL STATUS

43. RECOMMENDATIONS FOR RETROFIT

44. WORK-HOURS PER UNIT TO INSTALL RETROFIT KITS

a. ORGANIZATION	b. INTERMEDIATE	c. DEPOT	d. OTHER

45. WORK-HOURS TO CONDUCT SYSTEM TESTS AFTER RETROFIT

46. THIS CHANGE MUST BE ACCOMPLISHED □ BEFORE □ WITH □ AFTER THE FOLLOWING CHANGES:

47. IS CONTRACTOR FIELD SERVICE ENGINEERING REQUIRED? □ YES □ NO

48. OUT-OF-SERVICE TIME

49. EFFECT OF THIS ECP AND PREVIOUSLY APPROVED ECPs ON ITEM

50. DATE CONTRACTUAL AUTHORITY NEEDED FOR PRODUCTION: FOR RETROFIT:

DD Form 1692-5

ENGINEERING CHANGE PROPOSAL, PAGE 4

ORIGINATOR NAME AND ADDRESS

ECP NUMBER

51. ESTIMATED TOTAL COST IMPACT (*Use parentheses for savings*)

FACTOR	NON-RECURRING	RECURRING		TOTAL (Recurring)	TOTAL UNDER CONTRACT	OTHER COSTS/ SAVINGS TO THE GOVERNMENT
		UNIT	QUANTITY			
	(a)	(b)	(c)	(d)	(e)	(f)
a. PRODUCTION COST/SAVING						
(1) CONFIGURATION ITEM/CSCI	—	—	—	—	—	—
(2) FACTORY TEST EQUIPMENT	—	—	—	—	—	—
(3) SPECIAL FACTORY TOOLING	—	—	—	—	—	—
(4) SCRAP	—	—	—	—	—	—
(5) ENGINEERING, ENGINEERING DATA REVISION	—	—	—	—	—	—
(6) REVISION OF TEST PROCEDURES	—	—	—	—	—	—
(7) QUALIFICATION OF NEW ITEMS	—	—	—	—	—	—
(8) SUBTOTAL OF PROD. COSTS/SAVINGS	—	—	—	—	—	—
b. RETROFIT COSTS	—	—	—	—	—	—
(1) ENGINEERING DATA REVISION	—	—	—	—	—	—
(2) PROTOTYPE TESTING	—	—	—	—	—	—
(3) KIT PROOF TESTING	—	—	—	—	—	—
(4) RETROFIT KITS FOR OPERATIONAL SYSTEMS	—	—	—	—	—	—
(5) PREP. OF MWO/TCTO/SC/ALT/TD	—	—	—	—	—	—
(6) SPECIAL TOOLING FOR RETROFIT	—	—	—	—	—	—
(7) CONTRACTOR FIELD SERVICE ENGINEERING	—	—	—	—	—	—

(8) GOV'T PERSONNEL INSTALLATION	—			—	—	—
(9) TESTING AFTER RETROFIT	—			—	—	—
(10) MODIFICATION OF GFE/GFP	—			—	—	—
(11) QUALIFICATION OF GFE/GFP	—			—	—	—
(12) SUBTOTAL OF RETROFIT COSTS. SAVINGS	—	—	—	—	—	—
c. INTEGRATED LOGISTICS SUPPORT COSTS/SAVINGS						
(1) SPARES/REPAIR PARTS REWORK	—			—	—	—
(2) NEW SPARES AND REPAIR PARTS	—			—	—	—
(3) SUPPLY/PROVISIONING DATA	—			—	—	—
(4) SUPPORT/TEST EQUIPMENT	—			—	—	—
(5) RETROFIT KITS FOR SPARES	—			—	—	—
(6) OPERATOR TRAINING COURSES	—			—	—	—
(7) MAINTENANCE TRAINING COURSES	—			—	—	—
(8) REV. OF TECH. MAN./PROGRAMMING TAPES	—			—	—	—
(9) NEW TECH. MAN./PROGRAMMING TAPES	—			—	—	—
(10) TRAINING/TRAINERS	—			—	—	—
(11) INTERIM SUPPORT	—			—	—	—
(12) MAINTENANCE MANPOWER	—			—	—	—
(13) COMPUTER PROGRAMS/DOCUMENTATION	—			—	—	—
(14) SUBTOTAL OF ILS COSTS/SAVINGS	—	—	—	—	—	—
d. OTHER COSTS/SAVINGS	—	—	—	—	—	—
e. SUBTOTAL COSTS/SAVINGS	—	—	—	—	—	—
SUBTOTAL UNDER CONTRACT	—	—	—	—	—	—
f. COORDINATION OF CHANGES WITH OTHER CONTRACTORS					—	—
g. COORDINATION CHANGES BY GOVERNMENT					—	—
ESTIMATED NET TOTAL COSTS/SAVINGS	—	—	—	—	—	—

DD Form 1692-5

ENGINEERING CHANGE PROPOSAL, PAGE 5

ORIGINATOR NAME AND ADDRESS

ECP NUMBER

52. ESTIMATED COSTS SAVINGS/SUMMARY, RELATED ECPs (Use parentheses for savings)

N/A	CAGE CODE (a)	ECP NUMBER (b)	COSTS/SAVINGS UNDER CONTRACT (c)	OTHER COSTS/ SAVINGS TO THE GOVERNMENT (d)
PRODUCTION COST/SAVING (Subtotal of Costs/Saving Elements from block 51a applicable to aircraft, ship, tank, vehicle, missile, or its sub-system)				
SUBTOTAL PRODUCTION COSTS/SAVINGS				
RETROFIT COSTS (Applicable to aircraft, ship, tank, vehicle, missile, or its sub-system)				
SUBTOTAL RETROFIT COSTS				
INTEGRATED LOGISTICS SUPPORT COSTS/SAVING REVISED REQUIREMENTS				
(1) ITEM RETROFIT (If not covered under "b") (Applicable to aircraft, ship tank, vehicle, missile, or its sub-system)				
(2) ILS SUBTOTAL (Applicable to aircraft, ship, tank, vehicle, missile or its sub-system)				
(3) OPERATOR TRAINER (Net total cost/saving from each ECP covering operator trainer)				
(4) MAINTENANCE TRAINER (Net total cost/saving from each ECP covering maintenance trainer)				
(5) OTHER TRAINING EQUIPMENT				
(6) SUPPORT EQUIPMENT (Net total cost/saving from each ECP on support equipment)				
(7) ILS PLANS				
(8) MAINTENANCE CONCEPT, PLANS, SYSTEM DOCUMENTS				
(9) INTERIM SUPPORT PLAN				
PROCURING	NON- RECURRING COSTS			

NEW REQUIREMENTS	ACTIVITY CODE	RECURRING COSTS	UNIT	QTY	TOTAL		
(10) PROVISIONING DOCUMENTATION	—	—	—	—	—	—	—
(11) OPER TRNR/TRNG DEVICES/EQUIP	—	—	—	—	—	—	—
(12) MANUALS/PROGRAMMING TAPES, SPARES, REPAIR PARTS *(For 11)*	—	—	—	—	—	—	—
(13) MAINTENANCE TRNR/TRNG DEVICES/EQUIPMENT	—	—	—	—	—	—	—
(14) MANUALS/PROGRAMMING TAPES, SPARES, REPAIR PARTS *(For 13)*	—	—	—	—	—	—	—
(15) SUPPORT EQUIPMENT	—	—	—	—	—	—	—
(16) MANUALS/PROGRAMMING TAPES *(For 15)*	—	—	—	—	—	—	—
(17) PROVISIONING DOCUMENTATION *(For 15)*	—	—	—	—	—	—	—
(18) REPAIR PARTS *(For 15)*	—	—	—	—	—	—	—
(19) SUBTOTAL ILS COSTS/SAVINGS *(Sum of c. 1 through c. 18)*							

	CAGE CODE	ECP NUMBER		
d. OTHER COSTS/SAVINGS *(Total from block 48d of related ECPs)*	—	—	—	—
TOTAL OTHER COSTS/SAVINGS	—	—	—	—
SUBTOTALS OF COLUMNS	—	—		—
SUBTOTAL UNDER CONTRACT	—	—		—
e. ESTIMATED NET TOTAL COSTS/SAVING (a + b + c + d)	—	—		—

ENGINEERING CHANGE PROPOSAL
NOTICE OF REVISION (NOR) AND NEW DOCUMENT SUMMARY PAGE

ECP NUMBER

DOCUMENT TITLE	DOCUMENT AFFECTED		CURRENT REV. LTR.	NOTICE OF REVISION NO. SPECIFICATION CHANGE NOTICE NO.
	CAGE CODE	DOCUMENT NUMBER		
1.				
2.				
3.				
4.				
5.				
6.				
7.				
8.				
9.				

SHEET 1 OF 1

10.										
11.										
12.										
13.										
14.										
15.										
16.										
17.										
18.										
19.										
20.										

ENGINEERING CHANGE PROPOSAL (ECP) (HARDWARE), PAGE 6		DATE (YYMMDD)	Form Approved OMB No. 0704-0188

ECP NUMBER

53. CAGE CODE

54. CONFIGURATION NOMENCLATURE

55. TITLE OF CHANGE

56. DATE AUTHORIZATION TO PROCEED RECEIVED BY CONTRACTOR (YYMMDD) →▶

S START DELIVERY   C COMPLETE DELIVERY   ▼ PROGRESS POINT

a. CONFIGURATION		1	2	3	4	5	6	7	8	9	10	11	12	13	14	15	16	17	18	19	20	21	22	23	24	25	26	27	28	29	30	31	32	33	34	35	36
	(1) Production																																					
	(2) Tech Manuals/Prog. Tapes																																					
	(3) Retrofit																																					
	(4) MWO/TCTO/SC/ALT/TD																																					
	(5) Spares/Repair Parts																																					

		1	2	3	4	5	6	7	8	9	10	11	12	13	14	15	16	17	18	19	20	21	22	23	24	25	26	27	28	29	30	31	32	33	34	35	36
b. SUPPORT EQUIPMENT	(1) Production																																				
	(2) Tech Manuals/Prog. Tapes																																				
	(3) Retrofit																																				
	(4) MWO/TCTO/SC/ALT/TD																																				
	(5) Spares/Repair Parts																																				
c. TRAINER	(1) Operator																																				
	(2) Maintenance																																				

DD Form 1692-5

ENGINEERING CHANGE PROPOSAL (ECP) (SOFTWARE), PAGE 7

DATE (YMMDD)

Form Approved
OMB No. 0704-0188

ECP NUMBER

57. CAGE CODE

58. COMPUTER SOFTWARE ITEM NOMENCLATURE

59. TITLE OF CHANGE

60. DATE AUTHORIZATION TO PROCEED
RECEIVED BY CONTRACTOR (YYMMDD) → ▼

S START DELIVERY   **C** COMPLETE DELIVERY   ▼ PROGRESS POINT

a. CONFIGURATION	1	2	3	4	5	6	7	8	9	10	11	12	13	14	15	16	17	18	19	20	21	22	23	24	25	26	27	28	29	30	31	32	33	34	35	36
(1) Software Engineering																																				
(2) Software Documentation																																				
(3) Software Replication																																				
4) Software Distribution																																				

		1	2	3	4	5	6	7	8	9	10	11	12	13	14	15	16	17	18	19	20	21	22	23	24	25	26	27	28	29	30	31	32	33	34	35	36
b. SUPPORT EQUIPMENT	(1) Software Engineering Environment Upgrade																																					
	(2) Software Test Environment Upgrade																																					
c. TRAINER	(1) Operator																																					
	(2) Maintenance																																					

DD Form 1692-5

Appendix C

SAMPLE DATA DICTIONARY

Data Dictionary Entries for the ACME Library Management System

Configuration Identification: ACME.001.DD001

Name:	Asset Database
Aliases:	None
Where Used/How Used:	Used by the Database Management System to process requests and return results to the Inquiry and Administration Sub-systems
Content Description:	Attributes associated with each asset including: ■ Asset Number = 16 numeric digits ■ ISBN Number = 16 alphanumeric characters ■ Library of Congress Classification Number = 16 alphanumeric digits ■ Asset Title = 64 alphanumeric characters ■ Author = 32 alphanumeric characters ■ Dewey Decimal Classification Number = 16 numeric digits ■ Media Type = Enumeration {BOOK | MAGAZINE | CDROM | REFERENCE} ■ Status = Enumeration {IN | OUT | LOST | MISSING | DUE_DATE} ■ Category = Enumeration {FICTION | NONFICTION} ■ Published = 32 alphanumeric characters ■ Keywords = 64 alphanumeric characters ■ Date Acquired = Date ■ Location = 16 alphanumeric characters
Name:	Membership Database
Aliases:	None

Where Used/How Used:	Used by the Database Management System to process requests and return results to the Inquiry and Administration Sub-systems
Content Description:	■ Attributes associated with each asset including: ■ Membership Number = 10 numeric digits ■ Member Since Date = Date ■ Last Name = 16 alphanumeric characters ■ First Name = 16 alphanumeric characters ■ Address = 64 alphanumeric characters ■ Phone Number = 11 numeric digits (1, area code, phone number) ■ Assets on Loan = Array containing 10 strings, each containing 64 alphanumeric characters ■ Assets Overdue = Array containing 10 string,s each containing 64 alphanumeric characters ■ Late Fees Due = 10 numeric digits ■ Maximum Allowed Loans = 2 numeric digits
Name:	Member Data
Aliases:	None
Where Used/How Used:	A file used to validate username and passwords for members, librarians, and administrator when attempting to access the system. The username and password entered is compared with the username and password in this file. Access is granted only if a match is found.
Content Description:	Attributes associated with each asset including: ■ Member Username = 16 alphanumeric digits ■ Member Password = 16 alphanumeric digits
Name:	Library Data
Aliases:	None
Where Used/How Used:	Files maintained by the Administrator and used to provide general information about the library.
Content Description:	HTML files for: ■ General Library Information (Policy, etc.) ■ Coming Events ■ Library Floor Map ■ Library Directions Screen
Name:	Database Catalog
Aliases:	None
Where Used/How Used:	Used by the DDL Compiler process.
Content Description:	Contains detailed information about the various objects in the databases, including tables, indices, integrity constraints, security constraints, etc.

Appendix D

PROBLEM CHANGE REPORT

(Type or Print)

1. Date	2. P/CR No	3. Originator
4. Activity Code		5. Telephone/Ext.
6. Title		

7. Category: (Circle)

Plans	Concept	Requirements
Design	Code	DB/data file
Test Info	Manuals	
Other____		

8. Priority: (Circle)

1   2   3   4   5

9. Problem/Change Description:

10. Corrective Action:		
11. Actions Taken: Status	Date	
12. QA Sign-Off		

P/CR PREPARATION INSTRUCTIONS

1. TITLE

Problem/Change Report

2. DESCRIPTION/PURPOSE

2.1 The Problem/Change Report (P/CR) shows essential data on each software problem/change detected. It also shows errors on omissions in documentation. Sufficient detail of the problem shall be reported to enable analysis and isolation or replication if necessary.

3. APPLICATION INTERRELATIONSHIP

3.1 P/CRs are used to record and report problems found throughout development. They are also used to report errors or omissions found in documentation. The P/CR is the basic input to the quality assurance program during the test and acceptance phase of the development effort. P/CRs on interfaces with other systems require joint resolution action.

4. PREPARATION INSTRUCTIONS

1. Date. The date form is prepared.

2. P/CR Number. P/CR Number assigned for control purposes.

3. Originator. Printed name of person originating the P/CR form.

4. Activity Code. The activity and code name or number of individual originating the P/CR form.

5. Telephone/Ext. Originator's office telephone number, and extension (if applicable).

6. Title. Name used to identify problem/change.

7. Category. Circle appropriate category associated with problem/change being reported.

Categories:

a. Plans – One of the plans developed for the project

b. Concept – The operational concept

c. Requirements – The system or software requirements

d. Design – The design of the system or software

e. Code – The software code

f. Database/data file – A database or data file

g. Test information – Test plans, test descriptions, or test reports

h. Manuals – The user, operator, or support manuals

i. Other – Other software products

8. Priority. Circle appropriate priority code, 1 – 5.

   Priority Codes:

1 a. Prevent the accomplishment of an operational or mission essential capability

  b. Jeopardize safety, security, or other requirement designated "critical"

2 a. Adversely affect the accomplishment of an operational or mission-essential capability and no work-around solution is known

  b. Adversely affect technical, cost, or schedule risks to the project or to life-cycle support of the system, and no work-around solution is known

3 a. Adversely affect the accomplishment of an operational or mission-essential capability but a work-around solution is known

  b. Adversely affect technical, cost, or schedule risks to the project or to life-cycle support of the system, but a work-around solution is known

4 a. Result in user/operator inconvenience or annoyance but does not affect a required operational or mission-essential capability

  b. Result in inconvenience or annoyance for development or support personnel, but does not prevent the accomplishment of those responsibilities

5 Any other effect

9. Problem/Change Description. Write a description of the problem/change. Develop a word picture of events leading up to the problem. Structure statements so that the programmer/test analyst can duplicate the situation. Cite equipment being used, unusual configuration, etc. Indicate consoles online, modes, etc., if applicable. If continuation sheets are required, fill in page _____ of _____ at the top of the P/CR form.

10. Corrective Action: A description, by the programmer/tester, of actions taken to resolve the reported problem or to complete the requested change.

11. Actions Taken: Enter the status/disposition and date to indicate the current status. When the status changes, line out the old status and date and enter the appropriate new status and date.

12. QA Sign-off. Signature by designated quality assurance (QA) organization member authorizing implementation of the corrective change(s) and certifying the correctness and completeness of the change(s).

Appendix E

TEST PLAN

Table of Contents

1 REVISION HISTORY

The following is a revision history table for the Dog E-DayCare™ system's Software Test Cases document.

Date	Configuration ID	Version	Description	Author(s)

2 INTRODUCTION

Software testing is a critical quality assurance step in the software development process. Testing of the Dog E-DayCare™ system is undertaken to identify errors in the product before delivery to the client. Thorough testing ensures the product will meet user requirements, minimizing costs in the long run, bolstering client satisfaction, and promoting repeat business.

The purpose of this document is to provide the Test Plan for the Dog E-DayCare™ system. The Test Plan details the testing strategy, metrics, artifacts, schedule, procedures, and test cases. Two sets of sample test cases have been developed: class test cases and integration test cases. Class test cases focus on classes and their operations within a specific sub-system. Integration test cases take a larger view of the product, uncovering errors that could occur as sub-systems interact.

2.1 Goals and Objectives

Dog E-DayCare™ connects dog owners to dog-care service providers, providing a Web-based national forum to locate, purchase, and monitor pet-care services. The mission of the Dog E-DayCare™ project team is to fill a gap in the current market for online pet-care resources. For dog owners, finding a service that meets their immediate needs can be challenging and for dog-care service providers, there is a vibrant market to be reached. Dog E-DayCare™ envisions bringing together dog owners and service providers nationally to support this challenge.

2.2 Statement of Scope

While there are several online directories of pet-care services, there are few E-businesses offering a service locator as well as the ability to purchase and monitor pet-care services online.

The Dog E-DayCare™ system will be released in two phases. In the first phase, it will allow dog owners to search for services within a radius of their choice, and based on their specific needs, whether they are looking for ongoing in-home daycare, daycare outside the home, or an afternoon walk and grooming. Once a dog owner selects a service, the Dog E-DayCare™ system will allow them to submit all required information, schedule, and pay for service.

Dog-care service providers who have registered with Dog E-DayCare™ will have access to the system through two different forums: client software on their workstations and/or the Web. The system will notify service providers of potential clients, allowing them to communicate with dog owners, and access submitted information. Service providers will be able to coordinate scheduling of multiple clients, e-mail clients, and bill clients.

Phase II of the Dog E-DayCare™ system will introduce a range of additional tools to facilitate communication between the Customer and Service Provider. Discussion forums, chat rooms, and instant messaging will greatly enhance Customer-Service Provider relations. In addition, with selected Service Providers, Customers will be able to view their dogs online and receive an update of their dog's status. Dog E-DayCare™ users will also be able to access dog-care "tips of the day."

Dog E-DayCare™ also envisions partnering with community service organizations. For example, matching puppy raisers to puppies for Guiding Eyes for the Blind, or potential dog owners to rescued dogs on behalf of Lab Rescue. Community service is the foundation on which Dog E-DayCare™ is built.

2.3 Major Constraints

As identified in the Software Requirements Specification, the most obvious limitation in this project is the experience of the project team. This is our first attempt at going through the entire software development life cycle and presenting a product that satisfies requirements in a timely and efficient manner.

Thorough testing is particularly imperative in this context.

3 TEST PLAN

The Test Plan provides an incremental and iterative process of testing from small to large. The Dog E-DayCare™ system has been designed using an object-oriented approach. Its smallest components are the classes that encapsulate the responsibilities and attributes associated with the system's various functions. Sets of related classes have been organized into sub-systems. The testing process first examines the classes within sub-systems through class testing, and then examines the interactions among sub-systems through integration testing. Integration testing is followed by validation testing and system testing, which are not addressed in this plan.

The overall system description, the test strategy, testing resources and output, and the test schedule are detailed below.

3.1 System Description

The Dog E-DayCare™ system is composed of seven sub-systems. Each sub-system has an associated interface and represents a set of related responsibilities. The sub-systems comprise the following:

- Application Controller
- User Management
- Resource Management
- Order
- Accounting
- Customer Relationship Management[1]
- Persistence

The Application Controller sub-system provides a "core" for the entire application. The controller acts as a "grand central station" for each and every process that takes place within the scope of the application. The User Management sub-system provides a central location for handling each and every piece of user data. The Resource Management sub-system provides the application with its overall scheduling capabilities. The Order sub-system has responsibility for supporting the ordering of products and services from Service Providers by Dog E-DayCare™ clients. The Accounting sub-system is responsible for processing the financial transactions. The Customer Relationship Management sub-system provides the application with the ability to provide an opportunity for interaction between the customers and service care providers.[2] Finally, the Persistence Sub-system is responsible for the storage, retrieval, and update of data.

The following System Collaboration Diagram (see Figure E1) demonstrates the collaboration or "hand-shaking" that takes place throughout the major sub-systems within the application. The Application Controller is the core of the system — each sub-system generates a request and a corresponding response. The Application Controller must handle both the request and the response. It receives the request, processes a response,

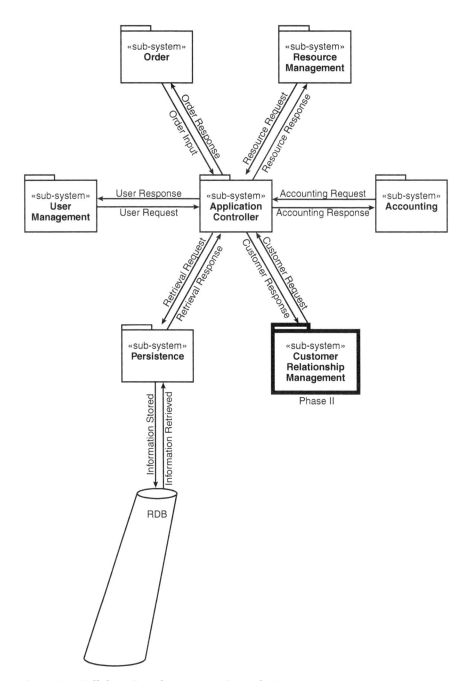

Figure E1 Collaborations between Major Sub-Systems

and returns the response to the calling function. This can also cross over into other layers of the system. For example, if the Accounting sub-system request requires information from the Ordering sub-system to accomplish its tasks, the Application Controller mediates between these sub-systems to formulate a response and provide it to the requester.

3.1.1 System Collaboration Diagram

Figure E1 depicts the collaborations that exist between the major Dog E-DayCare™ sub-systems.

3.2 Testing Strategy

In the object-oriented context, no operation can be tested in isolation. This poses a challenge to testers. The overall objective of testing is to uncover errors. The strategy for testing the Dog E-DayCare™ system entails first thoroughly testing the classes within sub-systems through Class Testing, and then testing interactions among sub-systems through scenario-based Integration Testing.

A set of test cases is developed for each testing method. Test cases for both Class and Integration Testing must exercise the requirements of the system. For the purpose of this Test Plan, a sample of tests has been developed and provided in Appendices E1 and E2.

Further details on Class Testing and Integration Testing in general are provided in Section 4: Testing Procedures, below.

3.3 Testing Resources

3.3.1 Staffing

The project team developing the Dog E-DayCare™ system consists of four members as detailed in the table below. Testing is a joint activity in which all team members participate. This activity is led by the Documentation Specialist.

Team Members:

- Web Software Developer, Sr.
- Web Designer, Sr.
- Documentation Specialist, Sr.
- Project Lead — Software Engineer

3.3.2 Tools

The hardware used for testing the Dog E-DayCare™ system will include:

- SQL Server 2000 to host the system
- Desktop (Pentium III processor) with a standard 56K modem to access the system
- Laptop to record test results

The software required for testing will include the stubs and drivers developed to support class testing.

3.4 Testing Metrics

It is envisioned that both Class Testing and Integration Testing will be carried out through several iterations, until all errors are corrected. For each iteration, Class Testing will involve recording the following metrics:

- For each class, indicators of test failure (as identified in the test cases)
- Number of failure indicators per class
- Number of failure indicators per sub-system
- A categorization of failure indicators by severity
- Number of repeat failures (not resolved in the previous iteration)
- Hours spent by test team in test process
- Hours spent by development team in correcting failures

Integration Testing will involve recording a similar set of metrics for each iteration; however, the level of analysis will be the scenario. In other words:

- For each scenario, indicators of test failure (as identified in the test cases)
- Number of failure indicators per scenario
- A categorization of failure indicators by severity
- Number of repeat failures (not resolved in the previous iteration)
- Hours spent by test team in test process
- Hours spent by development team in correcting failures

3.5 Testing Artifacts

The artifacts of testing that will be provided to the client include:

- Test Plan
- Test Cases
- Test Results
- Test Report

3.6 Testing Schedule

Class Testing will be undertaken as each set of sub-systems is completed. The following provides general information on how testing will be scheduled:

- PS+35 days: Class testing of Application Controller and Persistence sub-systems
- PS+49 days: Class testing of User Management and Order sub-systems
- PS+64 days: Class testing of Resource Management and Accounting sub-systems
- PS+86 days: Scenario-based Integration Testing

A detailed project schedule is provided in Appendix E3.

4 TEST PROCEDURES

4.1 Class Testing

Per the Project Schedule, class testing will take place as pairs of sub-systems have been completed. Test cases for class testing must be explicitly associated with the class to be tested. Effective class testing depends on well-articulated test cases. The test cases detail the:

- *Description.* The description includes the test's purpose (i.e., which class will be tested) and the particular responsibilities that will be tested.
- *Required stubs and/or drivers.* As stated previously, components of an object-oriented system cannot be tested in isolation. Because of the collaborations that must take place within and across sub-systems, class testing will likely require the use of stubs and drivers. In object-oriented testing, a stub is a stand-in for a subclass, and a driver is a sort of tester class that accepts test case data, passes data back to the class, and prints relevant results.
- *Test steps.* The test steps detail the events and states the system will move through from the beginning through to the end of the test.
- *Expected results.* The expected results provide the indicators of test success and test failure.

4.2 Integration Testing

Per the Project Schedule, Integration Testing will take place once all sub-systems have been developed and tested. Test cases are scenario based, reflecting what users need to do with the Dog E-DayCare™ system. Similar to the test cases above, the integration test cases detail the:

- *Description.* The description includes the test's purpose (i.e., which scenario or use case will be tested) and the particular sub-systems that must interact in order for the scenario to be completed.
- *Required stubs and/or drivers.* In object-oriented testing, stubs and drivers are critical for Class Testing. However, if Class Testing is thorough, stubs and drivers would not be necessary for completion of Integration Testing.
- *Test steps.* The test steps detail the events and states the system will move through from the beginning through to the end of the test.
- *Expected results.* The expected results provide the indicators of test success and test failure.

Sample Class and Integration Test Cases are provided in Appendices E1 and E2, respectively.

5 APPENDIX E1: CLASS TESTING TEST CASES

Class tests are developed for each sub-system of the Dog E-DayCare™ system. A sample of class test cases follows.

5.1 Application Controller Sub-system

The Application Controller sub-system provides a "core" for the entire application. The controller acts as a "grand central station" for each and every process that takes place within the scope of the application.

5.1.1 Test Case: ApplicationController:ApplicationController
CI: DD.0001.TEST001

5.1.1.1 Description

This test case tests to see if the user functions invoked by the Application user interface are handled correctly. This interface is invoked by the other sub-systems when actions are performed and requests are made from their respective user interfaces. This particular test focuses on the user who is attempting to search for a service care provider within their area.

5.1.1.2 Required Stubs/Drivers

The SearchUI will be invoked, which is part of the presentation layer.

5.1.1.3 Test Steps

1. The user will press the Search button within the Order sub-system, which is part of the presentation layer.
2. The user will be presented with a form to fill in his search criteria.
3. The search criteria will be concatenated to form a full select query against the database. ("Select * from ServiceSchedule where location = inputlocation and date/time = inputdatetime, and servicetype = inputservicetype order by location")
4. The user's search criteria will be evaluated and the results will be displayed.
5. The user may then select the desired result and schedule the service.

5.1.1.4 Expected Results

Test Success

The application controller sub-system successfully handles the routing of the information so that the query data goes from the presentation layer to the application controller layer, to the persistence layer, and ultimately is used to query the database. Success will be measured by the accuracy of the information (results) that is returned as a result of the query string.

Test Failure

1. The concatenation that must take place to form the query could be invalid, which would result in an error message when the query is executed against the database.
2. The route that the Application Controller must take may not be followed because of a flaw in the logic.
3. The query string concatenation may not be sufficient and the wrong data could be returned.

5.1.2 Test Case: ApplicationController:ApplicationController CI: DD.0001.TEST002

5.1.2.1 Description

This test case tests to see if the user functions invoked by the Application user interface are handled correctly. This interface is invoked by the other sub-systems when actions are performed and requests are made from their respective user interfaces. This particular test will verify that the user is able to view the Tip of the Day when the Tip of the Day button is pressed.

5.1.2.2 Required Stubs/Drivers

The CommunicationUI from the Customer Relationship Management module will be used heavily in conjunction with the communication class within that same sub-system.

5.1.2.3 Test Steps

1. The user will successfully log on to the system.
2. The user will press the Tip of The Day button.
3. The Tip of the Day will be displayed within the user interface.

5.1.2.4 Expected Results

Test Success

The success of the test must be measured based on the Application Controller sub-system's ability to use the system data to determine the date and use that as the query string to invoke the persistence sub-system that will use the query string against the database. The test passes if the Tip of the Day is returned with the correct Tip of the Day for today's date.

Test Failure

1. An exception may occur if the incorrect date is retrieved from the system time, and therefore the wrong Tip of the Day is returned.
2. An exception may also occur if the correct tip is displayed, but in an incorrect format.

5.1.3 Test Case: ApplicationController:ApplicationController CI: DD.0001.TEST003

5.1.3.1 Description

This test case tests to see if the user functions invoked by the Application user interface are handled correctly. This interface is invoked by the other sub-systems when actions are performed and requests are made from their respective user interfaces. This specific test will determine if the user's account balance is updated after a payment is made.

5.1.3.2 Required Stubs/Drivers

1. The PaymentUI, which is part of the presentation layer, must have been invoked and a payment must be attempted.
2. The Accounting sub-system and its interfaces will be invoked.

5.1.3.3 Test Steps

1. The user will successfully log on to the system.
2. The user will navigate to his account information.
3. The user will select the option to make a payment on his balance.
4. The user will be presented a form with which to indicate the amount of the payment and provide/change his credit card information.
5. The user will enter an amount and use his preregistered credit card information.
6. The user will press the Pay button.

5.1.3.4 Expected Results

Test Success

The success of this test can be measured by the user's new balance reflecting the recent payment on his account balance. Performing a query against the database to determine if the account balance is correct will test this. The ApplicationController is tested because it is its responsibility to ensure that the correct route is followed to ultimately commit the transaction and return a successful message.

Test Failure

1. An exception may occur if the query string is malformed. This could be caused by invalid data entry or faulty logic.
2. An exception may also occur if the update is unsuccessful and the query returns an invalid balance.

Test Case: ApplicationController:ApplicationController
CI: DD.0001.TEST004

5.1.4.1 Description

This test case tests to see if the user functions invoked by the Application user interface are handled correctly. This interface is invoked by the other sub-systems when actions are performed and requests are made from their respective user interfaces. This particular test will ensure that the service care provider can successfully update their scheduling information.

5.1.4.2 Required Stubs/Drivers

The Resource Management sub-system will be invoked, with particular attention to the resource class, which is used for scheduling.

5.1.4.3 Test Steps

1. The service care provider will successfully log on to the system.
2. The service care provider will press the Resource button.
3. A form will be presented, which will allow the service care provider to specify that it wants to edit its resource schedule.
4. The service care provider will modify its employee's schedule to exclude the dog shearer on a particular day.

5.1.4.4 Expected Results

Test Success

The success of this test can be determined by a query performed against the database, which is invoked when the user attempts to search for that particular service. The application controller will be tested because it is its responsibility to accept the query string and commit the transaction to the database via the Persistence sub-system.

Test Failure

1. An exception may occur if the concatenation of the query string is faulty, which will result in a database SQL error.
2. An exception may also occur if the user cannot see the changes updated via the user interface, which indicates that the test was unsuccessful.

5.2 User Management Sub-system

The User Management sub-system provides a central location for handling each and every piece of user data. This is very important in the parsing of the system.

5.2.1 Test Case: Security Manager :: addUser(in user : User) CI: DD.0001.TEST005

5.2.1.1 Description

The purpose of the test is to determine whether the Security Manager class is carrying out its responsibilities as expected. Security Manager is a critical class of the User Management sub-system, adding and removing users and their roles and authenticating users. This test will focus specifically on adding a user to the system.

5.2.1.2 Required Stubs/Drivers

Driver: IUserInterfaceDriver (smaller version of IUserInterface class)
   RegisterUIDriver (smaller version of RegisterUI class)

Stubs: UserStub (smaller version of User class)
   NextStub (captures next button clicks)

5.2.1.3 Test Steps

1. Open Register User Interface.
2. Input information "about you."
3. Click Next.
4. Input information "about your dog."
5. Click Next.
6. Input username and password.
7. Click Finish.
8. View results.

5.2.1.4 Expected Results

Test Success

1. Driver displays information entered for user.

Test Failure

1. Driver does not display information entered for user.

5.2.2 Test Case: Security Manager :: removeUser(in user : User)
CI: DD.0001.TEST006

5.2.2.1 Description

The purpose of the test is to determine whether the Security Manager class is carrying out its responsibilities as expected. Security Manager is a critical class of the User Management sub-system, adding and removing users and their roles and authenticating users. This test will focus specifically on removing a user.

5.2.2.2 Required Stubs/Drivers

Driver: IUserInterfaceDriver (smaller version of IUserInterface class)
    RegisterUIDriver (smaller version of RegisterUI class)

Stubs: UserStub (smaller version of User class)
    NextStub (captures next button clicks)

5.2.2.3 Test Steps

1. Open Register User Interface.
2. Select option to "cancel registration."
3. Input user id in appropriate field.
4. Click Remove.
5. View results.

5.2.2.4 Expected Results Description

Test Success

1. User id removed no longer appears in user id table.

Test Failure

1. User id removed persists in user id table.

5.2.3 Test Case: Security Manager :: authenticateUser(in user : User)
: Boolean
CI: DD.0001.TEST007

5.2.3.1 Description

The purpose of the test is to determine whether the Security Manager class is carrying out its responsibilities as expected. Security Manager is a critical class of the User Management sub-system, adding and removing users and their roles and authenticating users. This test will focus specifically on user authentication.

5.2.3.2 Required Stubs/Drivers

Driver: IUserInterfaceDriver (smaller version of IUserInterface class)
   LoginUIDriver (smaller version of LoginUI class)

Stubs: UserStub (smaller version of User class)
   NextStub (captures next button clicks)
   RoleStub (captures role assigned to user)

5.2.3.3 Test Steps

1. Open Login User Interface.
2. Input username and password.
3. Click Login.
4. View results.

5.2.3.4 Expected Results

Test Success

1. User enters a correct username and password, the welcome page appears, and the name of the user is displayed in the upper-right corner.
2. User enters an incorrect name and password. A login failure message is displayed asking the user to try again.

Test Failure

1. User enters a correct username and password. A login failure message is displayed.
2. User enters an incorrect username and password, the welcome page appears, and the name of the user is displayed in the upper-right corner.

5.2.4 Test Case: Customer :: getDogs() : Collection CI: DD.0001.TEST008

5.2.4.1 Description

The purpose of the test is to determine whether the Customer class is carrying out its responsibilities as expected. Customer's role in the User

Management sub-system is to receive, store, and return a range of information associated with a particular Customer. This test will focus specifically on retrieving a list of all dogs belonging to a particular Customer.

5.2.4.2 Required Stubs/Drivers

Driver: IUserInterfaceDriver (smaller version of IUserInterface class)
   SearchUIDriver (smaller version of SearchUI class)

Stubs: UserStub (smaller version of User class)
   NextStub (captures next button clicks)
   DogStub (small version of Animal Owner, Animal, and Dog classes)

5.2.4.3 Test Steps

1. Open Search User Interface (for Service Providers).
2. Input Customer ID.
3. Click Search.
4. View results.

5.2.4.4 Expected Results

Test Success

1. The names of all dogs owned by the customer are listed in the results page.

Test Failure

1. The names of dogs owned by other customers are listed in the results.
2. No dog names are listed in the results.

5.2.5 Test Case: Customer :: getInvoices() : Collection
CI: DD.0001.TEST009

5.2.5.1 Description

The purpose of the test is to determine whether the Customer class is carrying out its responsibilities as expected. Customer's role in the User Management sub-system is to receive, store, and return a range of information associated with a particular Customer. This test will focus specifically on retrieving a correct list of all invoices associated with a Customer.

5.2.5.2 Required Stubs/Drivers

Driver: IUserInterfaceDriver (smaller version of IUserInterface class)
 SearchUIDriver (smaller version of SearchUI class)

Stubs: UserStub (smaller version of User class)
 NextStub (captures next button clicks)
 InvoiceStub (smaller version of Invoice class)

5.2.5.3 Test Steps

1. Open Dog E-DayCare™ search interface (for Service Providers).
2. Enter Customer ID.
3. Click on Search.
4. View results.

5.2.5.4 Expected Results

Test Success

1. All invoices associated with the customer are listed.

Test Failure

1. Invoices associated with another customer are listed.
2. None of the invoices associated with the customer are listed.

5.2.6 Test Case: Service Provider :: addServiceOffering()
CI: DD.0001.TEST010

5.2.6.1 Description

The purpose of the test is to determine whether the Service Provider class is carrying out its responsibilities as expected. Service Provider's role in the User Management sub-system is to receive, store, and return a range of information associated with a particular Service Provider. This test will focus specifically on adding a service offering for a specific Service Provider.

5.2.6.2 Required Stubs/Drivers

Driver: IUserInterfaceDriver (smaller version of IUserInterface class)
 RegisterUIDriver (smaller version of RegisterUI class)

Stubs: ServiceProviderStub (smaller version of Service Provider class)
ServiceStub(smaller version of Service class)
NextStub (captures next button clicks)

5.2.6.3 Test Steps

1. Open Service Details page of Company Registration.
2. Input service information requested.
3. Click "add another service."
4. Input service information requested.
5. Click Next.
6. View results.

5.2.6.4 Expected Results

Test Success

1. Services information for particular company is present in Service Table.

Test Failure

1. Service information for particular company is not present in Service Table.

5.2.7 Test Case: Service Provider:: getAddress()
CI: DD.0001.TEST011

5.2.7.1 Description

The purpose of the test is to determine whether the Service Provider class is carrying out its responsibilities as expected. Service Provider's role in the User Management sub-system is to receive, store, and return a range of information associated with a particular Service Provider. This test will focus specifically on retrieving address information for a service provider.

5.2.7.2 Required Stubs/Drivers

Driver: IUserInterfaceDriver (smaller version of IUserInterface class)
SearchUIDriver (smaller version of SearchUI class)

Stubs: ServiceProviderStub (smaller version of ServiceProvider class)
NextStub (captures Next button clicks)

5.2.7.3 Test Steps

1. Open Dog E-DayCare™ search interface (for Customers).
2. Enter name of Service Provider.
3. Click on Search.
4. View results.

5.2.7.4 Expected Results

Test Success

1. If address information is available, correct address information is displayed in search results.
2. If address information is not available, no address information is displayed in search results.

Test Failure

1. If address information is available, incorrect address information is displayed in search results.
2. If address information is not available, someone's address information is displayed in search results.

5.3 Resource Management Sub-System

This Resource Management sub-system provides the application with its overall scheduling capabilities. It uses various respective classes and sub-systems to ensure that the user has up-to-date information regarding the services of interest.

5.3.1 Test Case: ResourceUI :: showCreate()
CI: DD.0001.TEST012

5.3.1.1 Description

The purpose of this test case is to test the Resource Management User Interface class' (ResourceUI) showCreate() method to determine if it can display the "Register Company – resource details" screen (see SDS section 11.22) as an add screen.

5.3.1.2 Required Stubs/Drivers

Driver: IUserInterfaceDriver (smaller version of IUserInterface class)

Stubs: ResourceStub (smaller version of Resource class)
  NextStub (captures next button clicks)
  OtherButtonsStub (captures other buttons clicked)

5.3.1.3 Test Steps

1. Execute the IUserInterfaceDriver in a Web browser.
2. Select "Staff" from the Resource Type drop-down list.
3. Enter a Staff Member's First Name (if resource type = Staff).
4. Enter a Staff Member's Last Name (if resource type = Staff).
5. Select an item in the Position drop-down list.
6. Determine that the Height, Width, and Length fields are protected.
7. Press the Next button.

5.3.1.4 Expected Results

Test Success

1. The IUserInterfaceDriver should display the "Register Company – resource details" screen in the Web browser.
2. The Resource Type drop-down list should contain an entry for Staff and permit its selection.
3. The Staff Member First Name should be enterable.
4. The Staff Member Last Name should be enterable.
5. The Position drop-down list should be enterable and permit the selection of one of its items.
6. The Height, Width, and Length fields should be protected.
7. The Next stub should return a basic Web page.

Test Failure

1. Report all failures.

5.3.2 Test Case: ResourceUI :: showEdit()
CI: DD.0001.TEST013

5.3.2.1 Description

The purpose of this test case is to test the Resource Management User Interface class' (ResourceUI) showEdit() method to determine if it can display the "Register Company – resource details" screen (see SDS section 11.22) as an edit screen.

5.3.2.2 Required Stubs/Drivers

Driver: IUserInterfaceDriver (smaller version of IUserInterface class)

Stubs: ResourceStub (smaller version of Resource class)
  NextStub (captures Next button clicks)
  OtherButtonsStub (captures other buttons clicked)

5.3.2.3 Test Steps

1. Execute the IUserInterfaceDriver in a Web browser.
2. Determine that "Staff" is displayed from the Resource Type drop-down list.
3. Update the Staff Member's First Name (if resource type = Staff).
4. Update the Staff Member's Last Name (if resource type = Staff).
5. Select another item in the Position drop-down list.
6. Determine that the Height, Width, and Length fields are protected.
7. Press the Next button.

5.3.2.4 Expected Results

Test Success

1. The IUserInterfaceDriver should display the "Register Company – resource details" screen in the Web browser.
2. The Resource Type drop-down list should display an entry for Staff.
3. The Staff Member First Name should be updated.
4. The Staff Member Last Name should be updated.
5. The Position drop-down list should be enterable and permit the selection of one of its items.
6. The Height, Width, and Length fields should be protected.
7. The Next stub should return a basic Web page.

Test Failure

1. Report all failures.

5.3.3 Test Case: ResourceUI :: showSearch()
CI: DD.0001.TEST014

5.3.3.1 Description

The purpose of this test case is to test the Resource Management User Interface class's (ResourceUI) showSearch() method to determine if it can display the Resource Search screen (example not present in SDS).

5.3.3.2 Required Stubs/Drivers

Driver: IUserInterfaceDriver (smaller version of IUserInterface class)

Stubs: ServiceProviderStub (smaller version of ServiceProvider class)
  ResourceStub (smaller version of Resource class)
  SearchStub (captures Search button clicks)
  OtherButtonsStub (captures other buttons clicked)

5.3.3.3 Test Steps

1. Execute the IUserInterfaceDriver in a Web browser.
2. Determine that the Service Provider drop-down list displayed.
3. Determine that the Resource Type drop-down list displayed.
4. Select a service provider from the Service Provider drop-down list.
5. Select a resource type from the Resource Type drop-down list.
6. Press the Search button.

5.3.3.4 Expected Results

Test Success

1. The IUserInterfaceDriver should display the "Register Company – resource details" screen in the Web browser.
2. The Service Provider drop-down list should display service providers.
3. The Resource Type drop-down list should display the resource types that the selected service provider supports.
4. The service provider selected should be visible in the drop-down list.
5. The resource type selected should be visible in the drop-down list.
6. The Search stub should return a basic Web page.

Test Failure

1. Report all failures.

5.4 Order Sub-system

The Order sub-system has responsibility for supporting the ordering of products and services from Service Providers by Dog E-DayCare™ clients.

5.4.1 Test Case: OrderUI :: showCreate()
CI: DD.0001.TEST015

5.4.1.1 Description

The purpose of this test case is to test the Order User Interface class' (OrderUI) showCreate() method to determine if it can display the "Order – initiate order" screen (see SDS section 11.10) and if the drop-down lists are populated.

5.4.1.2 Required Stubs/Drivers

Driver: IUserInterfaceDriver (smaller version of IUserInterface class)

Stubs: OrderStub (smaller version of Order class)
    ServiceProviderStub (smaller version of ServiceProvider class)
    ServiceStub (smaller version of Service class)
    AppointmentStub (smaller version of Appointment class)
    OtherButtonsStub (captures other buttons clicked)

5.4.1.3 Test Steps

1. Execute the IUserInterfaceDriver in a Web browser.
2. Select an item in the Service Provider drop-down list.
3. Select an item in the Service drop-down list.
4. Select an item in the Service Duration drop-down list.
5. Select an item in the Time Frame drop-down list.

5.4.1.4 Expected Results

Test Success

1. The IUserInterfaceDriver should display the "Order – initiate order" screen in the Web browser.
2. The Service Provider drop-down list should contain a list of service providers.
3. The Service drop-down list should contain a list of services offered by the selected service provider.
4. The Service Duration drop-down list should contain a list of service durations available for the selected service.
5. The Time Frame drop-down list should contain a list of all openings for the selected service.

Test Failure

1. Report all failures.

5.4.2 Test Case: OrderUI :: showEdit()
CI: DD.0001.TEST016

5.4.2.1 Description

The purpose of this test case is to test the Order User Interface class' (OrderUI) showEdit() method to determine if it can display the "Order – order details" screen (see SDS section 11.12).

5.4.2.2 Required Stubs/Drivers

Driver: IUserInterfaceDriver (smaller version of IUserInterface class)

Stubs: OrderStub (smaller version of Order class)
OtherButtonsStub (captures other buttons clicked)

5.4.2.3 Test Steps

1. Execute the IUserInterfaceDriver in a Web browser.
2. Determine if the correct Service Provider is displayed.
3. Determine if the correct Service is displayed.
4. Determine if the correct Location is displayed.
5. Determine if the correct Phone Number is displayed.
6. Determine if the correct Email Address is displayed.
7. Determine if the correct Appointment is displayed.

5.4.2.4 Expected Results

Test Success

1. The IUserInterfaceDriver should display the "Order – order details" screen in the Web browser.
2. The Service Provider name should display.
3. The Service name should display.
4. The Location should display.
5. The Phone Number should display.
6. The Email Address should display.
7. The Appointment should display.

Test Failure

1. Report all failures.

5.4.3 Test Case: OrderUI :: showSearch()
CI: DD.0001.TEST017

5.4.3.1 Description

The purpose of this test case is to test the Order User Interface class' (OrderUI) showSearch() method to determine if it can display the "Search" screen (see SDS section 11.26) and conduct a search using a stub to display the "results."

5.4.3.2 Required Stubs/Drivers

Driver: IUserInterfaceDriver (smaller version of IUserInterface class)

Stubs: SearchStub (captures Search button clicks)
OtherButtonsStub (captures other buttons clicked)

5.4.3.3 Test Steps

1. Execute the IUserInterfaceDriver in a Web browser.
2. Enter a value in the Customer ID field.
3. Press the Search button.
4. Enter a value in the Customer Name field.
5. Press the Search button.
6. Enter a value in the Order ID field.
7. Press the Search button.
8. Enter a value in the Invoice ID field.
9. Press the Search button.

5.4.3.4 Expected Results

Test Success

1. The IUserInterfaceDriver should display the "Search" screen in the Web browser.
2. The screen should permit entry of a Customer ID.
3. The Search stub should return a basic Web page.
4. The screen should permit entry of a Customer Name.
5. The Search stub should return a basic Web page.
6. The screen should permit entry of an Order ID.

7. The Search stub should return a basic Web page.
8. The screen should permit entry of an Invoice ID.
9. The Search stub should return a basic Web page.

Test Failure

1. Report all failures.

5.4.4 Test Case: OrderUI :: showList()
CI: DD.0001.TEST018

5.4.4.1 Description

The purpose of this test case is to test the Order User Interface class' (OrderUI) showList() method to determine if it can display the "Search Results – Customer Search Results" screen (see SDS section 11.27).

5.4.4.2 Required Stubs/Drivers

Driver: IUserInterfaceDriver (smaller version of IUserInterface class)

Stubs: OrderStub (smaller version of Order class)
    InvoiceStub (smaller version of the Invoice class)
    AddressStub(smaller version of the Address class)
    OtherButtonsStub (captures other buttons clicked)

5.4.4.3 Test Steps

1. Execute the IUserInterfaceDriver in a Web browser.
2. Determine if the correct Customer Name is displayed.
3. Determine if the correct Address is displayed.
4. Determine if the correct Email Address is displayed.
5. Determine if the correct Phone Number is displayed.
6. Determine if the correct Order Numbers are displayed.
7. Determine if the correct Invoice Numbers are displayed.

5.4.4.4 Expected Results

Test Success

1. The IUserInterfaceDriver should display the "Search Results – Customer Search Results" screen in the Web browser.
2. The Customer Name should display.

3. The Address should display.
4. The Email Address should display
5. The Phone Number should display.
6. The Order Numbers should display.
7. The Invoice Numbers should display.

Test Failure

1. Report all failures.

5.4.5 Test Case: OrderLineItem
CI: DD.0001.TEST019

5.4.5.1 Description

The purpose of this test case is to test the OrderLineItem class to determine if it correctly handles order-line-item related data.

5.4.5.2 Required Stubs/Drivers

Driver: OrderLineItem Test Driver: a small console application that assigns a value to the OrderLineItem and prints out the result in a console window.

Stub: N/A

5.4.5.3 Test Steps

1. Execute the OrderLineItem Test Driver in a console window. The test driver application should execute the following methods of OrderLineItem class:
   - SetServiceName()
   - SetUnitPrice()
   - SetQuantity()
   - GetServiceName()
   - GetUnitPrice()
   - GetQuantity()
   - GetTotalPrice()
   - GetTax()
   - GetTotalPriceWithTax()
2. Review the console printout to see if all property values are correctly assigned and returned.

3. Review the console printout to see if the getTotalPrice method return value is the result of Quantity multiply UnitPrice and then add Tax.

5.4.5.4 Expected Results

Test Success

1. All property values assigned match property value returned.
2. The total price matches the calculation from quantity, unit price, and tax values.

Test Failure

1. Property value assigned does not match property value returned.
2. Total price does not match the calculation from quantity, unit price, and tax values.

5.4.6 Test Case: ServiceResourceRequirement CI: DD.0001.TEST020

5.4.6.1 Description

The purpose of this test case is to test the ServiceResourceRequirement class to determine if it correctly handles the service resource requirement related data.

5.4.6.2 Required Stubs/Drivers

Driver: ServiceResourceRequirement Test Driver: a small console application that assigns a value to ServiceResourceRequirement and prints out the result in a console window.

Stubs: N/A

5.4.6.3 Test Steps

1. Execute the ServiceResourceRequirement Test Driver in a console window. The test driver application should execute the following methods of Order class:
   ■ SetQuantity()
   ■ SetPercentage()
   ■ SetResourceType()

■ GetQuantity()
■ GetPercentage()
■ GetResourceType()

2. Review the console printout to see if all property values are correctly assigned and returned.

5.4.6.4 Expected Results

Test Success

1. All property values assigned match property values returned.
2. If quantity value is less than 1, an exception is raised.
3. If percentage value is greater than 1, an exception is raised.

Test Failure

1. Property values assigned do not match property values returned.
2. If quantity value is less than 1, no exception is raised.
3. If percentage value is greater than 1, no exception is raised.

5.4.7 Test Case: Service
CI: DD.0001.TEST021

5.4.7.1 Description

The purpose of this test case is to test the Service class to determine if it correctly handles the service-related data.

5.4.7.2 Required Stubs/Drivers

Driver: Service Test Driver: a small console application that assigns a value to the order and prints out the result in a console window.

Stubs: ServiceResourceRequirement class or stub

5.4.7.3 Test Steps

1. Execute the Service Test Driver in a console window. The test driver application should execute the following methods of Order class:
   ■ SetName()
   ■ SetDescription()
   ■ SetUnitCost()
   ■ GetResourceRequirement()

- GetName()
- GetDescription()
- GetUnitCost()

2. Review the console printout to see if all property values are correctly assigned and returned.

5.4.7.4 Expected Results

Test Success

1. All property values assigned match property value returned.

Test Failure

1. Property values assigned do not match property value returned.

5.4.8 Test Case: Order
CI: DD.0001.TEST022

5.4.8.1 Description

The purpose of this test case is to test the Order class to determine if it correctly handles the order-related data.

5.4.8.2 Required Stubs/Drivers

Driver: Order Test Driver: a small console application that assigns a value to the order and prints out the result in a console window.

Stubs: OrderLineItem class or stub
    Invoice class or stub
    Payment class or stub
    Customer class or stub

5.4.8.3 Test Steps

1. Execute the Order Test Driver in a console window. The test driver application should execute the following methods of Order class:
   - SetOrderDateTime
   - SetCompletionDateTime
   - SetOrderStatus
   - GetOrderLineItems
   - GetTotalPrice

- GetCustomer
- GetPayment
- GetInvoice
2. Review the console printout to see if all property values are correctly assigned and returned.
3. Review the console printout to see if the getTotalPrice method return value is the total of all OrderLineItem prices.

5.4.8.4 Expected Results

Test Success

1. All property values assigned match property value returned.
2. The total price matches the calculation from order line items.

Test Failure

1. Property values assigned do not match property value returned.
2. Total price does not match the calculation from order line items.

5.5 Accounting Sub-system

The Accounting sub-system is responsible for processing the financial transactions.

5.5.1 Test Case: Accounting:InvoicePrint
CI: DD.0001.TEST023

5.5.1.1 Description

The purpose of this test is to determine if the service care provider is able to print the invoices for billing.

5.5.1.2 Required Stubs/Drivers

1. There must be orders placed against the service care provider in question via the order sub-system and the OrderService class.
2. The Accounting sub-system will be invoked, with the invoice class in particular.

5.5.1.3 Test Steps

1. A test customer order must be placed against a predetermined service care provider.
2. The service care provider must log on to the system successfully.
3. The service care provider must select the invoices that need to be printed.

5.5.1.4 Expected Results

Test Success

1. The invoices printing out successfully with the correct data will determine the success of the test.

Test Failure

1. The test can be deemed unsuccessful if the invoice does not print.
2. The test will also be unsuccessful if the format is incorrect.
3. The test will be unsuccessful if the wrong line items are printed.

5.5.2 Test Case: Accounting:Payment
CI: DD.0001.TEST024

5.5.2.1 Description

The purpose of this test is to determine if a representative of the service care provider can enter a payment receipt within the Accounting sub-system.

5.5.2.2 Required Stubs/Drivers

The Accounting sub-system will be invoked, with particular attention to the Payment class.

5.5.2.3 Test Steps

1. The service care provider must successfully log on to the system.
2. The service care provider must invoke the Accounting user interface to enter the payment receipt.
3. The service care provider must enter a payment receipt and press the button to commit the transaction.

5.5.2.4 Expected Results

Test Success

1. A subsequent query indicates the customer's balance reflecting the recent payment.
2. A successful message is displayed.

Test Failure

1. The customer's balance does not reflect the payment receipt.
2. The customer's balance reflects an incorrect amount that is a result of faulty logic within the program.

5.5.3 Test Case: Accounting:InvoiceList
CI: DD.0001.TEST025

5.5.3.1 Description

The purpose of this test is to ensure that every time a service care provider requests to view invoices, the correct invoices will be displayed.

5.5.3.2 Required Stubs/Drivers

The Application sub-system is required, with particular interest paid to the Invoice class.

5.5.3.3 Test Steps

1. The service care provider will successfully log on to the system.
2. The service care provider will select the button to view their invoices.
3. The system will determine who is logged on and display the appropriate invoices for that user.

5.5.3.4 Expected Results

Test Success

1. All invoices for that service care provider are displayed with the correct information.

Test Failure

1. The invoice(s) that are displayed are for the wrong service care provider.
2. The invoice(s) indicate an incorrect balance or other incorrect information.

5.6 Customer Relationship Management Sub-system

The Customer Relationship Management sub-system provides the application with the ability to provide an opportunity for interaction between the customers and service care providers. It also provides the system administrator with the ability to gain feedback from the customer in an effort to continually revamp the application.[3]

5.6.1 Test Case (This Feature Set Will Be Available in Phase II)

5.7 Persistence Sub-system

The Persistence sub-system has responsibility for supporting persistent data. The purpose of this group of test cases is to determine whether the PersistenceManager class is carrying out its responsibilities as expected. PersistenceManager is a critical part of the system that handles the persistence activities of all objects. Based on the system architecture design, the Persistence Layer Java code library from http://artyomr.narod.ru has been selected to execute the majority of the persistence functionality. The Persistence Layer code library uses an XML file to store the database map and class map information. So, the correctness of the XML file in terms of correctly mapping the class structure design with the database design will essentially determine whether the objects can be correctly persisted to the database. This will be a major area of potential fault of the implementation and hence one of the major focus areas of the testing of the Persistence sub-system.

Due to limited space, the document specifies in detail the example of Customer object persistence. Please be reminded that tests in similar patterns will need to be executed for EVERY object that needs to be persisted.

5.7.1 Test Case: PersistenceManager :: loadXMLConfig()
CI: DD.0001.TEST026

5.7.1.1 Description/Purpose

This test case tests the persistence manager's functionality to load the class map and the database map from the XML file. Potential errors are usually related to bad XML file entries: either file is a not valid XML file or it does not load correctly into the class map and database map.

5.7.1.2 Required Stubs/Drivers

DatabaseMap and ClassMap configuration XML file in format specified by http://artyomr.narod.ru/docs/pl/XMLConfigLoader.html

5.7.1.3 Test Steps

1. Edit Config.xml with all database map and class map information according to http://artyomr.narod.ru/docs/pl/XMLConfig-Loader.html
2. Start PersistenceManager application by running java Persistence-Manager.class from command prompt, loading Config.xml as the configuration.
3. Exit PersistenceManager application.

5.7.1.4 Expected Results

Test Success

1. The PersistenceManager application successfully starts without error messages.

Test Failure

1. XML parser error when loading Config.xml
2. Error parsing class map and database map information

5.7.2 Test Case: PersistenceManager :: saveObject()
CI: DD.0001.TEST027

5.7.2.1 Description/Purpose

This test case tests the persistence manager's functionality to save an object to the database.

5.7.2.2 Required Stubs/Drivers

1. DatabaseMap and ClassMap configuration XML file in format specified by http://artyomr.narod.ru/docs/pl/XMLConfigLoader.html
2. Customer registration screens

5.7.2.3 Test Steps

1. Edit Config.xml with all database map and class map information according to http://artyomr.narod.ru/docs/pl/XMLConfigLoader.html
2. Start PersistenceManager application by running java PersistenceManager.class from command prompt, loading Config.xml as the configuration.
3. Browse to DogEDayCare home page from the Web site.
4. Click Register button.
5. Input customer information.
6. Click Register to create a new Customer.
7. Use SQL Tool to open the database.
8. Execute "SELECT * FROM CUSTOMER" SQL statement and review the result.
9. Execute "SELECT * FROM DOG" SQL statement and review result.

5.7.2.4 Expected Results

Test Success

1. The customer and dog information should exist in the database.

Test Failure

1. RMI error when one clicks the Register button.
2. There is an error in executing SQL statement.
3. Customer and Dog did not get added to the database.

5.7.3 Test Case: PersistenceManager :: retrieveObject()
CI: DD.0001.TEST028

5.7.3.1 Description/Purpose

This test case tests the persistence manager's functionality to retrieve an object from the database.

5.7.3.2 Required Stubs/Drivers

1. DatabaseMap and ClassMap configuration XML file in format specified by http://artyomr.narod.ru/docs/pl/XMLConfigLoader.html
2. Customer information screens

5.7.3.3 Test Steps

1. Edit Config.xml with all database map and class map information according to http://artyomr.narod.ru/docs/pl/XMLConfigLoader.html
2. Start PersistenceManager application by running java Persistence-Manager.class from command prompt, loading Config.xml as the configuration.
3. Browse to DogEDayCare home page from the Web site.
4. Log on to DogEDayCare system.
5. Click Edit Customer Profile button.
6. Review the information retrieved from the persistence manager.

5.7.3.4 Expected Results

Test Success

1. The Customer and Dog information should be retrieved and match what was input.

Test Failure

1. RMI error when one clicks Edit Customer Profile button
2. Cannot retrieve Customer and Dog information
3. There is an error in executing SQL statement
4. Customer and Dog information retrieved but does not match the data that was input.

6 APPENDIX E2: INTEGRATION TESTING TESTS

Integration Tests are scenario based, capturing key activities that the Dog E-DayCare System™ allows the User to perform.

6.1 Test Case: Customer Registration
CI: DD.0001.TEST029

6.1.1 Description

Registering with the Dog E-DayCare™ System is the key task that allows users to take advantage of the services Dog E-DayCare™ has to offer. Registration requires collaboration among three sub-systems: User Management, Application Controller, and Persistence. The purpose of this test is to find errors in the interactions that must take place across these subsystems.

6.1.2 Required Stubs/Drivers

No stubs or drivers required.

6.1.3 Test Steps

1. User opens Dog E-DayCare™ welcome page.
2. User selects "Register."
3. The Register Customer/About You page displays.
4. User fills in fields and clicks Next.
5. The Register Customer/About Your Dog page displays.
6. User fills in fields and clicks Next.
7. Register Customer/User ID, Password page displays.
8. User fills in fields and clicks Next.
9. Register Customer/Verify Information page displays with appropriate information.
10. User reviews information and clicks Finish.
11. Register Customer/Thank You page displays.
12. User receives confirmation e-mail.

6.1.4 Expected Results

Test Success

1. User is able to successfully move through each step of the registration process.
2. The User information displayed in the Verify Information page is correct.
3. The Thank You page appears and User receives e-mail confirmation.

Test Failure

1. User cannot click from one step in the registration process to the next.
2. User information displayed in the Verify Information page is incorrect.
3. User does not receive a confirmation e-mail.

6.2 Test Case: Reallocate Resources
CI: DD.0001.TEST030

6.2.1 Description

One of the key services Dog E-DayCare™ provides to dog-care companies is the ability to manage their resources (e.g., staff, kennels, and play areas), allocating and reallocating resources in response to, for example, staff illness, rainy weather, etc.

Reallocating resources requires collaboration among several sub-systems: User Management, Order, Resource Management, Application Controller, and Persistence. The purpose of this test is to find errors in the interactions that must take place across these sub-systems.

6.2.2 Required Stubs/Drivers

No stubs or drivers required.

6.2.3 Test Steps

1. User opens Schedule/This Week page.
2. User selects appointment whose resources need to be reallocated.
3. Schedule/Appointment Details page displays.
4. User selects option to "reallocate" resources.
5. Schedule/Resource Details page displays.
6. User revises resource details as necessary and clicks Next.
7. Schedule/Confirm Changes page displays.
8. User clicks Finish.
9. Revised Schedule/Appointment Details page displays.

6.2.4 Expected Results

Test Success

1. User is able to successfully move through each step of the reallocation process.
2. Reallocation information displayed in the Confirm Changes page is correct.
3. Appointment Details have been updated.

Test Failure

1. User cannot click from one step in the reallocation process to the next.
2. User information displayed in the Confirm Changes page is incorrect.
3. Appointment Details have not been updated.

6.3 Test Case: Search for Service Provider and Initiate Order CI: DD.0001.TEST031

6.3.1 Description

The Dog E-DayCare™ System allows Customers to search for Service Providers based on geographic location and service desired. From the Search Results, a user can initiate an order.

Searching for a service provider and initiating an order requires collaboration among several sub-systems: User Management, Order, Application Controller, and Persistence. The purpose of this test is to find errors in the interactions that must take place across these sub-systems.

6.3.2 Required Stubs/Drivers

No stubs or drivers required.

6.3.3 Test Steps

1. User opens Search for Service Provider page.
2. User enters required information and clicks "search."
3. Search Results page displays all Service Providers that match criteria.
4. User selects "initiate order" button associated with the Service Provider of their choice.
5. Order/Initiate Order page displays.

6.3.4 Expected Results

Test Success

1. The Search Results page displays Service Providers matching the User's criteria.
2. The Order/Initiate Order page displays the name of the Service Provider selected and the services available from the selected Service Provider in the appropriate fields.

Test Failure

1. Search Results page does not display.
2. Search Results do not match criteria.
3. Order/Initiate Order page does not display correct Service Provider information.

6.4 Test Case: Place Order
CI: DD.0001.TEST032

6.4.1 Description

The Dog E-DayCare™ System allows Customers to place an order for the service they need, from a Service Provider of their choice, and within a desired timeframe.

Placing an order requires collaboration among several sub-systems: Order, User Management, Resource Management, Application Controller, and Persistence. The purpose of this test is to find errors in the interactions that must take place across these sub-systems.

6.4.2 Required Stubs/Drivers

No stubs or drivers required.

6.4.3 Test Steps

1. Order/Initiate Order page is displayed.
2. User fills in all fields.
3. User selects "view openings."
4. Order/Openings page displays.
5. User selects an available appointment time.
6. Order/Order Details page displays.
7. User selects "place order."
8. Order/Order Confirmation page displays.
9. An e-mail is sent to the User.

6.4.4 Expected Results

Test Success

1. The User is able to move successfully through each step in the process of placing an order.

2. The Order/Openings page displays the correct information on available appointment times.
3. The Order/Order Details page displays the correct information.
4. An e-mail is sent to the User.

Test Failure

1. The Order/Openings page displays incorrect information.
2. The Order/Order Details Page displays incorrect information.
3. An e-mail is not sent to the User.

6.5 Test Case: Pay for Service
CI: DD.0001.TEST033

6.5.1 Description

The Dog E-DayCare™ System allows Customers to pay online for the dog-care services they have received.

Paying for service requires collaboration among several sub-systems: Accounting, Order, User Management, Application Controller, and Persistence. The purpose of this test is to find errors in the interactions that must take place across these sub-systems.

6.5.2 Required Stubs/Drivers

No stubs or drivers required.

6.5.3 Test Steps

1. User opens the Payment/Initiate Payment page.
2. User enters the Order Id number and clicks "next."
3. The Payment/Payment Details page displays.
4. User reviews Payment Details and selects "next."
5. The Payment/Billing Address page displays.
6. User reviews information and clicks "next."
7. The Payment/Credit Card Details page displays.
8. User enters information and clicks "next."
9. The Payment/Make Payment page displays.
10. User reviews information and clicks "pay now."
11. The Payment/Payment Confirmation page displays.
12. An e-mail is sent to the User.

6.5.4 Expected Results

Test Success

1. The User is able to move successfully through each step in the process of making a payment for service.
2. The Payment/Payment Details page displays the correct information.
3. The Payment/Billing Address page displays the correct information.
4. The Payment/Make Payment page displays the correct information.
5. An e-mail is sent to the User.

Test Failure

1. The Payment/Payment Details page displays incorrect information.
2. The Payment/Billing Address page displays incorrect information.
3. The Payment/Make Payment page displays incorrect information.
4. An e-mail is not sent to the User.

7 APPENDIX E3: PROJECT SCHEDULE

Figure E2 is an example of a project schedule.

Notes

1. This feature set will be available in Phase II.
2. This feature set will be available in Phase II.
3. This feature set will be available in Phase II.

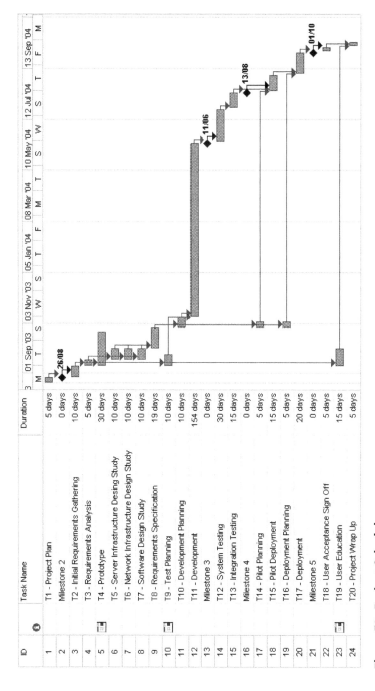

Figure E2 Project Schedule

Appendix F

PROGRAM CODE INSPECTION FORM

Code For Inspection:	Project:		
Author:	Project Manager:		
Date Of Inspection:			
CI:			

1	Criteria:	Inspected By	Pass ☐
			Fail ☐
	Notes:		
	Resolution & Date	Approved By & Date	

Appendix G

SAMPLE INSPECTION PLAN

CI:	Project:
Project Manager:	
Date Of Inspection:	

CONTENTS

PRODUCED FOR SAMPLE EXECUTIVE CONSULTANT GROUP

1 INTRODUCTION

This software inspection plan has been produced in conjunction with the current work we are carrying out for the Sample Executive Consultant Group to produce a Web-based interactive system to replace the existing computer system still in use. The purpose of the plan is to ensure SAMPLE are confident with the nature, scope, and level of the work being under-taken, that it adheres to the objectives of SAMPLE as per the original specification details, that the system produced will stand up by itself as a product that will work well in the marketplace for the client and candidate community, and that it will demonstrate to the SAMPLE com-petition that the organization is a worthy challenge to the marketplace. Further, it is the purpose of this work to demonstrate to SAMPLE that the output can stand the test of time by being rigorously produced to an industry standard, is maintainable, scalable, and a cost-effective business component.

A software inspection document needs to demonstrate that the product being worked on is relevant to the criteria as specified by the client. In this respect, this document needs to show that a methodology is being proposed that will ensure that the following criteria as specified by the SAMPLE senior management group have been met. In our original project plan, we detailed the provisions required to deliver the requirements of SAMPLE. These were, in brief:

■ To provide the SAMPLE Group with an interactive, secure, Web-enabled database application for the placement of candidates with client organizations.

■ To review current hardware, software, and security facilities at client premises and propose changes required to accommodate the secure Web application just mentioned.

■ To redesign the client's database to provide facilities in keeping with the secure Web application just mentioned.

Therefore, to ensure that this work is being productively actioned, the software inspection plan detailed here is proposed to give SAMPLE the confidence to monitor and review work completed to date, and work to be completed for the duration of this project. The software inspection is not a static process; rather, it is to continue for the life of the project, and as such SAMPLE are strongly urged to play a key role in the establishment of the inspection team — see below.

2 SCOPE OF THE SOFTWARE INSPECTION

As covered in the above introduction, the aim of this document is to demonstrate that the product being worked on is relevant to the criteria as specified by the client. It is also the aim to ensure that the software being built matches the design and development standards as outlined by the development project. To this end, the code needs to be inspected against a checklist of the project development standards.

The scope of this inspection is basically the overall development project and all that it encompasses. To facilitate this we will need the following documents as input into the inspection process:

- Complete and definitive user requirements document
- Complete and definitive list of development standards

To ensure that the inspection is comprehensive, a representative sample of code will be taken at regular intervals and delivered to the inspection team. To make this more acceptable and understandable, the section code will represent a specific part of the product (e.g., candidate entry).

The inspection of the code itself will ensure that the representative section of code:

- Meets the documentation standards for the project
- Meets the variable naming standards for the project
- Meets the general development standards for the project
- Meets maintainability standards for the project
- Is logically sound compared to the user requirements for the section of the product that it represents
- Is in line with the ethics and working practices of the customer
- Is compatible with the hardware requirements laid down on/by the customer

There will also be an inspection of the database structure to ensure that it meets the customer requirements. The database will be expected to:

- Meet the database normalization standards for the project
- Meet the database naming conventions for the project
- Be sized according to the expected growth of the product
- Contain the necessary elements to meet all the customer needs as defined in the user specification
- Have field sizes that meet the needs of the user specification document

3 SOFTWARE INSPECTION TEAM

It is important that the team that constitutes the inspection process is made up from a vertical slice of the organizations involved in the project. As already mentioned, the software inspection process is to involve more than just the validation and verification of the computer code being produced. To date, a number of significant findings have been encapsulated and recorded in a number of key documents, and all of this information is appropriate for inspection if we are to do full justice to the project being undertaken. To this end then, the inspection process needs to address:

Area to Address	Items to Examine	Appropriate Team
Computer code:	Database interfaces Web front-end code Database language code Application code	Technical
Risk data:	Risk documents	Risk
Environmental data:	Working locations (for computer storage)	Risk
Planning information:	Project plan	Management
User requirements:	Requirements documents	Management
Technical requirements:	Technical requirements documents Modeling specifications	Technical
Quality requirements:	Quality Plans	Risk

The Team profiles for the above inspection work are recommended thus:

Team	Membership	Team ID
Executive panel	Mary Sample – SAMPLE representative Steve Hyman – Consultant representative A. N. Other – independent	EP
Technical[a]	Sam Wilson – chair and chief moderator Martin Long – author and project consultant A. N. Other – reader/inspector	T
Risk[b]	John Small – chair and chief moderator Martyn Davies – author and project consultant A. N. Other – reader/inspector	R
Management[b]	Mary Sample – chair and chief moderator Mike Kennedy – project consultant and scribe A. N. Other – reader/inspector	M

[a]Note that we have already identified both a database team and a Web team in our project plan. These teams will be linking into this inspection process as it progresses.

[b]Note that we have already identified a security and reports team in our project plan. This team will be linking into this inspection process as it progresses.

The role of the Executive group is to oversee the work of the three other groups and report back to the project executive — as identified in the Quality documentation reported on in a previous stage of this project.

4 INSPECTION PROCESS

The inspection process is to last for the duration of the project. We have already provided a breakdown of the key project deliverables in terms of activity. Reproduced below is an appraisal of that work with the relevant inspection work added:

Based on the detailed plan (Above), the following analysis of the software inspection is given:

4.1 Inspection procedure

The approach to documentation inspection will be the same as program inspection. This is a generic process designed to aid continuity to the inspection process.

Figure G1 presents the overall approach we will be adopting for both documentation inspection and program inspection.

Each of the key steps in the inspection procedure are broken down thus:

- *Work products:* These can be anything to be considered under the remit of software inspection. This is not just computer code. A document used to define a computer system such as a requirements document or a technical specification could be submitted for inspection.
- *Planning:* The definition or roles and responsibilities for the inspection process.
- *Overview:* To be given by the author(s) of the work product to be inspected.
- *Preparation:* All involved in the inspection need to have a copy of what is to be inspected and some time to Sampleome familiar with t. This preparation stage is useful for independent evaluation prior to consensus of the group. An inspector will bring to this stage any checklists he or she may have.
- *Meeting:* A meeting for all the inspectors to get together to consider their findings and continue any detection of defect work. The defect list will be produced.

ID	Activity	Milestone	Deliverable
		High-Level Design	
A1	Requirements specification	Requirements defined	URD SRD
A2	Architectural design	Architecture design completed	System architecture
A3	User requirements analysis	User requirements fully understood	Base requirements for sizing
A4	Hardware sizing exercise	Hardware and database requirements analysis	H/w sizing doc DB sizing doc
SI 1		**Full Inspection – Benchmarking Function**	
	Technology		
A5	Formal hardware specification	Required hardware	Procurement form
A6	Purchase hardware	Hardware delivered	Hardware
A7	Purchase software	Software delivered	Software
SI 2		**Partial Inspection**	
	Security design		
A8	Interface design	Interface design complete	Interface specification
A9	Component design	Component design complete	Component specification
A10	Data structure design	Data structure design complete	Database map Entity relationship diagram
A11	Algorithm design	Algorithm design complete	Algorithm specification

SI 3	Partial Inspection		
Database Design			
A12	Component design	Component design complete	Component specification
A13	Data structure design	Data structure design complete	Data structure specification
A14	Algorithm design	Algorithm design complete	Algorithm specification
SI 4	Partial Inspection		
Web Design			
A15	Abstract specification	Abstract spec complete	Software specification
A16	Interface design	Interface design complete	Interface specification
A17	Component design	Component design complete	Component specification
A18	Algorithm design	Algorithm design complete	Algorithm specification
SI 5	Partial Inspection		
Reports Design			
A19	Requirements gathering	Requirements analysis complete	Report requirements
A20	Interface design	Interface design complete	Interface specification
A21	Component design	Component design complete	Component specification
A22	Data structure design	Data structure design complete	Data structure specification
A23	Algorithm design	Algorithm design complete	Algorithm specification

SI 6			**Partial Inspection**
Database coding			
A24	Create tables and queries	Database created	Database report
A25	Migrate test data	Migration complete	Migration report
A26	Develop stand-alone prototype	Prototype complete	Demonstrate prototype
SI 7			**Partial Inspection**
Web Coding			
A27	Site design	Site design complete	Site design report
A28	Look and feel	Look and feel complete	Look and feel report
A29	User interface – forms	User interface complete	UI report
A30	Database connectivity	Database connectivity complete	Database connectivity report
A31	Develop Web-enabled prototype	Prototype complete	Demonstrate prototype
SI 8			**Full Inspection**
Reports Coding			
A32	Reports design	Reports design complete	Reports design report
A33	User interface	Reports UI complete	Reports UI report
A34	Develop reports prototype	Prototype complete	Demonstrate prototype
SI 9			**Partial Inspection**

	Testing and Integration		
A35	Unit testing	Unit testing complete	Unit test report
A36	Component testing	Component testing complete	Component test report
A37	Integration testing	Integration testing complete	Integration test report
A38	End-to-end testing	End-to-end testing complete	End-to-end test report
A39	Load testing	Load testing complete	Load test report
A40	User testing	User testing complete	User test report[a]
A41	Acceptance testing	Acceptance testing complete	Acceptance test report
SI 10		**Partial Inspection**	
	User Documentation		
A42	Produce user documentation	Documentation complete	User documentation
SI 11		**Partial Inspection**	
	User Training		
A43	Train users	User training complete	Training report
	User Sign-Off		
A44	Produce sign-off document	Sign-off doc complete	Sign-off document
A45	Acquire signatures	Document signed	Signed document

[a] A user test report has been produced and is associated with this paper under Appendix G1. The report highlights the findings of the first pass of user acceptance and the corrective actions coming out of that first pass. An extensive human computer interface (HCI) exercise has been carried out as part of this process, and this information is provided in the report in Appendix G1.

ID	Action	Activity	Team(s)
SI 1	Full Inspection – Benchmarking function	To apply a full software inspection to all completed components to date constituting the project. All architectural plans, specifications, and objectives will have been delivered by this stage, and it is important that an inspection for benchmarking purposed takes place. This is benchmarking for the purposes of software inspection; that is, ensuring the process is sound and consigned, and that all four groups in the inspection process are calibrated and understand their terms of reference. Any computer code produced by this stage in whatever format will also be inspected.	T, R, M
SI 2	Partial Inspection	To test the details of the hardware delivery – delivery documentation, configuration details, and software specification – against delivery details.	T, R
SI 3	Partial Inspection	To test the database specification against beta production, the interface production against user requirements, and general math between algorithmic functions. Also to ensure that component approach is sound and integrated.	T
SI 4	Partial Inspection	Ensure continuity between findings from SI 3 and work in SI 4.	T
SI 5	Partial Inspection	To test the specification documentation for the Web interface aspect of the project and measure against stated deliverables as specified in the original user requirements and technical requirements.	T, R, M

SI 6	Partial Inspection	To ensure that the reporting measures adhere to those in keeping with the SAMPLE existing criteria and continuity between reports, reporting mechanisms, time scales, and scopes are all in tandem with each other.	M, R
SI 7	Partial Inspection	Database integrity checking, integration with Web aspect of project and adherence to existing SAMPLE standards. Also adherence to rules identified as part of SI 6.	T, D
SI 8	Full Inspection	Measure aspect of prototype in relation to look and feel, database connectivity, site navigation, human computer interface, quality, and overall adherence to SAMPLE standards.	T, R, M
SI 9	Partial Inspection	High-level inspection for overall context, integration with SAMPLE business approach. Also appraise results of work against outcomes of SI 6	T, M
SI 10	Partial Inspection	High-level inspection in relation to risk assessment of work completed to date, and appraisal of that work in relation to SI 6 and SI 9.	R, M
SI 11	Final Inspection	Inspection prior to sign-off. Executive Board inspection of SI 10 outputs, exception analysis, and identification of post-implementation review work.	M, EB

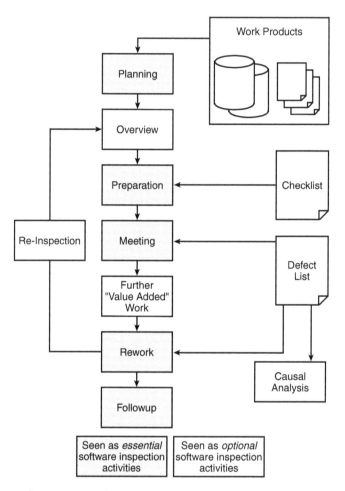

Figure G1 Software Inspection Steps

- *Further "value-added" work:* A chance for any improvements to be discussed.
- *Rework:* The author(s) start any reworking based on the defect list(s).
- *Re-inspection:* If necessary, the whole process or part of it will be repeated until all the defects have been eradicated, or a number suitable to pass the criteria set by the organization.
- *Causal analysis:* As an option, the inspection process may identify some underlying causes of some of the defects.
- *Follow-up:* Anything identified by the inspection team as requiring necessary follow-up work.

5 CONTINUING PROCESSES

As a result of this inspection, it is likely that some follow-up work will be required. This work needs to be monitored by the inspection team to ensure that all standards and needs are addressed throughout the life cycle of the project. Also, as change requests or other impacts on the product are encountered throughout the life cycle of the project, it will be necessary to ensure that no regression to the previous pre-inspection state of the code takes place as part of the resultant changes. As such, it is recommended that the following continuing processes are put into place:

- Regular random inspections of suspect code
- Monitoring revisits to code requiring follow-up work
- Regression inspections of code affected by change requests or other similar project impacts

It is also recommended that a chosen representative of the inspection team report back regularly to the project manager as to the state of the project code with regard to standards and user requirements to ensure that control of the process is maintained.

6 SUMMARY

As a summary, the author would like to point out the following:

1. This document was produced in conjunction with Sample Executive Consultant Group and must be signed by their representative to indicate acceptance of the aims of the document and the process it represents.
2. The inspection team will be made up of a cross-functional team to ensure that all aspects of the development are represented.
3. The process will originally focus on a first inspection of the requirements to ensure that they are complete and in a format that the inspection team can work with when inspecting the code.
4. A continuing process will remain in force for the life cycle of the project.
5. The continuing process will encompass follow-on actions from inspected code as well as regression inspections for highly modified code as a result of change requests or other such project impacts.
6. The inspection team is responsible to the project manager and should ensure that he or she is aware of the status of the inspections at all times.

7. Regular reporting will be in place between the inspection team and the project manager.

In short, this inspection is in place to protect the needs of the developers, the overall project team, and the customer. Its main aim is to ensure that the product delivered to the customer is what he requires, how he requires it, and written to a maintainable standard to ease the path of future upgrade, modification, and problem resolution.

Appendix H

QA HANDOVER DOCUMENT

QA Handover Document

Submitted: _____   Dept. _____   Phone # _____   Submission Date _____

Application/Module (CI #) _____   Product/Form to test: (required) _____   Implementation Date _____

Handover Item Name/Description _____   Version/Built: _____   New/Modified: _____

Brief but thorough description of the Modification, along with any special testing requirements

_____

_____

_____

_____

Testing done at the development stage. Attach documentation (required).

_____

_____

_____

_____

Known issues. Documentation attached (required).

TEAM MEMBER/DEVELOPER

PROJECT MANAGER

QA ANALYST

QA MANAGER

SYSTEMS MANAGER

QA001

Appendix I

SYSTEM SERVICE REQUEST

System Service Request

CI: _____

Requestor _____

Requestor Department _____

Secondary Contact _____

Request Date _____   Needed Date

Urgency: ☐ Low   ☐ Medium   ☐ High

Request Type: ☐ Maintenance (Fix or Modify System)

☐ New Development (New Capability)

Description:

☐ Please attach documentation: Screen shots with annotations for required changes are required for any maintenance to screens. This can be done by hitting the Print Screen key, and pasting into a Word document. Provide program or function name if known.

☐ Additional Information or interaction with other systems if pertinent.

☐ Can you provide test data?

Questions? Need Assistance? Call Ext. xxx or e-mail xxx@xxxx.com

SSR

Appendix J

DOCUMENT CHANGE REQUEST (DCR)

DOCUMENT CHANGE REQUEST (DCR)	
Document Title:	Tracking Number:
Name of Submitting Organization:	
Organization Contact:	Phone:
Mailing Address:	
Short Title:	Date:
Change Location: (use section #, figure #, table #, etc.)	
Proposed Change:	

Rationale for Change:

Note: For the Software Engineering Process Office (SEPO) to take appropriate action on a change request, please provide a clear description of the recommended change along with supporting rationale.

Send to:

Appendix K

PROBLEM/CHANGE REPORT

PROBLEM/CHANGE REPORT (Type or Print)		
1. Date	2. P/CR No	3. Originator
4. Activity Code		5. Telephone/Ext.
6. Title		
7. Category: (Circle) Plans Concept Requirements Design Code DB/data file Test Info Manuals Other _____		8. Priority: (Circle) 1 2 3 4 5
9. Problem/Change Description:		

10. Corrective Action:			
11. Actions Taken: Status	Date		
12. QA Sign-Off			

P/CR PREPARATION INSTRUCTIONS

1. TITLE
Problem/Change Report

2. DESCRIPTION/PURPOSE
2.1 The Problem/Change Report (P/CR) shows essential data on each software problem/change detected. It also shows errors on omissions in documentation. Sufficient detail of the problem shall be reported to enable analysis and isolation or replication if necessary.

3. APPLICATION INTERRELATIONSHIP
3.1 P/CRs are used to record and report problems found throughout development. They are also used to report errors or omissions found in documentation. The P/CR is the basic input to the quality assurance program during the test and acceptance phase of the development effort. P/CRs on interfaces with other systems require joint resolution action.

4. PREPARATION INSTRUCTIONS
1. Date. The date form is prepared.
2. P/CR Number. P/CR Number assigned for control purposes.
3. Originator. Printed name of person originating the P/CR form.
4. Activity Code. The activity and code name or number of individual originating the P/CR form.
5. Telephone/Ext. Originator's office telephone number, and extension (if applicable).
6. Title. Name used to identify problem/change.

7. Category. Circle appropriate category associated with problem/change being reported.
Categories:

   a. Plans – one of the plans developed for the project

   b. Concept – the operational concept

   c. Requirements – the system or software requirements

   d. Design – the design of the system or software

   e. Code – the software code

   f. Database/data le – a database or data le

   g. Test information – test plans, test descriptions, or test reports

   h. Manuals – the user, operator, or support manuals

   i. Other – other software products

8. Priority. Circle appropriate priority code, 1 – 5.
Priority Codes:

   1 a. Prevent the accomplishment of an operational or mission-essential capability

     b. Jeopardize safety, security, or other requirement designated "critical"

   2 a. Adversely affect the accomplishment of an operational or mission-essential capability and no work-around solution is known

     b. Adversely affect technical, cost, or schedule risks to the project or to life-cycle support of the system, and no work-around solution is known

   3 a. Adversely affect the accomplishment of an operational or mission-essential capability but a work-around solution is known

     b. Adversely affect technical, cost, or schedule risks to the project or to life-cycle support of the system, but a work-around solution is known

   4 a. Results in user/operator inconvenience or annoyance but does not affect a required operational or mission-essential capability

     b. Results in inconvenience or annoyance for development or support personnel, but does not prevent the accomplishment of those responsibilities

   5 Any other effect

9. Problem/Change Description. Write a description of the problem/change. Develop a word picture of events leading up to the problem. Structure statements so that the programmer/test analyst can duplicate the situation. Cite equipment being used, unusual configuration, etc. Indicate consoles online, modes, etc., if applicable. If continuation sheets are required, fill in page ____ of ____ at the top of the P/CR form.

10. Corrective Action: A description, by the programmer/tester, of actions taken to resolve the reported problem or to complete the requested change.

11. Actions Taken: Enter the status/disposition and date to indicate the current status. When the status changes, line out the old status and date and enter the appropriate new status and date.

12. QA Sign-off. Signature by designated quality assurance (QA) organization member authorizing implementation of the corrective change(s) and certifying the correctness and completeness of the change(s).

Appendix L

SOFTWARE REQUIREMENTS CHANGES

Software Requirements Changes (SRC)	CI:	
	Date raised:	
Source of SRC		
Description of SRC		
Consequence(s) of SRC		
Impact on project if SRC not actioned		
Responsibility for Actions		
Impact of each action on: ■ Risks ■ Project milestones ■ Project tolerance		
Recommendations		
Executive Board notification	Date	Action Required

Appendix M

PROBLEM REPORT (PR)

Problem Report (PR)	CI:	
	Date raised:	
Source of Problem (reported by and owner)		
Description of Problem		
Actual or potential consequence(s) of problem		
Action(s) taken to mitigate problem so far		
Responsibility for Action(s)		
Impact of each action on: ■ Risks ■ Project milestones ■ Project tolerance		
Recommendations		
Executive Board notification	Date	Action Required

Appendix N

CORRECTIVE ACTION PROCESSING (CAP)

Corrective Action Processing (CAP)		CI:	
		Date raised:	
Source of CAP (name, position in organization – project group)			
Area CAP relates to: ■ Software development ■ Quality ■ Training ■ Design of product ■ Management of project ■ Other			
Description of CAP			
Other areas this CAP could relate to			
Impact on organization if CAP not addressed			
Responsibility for actions relating to this CAP			
Impact of each action on : ■ Risks ■ Project milestones ■ Project tolerance ■ Future of BEC			
Recommendations			
Which forum should CAP be raised at? ■ Monthly meeting ■ Prototype demonstration ■ Training event ■ Software review ■ Ad hoc			
Executive Board notification	Date	Action Required	

Appendix O

SPECIFICATION CHANGE NOTICE

SPECIFICATION CHANGE NOTICE (SCN)

		1. DATE (YYMMDD)	FORM APPROVED OMB No. 0704-0188
			2. PROCURING ACTIVITY NO.
			3. DODAAC

4. ORIGINATOR

	5. SCN TYPE ☐ PROPOSED	☐ APPROVED
a. TYPED NAME (First, Middle Initial, Last)	6. CAGE CODE	7. SPEC. NO.
b. ADDRESS (Street, City, State, Zip Code)	8. CAGE CODE	9. SCN NO.

10. SYSTEM DESIGNATION	11. RELATED ECP NO.	12. CONTRACT NO.	13. CONTRACTUAL AUTHORIZATION
14. CONFIGURATION ITEM NOMENCLATURE			15. EFFECTIVITY

16. PAGES AFFECTED BY THIS SCN

PAGE(S) a.	TYPE OF CHANGE* b.	APPROVAL DATE (YYMMDD) c.

17. SUMMARY OF PREVIOUSLY CHANGED PAGES		DATE SUBMITTED (YMMDD) d.	TYPE OF CHANGE* e.	APPROVAL DATE (YMMDD) f.
SCN NO. a.	RELATED ECP NO. b.	PAGE(S) c.			

* "S" indicates earlier page. "A" indicates added page. "D" indicates deletion.

18.a. GOVERNMENT ACTIVITY	c. SIGNATURE	d. DATE SIGNED (YMMDD)
b. TYPED NAME (First, Middle Initial, Last)		

Previous editions are obsolete

DD Form 1696, APR 92

SPECIFICATION CHANGE NOTICE, CONTINUATION PAGE 2

SPEC. NO	SCN. NO	RELATED ECP NO.

17. SUMMARY OF PREVIOUSLY CHANGED PAGES (CONT.)

SCN NO. a.	RELATED ECP NO. b.	PAGE(S) c.	DATE SUBMITTED (YMMDD) d.	TYPE OF CHANGE* e.	APPROVAL DATE (YMMDD) f.

* "S" indicates earlier page. "A" indicates added page. "D" indicates deletion.

DD Form 1696, APR 92

Appendix P

PROJECT STATEMENT OF WORK

System Release # Project # CI

VERSION: *Draft*

Project Statement of Work

Project Manager: <name>

Created: <date>

Last Updated: <date>

Created By: <name>

TABLE OF CONTENTS

PROJECT INFORMATION

Project Request

This project has been requested to provide various Business Lines new and/or improved functionality within the <application name> System. Some of the requested changes will be beneficial for the customer also.

Project Number and Title

This project will be referred to as the "?? Project." The project number is ??.

Executive Sponsor or Delegate

The Business Group Head for this project is <group head name> of <company name> and the executive sponsor is <executive sponsor name>, Group Technology Executive.

PROJECT DEFINITION

Background

There are several requirements requested for Release ??. These requirements will be funded by various Business Lines and will benefit several different areas as well as the customer in many cases.

Release ?? is one of two remaining releases scheduled for <year> by the enterprise. The planned implementation date for Release ?? is <date>. This release will be coordinated with the <project name> scheduled between <month> and <month> <year>.

Project Objectives

To provide more functionality and data accessibility in the ?? System to the Business Lines and the customer in the least amount of time for the most reasonable cost.

Business Units Involved

Internal

Impacts to the following applications were determined in the initial data gathering phase of this project. Certain applications have been defaulted to testing only as no response was obtained during the data gathering phase. Formal sizing has been gathered from all impacted applications as a part of the requirements phase of this project. This list represents the internal interfaces.

Internal Applications/Areas: Impacts:

1. Application name: No development — set-up and testing needed
2. Application name: **Application name** — Development, testing needed
   Application name — Development
   Application name — Testing needed
3. Application name: Development, testing needed
   Sub-system name — Testing needed
   Sub-system name — No development; set-up, and testing needed
   Sub-system name — Testing needed

External

The external organizations impacted by this project include:

1. Third-Party Package name: New process and procedures; development, testing needed

Business Impacts

This project will have the following business impacts:

1. Changes for all <application name> customers
2. Changes for Wholesale Sales and Relationship Managers
3. Changes for Regional Managers
4. Changes for Operations
5. Changes for Central Implementation and Regional Implementation Centers

Business Benefits

This project will have the following business benefits:

1. Improved presentation of customer statements and reports
2. Productivity gains on automating various processes

3. Productivity gains on making specific data more readily available to analysts for problem resolution
4. Compliance with Corporate branding standards

Risks

Risk Rating

The risk score for this project is 82. As a result of the risk rating, this project has been rated as a medium-risk project. There is additional risk due to some of the requested changes to be implemented in conjunction with the release implementation date. There is a conflict between the release date and the upgrade date.

See Appendix P2: Risk Assessment form.

Identified Risks

The risks identified for this project include the following:

1. Late deliverables if resource constraints
2. Resource constraints if work needed on other higher priorities such as production issues
3. Retaining key project team resources
4. Conflicting project priorities
5. Communication, coordination, and task management of all impacted/affected applications are necessary for successful implementation
6. Risk of impacted customers due to the complexity of some changes

Risk Mitigation

The following actions will be taken to address the identified risks:

1. Hire contractors as necessary to assist the team in completing the assigned tasks.
2. Work with the Business Lines early in the requirements gathering phase to document detailed requirements.
3. More accurate estimates due to detailed business requirements.
4. Regularly scheduled meetings will be held to keep all impacted/affected applications up-to-date on tasks.
5. Include adequate checkpoint reviews in the project process to ensure accurate and complete information.

6. Testing will be coordinated with all impacted applications to ensure the changes are correct.

PROPOSED SOLUTION

Current

Not all functionality was built into the new <application name> System from the old <application name> System. This lack of functionality is causing many manual work-arounds and in some cases loss of revenue. Some of the requested changes also position <application name> in compliance with <company name> strategic standards.

Proposed Solution

The <application name> management team is working with the Project Manager to ensure that detailed Business Requirements are fully documented and to prioritize those requirements based on business need. Those requirements have been sized and presented to the various Business Lines. A resource plan will be updated to reflect the number of resources available during the Release ?? timeframe. The Business Lines will then obtain funding for the requirements that can be completed in that Release ?? timeframe.

The project plan will be updated and an issues log and task plan will be maintained throughout the term of the project.

PROJECT SCOPE

Inclusions

The scope of this project includes the following:

1. Defining and communicating the business requirements to all affected applications that are included in the Release ?? requirements
2. Assessing and managing the impacts to the various Operational/Support Groups/Business Lines
3. Participation in development of customer, department, and vendor communications
4. Participation in development of customer or internal training
5. Participation in development of user documentation and procedures
6. Participation in regression testing

7. Validation of requirements, design, development, and unit and system testing of application changes necessary to the applications listed in the Business Units Involved
8. Changes needed for other applications requirements

A list of the requirements scheduled for Release ?? is attached as Appendix P6.

Exclusions

The scope of this project does not include the following:

1. Any non-<APPLICATION NAME> accounts
2. <APPLICATION NAME> (??) application conversion (although it is a dependency)

Security Statement

1. The Security Plan is prepared to ensure that appropriate controls are being designed that meet security policy and standards. The plan should identify risks and exposures to information, systems, and networks that may result from any exceptions to the standards. The System Managers are responsible for ensuring that the security plans are updated or created for all systems.

PROJECT APPROACH

Project Management

<Project Manager name> has been assigned to manage the project. The responsibilities of the project manager will be:

1. Establish and execute a project plan
2. Ensure completion of project estimates, as required
3. Track actual costs against budget/planned costs
4. To assist in maintaining the overall project direction
5. First point of escalation of project issues
6. Obtain project resource commitments
7. Define project milestones
8. Create and maintain a project issues log

9. Schedule and conduct project status meetings
10. Complete project status meeting minutes
11. Complete project status reports
12. Contact lists for all project participants with defined roles and responsibilities
13. Ensure detailed test plans are complete
14. Participate in the post-event review
15. Communicate with the other End-to-End Project Managers
16. Close the project

Methodology

This project will follow the <methodology name> methodology.

One overall project manager will be assigned as the end-to-end project manager as well as the Technical Lead. This project manager will manage the details of the <APPLICATION NAME> System development efforts. The project manager will maintain a common format for issues, project plans, and technical requirements. The project manager will provide day-to-day management for the technical team and provide a roll-up of all issues, plans, and requirements.

Deliverables

Key Project Deliverables

Key deliverables from this project include:

1. Statement of Work
2. Risk Assessment
3. Project Change Requests
4. Project Requirements Document
5. Design Documents
6. Communication Plan
7. Data Security Plan
8. Resource Plan
9. Critical Success Factors Document
10. Master Test Plan
11. Training Plan
12. Implementation Plan
13. Post-Implementation Review

Approvals

Approval of key project deliverables must be received from the following individuals:

A = Approval Required; R = Review Only

Area	Deliverables												
	1	2	3	4	5	6	7	8	9	10	11	12	13
\<manager name\> Operations Manager	A	A	A	A	A	A	R	A	A	A	A	A	A
\<manager name\> Technical Manager	A	A	A	A	A	A	R	A	A	R	R	A	A
\<manager name\> TM Product Manager	A	A	A	A	A	A	A	A	A	A	A	R	A
\<manager name\> Operations Manager	A	A	A	A	A	A	R	A	A	A	A	A	A
\<manager name\> Project Manager	A	A	A	A	A	A	R	A	A	A	R	A	A
\<manager name\> Wholesale Services	A	A	A	A	A	A	R	A	A	R	A	R	A
\<manager name\> Wholesale Integration	A	A	A	A	A	A	R	A	A	A	A	R	A
Audit Representative	R	R	R	R	R	R	R	R	R	R	R	R	R

Acceptance Criteria

This project will be considered completed when the following acceptance criteria have been met:

1. Each system change has passed all levels of test successfully and is implemented into production successfully.
2. Delivered system functionality meets agreed-upon functionality
3. There is no undue fallout up to two weeks after implementation.

Assumptions

The following assumptions are being made for this project:

1. *Resources assumption.* The key resource assumptions for labor, space, and equipment are:
   - Technical Lead will be identified and assigned
   - A test coordination leader is identified and assigned for <APPLI-CATION NAME>.
   - Testing Assumptions in general:
     - Test coordination with all affected applications will be managed by an assigned resource from testing. Other testing resources will be drawn from each of the applications.
     - Testing by all affected applications will be conducted at the specified time established by Release Management for this release.
   - All Business Line resources are available to the overall project.
   - Project support resources are available to the overall project.
2. Production support has the highest priority for resources. Other resource issues will be addressed and prioritized at the Steering Committee Meeting level.
3. The Release ?? key dates will not be changed and the various phases of the project will start and end on time.

Key Facts

Key facts identified for this project include the following:

- If the ?? requirement is not implemented with this release, we will continue to lose revenue at the rate of approximately $?? a month.
- If the new statement paper and logo requirement is not implemented with this release, <APPLICATION NAME> will continue to be out of compliance with enterprise standards.
- If <requirement> is not implemented with this release, there will be staffing impacts to the Operations group.
- All <APPLICATION NAME> and <application name> related changes must be implemented concurrently.
- If <requirement> is not implemented, there will be customer and Operational impacts.
- If the file format changes are not made, there will be customer impacts.
- If the <requirement> changes are not made, there will be customer impact.

Issue Management

Project-related issues will be tracked, prioritized, assigned, resolved, and communicated as follows:

1. The project manager and participants will report issues that are identified throughout the life of the project.
2. The project manager will maintain a log of all issues and report on the status of issues.
3. The project manager will assign the priority and ownership to the issue. If necessary, the Executive Sponsors will assist the project manager in assigning appropriate ownership for resolution.
4. Individual team members assigned to resolve the issue will be responsible for communicating the issue status to the project manager.

See Appendix P5 for the Issue Log template.

Change Management

A change management procedure will be used by this project to help ensure that changes impacting the project are assessed, understood, and agreed upon by stakeholders before the change is made or before initiating specific actions to accommodate the change. The purpose of this procedure is to control change and impacts to the project and not to discourage change.

A Project Change Request form (PCR) must be submitted to the Project Manager for any changes that impact the project's cost, schedule, or scope. The Project Manager will review the proposed change request with the project team members impacted by the change to assess the impact of the change. The Project Manager will present the change request to the Steering Committee to approve or reject the request. The decision will be communicated to the requester and project team.

See Appendix P4 for the Project Change Request form and instructions.

Communication Plan

A project communication plan will be completed. This plan identifies the approach that will be used to share information with key internal and external parties throughout the project. The key elements of the communication plan include:

- Who must receive the information
- What intervals the information will be shared
- Who will provide the information
- What medium will be used

Project Status

The status of this project will be communicated in multiple ways. These include:

- Weekly project team status meeting
- Weekly project management status meeting
- Monthly project status reporting to the business lines
- Monthly online project status reporting to the PMO
- Project Plan Updates

A meeting agenda will be published prior to the meetings so participants can be prepared for the meeting. Meeting minutes will be distributed after the meeting has occurred so the team is aware of the discussion at the meeting.

PROJECT SCHEDULE AND MAJOR MILESTONES

Milestone	Start Date	Completion Date
Requirements	\<date>	\<date>
Analysis	\<date>	\<date>
Design	\<date>	\<date>
Development	\<date>	\<date>
Testing	\<date>	\<date>
Implementation	\<date>	\<date>
Post-Implementation Support	\<date>	\<date>
Project Closure	\<date>	\<date>

Project Team

Project Organization (Shaded Boxes in Figure P1 Are the Core Management Project Team)

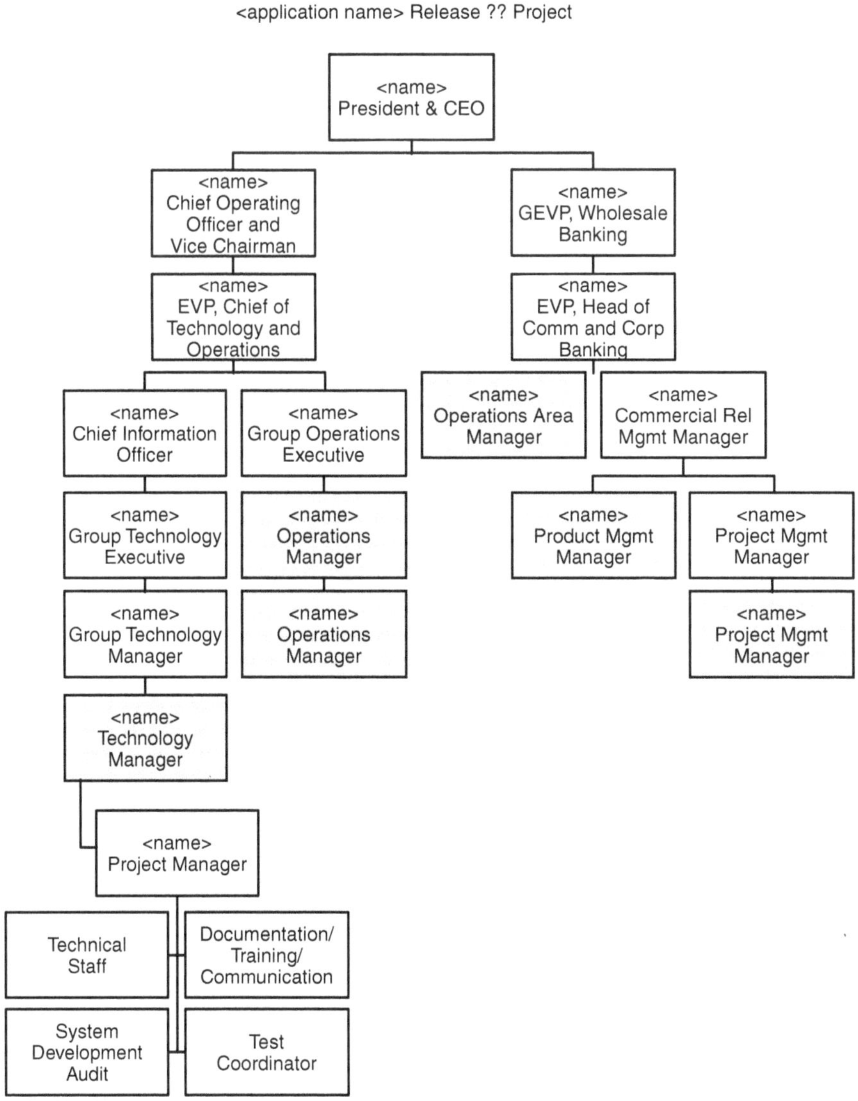

Figure P1 Project Organizational Chart

Project Team Roles/Responsibilities

Area	Individual(s)	Role/Responsibilities
Project Manager	\<name\>	First point of escalation of project issues Obtain project resource commitments Complete project estimates, as required Establish and execute a project plan Define project milestones Create and maintain a project issues log Schedule and conduct project status meetings Complete project status meeting minutes Compete project status reports Monitor and manage financial status of project Participate in the post-implementation review meeting Communicate with the other End-to-End Project Managers Close the project
Technical Lead	\<name\>	Review and approve Change Requests Create Systems project plan Participate in weekly project status meetings Conduct system training, as needed Conduct system status meetings Assist in User Acceptance Testing Ensure System Testing is completed Complete the Technical Design and Review Review and approve the project plan Develop the systems support plan Develop system conversion programs, as needed Complete system development and unit testing Update system documentation Complete production support plan Ensure technical activities are included in the project timeline Ensure technical resources are available to complete technical activities
Technical Systems Manager	\<name\>	Review and approve business requirements Approve project plan Review and approve Change Requests Review and approve project plan Review and approve User Design

Area	Individual(s)	Role/Responsibilities
		Review test plans
		Review and approve the project implementation plan
		Review and approve the support plan
Product Management Project Lead	\<name\>	Complete Product research and analysis
		Review product implementation workflow
		Define business requirements
		Approve project plan
		Review and approve Change Requests
		Review and approve project plan
		Communicate product changes and delivery plan to project team and line staff
		Review and approve User Design
		Perform gap analysis of old product versus new product
		Review and approve customer transition workflow
		Complete Product risk assessment
		Define product pricing structure
		Review test plans
		Resolve Product issues
		Assist with development of customer communications
		Review the project implementation plan
		Review and approve the support plan
Operations Project Leader	\<name\>	Review and approve Change Requests
		Create Operations project plan
		Participate in weekly project status meetings
		Conduct operations team status meetings, as necessary
		Participate in User Acceptance Testing
		Train Operations staff, as needed
		Provide Operations requirements
		Review and approve the Technical Design
		Review and approve User Design
		Review and approve the project plan
		Update Operations documentation
		Develop the operations support plan
		Review the project implementation plan
		Review and approve the support plan
		Ensure Operations resources are available to complete operation activities

Area	Individual(s)	Role/Responsibilities
Customer Services Project Leader	\<name\>	Review and approve Change Requests Participate in weekly project status meetings Participate in User Acceptance Testing Train Customer Services staff, as needed Provide Customer Service requirements Review and approve the Technical Design Review and approve User Design Review and approve the project plan Update Customer Service documentation Review the project implementation plan Review and approve the support plan Ensure Customer Services resources are available to complete customer service activities
Integration Project Leader	\<name\>	Review and approve Change Requests Participate in weekly project status meetings Participate in User Acceptance Testing Train Implementation staff, as needed Provide implementation requirements Review and approve the Technical Design Review and approve User Design Review and approve the project plan Update implementation documentation Review the project implementation plan Review and approve the support plan Ensure implementation resources are available to complete implementation activities
Documentation and Training	\<name\>	Coordinate with various bank training groups to ensure the proper updates are made to documentation, and to assess the need for training
Test Coordination	\<name\>	Identification of testing participants, organization of test team, and definition of responsibilities Coordinate cross-project testing dependencies with other testing project leads Identification of business/operation end users that may need to validate Confirm testing environment provided will meet needs Schedule testing with dependencies based on design, training, and conversion schedule

Area	Individual(s)	Role/Responsibilities
		Completion of test plan and approval
		Completion of test scripts and approval
		Establish and communicate testing schedule
		Communicate testing status with project team
		Monitoring of test cycles
		Ensure validation complete
		Track testing issues for fixes to be made and ensure appropriate resolution
		Obtain testing sign-offs
		Types of testing to manage for CTG:
		IAT (Integrated Application Testing)
		UAT (User Acceptance Testing)

PROJECT ESTIMATES/COSTS

Project Estimates and Costs

	Description	Dollars
Capital (hardware/software)	(if applicable)	N/A
Labor costs		
Employee	# hours	$
Contract labor	# hours	$
Total labor	hours	$
Test CPU	(if applicable)	N/A
Test DASD	(if applicable)	N/A
* Other (list all)	Travel/training	$
	Depreciation	N/A
	Software	N/A
	Teleconference	$ not budgeted
	Training	N/A
Total dollars		Total *$
		*Ball Park Estimate

Research and Experimentation Tax Credit Eligibility

An evaluation was completed for this project to determine if the project qualifies as an eligible R & E activity. The result of the evaluation indicates that this project does not qualify as an eligible R & E activity.

See Appendix P3 for the completed R & E Tax Credit evaluation.

APPENDICES:

Appendix P1: Statement of Work Approval

Project Number	??
Project Name	<APPLICATION NAME> Release ?? Project
Phase Name	Design

AUTHORIZATION

Name	**Signature**	**Approval Date**
<name>		

Operations Manager

<name>

Technology Manager

<name>

Project Manager

<name>

Treasury Management
 Product Management
<name>

Operations Manager

<name>

Client Services

<name>

Wholesale Integration

Appendix P2: Support Documentation Risk Assessment Form

Project Number	F1250	<APPLICATION NAME>
Project Title	<application name> Release ??	<name>
Date	<date>	
	Application Project Manager	

1.	Type of Project:	2
	Maintenance (correct problems)	1
	Enhancement (add new features)	2
	New development — replace existing automated system	3
	New development — replace manual system	5
	New development — develop system to support new business	6
	Implementation of software package in-house	6
	Outsourcing to external vendor	6
	Reengineering of system's architecture	6

11.	Number of Project Team Members:	8
	1–5	2
	6–10	4
	11–15	8
	16 or more	12

2.	Impact to Business Operations: (includes data/staffing/monetary)	10
	Limited change to business operation	5
	Medium change to business operation	10
	Major change to business operation	20

12.	Approximate Length of Time to Complete Project:	10
	<4 months	5
	4–7 months	10
	7–12 months	15
	>12 months	25

3.	Number of Years Business Organization Has Been in Business:	0	13.	Impact to Customer:	20
	>3	0		Limited product/portfolio customer base affected	5
	1–3	2		Partial product/portfolio customer base affected	10
	<1	4		Entire product/portfolio customer base affected	20
4.	Number of Years the Business Group and Technology Group Have Worked Together:	0	14.	Number of Years the Project Technology Has Been Used in the Organization:	4
	>3	0		>3	0
	1–3	2		1–3	4
	<1	4		<1	8
5.	Number of Years the Project Manager Has Been a Project Manager:	0	15.	Amount and Level of Documentation Currently Available:	5
	>3	0		Extensive, detailed documentation	1
	1–3	5		Extensive documentation, but not detailed	2
	<1	10		Limited documentation, but detailed	4
				Limited or no documentation, not detailed	5

6.	*Number of Years (on average) Business Group Area Has Worked with Specific Application to Be Developed:*	0	16.	*Number of Organizational Entities (besides systems) that Need to Be Involved:*	18
	>3	0		0–2	3
	1–3	5		3–5	9
	<1	10		>5	18
7.	*Number of Years (on average) Technology Project Team Has Worked with Specific Application to Be Developed:*	2	17.	*Availability of Business Partner to Technology Group:*	4
	>3	0		Assigned to desired level of involvement and available to dp immediately when needed	0
	1–3	2		Assigned to desired level of involvement, but likely not available immediately when needed	4
	<1	4		Not assigned to the desired level of involvement	16
8.	*Number of Years Technology Team Has Performed the Duties They Will Be Asked to Perform on the Project (i.e., analysis, design, coding, testing):*	0	18.	*Legal/Regulatory Impact:*	0

		Limited legal/regulatory ramifications	0
		Moderate legal/regulatory ramifications	5
		Significant legal/regulatory ramifications	10
9.	**Number of Years (average) Technology Team Has Worked with the Technology to Be Used on the Project (e.g., CICS, PACBASE, IMS):**	**0**	
	>3	0	
	1–3	4	
	<1	8	
19.	**Estimated Costs for Hardware/Software/Conversion:**	**0**	
	<$600,000	0	
	$600,000 to $3,000,000	3	5
	>$3,000,000	6	10
10.	**Number of Vendors Involved:**	**4**	
	1	2	
	2	4	
	≥3	8	
20.	**Number of Interfaces:**		**5**
	<4		0
	4–12		5
	≥12		10

TOTAL SCORE 82
RISK LEVEL __Medium__

Score Range	Risk
0 to 70	Low
71 to 120	Medium
121+	High

21.	Technology Options Explored/Researched:	0
	≥	0
	2	2
	1	5
	None	10
22.	Was This Technology Option Selected as a Second Choice Based upon Cost or Schedule?	0
	No	0
	Yes	4
23.	Technology Used in the Project:	0
	None of the technology used is new	0
	New to the business line	5
	New to Wells Fargo	10
	New to the industry	20

30.	Incorporation of the Corporate Business Continuity Planning Process into the Design of the Project.	4
	Extensive involvement in the systems design	0
	Minimal involvement in the systems design	4
	No involvement in the systems design	8
	No contingency plan exists	12
31.	Impact to the Customer and/or Environment if the Technology Fails:	5
	No impact	0
	Limited impact	5
	Moderate impact	10
	Significant impact	20
32.	Impact to the Customer and/or Environment if the Exit Plan Has to Be Executed:	4
	Limited impact	2
	Moderate impact	4
	Significant impact	8

24.	Project Requirements	0
	Requirements are clear, complete, and stable	0
	Requirements are documented, but some unclear, incomplete, or unstable information	5
	Minimal or no requirements documented	10
25.	Service or Functionality Provided to Customers or End Users by the Technology:	18
	Maintenance	3
	Standard enhancement	6
	Extended functionality	9
	New functionality/service/product/architecture	18
26.	Can Sizing and Capacity for Technology Be Evaluated and Incorporated into Design?	10
	Current and future sizing and capacity analysis is identified	2
	Only current sizing and capacity analysis is identified	5
	No sizing and capacity analysis can be identified	10

33.	Type of Third-Party Connectivity (non-Wells Fargo connectivity) Used in Project Or Technology:	5
	No third-party connectivity	0
	Existing third-party connectivity involved	5
	New third-party connectivity involved	10
34.	Outage during the Implementation of the Technology:	0
	No outage required	0
	Outage after business hours	4
	Outage during business hours	8
35.	Level of Training Necessary for Customers and End Users:	5
	None	0
	Limited training necessary	5
	Extensive training necessary	10

27.	**Changes to Existing Systems, Including Infrastructure, Necessary to Implement the Technology:**	*2*
	Limited	2
	Moderate	5
	Significant	10
28.	**Number of Dependencies on Other Projects, Changes, Services, Vendors, Suppliers, or Contractors:**	*15*
	None	0
	1	5
	≥2	15
29.	**Number of Applications or Systems Impacted:**	*10*
	≤1	5
	2–3	10
	4–12	15
	>12	25

Score Range	Risk
0 to 60	Low
61 to 110	Medium
111+	High

36.	**Amount of Training Materials and Documentation Budgeted and Necessary for Customers and End Users to Use the New Technology:**	*4*
	Limited or no documentation needed	2
	Limited documentation, but detailed	4
	Extensive documentation, but not detailed	6
	Extensive and detailed documentation	8
37.	**Formal RFP Process Used during Technology Selection:**	*0*
	RFP process followed	0
	RFP process followed, but only one response	3
	RFP process NOT followed	6
38.	**Level of Vendor Support Necessary for the Technology after Implementation:**	*5*
	No support necessary	0
	Minor support necessary (i.e., maintenance)	5
	Major support necessary (i.e., programming, upgrades, etc.)	10

TOTAL SCORE 87
RISK LEVEL <u>Medium</u>

Appendix P3: Potential Tax Credit Tests

The following analysis evaluates if this project qualifies as an eligible R & E activity.

Yes	No	Qualification Tests
☐	☒	*First Test* Do the activities qualify as research in the laboratory or experimental sense by: Relating to, or supporting, the development or improvement of a product; and Intending to discover information that would eliminate uncertainty concerning the development or improvement of a product or process?
☒	☐	*Second Test* Is the research undertaken for the purpose of discovering information that is technological in nature?
☒	☐	*Third Test* Do the activities undertaken include the elements of the process of experimentation (i.e., were alternative designs evaluated using the scientific method or did the development of the final design require experimentation)?
☒	☐	*Fourth Test* Is the activity being conducted for a permitted purpose: new or improved function, performance, reliability, quality, or significant cost reduction?

If software is developed for *internal management function* and technique it generally does not qualify for tax credit unless it meets the following **three-part test:**

Yes	No	
☐	☒	*First Test* Is the software innovative in that it results in a reduction of costs or improvement in speed that is substantial and economically significant?
☐	☒	*Second Test* Does the development involve significant economic risk in that the company commits substantial resources to the development and there is substantial uncertainty, because of technical risk, that such resources would not be recovered in a reasonable period?
☐	☒	*Third Test* Is the software being developed not commercially available (i.e., can the software be obtained elsewhere and used for the intended purpose without modifications that would satisfy the first and second tests above)?

Appendix P4: Change Management Form and Instructions

Procedure

At the conclusion of the requirement phase of the project, the requirements will be considered static and unchangeable because they will form the basis for subsequent project activities. In the event that a change is necessary, the following process must be followed to ensure that the change is implemented into the project plan and impacts are adequately assessed.

1. A change is identified as a result of an issue or of some change to the project environment (for example, regulatory and/or competitive changes).
2. The person who is requesting the change completes a Project Change Request Form and sends it to the Project Manager. This form will require the following information from the requester(s):
   - *Date of the Request* — this is the date the request form is filled out.
   - *Requester* — the name of the individual requesting the change.
   - *Description of Change* — a detailed description of the requested change.
   - *Business Reason for Change* — a detailed description of the business reason why the change must be implemented as part of this project.
3. The Project Manager will review the change request with all impacted team members to determine the project tasks that will either be added or impacted by the change request and estimate the impacts of the change.
4. After assessing the impact of the requested change on the project and completing estimated cost and schedule impacts, the request will be presented to the Executive Sponsors and either approved or denied.
5. The Project Manager will contact the requester by sending a completed change request form to the requester with the final decision and inform the impacted areas of the decision. If the change request is denied, the Project Manager will include a reason for denial in the Reason for Denial section.
6. A copy of the Project Change Request Form will be included in the project file for permanent record and the project task plan will be updated accordingly.

Project Change Request Form

<APPLICATION NAME> Release ??
Change Control Request Form

Instructions	Requester must complete this side of form.
Name of Change	
Date Requested	
Release Requested (cannot request change control on any release scheduled to move to ET in 60 days or less)	
Funding Source	
Estimate of Hours to Complete	
Estimated Dollars to Complete (number of hours multiplied by the current development rate of $100.00)	
Cost Savings Realized by Implementing this Request (describe in dollars the savings realized on a monthly or yearly basis)	
State the Requirements	
Current Work-around Being Employed	
Background or Other Important Facts	
Operations Approval Must have Operations Mgmt approval before being submitted to Systems for estimating	Insert approval e-mail in this section and copy Operations Mgmt on the e-mail when sent to Systems
Product Approval Must have Product Mgmt approval before being submitted to Systems for estimating	Insert approval e-mail in this section and copy Product Mgmt on the e-mail when sent to Systems
Systems Approval Approval will be granted after the estimate is completed	Insert approval e-mail in this section and copy Systems Mgmt on the e-mail when the response is e-mailed to Operations and Product within 10 business days of the request

Procedure:

1. Complete the Change Control Form.
2. Submit to <APPLICATION NAME> Application Systems Manager or Team Lead.
3. Systems will estimate the effort.
4. Systems will respond within 10 business days indicating if the change can be absorbed in the release requested:
   - If the request can be absorbed, work will be queued as appropriate.
   - If the request cannot be absorbed, the Systems group will call a meeting to discuss reprioritizing requirements or moving the request to another release.
5. See bottom of form for Approval Instructions.

Appendix P5: Issues Log

<APPLICATION NAME> Release ?? Issues Log

OPEN ISSUES

Issue #	Open Date	Opened By	Issue Description	Assigned To	Due Date	Closed Date	Status	Priority	Comments/Resolution

CLOSED ISSUES

Issue #	Open Date	Opened By	Issue Description	Assigned To	Due Date	Closed Date	Status	Priority	Comments/Resolution

Priority Codes:
High = Show Stopper — cannot continue without issue resolution.
Medium = Caution — may continue without immediate resolution.
Low = Not Critical — can continue without issue resolution.

Status Codes:
(A)ctive
(R)esolved
(D)eferred
(P)ending

Appendix P6: List of Requirements Scheduled for Release ??

- \<APPLICATION NAME\> New File Format
- New File Format
- New **\<APPLICATION NAME\>** Stmt Paper and Logo

Appendix Q

PROBLEM TROUBLE REPORT (PTR)

PROBLEM TROUBLE REPORT (PTR)

PROBLEM NO.: _____

CI: _____

DATE ISSUED: _____

PROGRAM/PROJECT/SCR: _____

TEST CYCLE/JOB: _____

TYPE: __ ONLINE/SCREEN

CONDITION NO.: _____

    __ BATCH/REPORT

    __ DOCUMENTATION

    __ DATABASE

CATEGORIES: __ A-CRITICAL/FIX IMMEDIATELY

             __ B-MAJOR/FIX BEFORE TEST COMPLETION

             __ C-FIX BEFORE DEPLOYMENT

             __ D-NEW OR REVISED REQUIREMENT

             __ E-PROBLEM EXISTS IN REAL WORLD

             __ F-USER DEFINED

SUBJECT: _____

PROBLEM DETAILS: (Attach examples) _____

ISSUED BY: _____

ISSUING ORG: _____

REQ. DEV. REPRESENTATIVE/LEAD RECOMMENDATIONS: _____
_____
_____

SIGNATURE: _____ DATE: _____

PROGRAMMER EVALUATION: _____
_____
_____

SOFTWARE PROGRAM/VERSION CHANGED: _____

FIXED: _____ RECOMMENDED CANCEL: _____ DATE: _____

PROGRAMMER SIGNATURE: _____

REQ. DEV. REPRESENTATIVE/ACQUIRER/USER EVALUATION:

RETEST DATE: _____

NOT RESOLVED: _____ CANCELED: _____ CLOSED: _____

    SIGNATURE: _____

Problem Trouble Report 10.2

Appendix R

LIBRARY/BASELINE CHANGE FORM

Library/Baseline Change Form

Project/Product Line:

Requested by:

DRCM Use

What Kind of Change?	☐ Promotion	☐ Demotion	☐ Addition	Request #:	Request Date:
Reason Why?	☐ Test passed ☐ Change Approved ☐ Milestone Passed	☐ Test failed ☐ Retreat to previous Version ☐ Customer rejected	☐ Establish Baseline ☐ Add new product to Baseline ☐ Received new product to add to the Baseline		

Products

CI/File Name	CI #	Ver/Rev	Type Soft/Doc	Current Location			Affected Library/Baseline Changed		
				Remote/Local File Path	Provided Media	Library or Baseline	Library or Baseline	Date	Authorities Name/Signature

Appendix S

SAMPLE MAINTENANCE PLAN

SAMPLE MAINTENANCE PLAN

Change Control Page

The following information is being used to control and track modifications made to this document.

1. Revision Date:

   CI:

   Author:

   Section(s):

   Page Number(s):

   Summary of Change(s):

TITLE PAGE

Document Name: Project Name

Maintenance Plan

Publication Date: Month Year

Contract Number: XX-XXXX-XXXXXXXXX

Project Number: Task: XXXXXXXXXXXXXX

Prepared by: XXXX XXXXXX

Approval: _____

                                      Name and Organization

Concurrence: _____

                                      Name and Organization

COMPANY

Organizational Title 1

Organizational Title 2

TABLE OF CONTENTS

PREFACE

Document Version Control: It is the readers' responsibility to ensure they have the latest version of this document. Questions should be directed to the owner of this document, or the project manager.

Life-cycle Stage: *Project Name* is in the maintenance stage of the project life cycle.

Approval: *An approval signature constitutes approval of this document when accepting a developed project(s) into the maintenance stage or for an existing project(s) that has been in the maintenance stage but did not have a documented plan.*

Document Owner: The primary contact for questions regarding this document is:

Author's Name, Author's Function, e.g., Project Planner

Project Name Team

Phone: (XXX) XXX-XXXX

E-mail: XXX.XXX@hq.doe.gov

Privacy Information

This document may contain information of a sensitive nature. This information should not be given to persons other than those who are involved in the *Project Name* project or who will become involved during the life cycle.

1 OVERVIEW

1.1 Background

Provide a high-level description of the project and its background. Clearly indicate if processes are already in place from the development of the system or whether the system has been in maintenance for some time and did not have documented processes. If the processes carried over from development, reference the documents that describe the process. If the processes were not documented before, describe each process in this maintenance plan.

1.2 Scope of Maintenance

Describe the software, hardware, documentation, and services that are included in the maintenance task assignment/contract.

State the parameters that are being set for the project(s). This may include areas such as work assignments; type and frequency of customer/client meetings; requirements analysis; project(s) characteristics, etc. Also, list any areas specifically excluded from the project(s) (i.e., acquisition of hardware/software, etc.).

Describe the nature of the maintenance to be performed. Is it ongoing (e.g., several resources are assigned and funded for a given period of time and they maintain the system) or is it for a specific project (e.g., a specific enhancement to be performed, or additional functionality to be added)?

1.3 References

Identify sources of information used to develop this document, such as IEEE or project documentation.

2 PRODUCT STATUS

Identify the status of the products included in the scope at the time the maintenance task assignment/contract is initiated. This would include version numbers, release numbers, and any known defects.

3 PROJECT TEAM

Identify all team members by functional job description (e.g., all maintenance team members, functional area members, and approvers). State approximate percentage of each team member's time that will be required to be devoted to the project(s).

3.1 Roles and Responsibilities

The person(s) responsible for ensuring that the maintenance activities are performed are identified in the in the chart below or the project(s) work breakdown structure that these persons are normally identified is referenced.

Role	Name	Org	Responsibility
System Owner/User Point of Contact (POC)			Has overall responsibility and accountability for systems and data. Assigns and approves all project activities.
Project Leader			Responsible for daily planning and control of project. Manages and coordinates technical effort. Evaluates all requests and assignments from system owner and assigns to the appropriate staff member. Provides consistent and timely communications with system owner. Responsible for final sign-off of all project assignments prior to forwarding to system owner for approval. Responsible for producing the Maintenance Plan and for obtaining the customer's agreement to the plan.
Project Leader's Manager			Provides support and guidance to the project leader and team. Ensures project staffing. Resolves and facilitates communications between client and support group.
Systems Programmer/ Analyst Support Staff			Analyzes assignments and performs the technical requirements of the task including coding, testing, documenting, and implementing.
Quality Analyst			Reviews deliverables from a QA perspective. Provides guidance and assistance on process matters.

4 MANAGEMENT APPROACH

Describe the priorities for managing the project; tracking and controlling the project; assumptions, constraints, or dependencies associated with the project; risk management issues; project estimates (sizing and time); staffing requirements (skills and resource load); and information on overall schedule and project deliverables. Provide an overview of how activities will be tracked to completion and how the project schedule/cost will be kept under control.

4.1 Management Priorities

Describe in general the approach for determining priorities.

4.2 Task Estimates

Describe the process for determining estimates for tasks received.

Estimate the task's size and the time required for completion. Estimates may be based on information such as the project's objectives, and information gathered during interviews, known requirements, and skill/experience levels. Estimating approaches may include a defined timeframe for each type of task based on tracking of actual times versus planned, over a period of time. Target response time and clearance time for problems/change requests.

4.3 Assumptions, Constraints, and Dependencies

List all known assumptions, constraints, and dependencies that could potentially affect maintenance of the project. An example of an assumption would be that the tasks for the project do not change significantly after they have been approved. A constraint is normally a situation that limits the resources that can be used to accomplish project maintenance. For example, the budget is restricted, requiring extra coordination to insure agreement on what tasks can be accomplished with the resources available. A dependency is an event or chain of events, outside the manager's control, that must happen for the project to be successful. For example, testing of project(s) will depend on installation, by 10-1-02, of a LAN backbone and connections by the Telecommunications area.

5 TECHNICAL APPROACH

5.1 Types of Maintenance Activities

The activities for maintenance changes are a shortened version of the development stages. The types of changes that are included in the maintenance task assignment/contract are: problem resolution (corrective), enhancements, interface modifications (adaptive).

5.2 Configuration Management

Describe the configuration management process. Describe the change control activities. This includes how the change is initiated by the customer or the maintenance team and the process for analysis, risk assessment, design, coding, testing, and installation of a new release of the software, including changes to project documents.

Include the process for corrective changes that are made on an emergency basis to keep the project operational. A sample change request form is in Attachment 1.

5.3 Risk Assessment

State all potential risks associated with the change being implemented. Describe the elements of the risk, and state how the risk will be handled during task implementation.

5.4 Testing

Describe the process for testing the changes.

5.5 System Protection

Describe the process for protecting unauthorized access to the project(s).

5.6 Special Processes

Identify special-purpose programs that are planned/regularly scheduled maintenance activities such as mass changes, database modifications, backup and recovery, etc.

5.7 Maintenance Records and Reports

Describe the format of records of maintenance activities performed and frequency of issue to customer.

List reports that will be produced and frequency of issue. These should include:

- List of requests for assistance or customer problems and the status of each
- List of corrective actions, including their priorities and results, if available
- Failure rates and maintenance activity metrics

Reference Attachment 2 for a sample Maintenance Log, instructions, and Maintenance Log — Detail Status Information.

5.8 Training

Describe the periodic or established training required for customers and maintenance team.

5.9 Documentation

Describe the documents that are maintained as part of the maintenance effort.

5.10 Quality Assurance Activities

Describe the activities and the process for reviewing the maintenance process to determine that activities are occurring as planned.

Attachment 1

Software Change Request Form

Software Change Request (SCR)

Requirement # : _____   SCR #: _____

Originator: _____

Date: _____   Release #: _____

Type:
( ) New Requirement   ( ) System Problem   ( ) Suggestion for Improvement
( ) Requirement Change   ( ) User Interface Problem   (_____)
( ) Design Change   ( ) Documentation Correction   Other: _____

Priority:
( ) High   ( ) Normal   ( ) Low

Description:

Please attach supporting documentation for the requested change
(screen/report printouts, document pages affected, etc.)

Status	Date	Initials/Comments
Reviewed & Estimated		

On Hold						
Canceled						
Approved for Change						
Code Updated						
Documentation Updated						
Completed						

SMR # _____

New Release # _____

Please attach supporting documentation for review & estimates (analysis, resource estimates, layouts, document pages affected, etc.)

Maintenance Log

Page #: _____ Log Date: ___/___/___

System Name:

Request #	Reqmnt #	Date Submitted	Priority (E,U,R) *	Approval			Status				
				Change Approved	Change Not Approved	Hold (Future Enhancement)	Technical Evaluation Phase	Change In-Progress	Canceled	Target Date	Date Complete

Maintenance Log V1.0 (6/22/98)

* E = Emergency, U = Urgent, R = Routine (as defined by the request form).

INSTRUCTIONS FOR COMPLETING THE MAINTENANCE LOG

This change control log form is included as a suggested format for recording and maintaining software change request data, including changes to documentation. A Detailed Status Information form is available to record supplementary details. The log and software change requests should be maintained in the Systems Project Notebook.

Field	Definition
Page #:	Enter the appropriate page number of the log sheet.
Log Date:	Enter the date control log was started.
System Name:	Enter the name and acronym of the system to be managed.
Request #:	Enter the unique sequential number assigned to each request on the request form (i.e., software change request form, etc.)
Reqmnt #:	Enter the unique number of the requirement to be changed (if known) on the request form.
Date Submitted:	Enter the date the request was submitted to the maintenance team.
Priority:	Enter the priority from the request form using the first character of the priority; e.g., E = Emergency, U = Urgent, and R = Routine.
Approval:	This area is for recording request approval information obtained from the request form.
	Change Approved: Enter the date the request was approved.
	Change Not Approved: Enter the date the request was disapproved.
	Hold (Future Enhancement): Enter the date the request was placed on "Hold."
Status:	This area is for recording basic information about the status of a request.
.	*Technical Evaluation Phase:* Enter the date the technical evaluation of the request commenced.
	Change In-Progress: Enter the date work began on the request. Usually, the areas "Technical Evaluation Phase" (if applicable) and "Change Approved" should be entered prior to posting the "Change In-Progress" date. Work on most requests should not be initiated without a technical evaluation and formal approval in the request form.
	Canceled: Enter the date the request was canceled.
	Target Date: Enter the estimated date that the request will be completed and ready for release/implementation.
	Date Complete: Enter the actual date the request was implemented.

MAINTENANCE LOG — DETAIL STATUS INFORMATION

Log Date: ___/___/___

Page #:

Request #:

System Name:

SCC-DS Log V1.0 (8/8/99)

Note: Use this form in conjunction with the Maintenance Log form to record supplementary details about a given software change request. Include the appropriate Page # and task # from the Maintenance Log form to maintain a cross-reference between logs. Keep all logs with the task request in the System Project Notebook.

REFERENCE

This document is an adaptation of a Maintenance Plan document template from the U.S. Department of Energy.

Appendix T

SOFTWARE CONFIGURATION MANAGEMENT PLAN (SCMP)

Software Configuration Management Plan (SCMP)
for
[System Title]

ORIGINATOR: _____   _____

            Author Name, Title   Date

            Code

REVIEWERS: _____   _____

            SCM Manager Name, Title   Date

            Code

                    _____   _____

            SQA Manager Name, Title   Date

            Code

APPROVAL: _____   _____

            Project Manager, Title   Date

            Code

SCM_PLANTEMPLATE:457F:1.00:30APR1998

TABLE OF CONTENTS

This Software Configuration Management (SCM) Plan (SCMP) describes the SCM organization and practices applied consistently and uniformly throughout the life cycle for Computer Software Configuration Items (CSCIs) that are developed or maintained by [originating organization].

   SCM is the process used during software development and maintenance to identify, control, and report functional and physical configurations of software products (e.g., source code, executable code, databases, test scenarios and data, and documentation).

1.1 Purpose

The purpose of this document is to define SCM responsibilities (requirements), resources, and processes used during the development and maintenance of the [system title] system. Figure T1 provides an overview of the SCM functions. In the figure, Data Management (DM) is shown connected to SCM with a broken line. DM is a sub-function of SCM with SCM having overall cognizant responsibility. Section 5 describes the DM responsibilities. Software Quality Assurance (SQA) is a separate function that works closely with SCM to ensure the integrity of the product (i.e., SCM controls the product; SQA certifies the integrity of the product).

1.2 Scope

This plan establishes the SCM methods used during the development and maintenance of the [system title] system.

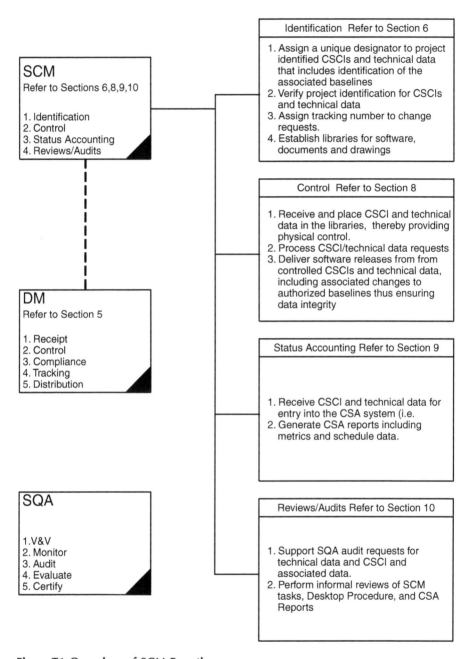

Figure T1 Overview of SCM Functions

Table T1 CSCI Nomenclature/Identification

Nomenclature	Acronym	CSCI Number
CSCI Name	Acronym	CSCI ID number
CSCI Name	Acronym	CSCI ID number
CSCI Name	Acronym	CSCI ID number

1.3 Approach

The SCM discipline is applied to those Configuration Items (CIs) for which the project organization has development and/or maintenance responsibilities. The SCM organization implements the processes described within this plan to ensure that products developed are correct, consistent, complete, and compliant with governing policies.

1.4 System Overview

<Provide a brief description of the system that this plan applies to.>

1.5 Project-Defined CSCIs

Table T1 shows the CSCIs that this plan applies to.

Listed below is a brief description of each of the CSCIs developed and maintained by [originating organization].

CSCI #1 — Include a brief description of the CSCI and its purpose.
CSCI #2 — Include a brief description of the CSCI and its purpose.
CSCI #3 — Include a brief description of the CSCI and its purpose.

The system includes entering the number of sub-systems within the system. Figure T2 identifies the CSCIs within each sub-system and highlights those that this SCMP applies. The current [system title] Software Development Plan (SDP) contains a detailed description of the software.

1.6 Document Overview

This SCMP establishes the plan for the configuration management of software and related documents produced by the [software development] organization. The processes developed in this SCMP are applicable to all personnel responsible for the analysis, design, development, maintenance, and testing of software embedded in or impacting on the operational capabilities of [system title].

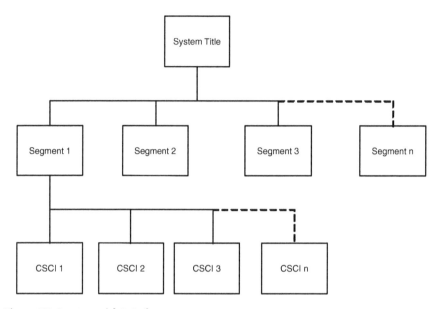

Figure T2 [system title] Software

This plan follows the process defined in the SCM Process Definition.

a. **Section 1** — provides the scope, the purpose, and a summary of the contents of the SCMP and a list of common configuration management terms and definitions.

b. **Section 2** — lists the standards and other publications referenced in this document and used in its preparation.

c. **Section 3** — outlines the project organization and responsibilities.

d. **Section 4** — describes the CM phasing and milestones.

e. **Section 5** — describes the activities associated with DM.

f. **Section 6** — describes the process of configuration identification of CSCIs, associated technical documentation, code, and media.

g. **Section 7** — describes the approach for identification and maintenance of system interfaces.

h. **Section 8** — describes the process for maintaining configuration control of CSCIs and their associated technical data.

i. **Section 9** — describes the Configuration Status Accounting (CSA) process used to record and report CSCI information.

j. **Section 10** — describes the approach used for performing physical and functional configuration audits and reviews of SCM activities and products.

k. **Section 11** — describes the methods used to ensure subcontractor and vendor compliance with SCM requirements.

l. **Appendix T1** — contains a list of all acronyms and abbreviations and their definitions used in this document.

m. **Appendix T2** — contains the format and preparation instructions for forms used by the SCM organization.

n. **Appendix T3** — describes the CM phasing and milestones.

1.7 SCM Terms and Definitions.

The terms and definitions listed below are provided as an aid to understanding and applying the SCM principles and processes used to manage software development and testing efforts.

Allocated Baseline (ABL) — The initially approved documentation that describes an item's functional, interoperability, and interface characteristics that are allocated from those of a system or a higher level configuration item, interface requirements with interfacing configuration items, additional design constraints, and the verification required to demonstrate the achievement of those specified characteristics.

Allocated Configuration Documentation (ACD) — The approved Allocated Baseline plus approved changes.

As-Built — Defines the initial software, hardware, or system configuration as it actually has been built.

Audit — An independent examination of a work product or set of work products to assess compliance with specifications, standards, contractual agreements, or criteria.

Baseline — A configuration identification document or set of such documents formally designated and fixed at a specific time during the configuration item's life cycle. Baselines, plus approved changes from those baselines, constitute the current configuration identification.

Change Request (CR) Form — A vehicle used to report deficiencies or enhancements generated against CIs or technical data; a document that requests a correction or change to the baselined documentation and software.

Computer Software (or Software) — A combination of associated computer instructions and computer data definitions required to enable the computer hardware to perform computational or control functions.

Computer Software Configuration Item (CSCI) — A configuration item that is software.

Configuration — The functional and physical characteristics of existing or planned hardware, firmware, or software or a combination thereof as set forth in technical documentation and achieved in a product.

Configuration Audit — A formal examination of a CSCI. Two types of configuration audits exist: the Functional Configuration Audit (FCA) and the Physical Configuration Audit (PCA).

Configuration Control — The systematic proposal, justification, evaluation, coordination, and approval or disapproval of proposed changes, and the implementation of all approved changes in the configuration of a Configuration Item (CI) after establishment of the baseline(s) for the CI.

Configuration Identification — The selection of CIs; the determination of the types of configuration documentation required for each CI; the issuance of numbers and other identifiers affixed to the CIs and to the technical documentation that defines the CI's configuration, including internal and external interfaces; the release of CI's and their associated configuration documentation; and the establishment of configuration baselines for CIs.

Configuration Item (CI) — An aggregation of hardware or software that satisfies an end-use function and is designated for separate configuration management.

Configuration Status Accounting (CSA) — The recording and reporting of information needed to manage configuration items (CI) effectively, including:

A record of the approved configuration documentation and identification numbers

The status of proposed changes, deviations, and waivers to the configuration

The implementation status of approved changes

The configuration of all units of the CI in the operational inventory

Deliverable — A system or component that is obligated contractually to a customer or intended user.

Developmental Configuration — The software and associated technical documentation that define the evolving configuration of a CSCI during development. The Developmental Configuration may be stored on electronic media.

Deviation — A specific written authorization to depart from a particular requirement(s) of an item's current approved configuration documentation for a specific number of units or a specified period of time.

Engineering Change Proposal (ECP) — A proposed engineering change and the documentation by which the change is described, justified, and submitted to the government for approval or disapproval.

Firmware — The combination of a hardware device and computer instructions or computer data that reside as read-only software on the hardware device. The software cannot be readily modified under program control.

Functional Baseline (FBL) — The initially approved documentation describing a system's or item's functional, interoperability, and interface characteristics and the verification required to demonstrate the achievement of those specified characteristics.

Functional Configuration Audit (FCA) — The formal examination of functional characteristics of a CI, prior to acceptance, to verify that the CI has achieved the requirements specified in its functional and allocated configuration documentation.

Functional Configuration Documentation (FCD) — The approved FBL plus approved changes.

Nondevelopmental Software (NDS) — Deliverable software that is not developed under the contract but is provided by the contractor, the government, or a third party. NDS may be referred to as reusable software, government-furnished software, or commercially available software, depending on its source.

Notice Of Revision (NOR) — A document used to define revisions to drawings, associated lists, or other referenced documents that require revision after ECP approval.

Physical Configuration Audit (PCA) — The formal examination of the "as-built" configuration of a CI against its technical documentation to establish or verify the CI's product baseline.

Product Baseline (PBL) — The initially approved documentation describing all of the necessary functional and physical characteristics of the CI and the selected functional and physical characteristics designated for production acceptance testing and tests necessary for support of the CI.

Product Configuration DocumentatioN (PCD) — The approved product baseline plus approved changes.

Program Management — The organization sponsoring the field activity project office.

Project Management — The designated government organization from the field activity project office responsible for the overall management of specific projects.

Release — A configuration management action whereby a particular version of software is made available for a specific purpose (e.g., released to test).

Reusable Software — Software developed in response to the requirements for one application that can be used, in whole or in part, to satisfy the requirements for another application.

Resources — The totality of computer hardware, software, personnel, documentation, supplies, and services applied to a given effort.

Software — *See* Computer Software.

Software Configuration Management (SCM) — A discipline that applies technical and administrative direction and surveillance to perform the functions listed below:

Identify and document the functional and physical characteristics of CSCIs.

Control the changes to CSCIs and their related documentation.

Record and report information needed to manage CSCIs effectively, including the status of proposed changes and the implementation status of approved changes.

Audit the CSCIs to verify conformance to specifications, interface control documents, and other contract requirements.

Software Development Library (SDL) — A controlled collection of software, documentation, and other intermediate and final software development products, and associated tools and procedures used to facilitate the orderly development and subsequent support of software.

Software-Related Group — Project members responsible for generating requirements, design, development, validation, verification, documentation, maintenance, and logistics of software.

Software Support — The sum of all activities that take place to ensure that implemented and fielded software continues to fully support the operational mission of the software.

Software Unit — An element in the design of a software item; for example, a major subdivision of a software item, a component of that subdivision, a class, object, module, function, routine, or database. Software units may occur at different levels of a hierarchy and may consist of other software units. Software units in the design may or may not have a one-to-one relationship with the code and data entities (routines, procedures, databases, data files, etc.) that implement them or with the computer files containing those entities.

Software Test Environment — A set of automated tools, firmware devices, and hardware necessary to test software. The automated tools may include but are not limited to test tools such as simulation software, code analyzers, test case generators, path analyzers, etc. and may also include the tools used in the software engineering environment.

Specification Change Notice (SCN) — A document used to propose, transmit, and record changes to a specification.

Technical Review — An activity by which the technical progress of a project is assessed relative to its technical or contractual requirements. The review is conducted at logical transition points in the development effort to identify and correct problems resulting from the work completed thus far before the problems can disrupt or delay the technical progress. The review provides a method for the contractor and government to determine that the development of a CSCI and its documentation have met contract requirements.

Version — An identified and documented body of software. Modifications to a version of software (resulting in a new version) require configuration management actions, by either the contractor, the government, or both.

Waiver — A written authorization to accept an item, which during manufacture, or after having been submitted for government inspection or acceptance, is found to depart from specified requirements, but nevertheless is considered suitable for use "as is" or after repair by an approved method.

1.8 SCMP Updates

This document will be periodically reviewed to ensure that all SCM functions are accurately described. Audit and review reports or changes to available resources may require this document to be updated. All changes will be incorporated in either change pages or a document revision. Updates to this document are recorded on the Record of Changes and List of Effective Pages sheets located at the front of this document.

SECTION 2: ORGANIZATION

This section describes the SCM organization in relation to the program and project organization structure.

2.1 Organizational Structure

Figure T3 is a graphic representation of the program and project organizational structure with respect to the SCM organization. Although SCM takes direction from the Project Manager, it operates within the policies and procedures established by [name of the organization establishing policies]. Listed below are the responsibilities of each of the organizations as related to [system title] development.

SCM interfaces with the functions listed below to control software configuration and release activities.

<Depending on the size of the organization, the functional groups defined below may be combined (e.g., the Software

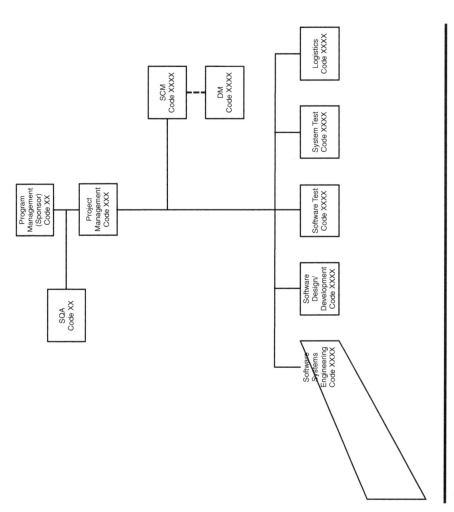

Figure T3 Organization Structure

Systems Engineering Group and the Software Design and Development Group may be one group known as software development). You will need to define the group interfacing with the SCM organization.>

Program Management (Code Number) — Responsible for and has the authority to ensure complete fulfillment of all program requirements. The Program Manager has the overall responsibility for acquisition, funding, and transitioning of the project.

Project Management (Code Number) — Responsible for the technical aspects of the project. The Project Manager has the responsibility for local funding, allocations, scheduling, tasking, and reporting to program management.

Software Systems Engineering (Code Number) — Responsible for systems design (and associated documentation) overview and guidance; detailed design and coding; test plans, procedures, and reports; software unit testing; and preliminary CSCI testing.

Software Design and Development (Code Number) — Responsible for software design (and associated documentation) overview and guidance; detailed design and coding; test plans, procedures, and reports; software unit testing; and preliminary CSCI testing.

Software Test (Code Number) — Responsible for the conduct of software testing, including preparation of test plan, description, procedures, and reports. The Software Test Group ensures that the correct configuration is undergoing test and incorporates approved changes into released test documentation based on change request baselining data from SCM. The Software Test Group confirms verification of change request corrective measures prior to change request closure. SCM identifies all change requests included in an Engineering Master (EM) that is to be tested. Test personnel then provide SCM a copy of the test report.

Software Quality Assurance (SQA) (Code Number) — Responsible for auditing the software development activities and products (FCA and PCA) and certifying of SCM compliance with this plan and DTPs.

System Test (Code Number) — Responsible for administering the verification and validation (V&V) testing prior to release of the software. The System Test Group is a separate organization from the Software Development Group (i.e., the Software Systems Engineering Group and the Software Design and Development Group).

Logistics (Code Number) — Responsible for ensuring that changes made to a system are supportable. SCM provides CSCI and associated technical data for logistics evaluation.

Data Management (DM) (Code Number) — Responsible for the receipt, distribution, and tracking of technical data associated with the project. DM also ensures compliance with contract requirements as defined in the Contract Data Requirements List (CDRL).

<If the list of organizations exceeds the list above, it may be appropriate to create numbered paragraph headings for each organization.>

2.1.1 SCM Responsibilities

SCM is responsible for maintaining configuration control over software Developmental Configurations and Baselines and for processing changes to the software configuration. SCM functions include Software Development Library (SDL) operation, software product release coordination, and change request processing and tracking.

The responsibilities of each SCM function are listed in the paragraphs below.

<Tailor these responsibilities to be project specific.>

2.1.1.1 Configuration Identification

1. Establish methods and procedures for unique identification of CSCIs.
2. Establish and maintain Functional, Allocated, and Product Baselines and the Developmental Configuration (identify, document, archive, and track changes to system releases).
3. Establish and follow release procedures to obtain Product Baselines for new version releases.
4. Coordinate assignment of identifying numbers for CSCIs and documents.
5. Provide documentation that reflects the release software package.
6. Coordinate release of software and associated documentation to release organizations.
7. Maintain records and prepare reports on release coordination activities.

2.1.1.2 Configuration Control

1. Serve as a member of the Software Configuration Control Board (SCCB). SCM is responsible for preparing and distributing the meeting agenda and minutes and for recording action items and their resolution.
2. Establish and document configuration change control procedures.
3. Establish and follow configuration controls for software and documentation.
4. Place contents of baseline and Developmental Configurations under configuration control in the SDL.
5. Generate executable load modules from controlled source code.
6. Ensure that the contents of the SDL are changed by SCM personnel and only upon receipt of the appropriate paperwork signed by the SCM Manager.
7. Prepare and maintain master(s) of the currently active version of each CI until superseded by a new version. Retain superseded versions of the master(s) in the SDL archive files.
8. Maintain records and prepare reports on SDL activities and software products.
9. Perform nontechnical check of software documentation.
10. Interface with the Software Change Review Board (SCRB) Chairperson to schedule SCRB meetings, prepare SCRB agendas, and record SCRB meeting minutes.

2.1.1.3 Configuration Status Accounting (CSA)

1. Provide CSA recording and reporting.
2. Maintain accounting of software changes by tracking change requests, ensuring traceability to a formal change proposal (i.e., ECP) from initiation through resolution and disposition.
3. Prepare status reports on change requests, formal change proposals (i.e., ECPs), and changes.

2.1.1.4 Configuration Audits

1. Support requests for audit and certification of software systems by SQA or the independent auditor.
2. Perform reviews of SCM activities and products.
3. Review and update SCM documentation as required to ensure that current applicability is maintained.

2.1.1.5 Training

<Tailor this section to list specifics of project organization training.>

The SCM Manager is responsible for identifying, establishing, coordinating, and revising training as required to ensure effective performance of SCM activity by the SCM organization and software-related groups.

2.2 Boards

<Identify the configuration control boards (CCBs) established for the project and program organization (e.g., CCB, SCCB, SCRB). Reference any charters, Memorandum of Understanding, or any program directives that establish CCBs.>

The paragraphs below provide an overview of the functions, responsibilities, and authority of the CCBs.

2.2.1 Software Change Review Board (SCRB)

The SCRB functions in a technical advisory capacity to the Program Manager. The SCRB considers the recommendations of the project's SCCB for final approval or disapproval of proposed engineering changes to a CSCI's current approved configuration and its documentation. The board also approves or disapproves proposed waivers and deviations.

SCM provides status accounting reports to the program's SCRB and updates the status accounting database to reflect SCRB decisions. [SCM or designate] serves as secretariat to the board.

2.2.2 Software Configuration Control Board (SCCB)

The SCCB supports the Project Manager and is composed of technical and administrative representatives who recommend approval or disapproval of proposed engineering changes to a CSCI's current approved configuration and its documentation. The board also recommends approval or disapproval of proposed waivers and deviations from a CSCI's current approved configuration and its documentation.

Issues that the project's SCCB is unable to resolve or that involve a change in scheduling or fiscal costs are initially addressed by the SCCB and forwarded to the program's SCRB for final approval or disapproval and recommendations.

SCM provides status accounting reports to the project's SCCB and updates the status accounting database to reflect SCCB decisions. SCM or designate serves as secretariat to the board.

SECTION 3: CM PHASING AND MILESTONES

This section describes the software development activity for software-related groups and the SCM responsibilities in relation to this activity and program events. These activities occur within the Engineering and Manufacturing Development phase of the software life cycle. The software life cycle includes five phases: Concept Exploration and Definition, Demonstration and Validation, Engineering and Manufacturing Development, Production and Deployment, and Operations and Support. Some of the Engineering and Manufacturing Development activities may be applicable to and overlap with other life-cycle phases. For this reason, the objectives of each life-cycle phase are presented. Table T2 defines the SCM milestones in relation to software-related group activity for [project name].

3.1 Concept Exploration and Definition

> <Individual projects must tailor this section to describe software development activities derived from applicable software development standards and phasing consistent with the project's software development plan.>

Objectives of the Concept Exploration and Definition phase are to:

1. Explore various material alternatives to satisfying the documented mission need.
2. Define the most promising system concept(s).
3. Develop supporting analyses and information to include identifying high-risk areas and risk management approaches to support project decisions.
4. Develop a proposed acquisition strategy and initial program objectives for cost, schedule, and performance for the most promising system concept(s).

SCM responsibilities are to:

1. Develop a CM Plan for the Acquirer, if tasked.
2. Charter the SCCB.
3. Document the Functional and Physical Characteristics (FPC).

Table T2 SCM Milestones

Software-Related Group Activity	SCM Milestone
Concept and Exploration	Plan how project will affect program products and their CM
	Baseline product identification
Project Planning and Oversight	Draft SCMP (new system) or SCMP update (existing system)
	SCM organization established, staffed
	Management and technical review participation
	Configuration identification
	Planning documents under configuration control
	Establish SCRB and SCCB
Software Development Environment	SCM staff training
	SDL and SDFs established
System Requirements Analysis	System requirements documents under configuration control
	SCCB and SCRB support
System Design	Approved SCMP implemented
	SCM tasks identified
	DTPs created and/or maintained
	System design documents baselined and maintained
	Functional Baseline established and maintained
	CSA system established and maintained
	CM Document Library established and maintained
Software Requirements Analysis	Software requirements documents baselined
	Allocated Baseline established
	CM Drawing Library established and maintained
Software Design	Development Configuration products maintained
	Development Configuration corrective action process established
Software Implementation and Unit Testing	
Unit Integration and Testing	
CSCI Qualification Testing	Test documents baselined
CSCI/HWCI Integration and Testing	FCA and PCA support

System Qualification Testing	
Software Use Preparation	Product Baseline established and maintained
	Software user documents and manuals baselined
Software Transition Preparation	Product Baseline archived
	Product Baseline transferred to SSA

4. Ensure contractor control and accounting of the FPC.
5. Participate in System Requirements Review.

3.2 Demonstration and Validation

<Individual projects must tailor this section to describe software development activities derived from applicable software development standards and phasing consistent with the project's software development plan.>

Objectives of the Demonstration and Validation phase are to:

1. Define critical design characteristics and expected capabilities of system concept(s).
2. Demonstrate that the technologies critical to the most promising concept(s) can be incorporated into system design(s) with confidence.
3. Prove that the processes critical to the most promising system concept(s) are understood and attainable.
4. Develop the analysis/information needed to support project decisions.
5. Establish a proposed Development Baseline containing refined program cost, schedule, and performance objectives for the most promising design approach.

SCM responsibilities are to:

1. Update the CCB charter and CM Plan.
2. Continue documentation of the FPC.
3. Ensure contractor control and accounting of the FPC.

4. Ensure government control and accounting of the FPC.
5. Participate in System Design Review.

3.3 Engineering and Manufacturing Development

<Individual projects must tailor this section to describe software development activities derived from applicable software development standards and phasing consistent with the project's software development plan.>

Table T2 shows SCM milestones for the Engineering and Manufacturing Development phase of a software life cycle.

3.3.1 Concept and Exploration

During concept and exploration, software-related groups are concerned with the following activities:

1. Provide sponsors with estimates of cost, schedule, risk items, etc.
2. Assist with generation of an action plan to include initial estimates for cost, schedule, risk, and system size.
3. Involve Software Quality Assurance in planning.

SCM responsibilities are to:

1. Plan how this project will affect other program products and the configuration management of them.
2. Baseline the product identification.

3.3.2 Project Planning and Oversight

During project planning and oversight, software-related groups are concerned with the following activities:

1. *Software development planning:* development and documentation of plans to conduct software development process activities identified in the following sections; development of program and project plans including a Software Development Plan (SDP) and development and implementation of a CM policy.
2. *CSCI test planning:* development and documentation of plans for conducting CSCI qualification testing and the generation of a Software Test Plan (STP).

3. *System test planning:* participation in developing and documenting plans to conduct system qualification testing.
4. *Software installation planning:* development and documentation of plans to perform software installation and training at user sites and generation of a Software Installation Plan (SIP).
5. *Software transition planning:* identification of all software development resources needed by the support agency to fulfill support concept, and development and documentation of a Software Transition Plan (STrP).
6. *Following and updating plans:* conduct of relevant activities in accordance with approved plans, supporting management reviews of the software development process, and updating plans as needed.
7. Establishment of the SCRB and SCCB.

SCM responsibilities are to:

1. Create a draft SCMP or update an SCMP for existing system.
2. Establish and staff the project SCM functional organization.
3. Apply and maintain the identification scheme for project products.
4. Place planning documents (SDP, STP, SIP, STrP, SCMP) under configuration control.
5. Participate in joint management and technical reviews.

3.3.3 Establishment of Software Development Environment

During establishment of a software development environment, software-related groups are concerned with the following activities:

1. *Software engineering environment:* establishment, control, and maintenance of the environment.
2. *Software test environment:* establishment, control, and maintenance of the environment.
3. *Software Development Library (SDL):* establish, control, and maintain an SDL to facilitate the orderly development and subsequent support of software.
4. *Software Development Files (SDFs):* establishment, control, and maintenance of an SDF for each software unit or logically related group of software units.
5. *Nondeliverable software:* verification that the nondeliverable software performs the intended functions.

SCM responsibilities are to:

1. Train staff on the SCM processes.
2. Establish and maintain the SDL and SDFs.
3. Participate in joint management and technical reviews.

3.3.4 System Requirements Analysis

During system requirements analysis, software-related groups are concerned with the following activities:

1. *Analysis of user input:* analysis provided by acquirer and generation of need surveys, problem/change reports, feedback on prototypes, interviews, or other user input.
2. *Operational concept:* participation in the definition and documentation of the operational concept for the system and generation of an Operational Concept Description (OCD).
3. *System requirements:* participation in the definition and documentation of system requirements and methods used to ensure that each requirement has been met; and, depending on CDRL provisions, generation of a System/Sub-system Specification (SSS) or an Interface Requirements Specifications (IRSs).
4. Participation in joint management and technical reviews.

SCM responsibilities are to:

1. Participate in joint management and technical reviews to provide status on SCM activities.
2. Place system requirements documents (OCD, SSS, IRSs) under configuration control.
3. Support the SCCB and SCRB.

3.3.5 System Design

During system design, software-related groups are concerned with the following activities:

1. *System-wide design decisions:* participation in definition and documentation of system-wide design decisions, and generation of a System/Sub-system Design Description (SSDD), Interface Design Descriptions (IDDs), or Database Design Descriptions (DBDDs), depending upon CDRL requirements.
2. *Architectural design:.* participation in definition and documentation of architectural design and traceability between system components and system requirements.

3. Convene the SCCB to establish the Functional Baseline.
4. Convene the SCRB, when required, to exercise software configuration control upon establishment of the Functional Baseline.
5. Participation in joint management and technical reviews.
6. *Approve project plans:* Program and Project Plans, Software Development Plan, and SCMP.

SCM responsibilities are to:

1. Implement the approved SCMP.
2. Identify tasks stated in SCMP.
3. Create or update DTPs.
4. Participate in joint management and technical reviews.
5. Place system design documents (SSDD, IDDs, DBDDs) under configuration control.
6. Maintain configuration control of the Functional Baseline.
7. Support the SCCB and SCRB.
8. Establish and maintain the CSA system.
9. Provide access procedures to project personnel on use of CSA system.
10. Generate and distribute CSA reports.
11. Establish and maintain the CM Document Library.

3.3.6 Software Requirements Analysis

During software requirements analysis, software-related groups are concerned with the following activities:

1. *Software requirements.* Participate in the definition and documentation of CSCI software requirements in Software Requirements Specifications (SRSs) or the IRSs, methods used to ensure requirements have been met, and traceability between CSCI requirements and system requirements.
2. Convene the SCCB to establish the Allocated Baseline.
3. Convene the SCRB, when required, to exercise software configuration control upon establishment of the Allocated Baseline.
4. Participation in joint management and technical reviews.

SCM responsibilities are to:

1. Place software requirements documents (SRSs, IRSs) under configuration control.

2. Maintain configuration control of the Functional and Allocated Baselines.
3. Participate in joint management and technical reviews.
4. Support the SCCB and SCRB.
5. Maintain the CSA system.
6. Generate and distribute CSA reports.
7. Maintain the CM Document Library.
8. Establish and maintain the CM Drawing Library.

3.3.7 Software Design

During software design, software-related groups are concerned with the following activities:

1. *CSCI-wide design decisions:* participation in definition and documentation of CSCI-wide design decisions in design documentation.
2. *CSCI architectural design:* participation in definition and documentation of CSCI architectural design in SDDs or IDDs and traceability between software units and CSCI requirements.
3. *CSCI detailed design:* participation in development and documentation of descriptions for each software unit in design documentation.
4. Convene the SCCB to establish Developmental Configuration.
5. Participation in joint management and technical reviews.

SCM responsibilities are to:

1. Establish and maintain corrective action process for Developmental Configuration.
2. Place software design documents (SDDs, IDDs, DBDDs) under developmental configuration control.
3. Maintain configuration control of developmental configuration products.
4. Maintain configuration control of Functional and Allocated Baselines.
5. Participate in joint management and technical reviews.
6. Support the SCCB and SCRB.
7. Maintain the CSA system and distribute CSA reports.
8. Maintain the CM Document and Drawing Libraries.

3.3.8 Software Implementation and Unit Testing

During software implementation and unit testing, software-related groups are concerned with the following activities:

1. *Software implementation:*. development and documentation of software corresponding to each software unit in the CSCI design.
2. *Preparation for unit testing:* establishment of test cases, test procedures, and test data for testing the software corresponding to each software unit, and documentation of test case information in SDFs.
3. *Performance of unit testing:* testing the software corresponding to each software unit in accordance with unit test cases and procedures.
4. *Revision and retesting:* software revision, retesting, and SDF update based on unit testing results.
5. *Analyzing and recording unit testing results:* analyzing unit testing results and documentation of test and analysis results in appropriate SDFs.
6. Participation in joint management and technical reviews.

SCM responsibilities are to:

1. Maintain corrective action process and provide status reports.
2. Maintain configuration control of developmental configuration products (including source code and source code listings).
3. Maintain configuration control of the Functional and Allocated Baselines.
4. Participate in joint management and technical reviews.
5. Support the SCCB and SCRB.
6. Maintain the CSA system and distribute CSA reports.
7. Maintain the CM Document and Drawing Libraries.
8. Maintain the SDL and SDFs.

3.3.9 Unit Integration and Testing

During unit integration and testing, software-related groups are concerned with the following activities:

1. *Preparation for unit integration and testing:* establishment of test cases, test procedures, and test data to conduct unit integration and testing, and documentation of information in appropriate SDFs.

2. *Performance of unit integration and testing:* performance of unit integration and test in accordance with unit integration test cases and procedures.
3. *Revision and retesting:* revision of software, retesting, and updating of SDFs and other software products based on results of unit integration and testing.
4. *Analysis and recording unit integration and test results:* analysis of unit integration and testing results and documentation of these results in appropriate SDFs.
5. Participation in joint management and technical reviews.

SCM responsibilities are to:

1. Maintain corrective action process and provide status reports.
2. Maintain configuration control of developmental configuration products.
3. Maintain configuration control of the Functional and Allocated Baselines.
4. Participate in joint management and technical reviews.
5. Support the SCCB and SCRB.
6. Maintain the CSA system and distribute CSA reports.
7. Maintain the CM Document and Drawing Libraries.
8. Maintain the SDL and SDFs.

3.3.10 CSCI Qualification Testing

During CSCI qualification testing, software-related groups are concerned with the following activities:

1. *Independence in CSCI qualification testing:* assurance that qualification testing is performed by nonparticipant in the CSCI detailed design and implementation.
2. *Testing on target computer system:* inclusion of CSCI qualification testing on target computer system or approved alternative system.
3. *Preparation for CSCI qualification testing:* definition and documentation of test preparations, cases, and procedures for CSCI qualification testing, traceability between test cases and the CSCI requirements, and generation of a Software Test Description (STD).
4. *Dry run of CSCI qualification testing:* testing in preparation for witnessing by the acquirer, documentation of results in SDFs, and update of CSCI test cases and procedures.
5. *CSCI qualification testing:* performance of CSCI qualification testing in accordance with the CSCI test cases and procedures.

6. *Revision and retesting:* revision of software, perform all necessary retesting, and update of SDFs and other software products, based on results of CSCI qualification testing.
7. *Analysis and recording of CSCI qualification test results:* analysis and documentation of test results in a Software Test Report (STR).
8. Participation in joint management and technical reviews.

SCM responsibilities are to:

1. Maintain corrective action process and provide status reports.
2. Place testing documents (STD, STR) under developmental configuration control.
3. Maintain configuration control of developmental configuration products.
4. Maintain configuration control of the Functional and Allocated Baselines.
5. Participate in joint management and technical reviews.
6. Support the SCCB and SCRB.
7. Maintain the CSA system and distribute CSA reports.
8. Maintain the CM Document and Drawing Libraries.
9. Maintain the SDL and SDFs.

3.3.11 CSCI/Hardware Configuration Item (HWCI) Integration and Testing

During CSCI/HWCI integration and testing, software-related groups are concerned with the following activities:

1. *Preparation for CSCI/HWCI integration and testing:* participation in development and documentation of test cases, test procedures, and test data for conduct of CSCI/HWCI integration and testing, and documentation of software-related information in the appropriate SDFs.
2. *Performance of CSCI/HWCI integration and testing:* participation in CSCI/HWCI integration and testing in accordance with the CSCI/HWCI integration test cases and procedures.
3. *Revision and retesting:* revisions to software, participation in all necessary retesting, and update of appropriate SDFs and other software products, based on CSCI/HWCI integration and testing results.
4. *Analysis and recording CSCI/HWCI integration and test results:* participation in analysis of CSCI/HWCI integration and testing results, and documentation in appropriate SDFs.

5. Participation in joint management and technical reviews.
6. Conduct of FCA and PCA.

SCM responsibilities are to:

1. Maintain corrective action process and provide status reports.
2. Maintain configuration control of developmental configuration products.
3. Maintain configuration control of the Functional and Allocated Baselines.
4. Participate in joint management and technical reviews.
5. Support the FCA and PCA.
6. Support the SCCB and SCRB.
7. Maintain the CSA system and distribute CSA reports.
8. Maintain the CM Document and Drawing Libraries.
9. Maintain the SDL and SDFs.

3.3.12 System Qualification Testing

During system qualification testing, software-related groups are concerned with the following activities:

1. *Independence in system qualification testing:* assurance that system qualification testing is performed by nonparticipant in the detailed design and implementation of system software.
2. *Testing on target computer system:* qualification testing on target computer system or approved alternative system.
3. *Preparation for system qualification testing:* participation in development and documentation of test preparations, test cases, and test procedures to be used for system qualification testing, traceability between test cases and system requirements, and documentation of all applicable items in the Software Test Description (STD).
4. *Dry run of system qualification testing:* testing in preparation for witnessing by the acquirer, documentation of results in SDFs, and update of system test cases and procedures.
5. *Performance of system qualification testing:* participation in system qualification testing in accordance with the system test cases and procedures.
6. *Revision and retesting:* participation in all software revision, retesting, and update of appropriate SDFs and other software products, based on results of system qualification testing.

7. *Analysis and recording of system qualification test results:* participation in analysis and documentation of system qualification test results.
8. Participation in joint management and technical reviews.

SCM responsibilities are to:

1. Maintain corrective action process and provide status reports.
2. Maintain configuration control of Functional and Allocated Baselines.
3. Participate in joint management and technical reviews.
4. Support the SCCB and SCRB.
5. Maintain the CSA system and distribute CSA reports.
6. Maintain the CM Document and Drawing Libraries.
7. Maintain the SDL and SDFs.

3.3.13 Software Use Preparation

During software use preparation, software-related groups are concerned with the following activities:

1. *Preparation of executable software:* preparation of executable software for each user site and documentation of all applicable items in the Software Product Specification (SPS).
2. *Preparation of version descriptions for user sites:* identify and document the exact version of software prepared for each user site in a Software Version Description (SVD).
3. *Preparation of user manuals:* user manuals may include System User Manual (SUM), Software Input/Output Manual (SIOM), Software Center Operator Manual (SCOM), and Computer Operation Manual (COM).
4. *Installation at user sites:* installation, check-out of executable software at specified user sites, training, and other specified assistance.
5. Convene the SCCB to establish the Product Baseline.
6. Convene the SCRB to exercise software configuration control upon establishment of the Product Baseline.

SCM responsibilities are to:

1. Place software user documents (SPS, SVD) and user manuals (SUM, SIOM, SCOM, COM) under configuration control.
2. Maintain corrective action process and provide status reports.

3. Maintain configuration control of Functional, Allocated, and Product Baselines.
4. Participate in joint management and technical reviews.
5. Support the SCCB and SCRB.
6. Maintain the CSA system and distribute CSA reports.
7. Maintain the CM Document and Drawing Libraries.
8. Maintain the SDL and SDFs.

3.3.14 Software Transition Preparation

During software transition preparation, software-related groups are concerned with the following activities:

1. *Preparation of executable software:* preparation of executable software for transition to support site and documentation of applicable items in the SPS.
2. *Preparation of source files:* preparation of source files for transition to the support site and documentation of applicable items in the SPS.
3. *Preparation of version descriptions for support site:* identification and documentation of the exact version of software prepared for the support site in the SVD.
4. *Preparation of the "as-built" CSCI design and related information:* update of each CSCI design description to match the "as-built" software. Definition and documentation of all information (in the SPS) needed to support the software, and traceability between the CSCI's source files and software units and between the computer hardware resource utilization measurements and the CSCI requirements concerning them.
5. *Update of system design description:* participation in updating system design description to match the "as-built" system in the SSDD.
6. *Preparation of support manuals:* support manuals may include Computer Programming Manuals (CPMs) and Firmware Support Manuals (FSMs).
7. *Transition to designated support site:* installation and check-out of deliverable software in the support environment, training, and miscellaneous assistance to support agency.

SCM responsibilities are to:

1. Archive Product Baseline.
2. Transfer Product Baseline to support site.

3.4 Production and Deployment

<Individual projects must tailor this section to describe software development activities derived from applicable software development standards and phasing consistent with the project's software development plan.>

Objectives of the Production and Deployment phase of the software life cycle are to:

1. Establish a stable, efficient production and support base.
2. Achieve an operational capability that satisfies the mission need.
3. Conduct follow-on operational and production verification testing to confirm and monitor performance and quality and verify the correction of deficiencies.

SCM responsibilities are to:

1. Update CCB charter, CM Plan(s), Functional, Allocated, and Product Baselines.
2. Ensure contractor and government control of FPC, Functional, Allocated, and Product Baselines.
3. Provide training in the CM process to the operating forces.

3.5 Operations and Support

<Individual projects must tailor this section to describe software development activities derived from applicable software development standards and phasing consistent with the project's software development plan.>

Objectives of the Operations and Support phase of the software life cycle are to:

1. Ensure that the fielded system continues to provide the capabilities required to meet the identified mission need.
2. Identify shortcomings or deficiencies that must be corrected to improve performance.

SCM responsibilities are to:

1. Update CCB charter, CM Plan(s), Functional, Allocated, and Product Baselines.
2. Continue control and accounting of FPC, Functional, Allocated, and Product Baselines.
3. Participate in conduct of audits as required.
4. Provide training in the CM process to the operating forces.

SECTION 4: DATA MANAGEMENT

The section describes the data handling, processing, storage, integrity, transfer, security, and maintenance of configuration management technical data.

Data management responsibilities are to:

1. Receive/obtain CDRL documents, software, or project technical data.
2. Implement and apply the configuration identification scheme in accordance with Section 6 of this plan.
3. Catalog the CDRL documents, software, or project technical data.
4. Maintain status records or database of CDRL documents, software, or project technical data.
5. Perform security access and control.
6. Provide change control.
7. Provide distribution copies for project personnel or for outside distribution.
8. Maintain review comments or files, and forward comments to document originators.
9. Prepare and distribute status and inventory reports.
10. Archive CDRL documents, software, or project technical data.
11. Track CDRL documents, software, or project technical data requiring response or action.

4.1 Data Distribution and Access

Access to project technical data is limited in accordance with the applicable distribution statements defined by the contract or Project Manager and by data rights, CDRL distribution security requirements, and data status level (released or submitted for approval unless otherwise specified). Distribution lists of projects technical data are maintained as part of the data status reporting function. Requests for project technical data by activities outside this project require approval by the Project Manager or designated authority.

4.2 Automated Processing and Submittal of Data

The following requirements are used to identify and control data during the review and update cycle:

1. Data files are uniquely identified and include file version and "submitted" status (e.g., "working," "released," etc.). File-naming conventions are used to indicate changes from previous versions or to distinguish an altered (annotated, redlined) file version from the originally submitted file version (e.g., filename.srs;2, or filename_srs.ann;6).
2. Data and changes are transmitted in accordance with the submittal date specified in the contract.
3. An acknowledgment of receipt from the receiving party is required when electronic data is being sent. The required time to respond is 24 hours. A follow-up is made after the 24-hour period.
4. Data that is electronically transferred is identified and defined as follows:
   - "Working": work in progress, not formally submitted or made accessible; provided for information or communication; subject to internal CM (version control).
   - "Released": CM controlled version released or made accessible after internal interview and approval.
   - "Submitted": CM controlled master version formally submitted or made accessible.
   - "Approved": CM controlled master version approved.
5. Records are kept for each data transaction.

4.3 Interactive Access to Digital Data

Define the following processes:

1. How data is to be accessed
2. Request for access and logging of access for read-only or annotations
3. Naming of temporary working version of files for the purpose of annotation or mark-up
4. Means of indicating whether a comment or annotation is essential or suggested
5. Reidentification of marked-up versions, as required
6. Method of indicating acceptance, provisional acceptance, approval, or rejection
7. Automated status accounting, including tracking the disposition of required changes

8. Reidentification of changed files

4.4 Status Reporting

Data requirements defined by the CDRL are incorporated into the [name of the database used to track CDRLs] database. The database is used to identify all CDRL data, to prepare status reports, and to track approval history. The database contains each contractually required data item and information on data submission. In addition to the CDRL item, the title of the data item and source references (e.g., Data Item Description [DID] number, paragraph number of applicable addendum) are included. Listed below are the main areas addressed in the status reports.

1. Data deliveries completed in the previous period
2. Data scheduled for submission
3. Data due but not yet delivered
4. Status of delinquent data

4.5 Data Security and Classification Management

Data security and classification management are an integral part of data management. Security requirements are considered during all areas of data management control.

SECTION 5: CONFIGURATION IDENTIFICATION

This section describes the process for configuration identification.

5.1 Selection of CSCIs

The selection of CSCIs is the responsibility of project management or the developer. CSCIs are placed under configuration management in accordance with this plan. Once the CSCI has been identified and provided to the SCM organization, the SCMP will be updated.

5.2 Formal Baseline Establishment

For each CSCI, configuration identification is established for software technical documentation, code, and media. The initially approved configuration identifications establish baselines from which subsequent changes are controlled. The configuration identifications and baselines to be established for [system title] CSCIs are defined as shown below.

1. *Functional Baseline.* Listed below are the documents that comprise the Functional Baseline for [system title].
   - Document 1
   - Document 2
   - Document 3
2. *Allocated Baseline.* Listed below are the documents that comprise the Allocated Baseline for [system title].
   - Document 1
   - Document 2
   - Document 3
3. *Product Baseline.* Listed below are the documents that comprise the Product Baseline for [system title].
   - Document 1
   - Document 2
   - Document 3

5.3 Identification Methods

The paragraphs below describe the methods used in identifying the CSCI and associated technical data and project-developed support software required for development, test, and maintenance.

5.3.1 Document Identification

SCM assigns unique numbers to CSCI documents. Each page of the document contains the identification number with the applicable revision letter.

5.3.1.1 Document Revision

SCM assigns identifiers to document revisions.

5.3.1.2 Document Change Pages

SCM assigns numbers to document change pages.

5.3.2 Drawing Identification

SCM assigns unique numbers to drawings.

5.3.3 Software Identification

SCM assigns unique numbers to drawings.

5.3.3.1 Copy Number

Each accountable copy of a software product (e.g., source code tape), with the exception of the EM and listings, is assigned a unique copy number, both externally and embedded within the software.

5.3.3.2 Volume Number

For software products that require more than one unit of physical storage per copy, a volume number is assigned to each unit of storage, both externally and embedded on the software.

5.3.3.3 Labels

[system title] software is labeled for ease in identification. Describe the specific labeling practices being used.

> <The types of information needed for this paragraph include the color of labels being used, the meaning associated with each color, etc. This information may be presented in a table.>

Listed below is the minimum information necessary to adequately identify software media.

1. Identify each of the elements required on a label.

5.3.4 Firmware Identification

The components of firmware, the hardware device, and the computer instructions or computer data that reside as read-only software on the hardware device are each uniquely identified. Firmware identification includes the top-level document/drawing that defines how these components fit together for the firmware assembly. Firmware is assigned a unique identifier.

5.3.5 Change Request Form Identification

Each change request form received by SCM is assigned a unique identifier.

5.3.6 Engineering Release

The software release process begins at the start of system integration and testing. At the initiation of this phase, the software Product Baseline is established by the project's SCCB. The software release identified as part of the Product Baseline is provided for integration with the operational hardware. Final testing is accomplished by Operational Test and Evaluation (OT&E). Issues found by OT&E are resolved using the baseline change process. Upon satisfactory completion of OT&E, the software release is approved as the Product Baseline Configuration. Approval for service use initiates distribution to Fleet users. CM/DM is responsible for making and distributing copies of software products. The copies are made from the EM. SCM is responsible for ensuring that the correct software product and release documentation are distributed through DM.

5.4 Developmental Configuration — Corrective Action Process

Anomalies or discrepancies against the Developmental Configuration are resolved through a corrective action process. The corrective action process is a closed-loop process, ensuring that all detected problems are promptly reported and entered into the process, action is initiated on them, resolution is achieved, status is tracked and reported, and records of the problems are maintained for the life of the product.

The corrective action process is the development team's internal control over software that is evolving from requirements and being developed through design, code and unit test, integration test, and software system test.

The Development Group is responsible for the Developmental Configuration and therefore provides status of implementing change proposals and closing out the change request form. The paragraphs below describe the steps in processing a change request form.

1. The initiator reports a problem using a change request form and submits it to the SCM organization.
2. SCM assigns a change request form tracking number, updates the change request form tracking database, and provides a copy to the development team for problem analysis and proposed solution. A master copy of the change request form is maintained by the library.
3. The approval authority determines the corrective action to be taken and the priority of the action. Corrective actions may be returned to the Development Group for implementation or sent to another group for review or action.
4. The Development Group implements the approved solution and provides status of the implementation and completion to the SCM organization. Implementation includes updating the software and configuration documents. Implementation is considered complete

when the integration and testing of the change request "passes" test criteria.

5.5 Configuration Management Libraries

The Developmental Configuration management process includes the responsibility to control documentation and repositories containing elements of the Developmental Configuration. The [project organization], in response to this requirement, has established the following libraries: Software Development Library, Documentation Library, and Drawing Library. The following paragraphs describe the functions of each of the libraries.

Project management authorizes access to each of the [project organization] libraries. Access includes types of user privileges granted (e.g., for software: read, write, execute; for documentation: loan copy, distribution copy).

5.5.1 Software Development Library

The SDL is the controlled collection of documentation, intermediate software development products, associated tools, and procedures that comprise a Developmental Configuration CSCI. The SDL provides storage of and controlled access to software development products in human-readable form, machine-readable form, or both. SDL components are initially documented in an identification list for the Allocated Baseline.

> <The following description outlines the typical SDL control for software produced under the "waterfall" software development methodology. A graphic showing the product development evolution would be helpful as can be seen in Figure T4.>

The [project organization] SDL consists of a series of phases through which the software is developed. Before software is released from one development phase to the next, it must be validated by a Quality Assurance function and verified by SCM. SCM uses the [name the tool or briefly explain the process] to perform this verification. SCM verifies that approved software changes have been incorporated into the proper phase of the SDL, reports status to the SCCB, and performs the release function upon SCCB authorization.

> <The release function for software should be detailed in the DTPs for Configuration Identification, both for engineering

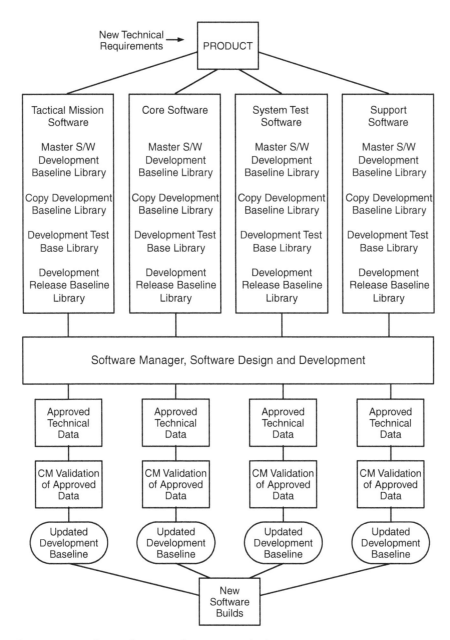

Figure T4 Sample Product Development Evolution

release to a user and for internal release from one development phase to the next.>

5.5.2 Documentation Library

The [project organization] Documentation Library contains the controlled collection of all the project's document inventory, in any media, for both released and development versions; it houses both deliverable and non-deliverable products (e.g., preliminary versions of baseline documents, specifications on commercial off-the-shelf [COTS] tools). The Documentation Library for a newly designated baseline is established at the same time as its Developmental Configuration, and its components are initially documented in an identification list for the Allocated Baseline. SCM verifies that new documents that are entered into the library as CSCIs have been approved by the SCCB and that only approved document changes have been incorporated into all controlled documents. SCM activates the release process upon SCCB authorization.

> <The DTPs for Configuration Identification should include a procedure for Documentation Library control that includes the document release function.>

5.5.3 Drawing Library

The [project organization] Drawing Library contains the controlled collection of all of the project's drawings, Computer-Aided Design (CAD), and Computer-Aided Manufacturing (CAM) instructions. The Drawing Library for a newly designated baseline is established at the same time as its Developmental Configuration, and its components are initially documented in an identification list for the Allocated Baseline. SCM verifies that approved changes have been incorporated into drawings originated by and under control of the [project organization].

> <The DTPs for Configuration Identification should include a procedure for Drawing Library control that includes the drawing release function. If Hardware Drawing Library is discussed in another CM Plan, reference that plan. If drawings are not applicable to the project, then this paragraph should be omitted.>

SECTION 6: INTERFACE MANAGEMENT

> <This section may not apply to all systems. If it does not apply, insert a statement to the effect that currently no interface requirements have been established for the system.>

This section identifies the interface requirements and establishes the Interface Control Working Group. Interface management is performed to ensure compatibility and interoperability among various hardware and software components in a system as specified in the baselined configuration documentation.

6.1 Interface Requirements

Listed below are the interface requirements for [system title].

> <List your interface requirement specification and/or document.>

1. Interface Requirement number 1
2. Interface Requirement number 2
3. Interface Requirement number 3

6.2 Interface Control Working Group (ICWG)

The ICWG is chartered to ensure the compatibility of the software and hardware components. The ICWG is composed of members of the systems outlined above and representatives from the system design group. The ICWG meetings will include discussions of the interface control documentation.

SCM may be required to generate and distribute CSA reports and technical data.

> <SCM may provide administrative support.>

SECTION 7: CONFIGURATION CONTROL

This section describes the process for maintaining configuration control of all identified CSCIs developed or maintained by [originating organization].

The purpose of configuration control is to maintain the integrity of baselined CSCIs and their associated documentation by ensuring that only authorized changes are incorporated. This requires the systematic evaluation, processing, and approval or disapproval of all proposed changes. Configuration control begins when a CSCI is baselined and continues as further baselines are established.

SCM is responsible for maintaining software configuration control over software products in the Functional, Allocated, Developmental Configuration, and Product Baselines. In addition, SCM is responsible for administering the process by which a request for change to products under control is submitted, reviewed, and approved or disapproved.

7.1 Boards

The [originating organization] is subject to a hierarchy of control boards for baseline integrity. A description of each of these boards, along with their functions and responsibilities, is presented in the paragraphs below.

> <It is understood that each organization will have a unique hierarchy and linkage among boards. A separate numbered paragraph should be dedicated to each of these boards. It may also be helpful to include a figure that illustrates the linkage among the boards.>

7.1.1 SCCB

A Software Configuration Control Board (SCCB) has been established to authorize changes to baselined documentation and software for delivered products and for in-development products. The specific procedures for conducting an SCCB meeting are detailed in [document name].

7.1.1.1 SCCB Responsibilities

The SCCB has authority for managing the project's software through the performance of the functions listed below.

1. Authorize establishment of software baselines and identification of CSCIs.
2. Represent interests of project management and all groups who may be affected by software changes to the baselines.
3. Assign, review, and provide for disposition of action items.
4. Provide required staff coordination on all proposed or reviewed changes or modifications.
5. Serve as a source for the coordination of software technical expertise for the project.
6. Determine or review the availability of resources required to complete the proposed change or modification, assess the impact of the proposed change upon the system, examine cost considerations, and determine the impact of the change on development and test schedules.
7. Monitor the design, production, and validation process for approved modifications, and initiate, when required, the corrective actions

necessary to ensure design compatibility and integrity, cost-effectiveness, and conformance to scheduled milestones.

8. Direct software change implementation on changes approved by the SCCB.
9. Exercise interface management support and control for project software.

7.1.1.2 SCCB Composition

The SCCB is chaired by an SCCB Chairperson or a designated representative. Board members include representatives of the functions designated below:

1. SCM
2. Software Requirements
3. Software Design/Development
4. Software Test
5. SQA
6. Software Systems Engineering
7. Logistics
8. System Test
9. Technical personnel directly associated with problems or proposed changes to be reviewed

SCM schedules and coordinates SCCB meetings, including the creation and distribution of meeting agenda and minutes. For time-critical software problems, an emergency SCCB meeting may be convened. The required attendees are listed below.

1. SCCB Chairperson
2. SCM Manager
3. Software Requirements Manager
4. Software Design Manager
5. If applicable, the manager of the group that documented the problem

7.1.1.3 Roles of SCCB Members

The paragraphs below describe the roles of SCCB members.

7.1.1.3.1 SCCB Chairperson   Ultimate authority for the SCCB rests with project management. An SCCB Chairperson is appointed by the Project Manager to serve as Project Manager agent for SCCB functions. The SCCB

Chairperson reports all SCCB functions to the Project Manager. The responsibilities of the SCCB Chairperson are listed below.

1. Schedule and conduct SCCB meetings.
2. Ensure that notice of each SCCB meeting is furnished sufficiently in advance so that representatives may attend completely prepared.
3. Evaluate and act on proposed changes.
4. Present recommended changes to the Project Manager to assist in determining which change requests will be processed for implementation.
5. Coordinate implementation of software changes approved by the Project Manager.
6. Sign the written synopsis of matters considered and recommendations made by the SCCB. (The synopsis is made a permanent part of the proceedings of the SCCB, and copies of the synopsis are distributed to all SCCB members.)

7.1.1.3.2 SCCB Secretariat   The [originating organization] provides a secretariat (i.e., the SCM Manager) to perform the administrative functions listed below.

1. Prepare, coordinate, and distribute the SCCB meeting agenda.
2. Act as recording secretary during SCCB meetings.
3. Prepare and distribute the SCCB meeting minutes.
4. Perform additional staffing functions as directed by the SCCB Chairperson.
5. Prepare the written synopsis of matters considered and recommendations made by the SCCB.
6. Distribute copies of signed synopsis to all SCCB members.

7.1.1.3.3 Other SCCB Members   All SCCB members represent their respective activities regarding all proposed software changes brought before the SCCB. Their duties include those listed below.

1. Receive copies of all proposed changes submitted for SCCB consideration.
2. Review, evaluate, and coordinate with other offices as required to determine impact of all proposed changes.
3. Attend meetings of the SCCB to present position statement on proposed changes.
4. Assist in the preparation of composite ECP or local form.

5. Assist the [originating organization] in the analysis of the impact of proposed changes in their area of expertise.
6. Perform other tasks as assigned by the SCCB Chairperson.

7.1.2 Other Local Boards

<Add an additional paragraph heading and subheadings for responsibilities and composition for each local board (e.g., Developmental Configuration Review Board, Technical Review Board, Developmental Change Review Board).>

7.1.3 Other Boards

<Add an additional paragraph heading and subheadings for responsibilities and composition for each external board (e.g., Operational Advisory Group/Maintenance Advisory Group [OAG/MAG]).>

7.1.4 SCRB

The management team required to establish and maintain configuration control of software consists of the sponsor and an established SCRB.

7.1.4.1 SCRB Responsibilities

The SCRB is responsible for evaluating and approving or disapproving proposed software changes. The evaluation of proposed changes must consider, as a minimum, such factors as documentation, equipment interfaces, training equipment, implementation costs, and performance requirements.

Proposed changes submitted for SCRB action must be complete with respect to technical requirements, justification, cost information, logistic requirements, interface requirements, retrofit requirements, and other applicable information. When a proposed change affects any system or item under the cognizance of another SCRB, joint SCRB meetings will be held as required.

7.1.4.2 SCRB Composition

The organization of the SCRB consists of the members listed below.

1. Program Manager (PM) or Acquisition Manager (AM)

2. SCRB Chairperson (designated by the PM or AM)
3. Sponsor Representative
4. Representatives of participating Navy field activities
5. Representatives of the [originating organization]

In addition, advisory personnel from each of the areas listed below are included in the SCRB as required.

1. Fleet users
2. Test and evaluation personnel
3. Contractor and Navy developer
4. Interfacing systems SCRB representatives

In specific cases, representatives of other divisions and offices of NAVAIR TEAM may be required to serve as advisors to the board. Participation of these divisions is coordinated by the SCRB Chairperson.

7.1.4.3 Roles of SCRB Members

The following paragraphs describe the roles of SCRB members.

7.1.4.3.1 SCRB Chairperson
Ultimate authority for the SCRB rests with the [SCRB program management]. An SCRB Chairperson is appointed by the Program Manager to serve as the program management agent for SCRB functions. The SCRB Chairperson reports all SCRB functions to the Program Manager. The responsibilities of the SCRB Chairperson include:

1. Schedule and conduct SCRB meetings.
2. Ensure that notice of each SCRB meeting is furnished sufficiently in advance so that representatives may attend completely prepared.
3. Ensure that task statements, work unit assignments, and contract changes are issued to fund SCRB members for direct SCRB participation.
4. Evaluate budgetary estimates of SCRB members for proposed software changes.
5. Evaluate and act on proposed changes (i.e., approve/disapprove).
6. Present recommended changes to the PM and AM to assist them in determining which change requests will be processed for implementation.
7. Coordinate implementation of software changes approved by the PM and AM.
8. Present composite ECPs for new baseline to the appropriate SCCB.

9. Sign the written synopsis of matters considered and recommendations made by the SCRB. (The synopsis is made a permanent part of the proceedings of the SCRB, and copies of the synopsis are distributed to all SCRB members.)

7.1.4.3.2 SCRB Secretariat The [originating organization] provides a secretariat (i.e., the SCM Manager) to perform the administrative functions listed below.

1. Prepare, coordinate, and distribute the SCRB meeting agenda.
2. Act as recording secretary during SCRB meetings.
3. Prepare and distribute SCRB meeting minutes.
4. Prepare the composite ECP or local form.
5. Perform additional staffing functions as directed by the SCRB Chairperson.
6. Prepare written synopsis of matters considered and recommendations made by the SCRB.
7. Distribute copies of signed synopsis to all SCRB members.

7.1.4.3.3 Other SCRB Members All SCRB members represent their respective activities regarding all proposed software changes brought before the SCRB. Their duties include:

1. Receive copies of all proposed changes submitted for SCRB consideration.
2. Review, evaluate, and coordinate with other offices as required to determine impact of all proposed changes.
3. Attend SCRB meetings to present position statement on proposed changes.
4. Assist with the analysis of the impact of proposed changes.
5. Perform other tasks as assigned by the SCRB Chairperson.

7.2 Baseline Change Process

The [project organization] baseline change process is a continuous function that involves the preparation, implementation, and distribution of CSCI and associated documentation changes. It has been approved by the [sponsor organization] and involves activity at both the project and program levels.

> <These statements and the following paragraphs assume that the project organization is both the developmental activity and

SSA for the software product. If this is not the case, tailor your document accordingly.>

The assigned responsibilities and approval authority for accomplishing changes to baselines are detailed in a project-originated SCCB charter documented in [list the document name]. This charter interfaces with the [sponsor organization] charter. The charter establishes the processing of change requests and their resolution by local and [sponsor organization] boards.

Changes to a [project organization] baseline configuration are initiated through a change request process that involves the preparation of a defined series of documents (change forms) whose status is determined by a hierarchy of control boards. Change requests are used to report problems and propose changes or enhancements to software or documentation. A change request must be documented, submitted, reviewed, and approved prior to implementation. Change requests against developmental baselines are resolved by the [project organization] SCCB <*if not the SCCB, identify the board*>. Change requests against established baselines require approval of the [sponsor organization] SCRB.

7.2.1 Change Request Forms

The [project organization] uses the following change forms for control of its software baselines:

1. Engineering Change Proposals (ECPs)
2. Specification Change Notices (SCNs)
3. Notices of Revisions (NORs)
4. Deviation and Waiver
5. Local change requests — insert title of local change request

7.2.1.1 Engineering Change Proposal

The ECP is used to document all proposed changes to established baselines. The completed ECP must include detailed descriptions, justifications, and costs for the proposed change.

7.2.1.2 Specification Change Notice

The SCN is used to correct or update specifications. The SCN identifies the document to be changed, the SCN number, its status (proposed or approved), the related ECP, and other [project organization] identifying data.

7.2.1.3 Notice of Revision

The NOR is primarily intended for use when the master drawing list and other documents comprising the configuration identification are not held by the originator of the ECP. NORs permit the ECP previewing or approving activity to direct the custodian of an applicable document to make specific revisions in affected documents. A separate NOR is prepared for each drawing, associated list, or other referenced document that requires revision when the related ECP is approved. The description of the revision consists of a detailed statement covering each required correction, addition, or deletion.

7.2.1.4 Deviation and Waiver

A request for deviation or waiver is designated as minor, major, or critical.

7.2.1.5 Local Change Request

> <Use this paragraph to describe your local change request form and a high-level description of its processing. An accompanying table with instructions for its completion is recommended.>

Table T3 describes the baseline change process used by the [project organization]. Table T4 displays problem priorities.

> <Each standard has its own unique problem priority definitions and should be referenced as applicable.>

Table T5 shows categories to be used for classifying problems in software products.

> <Table T5 presents a typical baseline change process used by a software development activity. Modify the description to reflect the process used by your project organization for controlling changes to baselines. If your project's responsibility is for product development only, then your baseline change process will not include the starred (*) activities.>

SECTION 8: CONFIGURATION STATUS ACCOUNTING

This section describes the process used to provide configuration status accounting (CSA). CSA is the recording and reporting of information needed to manage CSCIs effectively, including the items listed below.

Table T3 Baseline Change Process

Activity	Responsibility	SCM Interface	Comments
Change Request Initiator	Use (local) change request to report problem, error, deficiency; request enhancement, change, new requirement. Submit change request to SCM.	Assign tracking identification. Input appropriate data to CSA database. Provide copies of change request for review. Place master change request in library.	SCM should automate this process to the fullest extent of its capabilities. Eliminate paper whenever possible.
Project Technical Evaluation Team	Evaluate change request for technical feasibility. Provide analysis of change request.	Gather and distribute additional documentation in support of change request when needed. Perform secretariat duties for Project Technical Evaluation Team when requested. Update CSA databases.	Composition of the Project Technical Evaluation Team is determined by project management. This may be a CCB activity.
SCCB	Convene meeting. Disposition, prioritize, and categorize Direct implementation of change requests to developmental baselines. Direct preparation of preliminary change proposals to delivered baselines for SCRB working group consideration.	Distribute relevant CSA reports. Update CSA databases. Perform secretariat duties when requested.	

SCRB Working Group	Convene meeting. Disposition and prioritize change proposals. Identify approved change proposals for new baseline configuration. Preparation of ECP.	Distribute change proposals and associated documentation. Perform secretariat duties when required.	SCM will provide and prepare, as requested, the appropriate documentation.
Software Requirements Group	Prepare ECP for SCRB review. Determine whether deviations or waivers are required; prepare if necessary.	Provide CSCI and associated technical data required for ECP development. Assign identification or tracking number to ECP. Prepare SCNs and NORs for submittal with completed ECP. Prepare ECP release package to SCRB. Update CSA database.	
SCRB	Convene meeting. Review ECP. Direct implementation of acceptable ECP. Return unacceptable ECP for rework by project organization.	Provide appropriate tracking for ECP. Update CSA database.	
Software Design Group	Implement approved ECP. Provide design status and information to SCCB.		

Table T3 Baseline Change Process

Activity	Responsibility	SCM Interface	Comments
SCCB	Begin SCCB oversight of new Developmental Configuration. Initiate corrective action process. Determine development milestones.	Identify, process, and track change requests. Provide SCCB secretariat function. Assist with reviews and audits as required.	
Software Requirements Group	Update software and configuration documents.	Receive and process software and documentation changes.	
Software Test Group	Perform V&V of project developed software based on test plans and procedures. Generate change requests for problems detected during test.	Receive test documents for configuration control. Identify, process, and track change requests reported during testing.	
Quality Assurance Group	Perform review and audits of baseline software.	Assist SQA in conduct of reviews and audits as required.	
SCCB	Release Developmental configuration as Product Baseline.	Perform release function for accepted Product Baseline.	

Table T4 Explanation of Priorities

Priority	Applies if a Problem Could:
1	a. Prevent the accomplishment of an operational or mission-essential capability. b. Jeopardize safety, security, or other requirement designated "critical."
2	a. Adversely affect the accomplishment of an operational or mission-essential capability and no work-around solution is known. b. Adversely affect technical, cost, or schedule risks to the project or to the life-cycle support of the system, and no work-around solution is known.
3	a. Adversely affect the accomplishment of an operational or mission-essential capability but a work-around solution is known. b. Adversely affect technical, cost, or schedule risks to the project or to the life-cycle support of the system but a work-around solution is known.
4	a. Result in user/operator inconvenience or annoyance but does not affect a required operational or mission-essential capability. b. Result in inconvenience or annoyance for development or support personnel but does not prevent the accomplishment of those responsibilities.
5	Result in any other effect.

Table T5 Categories Used for Classifying Problems in Software Products

Category	Applies to Problems in:
Plans	One of the plans developed for the project
Concept	The operational concept
Requirements	The system or software requirements
Design	The design of the system or software
Code	The software code
Database/data file	A database or data file
Test information	Test plans, test descriptions, or test reports
Manuals	The use, operator, or support manuals
Other	Other software products

1. A record of the approved configuration documentation and identification numbers
2. The status of proposed changes, deviations, and waivers to the configuration
3. The implementation status of approved changes
4. The configuration of all units of the CSCI in the operational inventory
5. Results of audits

CSA documentation is the means through which actions affecting CSCIs are recorded and reported to the Software Systems Engineering Manager of the [system title] system. It principally records the "approved configuration" (baseline) and the implementation status of changes to the baseline. It is the bookkeeping part of SCM that provides managers with feedback information to determine whether decisions of the SCCB are being implemented as directed.

To automate CSA, SCM uses [identify the software tool], a relational database management system, to define the data content and format. [Identify the software tool] is an approved, baselined CSCI, so any proposed change to it requires a change request and SCCB approval for implementation.

<If the above paragraph does not reflect current practices, modify the paragraph as required.>

Input data includes SCCB decisions, such as approving or disapproving change requests, establishing configuration baselines, and approving the release of software for distribution. Input data also includes status information of CSCIs and change requests. Output data is formatted as CSA reports.

8.1 Records

The records maintained by SCM contain detailed data that documents that the as-built software conforms to its technical description and specified configuration. They include the information listed below.

1. Approved technical documentation for each CSCI
2. Status of proposed changes
3. Implementation status of approved changes
4. Status of software problems
5. A record of change request status

8.1.1 Change Request Table

The change request table contains a record of all change requests and related information. It includes, but is not limited to, the data listed below.

> <It may be beneficial to include a description or figure showing the format of this form.>

1. Change request number
2. Title
3. Date
4. Software product name or acronym
5. Part number or revision in error
6. Originator
7. Change source (e.g., ECP), if applicable
8. Current change request status
9. Change request disposition

8.1.2 Library(ies) Inventory Table

The library inventory table contains a record of each software product stored in the library(ies). It includes, but is not limited to, the data listed below.

<It may be beneficial to include a description or figure showing the format of this form.>

1. Product name
2. Part or document number and revision
3. Date of creation, last modification, and last access
4. "Master" or "Copy" designation
5. Authorizing paperwork type and number
6. Type of media
7. Location
8. Classification

8.1.3 Data Distribution Table

The data distribution table contains a record of all data (e.g., documents and drawings, including CDRL items) distributed by the software organization through DM. The table includes, but is not limited to, the information listed below.

1. Type and identification number of distribution request
2. Date of submittal
3. Media identification
4. Reason for distribution
5. Classification

8.1.4 Release Table

The release table contains a record of all releases made by the software organization (e.g., drawings, documents, software documents, tape). It includes, but is not limited to, the information listed below.

1. Date of release
2. Type of release
3. Software product released
4. Changes incorporated into the release
5. Approval signatures
6. Location of masters

8.1.5 Archive Records Table

SCM maintains a record of all archived material. Archived material includes obsolete material and data not required for current use and off-site stored backup data in case of loss of online data.

8.2 Reports

SCM has the prime responsibility for managing, compiling, maintaining, and publishing the [system title] detailed software CSA reports. These reports provide the status to management that all changes between the software technical description and the software itself are being accounted for on a one-to-one relationship. This status information, together with the CSA reports maintained by the SCM organization, is an input for the final review for product acceptance.

Project management determines the frequency of distribution and recipients of the CSA reports. These reports include the information listed below.

1. Identification of currently approved configuration documentation and configuration identifiers associated with each CSCI
2. Status of proposed change requests from initiation to implementation
3. Results of configuration audits; status and disposition of discrepancies
4. Traceability of changes from baselined documentation of each CSCI
5. Effectivity and installation status of configuration changes to all CSCIs at all locations

The above reports answer basic questions regarding the approved configuration (baseline) and the implementation status of changes to the baseline.

8.3 Requests for CSA Reports

Requests for CSA reports originating outside the project are directed for approval to Project Management, which authorizes need-to-know access.

SECTION 9: CONFIGURATION AUDITS

This section describes the approach used in performing configuration audits.

Configuration audits validate that the design and the final product conform to approved functional requirements defined in specifications and drawings and that the changes to the initially approved specifications and drawings have been incorporated.

The SCM assists in the conduct of two audits for developed baselines prior to their release: the FCA and PCA. These audits ensure that baseline changes are validated and the new baseline meets new requirements and specifications.

SCM personnel provide assistance through the specific activities listed below, as required by the project.

1. Assist in the audit.
2. Review audit checklists.
3. Prepare SCM reports, logs, or records required to support the audit.
4. Establish and maintain baseline specification and product files.
5. Follow up on audit reports to assess possible SCM impact.
6. Provide storage for audit documentation, records, and products.
7. Ensure audit report action items are resolved.

9.1 Functional Configuration Audit (FCA)

SCM ensures that the released version of the software products is available for the audit so that the inspectors can verify that the software performs as required by its allocated configuration.

FCAs are usually conducted after a major change or a significant number of minor changes have occurred or before the establishment of the Product Baseline. The SCM Manager is responsible for assisting SQA in the preparation of the FCA plan. The FCA plan identifies specific tasks and procedures to accomplish those tasks. The FCA plan identifies documents, hardware, software, test sets, etc. required for performing the audit. The SCM Manager records differences between the SRS and the CSCI under audit for incorporation into the minutes of the FCA for post-audit action.

9.2 Physical Configuration Audit (PCA)

This audit ensures that the as-built configuration is accurately reflected by the released documentation to establish the Product Baseline. SCM audits the released engineering documentation and quality control records to make sure the as-built or as-coded configuration is reflected by this documentation.

PCAs are usually conducted concurrently with FCAs or immediately following an FCA. The SCM Manager is responsible for assisting SQA in the preparation of the PCA plan. The PCA plan identifies specific tasks and procedures to accomplish those tasks. The PCA plan also identifies the software and technical documentation to be examined.

9.3 Audits and Reviews of SCM

To ensure that SCM efforts are adequate and completed as detailed in this document, audits and reviews of SCM processes and products are performed as described in the following paragraphs.

9.3.1 SCM Audits

To ensure that the SCM program complies with the requirements specified in this plan, an independent audit of SCM processes, procedures, and products is required. Normally, this type of audit is performed by a QA representative. Products generated or tracked by SCM are listed below.

1. CSA reports
2. Identified CSCIs
3. Change requests
4. Software version releases
5. Libraries
6. Documented SCM processes and procedures
7. SCM review reports

The audit findings are documented in an audit report and provided to the SCM Manager. The audit report is used by the SCM Manager to correct deficiencies or identify changes in the SCM requirements. Correcting deficiencies would include updating SCM processes and procedures, records, configuration documents, software, or tools. Identifying changes in the SCM requirements would result in adding, modifying, or deleting a requirement in this SCMP.

9.3.2 SCM Reviews

The SCM Manager periodically performs internal reviews of SCM processes, procedures, and products. An SCM review serves as a method to determine how effectively and efficiently the SCM processes and procedures fulfill the SCM requirements as defined in this plan. SCM reviews also include verification of the products generated by SCM. Verification is the process of evaluating the products to ensure correctness and consistency with respect to the SCMP, tasks, processes, and procedures. The review findings are documented in a report that is used by the SCM Manager to correct deficiencies or identify changes in SCM requirements.

It is the SCM Manager's responsibility to perform or assign SCM personnel to perform the SCM reviews and to specify the SCM processes or procedures to be reviewed. The review report includes what actions were taken to resolve the deficiency or requirements change. The review report is filed with the appropriate DTP and serves as a record to show that an internal SCM review was performed and corrective action was taken as required. Review reports may be audited.

SECTION 10: SUBCONTRACTOR/VENDOR CONTROL

This section describes the methods used to ensure subcontractor/vendor compliance with configuration management requirements.

Each contractor working on this system is required to develop a configuration management plan that is in conformance to this document. The development contractor ensures that nondeliverable software will functionally meet the requirements of the system.

Vendors' products are inspected at delivery to ensure that their products meet the requirements as specified. The vendors' quality control procedures may be obtained to aid in the evaluation of the COTS software by the system developer.

Configuration management personnel are acquired as a team through competitive contract negotiation. The SCM staff has responsibility for conducting the SCM function under the management of [name of the supervising organization or function assigned by the program]. The staff is required to be fully knowledgeable in all aspects of the program's configuration management function and to maintain and upgrade the SCM program whenever they can.

APPENDIX T1: ACRONYMS AND ABBREVIATIONS

This appendix includes an alphabetical listing of all acronyms, abbreviations, and their meanings as used in this document.

ABL — Allocated Baseline
ACD — Allocated Configuration Documentation
AM — Acquisition Manager
CAD — Computer-Aided Design
CALS — Continuous Acquisition and Life-Cycle Support
CAM — Computer-Aided Manufacturing
CCB — Configuration Control Board
CDR — Critical Design Review
CDRL — Contract Data Requirements List
CI — Configuration Item
CITIS — Contractor Integrated Technical Information Service
CM — Configuration Management
CMU — Carnegie Mellon University
COM — Computer Operation Manual
COTS — Commercial Off-The-Shelf
CPM — Computer Programming Manual
CSA — Configuration Status Accounting
CSC — Computer Software Component
CSCI — Computer Software Configuration Item
CSU — Computer Software Unit
DBDD — Database Design Description
DID — Data Item Description
DM — Data Management
DoD — Department of Defense
DTP — Desktop Procedure
ECP — Engineering Change Proposal
EM — Engineering Master
FBL — Functional Baseline
FCA — Functional Configuration Audit
FCD — Functional Configuration Documentation
FPC — Functional and Physical Characteristics
FQT — Functional Qualification Testing
FSM — Firmware Support Manual
HWCI — Hardware Configuration Item
ICWG — Interface Control Working Group
ID — Identification
IDD — Interface Design Document
IRS — Interface Requirements Specification

MAG — Maintenance Advisory Group
MCCR — Mission Critical Computer Resources
NAVAIR — Naval Air Systems
NDS — Non-Developmental Software
NOR — Notice of Revision
OAG — Operational Advisory Group
OCD — Operational Concept Description
OT&E — Operational Testing and Evaluation
PBL — Product Baseline
PCA — Physical Configuration Audit
PCD — Product Configuration Documentation
PDR — Preliminary Design Review
PM — Program Manager
QA — Quality Assurance
SCCB — Software Configuration Control Board
SCM — Software Configuration Management
SCMP — Software Configuration Management Plan
SCN — Specification Change Notice
SCOM — Software Center Operator Manual
SCP — Software Change Proposal
SCR — Software Change Request
SCRB — Software Change Review Board
SDD — Software Design Document
SDF — Software Development File
SDL — Software Development Library
SDP — Software Development Plan
SDR — System Design Review
SEI — Software Engineering Institute
SEP — Software Enhancement Proposal
SIOM — Software Input/Output Manual
SIP — Software Installation Plan
SPS — Software Product Specification
SQA — Software Quality Assurance
SRR — Software Requirements Review
SRS — Software Requirements Specification
SSA — Software Support Activity
SSDD — System/Segment Design Document
SSR — Software Specification Review
SSS — System/Sub-system Specification
STD — Standard
STP — Software Test Plan
STR — Software Test Report
STR Form — System Trouble Report Form

STrP — Software Transition Plan
SUM — Software User's Manual
SVD — Software Version Description
TRR — Test Readiness Review
V&V — Verification and Validation
VDD — Version Description Document

APPENDIX T2: FORMS

Software Change/Software Enhancement Proposal

1. SYSTEM/PROJECT NAME	2. DATE PREPARED	3. SCP NUMBER
4. TITLE OF SCP		
5. ORIGINATOR	6. COMPONENT AFFECTED	
7. DESCRIPTION OF PROBLEM/NEED FOR SCP		
8. DESCRIPTION OF RECOMMENDED SCP		
9. ALTERNATIVES/IMPACT IF NOT APPROVED		
10. BASELINE AFFECTED	11. DOCUMENTATION/SPECIFICATIONS AFFECTED	
12. OTHER SYSTEMS, CONFIGURATION ITEMS, CONTRACTORS AFFECTED, ETC.		
13. EFFECT OF SCP ON SYSTEM EMPLOYMENT, ILS, TRAINING, EFFECTIVENESS, ETC.		
14. NET EFFECT ON SYSTEM RESOURCES (E.G., PROCESSING TIME, MEMORY, DISK SPACE)		

15. DEVELOPMENTAL REQUIREMENTS		
16. SCP EFFECTIVITY POINT		17. DATE APPROVAL NEEDED BY
18. THIS SCP MUST BE ACCOMPLISHED BEFORE/WITH/AFTER THE FOLLOWING ECP/SCP/SEP/STR(S)		
19. SUPERSEDES OR REPLACES ECP/SCP/SEP/STR		
20. COST, SCHEDULE OR INTERFACE IMPACT ☐ NO ☐ YES (See attached DD Form 1692 ECP) ☐ NO		
21. CONTRACTOR SCCB ACTION ☐ Approve ☐ Disapprove ☐ ECP		
AUTHORIZED SIGNATURE	TITLE	DATE
22. GOVERNMENT SCCB ACTION ☐ No Action Required ☐ Approve ☐ Disapprove ☐ Withdrawn		
RETURNED TO CONTRACTOR FOR		
GOVERNMENT AGENCY/TITLE	SIGNATURE	DATE

Software Trouble/Change Request (STR/SCR)

1. NAME	2. DATE
3. ORGANIZATION	
4. PHONE COM	DA
5. REPORT TYPE 6. SYSTEM AFFECTED	7. COMPUTER PROGRAM IDs
☐ SOFTWARE TROUBLE	
REPORT	
☐ SOFTWARE CHANGE	
REQUEST	
8. BRIEF TITLE	

9. DETAILED NARRATIVE DESCRIPTION OF SOFTWARE TROUBLE EXISTING (AND STATUS OF DISPLAYS AND CONTROLS) OR ENHANCEMENT DESIRED. INCLUDE A STATEMENT REGARDING IMPACT.

DOCUMENT CHANGE REQUEST

Tracking No.: _____

Submitting Organization: _____

Contact Person: _____

Telephone: _____

Mailing Address: _____
_____
_____

Date: _____

Short Title: _____

Change Location Tag: _____

(Section No., Figure No., Table No., Page No., etc.)

Proposed Change:	
Reason for Change:	

APPENDIX T3: SOFTWARE CONFIGURATION MANAGEMENT PHASING AND MILESTONES

This section describes the sequence of events and milestones for implementation of SCM in phase with major software and development milestones and events. SCM milestones are achieved upon completion of individual SCM activities.

> <The deliverable products given below can be modified or deleted as stated in the governing SDP or software tailoring plan.>

T3.1 System Requirements Analysis Phase

This is the first phase of system-level planning. During the system requirements analysis phase, the top-level (system) requirements are established, analyzed, and approved. The requirements describe the major functions that the system must fulfill.

The outputs of this phase consist of one preliminary product (Preliminary System Specification) and a program review (System Requirements Review [SRR]). No baselines are established at this point. The SCRB and SCCB are established.

SCM activities during this phase are listed below.

1. Establish project SCM.
2. Train staff.
3. Create draft SCMP or update SCMP for existing system.
4. Attend SRR as required.

T3.2 System Design Phase

This is the second phase of the system-level planning. During the system design phase, a top-level (system) design is formulated and documented. The outputs of this phase consist of four final deliverable products (System Specification, System/Segment Design Document, Software Development Plan, and Software Configuration Management Plan); two preliminary deliverable products (Preliminary Software Requirements Specification and Preliminary Interface Requirements Specification); one program review (System Design Review); and the establishment of the first of three baselines (Functional Baseline).

> <Hereinafter, the acronym FBL may be used in place of Functional Baseline.>

The SCCB meets to establish the Functional Baseline. The SCRB meets to exercise software configuration control upon establishment of the Functional Baseline.

SCM activities during this phase are listed below.

1. Implement approved SCMP:
   - Identify the tasks stated in SCMP.
   - Identify processes from the tasks in the SCMP.
   - Create or update DTPs from the processes.
2. Establish complete number scheme for project-defined version identification (ID).
3. Exercise configuration control of the functional configuration documentation.
4. Attend System Design Review.
5. Establish and maintain CSA system.
6. Establish and maintain CM library(ies).
7. Support SCCB throughout the software life cycle.

T3.3 Software Requirements Analysis Phase

During the software requirements analysis phase, the software performance and interface requirements that must be met are formulated and analyzed. This phase is similar to the system requirements analysis phase except that it focuses on the software requirements derived from the system requirements.

The outputs from this phase consist of two final deliverable products (Software Requirements Specification and Interface Requirements Specification), one program review (Software Specification Review), and the establishment of the second of three baselines (Allocated Baseline).

> <Hereinafter, the acronym ABL may be used in place of Allocated Baseline.>

SCM activities during this phase are listed below.

1. Attend Software Specification Review (SSR).
2. Exercise control of allocated configuration documentation.

T3.4 Preliminary Design Phase

During the preliminary design phase, the system-level architecture, interfaces, and design are developed. A Preliminary Design Review (PDR) is held, and approval is obtained before proceeding with the detailed (low-level) design phase.

The outputs from this phase consist of one final deliverable product (Software Test Plan [Test Ids]), two preliminary deliverable products (Preliminary Software Design Documents and Preliminary Interface Design Document), one program review (Preliminary Design Review), and the establishment of the Developmental Configuration.

SCM activities during this phase are listed below.

1. Establish and maintain SDL.
2. Establish corrective action process for Developmental Configuration.
3. Attend PDR.
4. Exercise configuration control of Developmental Configuration Products.

T3.5 Detailed Design Phase

During the detailed design phase, the design team develops the detailed design, and a Critical Design Review (CDR) is held for review and approval of the total design. The design is completed and approved at the CDR. By the time the CDR occurs, the software constituting the system has been decomposed into a hierarchical structure of CSCIs, Computer Software Components (CSCs), and CSUs.

The preceding phases ensure that design requirements have been identified, validated, and allocated to the approved design and to their respective baselines.

The outputs from this phase consist of three final deliverable products (detailed Software Design Documents, Software Test Descriptions [Cases[, and Interface Design Document); one program review (Critical Design Review); and the continuance of the Developmental Configuration.

SCM activities during this phase are listed below.

1. Attend CDR.
2. Exercise configuration control of Developmental Configuration Products.

T3.6 Coding and CSU Testing Phase

During the coding and CSU testing phase, coding and unit (CSU) testing is accomplished. All design data, programmer notes, and CSU test results are kept in the Software Development Files (SDFs). This is for programmer and peer review only. SQA can perform audits of the SDFs.

The outputs from this phase result in completed CSU development and testing evidenced by source code and source code listings. The Developmental Configuration continues.

SCM activities during this phase are listed below.

1. Exercise configuration control of Developmental Configuration Products.

T3.7 CSC Integration and Testing Phase

During the CSC integration and testing phase, coding and testing of CSCs is accomplished. CSUs are integrated into their next-higher structures and tested to ensure proper processing. Test drivers and stubs are written to perform these tests. All design data, programming notes, and test results are added to the SDFs. This is for programmer and peer review only. SQA can perform audits of the SDFs.

The outputs from this phase consist of one final deliverable product (Software Test Description (Procedures)), one program review (Test Readiness Review [TRR]), plus updated source code, source code listings, and command files. Successful completion of these activities indicates the conclusion of the Developmental Configuration.

SCM activities during this phase are listed below.

1. Support TRR by providing the items listed below:
   ▪ CSCI and associated technical data
   ▪ Status of reported software and documentation anomalies
2. Exercise configuration control of Developmental Configuration products.

T3.8 CSCI Testing Phase

During the CSCI testing phase, testing of CSCIs is accomplished to demonstrate that the software system is reliable and maintainable. All lower-level (CSU and CSC) coding and testing have been completed. This final software testing ensures that each CSCI functions as designed.

<If the System Test Group has been established, the following statement applies.>

The V&V process is a software quality check to ensure that the design is complete and that the software fulfills all approved requirements and may be performed by the Systems Test Group.

Formal Qualification Testing (FQT) is performed in this phase. The CSCI testing is basically the FQT, whereby the customer accepts the tested integrity of the developed system. The completed Software Test Plan includes tests of user identification and access to the system, as well as test plans for any identified safety issues.

The outputs from this phase consist of the following final deliverable products (Software Test Reports, Operation and Support Documents, Version Description Documents, Software Product Specifications, and updated source code and listings); two audits (PCA and FCA); and establishment of the last of the three baselines (Product Baseline).

> <Hereinafter, the acronym PBL may be used in place of Product Baseline>

When the FCA/PCA is approved, the customer accepts the Product Baseline.

SCM activities during this phase are listed below.

1. Support FCA and PCA. These audits may be deferred until after system integration and testing.
2. Release product configuration documentation.
3. Exercise configuration control of product configuration documentation.

T3.9 System Integration and Testing phase

During the system integration and testing phase, the software is integrated into the operational hardware and tested. DOD-STD-2167A development activities end with CSCI testing and the establishment of the software Product Baseline. After software Product Baseline, the software must be integrated into the operational hardware and final testing (Operational Testing and Evaluation [OT&E]) accomplished by the customer before placing the system into operation.

REFERENCES

This document is an adaptation of a document developed at the request of Naval Air Systems Command (NAVAIR) TEAM. The original document can be found at http://sepo.nosc.mil/sepo/GenSCMP/GenSCMP.html.
SPAWAR Systems Center San Diego, Systems Engineering Process Office, http://sepo.spawar.navy.mil/sepo/index2.htm.

APPENDIX T4: CONFIGURATION MANAGEMENT PHASING AND MILESTONES

Development Phase	SCM Activity	SCM Control	Milestones	Product
System Requirements Analysis	Establish project SCM Train staff Create draft or update SCMP for existing system Attend SRR as required		SRR SCM established Program SCRB established Project SCCB established	Preliminary System Specification Preliminary SCMP
System Design	Implement approved SCMP Identify tasks stated in SCMP Identify processes from tasks Create/update DTPs Establish complete number scheme for project-defined version ID Attend SDR Establish and maintain CSA system Establish and maintain CM library(ies) Support SCCB throughout software life cycle	System Specification SSDD SDP SCMP	SDR Functional Baseline	System Specification SSDD SDP SCMP Preliminary SRS Preliminary IRS
Software Requirements Analysis	Attend SSR	SRS IRS	SSR Allocated Baseline	SRS IRS
Preliminary Design	Establish and maintain Software Development Library Establish corrective action process Attend PDR Exercise configuration control of Developmental Configuration products	STP (Test IDs)	PDR Developmental Configuration	Preliminary SDD Preliminary IDD STP

Detailed Design	Attend CDR Exercise configuration control of Developmental Configuration Products	SDD IDD STD (Test Cases)	CDR	Detailed SDD IDD STD (Test Cases)
Coding and CSU Testing	Exercise configuration control of Developmental Configuration Products	Tested Source Code (CSUs) Source Code Source Code Listings		Source Code Source Code Listings
CSC Integration and Testing	Exercise configuration control of Developmental Configuration Products Support TRR by providing CSCI and associated technical data and status of reported software and documentation anomalies Exercise configuration control of developmental configuration products	STD (Test Procedures) Updated Source Code Updated Source Code Listings Command Files	TRR	STD (Procedures) Updated Source Code Source Code Listings Command Files
CSCI Testing	Exercise configuration control of product configuration documentation Support FCA and PCA Release product configuration documentation	Updated Source Code Updated Source Code Listings Command Files STR Operation and Support Documents VDD SPS	FCA PCA Product Baseline	Updated Source Code Command Files Software Test Report Operation and Support Documents VDD SPS

Appendix U

ACRONYMS AND GLOSSARY

ACRONYMS

AA — Application Activity
ABL — Allocated Baseline
ACD — Allocated Configuration Documentation
ACO — Administrative Contracting Officer
AECMA — Association Europeenne des Construceurs de Materiel Aerospace
AFB — [U.S.] Air Force Base
AFM — [U.S.] Air Force Manual
AFR — [U.S.] Air Force Regulation
AGE — Aerospace Ground Equipment
AIA — Aeronautical Industry Association
AIS — Automated Information System
ALT — Alteration Instruction
AMSDL — Acquisition Management Systems and Data Requirements Control List
ANSI — American National Standards Institute
AR — [U.S.] Army Regulation
ARDEC — [U.S. Army] Armament Research, Development and Engineering Center
ASCII — American Standard Code for Information Interchange
ASTM — American Society for the Testing of Materials
BOM — Bill of Materials
CAGE — Commercial and Government Entity
CALS — Continuous Acquisition and Life-Cycle Support
CCB — Configuration Control Board, Configuration Change Board
CDCA — Current Document Change Authority
CDR — Critical Design Review

CDRL — Contract Data Requirements List

CFR — Code of Federal Regulations

CI — Configuration Item

CITIS — Contractor Integrated Technical Information Service

CLIN — Contract Line Item Number

CM — Configuration Management

CMP — Configuration Management Plan

CNWDI — Critical Nuclear Weapons Design Information

CPIN — Computer Program Identification Number

CRYPTO — Cryptographic information

CSA — Configuration Status Accounting

CSCI — Computer Software Configuration Item

DCMC — [U.S.] Defense Contract Management Command

DDRS — [U.S.] Department of Defense Data Repository System

DED — Data Element Definition

DFARS — [U.S.] Defense Department Supplement to the Federal Acquisition Regulation

DID — Data Item Description

DIN — Deutsches Institute fur Normung

DLA — [U.S.] Defense Logistics Agency

DoD — [U.S.] Department of Defense

DODISS — [U.S.] Department of Defense Index of Specifications and Standards

DOE — [U.S.] Department of Energy

DOT — [U.S.] Department of Transportation

DTIC — [U.S.] Defense Technical Information Center

ECN — Engineering Change Notice

ECO — Engineering Change Order

ECP — Engineering Change Proposal

ECS — Embedded Computer Software

EDM — Enterprise Data Model

EEPROM — Electronically Erasable Programmable Read-Only Memory

EIA — Electronic Industries Association

ELIN — Exhibit Line Item Number

E-mail — Electronic mail

FBL — Functional Baseline

FCA — Functional Configuration Audit

FCD — Functional Configuration Documentation

FFT — First Flight Test

FSC — [U.S.] Federal Supply Class

FSCM — [U.S.] Federal Supply Code for Manufacturers

GFD — Government-Furnished Documents

GFE — Government-Furnished Equipment

GFP — Government-Furnished Property
GLAA — Government Lead Application Activity
GPLR — Government Purpose License Rights
GPO — Government Printing Office
GSN — Government Serial Number
HEI — High Explosive Incendiary
HTML — Hypertext Mark-up Language
HWCI — Hardware Configuration Item
ICD — Interface Control Drawing, Interface Control Documentation
ICWG — Interface Control Working Group
IEEE — Institute of Electrical and Electronics Engineering
IFF — Identify Friend or Foe
IGES — Initial Graphics Exchange Specification
IPT — Integrated Product Team
IRPOD — Individual Repair Part Ordering Data
ISO — International Standardization Organization
MACHALT — Machinery Alteration
MACHALTINST — Machinery Alteration Instruction
MICOM — [U.S. Army] Missile Command
MIL-STD — Military Standard
MIP — Modification Improvement Program
MRB — Material Review Board
MS — Military Standard
MSN — Manufacturer's Serial Number
MWO — Modification Work Order
NAS — [U.S.] National Aerospace Standard
NASA — [U.S.] National Aeronautics & Space Administration
NATO — North Atlantic Treaty Organization
NAVAIR — [U.S.] Naval Air Systems Command
NAVMATINST — [U.S.] Naval Materiel Systems Command Instruction
NAVSEA — [U.S.] Naval Sea Systems Command
NIIN — [U.S.] National Item Identification Number
NIST — [U.S.] National Institute of Standards and Technology
NOR — Notice of Revision
NSA — [U.S.] National Security Agency
NSCM — NATO Supply Code for Manufacturers
NSN — National Stock Number
NTIS — National Technical Information Service
NUCALTINST — Nuclear Alteration Instruction
NWS — [U.S.] Naval Weapons Station
ORDALTINST — Ordnance Alteration Instruction
OSD — [U.S.] Office of the Secretary of Defense
OSHA — [U.S.] Occupational Safety & Health Agency

PAN — Procuring Activity Number
PBL — Product Baseline
PCA — Physical Configuration Audit
PCD — Product Configuration Documentation
PCO — Procurement Contracting Officer
PCTSS — Provisioning & Cataloging Technical Support System
PDM — Product Data Management [System]
PDF — Page Description File
PDR — Preliminary Design Review
PHST — Packaging, Handling, Storage, and Transportation
PIN — Part or Identification Number
POC — Point of Contact
PROM — Programmable Read-Only Memory
RAC — Rapid Action Change [order]
RFD — Request for Deviation
SAE — Society of Automotive Engineers
SBIR — Small Business Innovative Research
SCN — Specification Change Notice
SDR — System Design Review
SFR — System Functional Review
SGML — Standard Generalized Markup Language
SHIPALT — Ship Alteration
SHIPALTINST — Ship Alteration Instruction
SIE — Special Inspection Equipment
SOW — Statement of Work
SRR — System Requirements Review
SSAN — Social Security Account Number
SSR — Software Specification Review
STANAG — Standard NATO Agreement
STEP — Standard for the Exchange of Product model data
TA — Tasking Activity
TCTO — Time-Compliance Technical Order
TD — Technical Directive
TDP — Technical Data Package
TM — Technical Manual
TOPS — Technical Order Page Supplement
TPS — Test Program Set
U.S. — United States [of America]
USAF — United States Air Force
VDD — [Software] Version Description Document
VECP — Value Engineering Change Proposal
VHSIC — Very High Speed Integrated Circuit
WINTEL — Warning: Intelligence methods and sources disclosed

DEFINITIONS

De nitions for con guration management terms used in this stand ard are consistent with ANSI/EIA 649.

Allocated Baseline (ABL) — The approved allocated configuration documentation.

Allocated Configuration Documentation (ACD) — The documentation describing a CI's functional, performance, interoperability, and interface requirements that are allocated from those of a system or higher-level configuration item; interface requirements with interfacing configuration items; and the verifications required to confirm the achievement of those specified requirements.

Application Activity (AA) — An activity that has selected an item or a document for use on programs under its control. However, it is not the current document change authority for the document(s).

Approval — The agreement that an item is complete and suitable for its intended use.

Approved Document (or Data) — Document that has been approved by an appropriate authority and is the official (identified) version of the document until replaced by another approved version.

Archived Document (or Data) — Released or approved document that is to be retained for historical purposes.

Assembly — A number of basic parts or subassemblies, or any combination thereof, joined together to perform a specific function. Typical examples are electric generator, audio-frequency amplifier, and power supply.

Computer database — *See* Database.

Computer software — *See* Software.

Computer Software Configuration Item (CSCI) — A configuration item that is computer software.

Computer software documentation — Technical data or information, including computer listings, regardless of media, that document the requirements, design, or details of computer software; explain the capabilities and limitations of the software; or provide operating instructions for using or supporting computer software.

Configuration — The performance, functional, and physical attributes of an existing or planned product, or a combination of products.

Configuration audit — *See* Functional Configuration Audit (FCA), and Physical Configuration Audit (PCA).

Configuration baseline (baseline) — (1) An agreed-to description of the attributes of a product, at a point in time, which serves as a basis for defining change. (2) An approved and released document, or a set of documents, each of a specific revision, the purpose of which is to provide a defined basis for managing change. (3) The currently approved and released configuration documentation. (4) A released set of files comprising a software version and associated configuration documentation. *See* Allocated Baseline (ABL), Functional Baseline (FBL), and Product Baseline (PBL).

Configuration control — (1) A systematic process that ensures that changes to released configuration documentation are properly identified, documented, evaluated for impact, approved by an appropriate level of authority, incorporated, and verified. (2) The configuration management activity concerning: the systematic proposal, justification, evaluation, coordination, and disposition of proposed changes; and the implementation of all approved and released changes into (a) the applicable configurations of a product, (b) associated product information, and (c) supporting and interfacing products and their associated product information.

Configuration Control Board (CCB) — A board composed of technical and administrative representatives who recommend approval or disapproval of proposed engineering changes to, and proposed deviations from, a CI's current approved configuration documentation.

Configuration Control Board Directive (CCBD) — The document that records the Engineering Change Proposal (ECP) approval (or disapproval) decision of the CCB and that provides the direction to the contracting activity either to incorporate the ECP into the contract for performing activity implementation or to communicate the disapproval to the performing activity.

Configuration documentation — Technical documentation, the primary purpose of which is to identify and define a product's performance, functional, and physical attributes (e.g., specifications, drawings). (*See also* Allocated Configuration Documentation [ACD], Functional Configuration Documentation [FCD], and Product Configuration Documentation [PCD].)

Configuration identification — (1) The systematic process of selecting the product attributes, organizing associated information about the attributes, and stating the attributes. (2) Unique identifiers for a product and its configuration documents. (3) The configuration management activity that encompasses the selection of CIs; the determination of the types of configuration documentation required for each CI; the issuance of numbers and other identifiers affixed to the CIs and to the technical documentation that defines the CI's configuration; the release of CIs and their associated configuration documentation; and the establishment of configuration baselines for CIs.

Configuration Item (CI) — A Configuration Item is any hardware, software, or combination of both that satisfies an end use function and is designated for separate configuration management. Configuration items are typically referred to by an alphanumeric identifier, which also serves as the unchanging base for the assignment of serial numbers to uniquely identify individual units of the CI. (*See also* Product-Tracking Base-Identifier.)

Configuration Management (CM) — A management process for establishing and maintaining consistency of a product's performance, functional, and physical attributes with its requirements, design and operational information throughout its life.

Configuration Management Plan (CMP) — The document defining how configuration management will be implemented (including policies and procedures) for a particular acquisition or program.

Configuration Status Accounting (CSA) — The configuration management activity concerning capture and storage of, and access to, configuration information needed to manage products and product information effectively.

Contract — As used herein, denotes the document (for example, contract, memorandum of agreement/understanding, purchase order) used to implement an agreement between a tasking activity (e.g., buyer) and a performing activity (e.g., seller).

Contractual acceptance of data — The action taken by the tasking activity signifying that an item submitted or delivered by the performing activity complies with the requirements of the contract.

Current Document Change Authority (CDCA) — The authority currently responsible for the content of a drawing, specification, or other document and which is the sole authority for approval of changes to that document. (*See also* Application Activity [AA], Approval, Document Custodian Activity.)

Customer Repair (CR) Item — Any part or assembly that, upon failure or malfunction, is intended to be repaired or reworked.

Data — Recorded information of any nature (including administrative, managerial, financial, and technical) regardless of medium or characteristics. (*See also* Data item, Document.)

Database — A collection of related data stored in one or more computerized files in a manner that can be accessed by users or computer programs via a database management system.

Data item — A document or collection of documents that must be submitted by the performing activity to the procuring or tasking activity to fulfill a contract or tasking directive requirement for the delivery of information.

Defect — Any nonconformance of a characteristic with specified requirements.

Deficiencies — Deficiencies consist of two types:
  a. Conditions or characteristics in any item which are not in accordance with the item's current approved configuration documentation; or
  b. Inadequate (or erroneous) configuration documentation which has resulted, or may result, in units of the item that do not meet the requirements for the item.

Design change — *See* Engineering change.

Deviation — A specific written authorization to depart from a particular requirement(s) of an item's current approved configuration documentation for a specific number of units or a specified period of time, and to accept an item that is found to depart from specified requirements, but nevertheless is considered suitable for use "as is" or after repair by an approved method. (A deviation differs from an engineering change in that an approved engineering change requires corresponding revision of the item's current approved configuration documentation, whereas a deviation does not.)

Distribution Statement — A statement used in marking a technical document to denote the extent of its availability for distribution, release, and disclosure without need for additional approvals and authorizations from the controlling DoD office.

Document — A self-contained body of information or data that can be packaged for delivery on a single medium. Some examples of documents are: drawings, reports, standards, databases, application software, engineering designs, virtual part-models, etc.

Document custodian activity — The custodian of a document is the activity that is charged with the physical and electronic safekeeping and maintenance of the "original" document.

Document representation — (1) A set of digital files that, when viewed or printed together, collectively represent the entire document. (For example, a set of raster files or a set of IGES files.) A document may have more than one document representation. (2) A document in a nondigital form. (For example, paper, punched card set, or stable-base drawing.)

Engineering change — (1) A change to the current approved configuration documentation of a configuration item. (2) Any alteration to a product or its released configuration documentation. Effecting an engineering change may involve modification of the product, product information, and associated interfacing products.

Engineering Change Directive (ECD) — An internal performing activity document that indicates the approval of and direction to incorporate or implement engineering change.

Engineering Change Proposal (ECP) — The documentation by which a proposed engineering change is described, justified, and submitted to (a) the current document change authority for approval or disapproval of the design change in the documentation and (b) to the procuring activity for approval or disapproval of implementing the design change in units to be delivered or retrofit into assets already delivered.

Exchangeability of items — *See* Interchangeable item, Replacement item, and Substitute item.

Firmware — The combination of a hardware device and computer instructions or computer data that reside as read-only software on the hardware device.

Fit — The ability of an item to physically interface or interconnect with or become an integral part of another item.

Form — The shape, size, dimensions, mass, weight, and other physical parameters that uniquely characterize an item. For software, form denotes the language and media.

Function — The action or actions that an item is designed to perform.

Functional Baseline (FBL) — The approved functional configuration documentation.

Functional characteristics — Quantitative performance parameters and design constraints, including operational and logistic parameters and their respective tolerances. Functional characteristics include all performance parameters, such as range, speed, lethality, reliability, maintainability, and safety.

Functional Configuration Audit (FCA) — The formal examination of functional characteristics of a configuration item, or system, to verify that the item has achieved the requirements specified in its functional and/or allocated configuration documentation.

Functional Configuration Documentation (FCD) — The documentation describing the system's functional, performance, interoperability, and interface requirements and the verifications required to demonstrate the achievement of those specified requirements.

Hardware — Products made of material and their components (mechanical, electrical, electronic, hydraulic, pneumatic). Computer software and technical documentation are excluded.

Hardware Configuration Item (HWCI) — *See* Configuration Item (CI).

Interchangeable item — A product that possesses such functional and physical attributes as to be equivalent in performance to another product of similar or identical purposes, and is capable of being exchanged for the other product without selection for fit or performance, and without alteration of the products themselves or of adjoining products, except for adjustment.

Interface — The performance, functional, and physical characteristics required to exist at a common boundary.

Interface control — The process of identifying, documenting, and controlling all performance, functional and physical attributes relevant to the interfacing of two or more products provided by one or more organizations.

Interface Control Documentation (ICD) — Interface control drawing or other documentation that depicts physical, functional, performance, and test interfaces of related or co-functioning products.

Interface Control Working Group (ICWG) — For programs that encompass a system, configuration item, or a computer software configuration item design cycle, an ICWG is established to control interface activity among the tasking activity, performing activities, or other agencies, including resolution of interface problems and documentation of interface agreements.

Interoperability — The ability to exchange information and operate effectively together.

Item — A nonspecific term used to denote any product, including systems, materiel, parts, subassemblies, sets, accessories, etc.

Life-cycle cost — The total cost to the tasking activity of acquisition and ownership of an item over its life cycle. As applicable, it includes the cost of development, acquisition, support, and disposal.

Lot number — An identifying number consisting of alpha and numeric characters which, in conjunction with a manufacturer's identifying code and a Product-Tracking Base-Identifier, uniquely identifies a group of units of the same item which are manufactured or assembled by one producer under uniform conditions and which are expected to function in a uniform manner.

Manufacturer Repair (MR) Item — Any part or assembly for which user-maintenance is limited to replacement of consumables and that, upon failure or malfunction, is returned to the original manufacturer for repair.

Materiel — A generic term covering systems, equipment, stores, supplies, and spares, including related documentation, manuals, computer hardware, and software.

Modification Directive — The documentation that indicates the approval of, and direction to implement, a modification request.

Modification Request — The documentation by which a proposed modification of an asset is described, justified, and submitted to the asset owner (who is not the Current Document Change Authority for the asset design documentation) for approval or disapproval of implementing the modification in one or more units. A modification request may result in modification or installation drawings being created to describe the new configuration, but does not result in a revision of the existing design documentation for which an Engineering Change Proposal would be required.

Nomenclature — (1) The combination of an assigned designation and an approved item name. In certain cases, the designation root serves as the basis for assignment of serial and/or lot numbers. (2) Names assigned to kinds and groups of products. (3) Formal designations assigned to products by customer or supplier (such as model number, model type, design differentiation, specific design series, or configuration).

Nonconformance — The failure of a unit or product to meet a specified requirement.

Nonrecurring costs — As applied to an ECP, one-time costs that will be incurred if an engineering change is approved and which are independent of the quantity of items changed, such as cost of redesign or development testing.

Nonrepairable Item — Any part or assembly for which user-maintenance is limited to replenishment of consumables and replacement of the part or assembly upon failure or malfunction.

Notice of Revision (NOR) — A document used to define revisions to configuration documentation which require revision after Engineering Change Proposal approval. *(See also* Engineering Change Proposal [ECP].)

Original — The current design activity's documents or digital document representation and associated source data file(s) of record.

Performing Activity — Denotes an activity performing any of the requirements contained in a contract or tasking directive. A "Performing Activity" can be either a contractor or government activity.

Physical characteristics (attributes) — Quantitative and qualitative expressions of material features, such as composition, dimensions, finishes, form, fit, and their respective tolerances.

Physical Configuration Audit (PCA) — The formal examination of the "as-built" configuration of a configuration item against its technical documentation to establish or verify the configuration item's product baseline.

Product Baseline (PBL) — The approved product configuration documentation.

Product Configuration Documentation (PCD) — A CI's detail design documentation, including those verifications necessary for accepting product deliveries (first article and acceptance inspections). Based on program production/procurement strategies, the design information contained in the PCD can be as simple as identifying a specific part number or as complex as full design disclosure.

Product-Tracking Base-Identifier — An unchanging identifier used as a base for the assignment of serial numbers to uniquely identify individual units of an item or lot numbers to uniquely identify groups of units of an item. The product-tracking identifier is used rather than the Part or Identifying Number (PIN) because the PIN is altered to reflect a new configuration when the item it identifies is modified. The same product-tracking base-identifier may be used for several similar items (usually defined by a common document) and requires that each such item is assigned serial or lot numbers distinct from each other such item.

Product Tracking Identifier — A generic term that refers to the sequentially assigned alphanumeric identifier applied to a product to differentiate units of the product or groups of the product. This may be a government serial (or hull) number, manufacturer's serial number, lot number, or date code.

Recurring costs — Costs that are incurred on a per-unit basis for each item changed or for each service or document ordered.

Release — The designation by the originating activity that a document representation or software version is approved by the appropriate authority and is subject to configuration change management procedures.

Released Document (Data) — (1) Document that has been released after review and internal approvals. (2) Document that has been provided to others outside the originating group or team for use (as opposed to for comment).

Repair — A procedure that reduces, but does not completely eliminate, a nonconformance. Repair is distinguished from rework in that the characteristic after repair still does not completely conform to the applicable drawings, specifications, or contract requirements.

Repairable Item — Any part or assembly that, upon failure or malfunction, is intended to be repaired or reworked.

Replacement item — One that is interchangeable with another item, but differs physically from the original item in that the installation of the replacement item requires operations such as drilling, reaming, cutting, filing, shimming, etc., in addition to the normal application and methods of attachment.

Retrofit — The incorporation of new design parts or software code, resulting from an approved engineering change, to a product's current approved product configuration documentation and into products already delivered to and accepted by customers.

Retrofit Instruction — The document that provides specific, step-by-step instructions about the installation of the replacement parts to be installed in delivered units to bring their configuration up to that approved by an ECP. (Sometimes referred to Alteration Instruction, Modification Work Order, Technical Directive, or Time Compliance Technical Order.)

Rework — A procedure applied to a product to eliminate a nonconformance to the drawings, specifications, or contract requirements that will completely eliminate the nonconformance and result in a characteristic that conforms completely.

Serial number — An identifying number consisting of alpha and numeric characters which is assigned sequentially in the order of manufacture or final test and which, in conjunction with a manufacturer's identifying CAGE code, uniquely identifies a single item within a group of similar items identified by a common product-tracking base-identifier.

Software — Computer programs and computer databases.

Specification — A document that explicitly states essential technical attributes/requirements for a product and procedures to determine that the product's performance meets its requirements/attributes.

Specification Change Notice (SCN) — *See* Engineering Change Proposal (ECP).

Submitted Document (Data) — Released document that has been made available to customers.

Substitute item — An item that possesses such functional and physical characteristics as to be capable of being exchanged for another item only under specified conditions or in particular applications and without alteration of the items themselves or of adjoining items.

Support equipment — Equipment and computer software required to maintain, test, or operate a product or facility in its intended environment.

Survivability — The capability of a system to avoid or withstand a hostile environment without suffering an abortive impairment of its ability to accomplish its designated mission.

System — A self-sufficient unit in its intended operational environment, which includes all equipment, related facilities, material, software, services, and personnel required for its operation and support.

Tasking activity — An organization that imposes the requirements contained in a contract or tasking directive on a performing activity. (For example, a Government Contracting Activity that awards a contract to a contractor, a Government Program Management Office that tasks another Government activity, or a contractor that tasks a subcontractor.)

Technical data — Technical data is recorded information (regardless of the form or method of recording) of a scientific or technical nature (including computer software documentation).

Technical data package — A technical description of an item adequate for supporting an acquisition strategy, production, engineering, and logistics support. The description defines the required design configuration and procedures required to ensure adequacy of item performance. It consists of all applicable technical data such as drawings and associated lists, specifications, standards, performance requirements, quality assurance provisions, and packaging details.

Technical documentation — *See* Technical data.

Technical reviews — A series of system engineering activities by which the technical progress on a project is assessed relative to its technical or contractual requirements. The reviews are conducted at logical transition points in the development effort to identify and correct problems resulting from the work completed thus far before the problems can disrupt or delay the technical progress. The reviews provide a method for the performing activity and tasking activity to determine that the development of a configuration item and its documentation have a high probability of meeting contract requirements.

Training equipment — All types of maintenance and operator training hardware, devices, audio-visual training aids, and related software that:

Are used to train maintenance and operator personnel by depicting, simulating, or portraying the operational or maintenance characteristics of an item or facility.

Are kept consistent in design, construction, and configuration with such items in order to provide required training capability.

Version — (1) One of several sequentially created configurations of a data product. (2) A supplementary identifier used to distinguish a changed body or set of computer-based data (software) from the previous configuration with the same primary identifier. Version identifiers are usually associated with data (such as files, databases, and software) used by, or maintained in, computers.

Waiver — *See* Deviation.

Working Document (Data) — Document that has not been released; any document that is currently controlled solely by the originator including new versions of the document that were previously released, submitted, or approved.

Appendix V

FUNCTIONAL CONFIGURATION AUDIT (FCA) CHECKLIST

Functional Configuration Audit (FCA) Checklist

CI Nomenclature: _____ Date: _____
CI/CSCI Identifier: _____ Release # _____

Requirements	Yes	No	NA
1. Facilities for conducting FCA available			
2. Audit Team members have been identified and informed of audit			
3. Audit Team members are aware of their responsibilities			
4 General Requirements Specification (GRS) or all of the following two documents: Software Requirements Specification (SRS), System Specification (SS)			
5. Waiver or Deviation list prepared			
6. Verification Test Procedures submitted (test transactions)			
7. Verification Test Procedures reviewed and approved (test transactions)			
8. Verification Testing completed and results available (System Qualification Test)			
9. Verification Test data and results reviewed and approved			
10. Test Results submitted (if available or applicable)			
11. Verification Testing witnessed			
12. Test Readiness Review I and II (TRR I and TRR II) completed			
13. Test Readiness Review I and II (TRR I and TRR II) minutes and open action items from past reviews available			
14. Copy of baseline and database change requests with their associated status accounting records along with all design (Problem Reports and Deficiency Reports [PRs and DRs], etc.) provided			
15. Other inputs as specified by the functional requirements and planning documents (i.e., ORD, RTM)			

Signature of FCA Team Members: Date:

_____   _____
_____   _____
_____   _____
_____   _____
_____   _____
_____   _____
_____   _____
_____   _____
_____   _____
_____   _____
_____   _____
_____   _____
_____   _____

Check one:
☐ Results reviewed satisfy the requirements and are accepted (see attached comments).
☐ Results reviewed do not satisfy requirements (see attached comments and list of deficiencies).
Approved by: _____ Date: _____

Appendix W

PHYSICAL CONFIGURATION AUDIT (PCA) CHECKLIST

Physical Configuration Audit (PCA) Checklist

The following requirements and tasks shall be available and accomplished at the PCA.

Requirements	Yes	No	NA
1. Approved final draft of the configuration item product specification.			
2. A list delineating both approved and outstanding changes against the configuration item.			
3. Complete list of shortages in CSCI production.			
4. Acceptance test procedures and associated test data.			
5. Findings/status of quality assurance programs.			
6. Manuscript copy of all software CI manuals (*i.e., SSS, SRS, STP, STD, SCOM, SUM, etc.*).			
7. Computer Software Version Description Document.			
8. Current set of listings and updated design descriptions or other means of design portrayal for each software CI.			
9. FCA minutes for each configuration item.			
Tasks			
1. Define Product Baseline.			
2. Specification Review and Validation.			
3. Record in the minutes of the PCA the differences between the CSCI being audited and its CM records.			
4. Ensure the discrepancies noted during the FCA on each CSCI have been corrected.			
5. Ensure CSCI design descriptions properly reflect labels, references, and data descriptions.			
6. Ensure each CSCI design description is consistent.			
7. Review acceptance test plan, procedures, records, and results, as well as specification records to ensure the product complies with its design requirements.			
8. Review shortages and design changes.			
9. Review deviations/waivers.			
10. Ensure each CSCI's system evaluation documents are completed and properly formatted.			
11. Ensure all system documentation is complete and conforms to its data item description.			
12. Review system allocation document.			
13. Review Software User's Manuals and Software Programmer's Manuals.			

14. Review software CIs for the following:
  a. Preliminary and detail Software Component design descriptions
  b. Preliminary and detail Software Interface requirements
  c. Database characteristics, storage allocation charts, and timing and sequencing characteristics			

15. Review packaging plan and requirements.			
16. Review release records and procedures.			
17. Ensure that approved software coding standards have been used and documented.			
18. Certify that each CSCI accepted has been built in accordance with the specifications.			

Signature of PCA Team Members: Date:

_____   _____

_____   _____

_____   _____

_____   _____

_____   _____

_____   _____

_____   _____

Check one:
☐ Results reviewed satisfy the requirements and are accepted (see attached comments).
☐ Results reviewed do not satisfy requirements (see attached comments and list of deficiencies).

Approved by: _____   Date: _____

Source: Adapted from Military Standard Configuration Management, MIL-STD-973.

Appendix X

SCM GUIDANCE FOR ACHIEVING THE "REPEATABLE" LEVEL ON THE SOFTWARE

Table of Contents

1 INTRODUCTION

1.1 Scope

This document provides information and guidance to personnel involved in SCM of computer software. This document assumes that each project performs the tasks listed below.

1. Implements SCM for the full life cycle of the product
2. Assigns a manager with specific SCM responsibilities.
3. Requires contractors who produce software products to implement SCM to at least the same degree as the approved project SCMP and procedures and comply with other instructions of the SCMP

The activities in the SCM process outlined in this document are not sequential. More than one activity may be accomplished at the same time; an activity begins when the entry criteria are met, controls are imposed on the activity, inputs are provided so that action(s) can be taken, and an identified individual(s) or groups clearly understand their roles and responsibilities for accomplishing the process activity and/or generating an output.

1.2 Purpose

The purpose of this document is to describe the process activities common to all organizations required to **Provide SCM Support.** The title of each process appears in boldface throughout this document to aid in identification of the process activity. This document identifies and describes an SCM process to achieve a repeatable level of SCM maturity. Repeatability requires that: "Basic project management processes are established to track cost, schedule, and functionality. The necessary process discipline is in place to repeat earlier successes on projects with similar applications."[1]

To further assist in a repeatable SCM process, two additional documents have been developed based on the information contained within this document: (1) a Generic SCMP used to generate an SCMP that is project specific and (2) a Sample DTP describing a configuration control task. The sample DTP includes information to guide an author through the development of task-specific DTP.

1.3 Document Overview

This document is intended to provide an overview of a repeatable process(es) that SCM personnel can use in providing SCM support to a project. It describes the SCM process down to project-specific activities. This

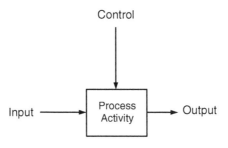

Figure X1 Sample Control Activity Diagram

document describes the responsibilities of SCM personnel and the tasks associated with each SCM activity.

Figure X1 is a sample control activity diagram. Control to an activity is indicated by an arrow entering the top of the box. Input to an activity is indicated by an arrow entering the left-side of the box. Output from an activity is indicated by an arrow exiting from the right side of the box.

Figure X2 identifies SCM interfaces. It shows (1) identified external sources that interface with SCM, (2) inputs provided to the process activity that **Provide SCM Support**, and (3) outputs generated by SCM as a result of **Provide SCM Support**. The external sources shown in Figure X2 will be updated as other interfaces are identified.

Figure X3 is a diagram of the SCM Process Definition. Each box in the diagram represents a process activity and is identified by a title of the activity and a label identifier (the letter A followed by a numeric identifier). The first-level activity is titled **Provide SCM Support** and labeled A0 (Figure X3a). The second level of **Provide SCM Support** is comprised of two activities: **Manage SCM** (labeled A1; Figure X3b) and **Perform SCM** (labeled A2; Figure X3b). Third-level activities, derived from A1, are **Create and Maintain Project SCMP** (labeled A11; Figure X3c), **Manage Implementation of SCMP** (labeled A12; Figure X3c), and **Provide SCM Training** (labeled A13; Figure X3c). Third-level activities, derived from A2, are **Perform Configuration Identification** (labeled A21; Figure X3d), **Perform Configuration Control** (labeled A22; Figure X3d), **Perform Configuration Status Accounting** (labeled A23; Figure X3d), and **Perform Configuration Audits and Reviews** (labeled A24; Figure X3d). Fourth-level activities, derived from A12, are **Manage SCM Tasks** (labeled A121; Figure X3e), **Create and Maintain DTP** (labeled A122; Figure X3e), and **Manage Resources and Personnel to Perform SCM** (labeled A123; Figure X3e).

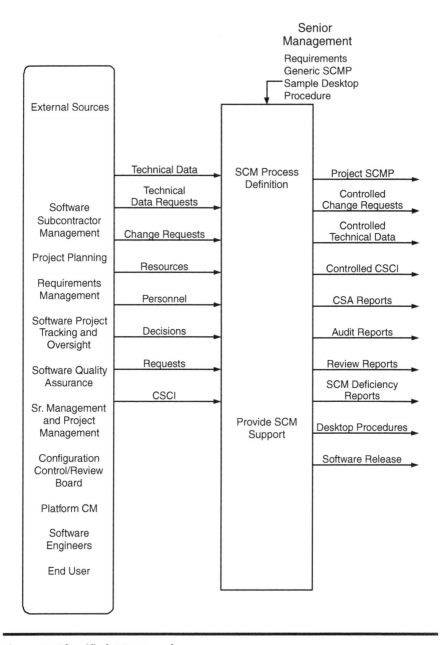

Figure X2 Identified SCM Interfaces

This document is organized into the sections listed below.

Section 1 provides the scope and purpose of this document.
Section 2 lists the government standards and other publications referenced in this document and used in its preparation.

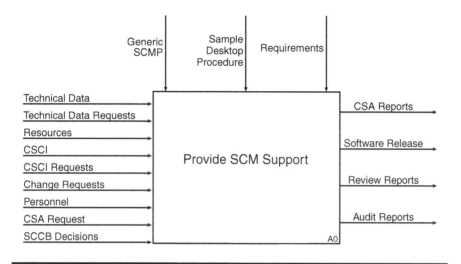

Figure X3a SCM Process Definition Diagram: Level 0 — SCM Process

Section 3 lists the configuration management (CM) terms and definitions as they are used in this document. To effectively use this document, the reader should first become familiar with the definitions.

Section 4 describes the process activities. The following provides the format definitions for describing a process activity of the SCM Process Definition and the diagram in Figure X3.

- *Purpose:* the objective of the process activity. If a subprocess activity exists, the details are described in that specific paragraph description.
- *Role and responsibility:* the responsibilities of individuals or groups for accomplishing a process activity.
- *Entry criteria:* the elements and conditions necessary to be in place to begin a process activity. Reading lower-level activities assumes that the entry criteria for all higher-level activities have been satisfied.
- *Control:* data that constrains or regulates a process activity. Controls regulate the transformation of inputs into outputs.
- *Input:* data or material with which a process activity is performed.
- *Process activity:* actions to transform an input, as influenced by controls, into a predetermined output.
- *Output:* data or material produced by or resulting from a process activity. It must include the input data in some form. The output title differs from the input title in order to indicate that an activity has been performed.
- *Exit criteria:* elements and/or conditions necessary to be in place to complete a process activity.

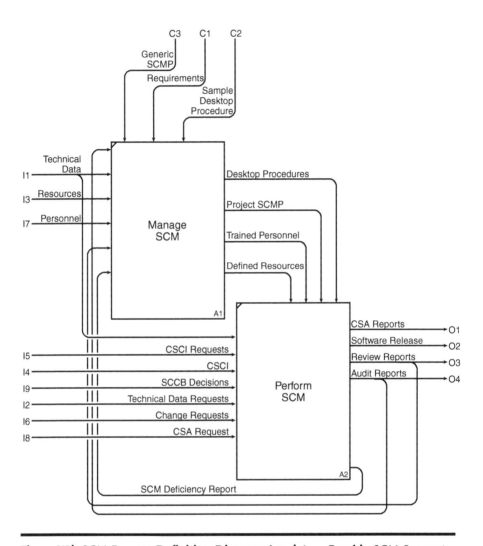

Figure X3b SCM Process Definition Diagram: Level 1 — Provide SCM Support

Appendix A contains a list of all acronyms and abbreviations and their definitions used in this document.

Appendix B contains a traceability matrix between the process activities defined in this document and the SCM *Briefing Evaluation Check Sheet* for Level 2, Repeatability.

2 TERMS AND DEFINITIONS

The terms and definitions listed below are provided as an aid to understanding and applying the SCM principles and processes used to manage software development and testing efforts.

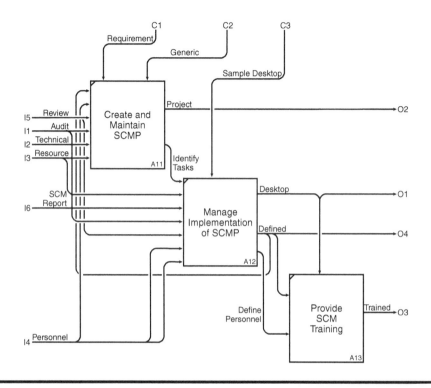

Figure X3c SCM Process Definition Diagram: Level 2 — Manage SCM

Audit — An independent examination of a work product or set of work products to assess compliance with specifications, standards, contractual agreements, or criteria.

Audit reports — Independent group findings that are the results of reviewing compliance with specifications, standards, contractual agreements, or other specified criteria.

Baseline — A configuration identification document or set of such documents formally designated and fixed at a specific time during the configuration item's (CI's) life cycle. Baselines, plus approved changes from those baselines, constitute the current configuration identification.

Capability Maturity Model (CMM) — A Software Engineering Institute document that describes the stages that software organizations evolve as they define, implement, measure, control, and improve their software processes. The model is a guide for selecting the process improvement strategies by facilitating the determination of current process capabilities and identification of the issues most critical to software quality and process improvement.

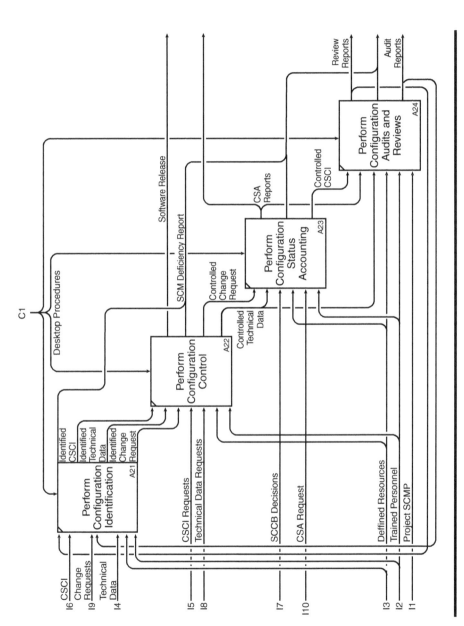

Figure X3d SCM Process Definition Diagram: Level 2 — Perform SCM (Cont'd)

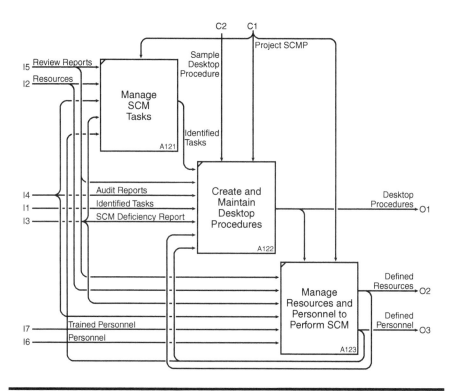

Figure X3e SCM Process Definition Diagram: Level 3 — Manage Implementation of SCMP

Change Request (CR) — Reports of deficiencies or enhancements generated against product Computer Software Configuration Items (CSCIs) or technical data; a document that requests a correction or change to the baselined documentation or software. Examples are Software Change Proposals, Software Trouble Reports, Software Problem Reports, Engineering Change Proposals, and other local forms that communicate problems in a product. A CR becomes "controlled" when the master copy of the CR is received, processed, and maintained by the SCM organization (e.g., SCM assigns a tracking number or identifier, enters the information into the configuration status accounting [CSA] system, distributes copies, files, ensures updates to master copy by authorized personnel, etc.).

Configuration Audit — A formal examination of a CSCI. Two types of configuration audits exist: the Functional Configuration Audit (FCA) and the Physical Configuration Audit (PCA). (See Appendices V and W.)

Configuration Control — The systematic proposal, justification, evaluation, coordination, and approval or disapproval of proposed changes, and the implementation of all approved changes in the configuration of a CI after establishment of the baseline(s) for the CI.

Configuration Identification — The selection of CIs; the determination of the types of configuration documentation required for each CI; the issuance of numbers and other identifiers affixed to the CIs and to the technical documentation that defines the CI's configuration, including internal and external interfaces; the release of CIs and associated configuration documentation; and the establishment of configuration baselines for CIs.

Controlled CR — Maintenance of the master copy of the CR.

Computer Software Configuration Item (CSCI) — A CI that is software.

Configuration Status Accounting (CSA) — The recording and reporting of information needed to manage CIs effectively, including:

■ A record of the approved configuration documentation and identification numbers

■ The status of proposed changes, deviations, and waivers to the configuration

■ The implementation status of approved changes

■ The configuration of all units of the CI in the operational inventory

CSA Reports — Formatted output of the CSA system database.

Desktop Procedure (DTP) — Step-by-step instructions describing a course of action to be taken to perform a given process.

End Product — The authorized and approved complete set, or any of the authorized and approved individual items of the set, of computer programs, procedures, and associated documentation and data designated for delivery to a customer or end user.

Field Activity — A designated government agency that performs a task in accordance with a contractual agreement with a sponsoring government organization.

Identified CR — A CR to which a tracking number has been assigned.

Life Cycle — A generic term covering all phases of acquisition, operation, and logistics support of an item beginning with concept definition and continuing through disposal of an item.

Nondevelopmental Software (NDS) — Deliverable software that is not delivered under the contract but is provided by the contractor, the government, or a third party. NDS may be referred to as reusable software, government-furnished software, or commercially available software, depending on its source.

Personnel — A pool of potential workers available to perform SCM tasks. "Defined personnel" are individuals who have been selected to staff or support SCM tasks. "Trained personnel" are individuals having the knowledge, skills, and abilities required to perform SCM tasks.

Program Management — The government organization sponsoring the field activity project office.

Project Management — The designated government organization from the field activity project office responsible for the overall management of specific projects.

Repeatable — Basic project management processes are established to track cost, schedule, and functionality. The necessary process discipline is in place to repeat earlier successes on projects with similar applications.

Requirements — Direction provided by standards, specifications, instructions, etc.; by data item descriptions; and by program management or field activity.

Resources — Funding, facilities, tools, and nondevelopmental software as determined on a project-by-project basis. Personnel have been separated from resources to highlight the training aspects related to personnel. "Defined resources" are identified resources such as funding, facilities, tools, and nondevelopmental software allocated to perform any given SCM task.

Review Reports — Findings of an internal SCM or independent group that result from informal checks of SCM procedures or of formal reviews by Software Quality Assurance (SQA).

Retired — The removal of support from an operational system or component.

Software Configuration Control Board (SCCB) — A group of individuals responsible for and empowered by project management to evaluate and make decisions that affect software baselines.

Software Configuration Management (SCM) — A discipline that applies technical and administrative direction and surveillance to perform the functions listed below:

- Identify and document the functional and physical characteristics of CSCIs.
- Control the changes to CSCIs and their related documentation.
- Record and report information needed to manage CSCIs effectively, including the status of proposed changes and the implementation status of approved changes.
- Audit the CSCIs to verify conformance to specifications, interface control documents, and other contract requirements.

SCM Deficiency Reports — Problems or enhancements that are written against SCM tools, processes, procedures, and CSA reports. The SCM manager remains cognizant of these reports until resolution.

SCM Plan (SCMP) — The document defining how SCM will be implemented (including policies and procedures) for a particular acquisition or program.

Software Product — The complete set, or any of the individual items of the set, of computer programs, procedures, and associated documentation and data designated for delivery to a customer or end user.

Software-Related Group — Project members responsible for generating requirements, design, development, validation, verification, documentation, maintenance, and logistics of software.

Software Release — An end product delivered to a customer, including end-user documentation.

Software Unit — An element in the design of a software item; for example, a major subdivision of a software item, a component of that subdivision, a class, object, module, function, routine, or database. Software units may occur at different levels of a hierarchy and may consist of other software units. Software units in the design may or may not have a one-to-one relationship with the code and data entities (routines, procedures, databases, data files, etc.) that implement them or with the computer files containing those entities.

Tasks — Well-defined units of work that provides configuration management guidelines to accomplish given requirements.

Technical Data — Recorded information (regardless of the form or method of recording) of a scientific or technical nature (including computer software documentation) relating to supplies procured by an agency. Technical data does not include computer software, financial data, administrative data, cost data, pricing data, management data, or other information incidental to contract administration.

3 PROVIDE SCM SUPPORT

3a Purpose

The purpose of this process activity (A0) is to establish and maintain a product's integrity throughout its life cycle. SCM support will be provided through implementation of the process included in the tasks listed below.

1. Manage SCM.
2. Perform SCM.

3b Roles and Responsibilities

The following are responsible for **Provide SCM Support**:

Role	Responsibility
Program Management	Provide technical data and requirements to SCM. Provide resources for SCM.
Project Management	Provide technical data and requirements to SCM. Provide resources for SCM. Establish (project level) SCCB, appoint chairperson. Review SCM activity status and aid in problem resolution for audit findings. Assign SCM manager with specific SCM responsibilities.
SCM Manager	Manage SCM Establish SCM organization to perform SCM.
SCM Organization	Implement and perform SCM throughout the life cycle of the software product.

3c Entry Criteria

SCM support is initiated upon project authorization.

3d Control

Controls for this activity are listed below.

1. Requirements determine the scope and depth of SCM responsibilities.
2. The Generic SCMP provides a basis for a project SCMP.
3. The Sample DTP provides the basis for developing detailed instructions required to complete SCM tasks.

3e Input

Inputs to this activity are listed below.

1. CSCI
2. Technical Data
3. CSCI Requests
4. Technical Data Requests
5. CRs
6. Resources
7. Personnel
8. SCCB Decisions
9. CSA Requests

3f Process Activities

The process activities for **Provide SCM Support** are as follows:

1. Technical data, resources, personnel, and SCCB decisions are used to create and implement the project SCMP and DTP.
2. Technical data, resources, personnel, SCCB decisions, and CRs that affect SCM requirements may require changes to maintain a current SCMP and DTP.
3. SCCB decisions and CRs are used to identify and track the creation and modification of products.
4. CSCI and technical data requests are processed by SCM to supply the requested CSCI and technical data.
5. CSA requests are processed to produce reports.
6. Technical data, SCMP, tasks, and DTP are audited and reviewed with results documented in audit and review reports.

3g Output

Outputs of this activity are listed below.

1. Project SCMP
2. Controlled CSCI
3. Controlled CRs
4. Controlled Technical Data
5. CSA Reports
6. Audit Reports
7. Review Reports
8. SCM Deficiency Reports
9. Software Release
10. DTP

3h Exit Criteria

Retiring a software product satisfies the exit criteria.

3.1 Manage SCM (A1)

3.1a Purpose

The purpose of this process activity (A1) is to manage SCM support. SCM is managed through the functions listed below.

1. Create and Maintain the Project SCMP.

2. Manage Implementation of the SCMP.
3. Provide SCM Training.

3.1b Role and Responsibility

The following is responsible for **Manage SCM**:

Role	Responsibility
SCM Manager	Create and maintain the project SCMP.
	Identify tasks to be accomplished.
	Oversee generation, implementation, and maintenance of DTP in accordance with the project SCMP.
	Provide SCM training.
	Evaluate and use measurements gathered against the SCM procedures to improve the processes.
	Periodically review and provide status on SCM activities with field activity management.
	Respond to audit and review findings on SCM activities.
	Interface with appropriate internal and external agencies.

3.1c Entry Criteria

An individual is assigned the responsibilities of SCM Manager to provide SCM support to the project.

3.1d Control

Controls for this activity are listed below.

1. Requirements determine the SCM responsibilities.
2. The Generic SCMP provides a basis for a project-specific SCMP.
3. The Sample DTP provides the basis for developing detailed instructions required to complete SCM tasks.

3.1e Input

Inputs to this activity are listed below.

1. Technical data.
2. Resources
3. Audit Reports
4. Review Reports
5. Trained Personnel
6. Defined Personnel

7. SCM Deficiency Reports
8. Identified Tasks
9. Defined Resources
10. Personnel

3.1f Process Activities

The process activities for **Manage SCM** are as follows:

1. Oversee the creation, implementation, and maintenance of the project SCMP and DTP. Identify the tasks to be accomplished.
2. Provide for the training of personnel as required for the project to perform the SCM activities.

3.1g Output

Outputs from this activity are listed below.

1. Project SCMP
2. Identified Tasks
3. DTP
4. Defined Resources
5. Defined Personnel
6. Trained Personnel

3.1h Exit Criteria

Retiring a software product satisfies the exit criteria.

3.1.1 Create and Maintain Project SCMP (A11)

3.1.1a Purpose

The purpose of this process activity (A11) is to document the plan that defines how configuration management will be implemented for a project, submit the plan for program management and SCCB approval, and update the plan to reflect current project requirements, processes, and practices.

3.1.1b Roles and Responsibilities

The following are responsible for **Create and Maintain Project SCMP**:

Role	Responsibility
Program Management	Provide overall approval to the project SCMP as approved by the SCCB.
SCCB	Approve the project SCMP and changes to the baselined project SCMP.
SCM Manager	Oversee creation, implementation, and maintenance of the project SCMP throughout the product's life cycle.
	Place the approved project SCMP under configuration control.
Software-Related Groups	Review project SCMP and updates.

3.1.1c Entry Criteria

The SCM Manager has the following sources available:

1. Identified SCM interfaces within the project organization and within external organizations.
2. The Generic SCMP is used as a template in the development of a project SCMP.
3. Technical data outlining project requirements.

3.1.1d Control

Controls of this activity are listed below.

1. Requirements determine the scope and depth of SCM responsibilities.
2. The Generic SCMP provides a basis for the creation and maintenance of a project SCMP.

3.1.1e Input

Inputs to this activity are listed below.

1. Technical Data
2. Resources
3. Audit Reports
4. Review Reports
5. Trained Personnel

3.1.1f Process Activities

The process activities for **Create and Maintain Project SCMP** are as follows:

1. Use the inputs of technical data, resources, and personnel as stated by the requirements and the Generic SCMP to manage the creation of a project SCMP.
2. Review and respond to audit and review reports to maintain the project SCMP. Technical data, resources, and personnel as stated in the requirements and the Generic SCMP are also used to maintain the project SCMP.
3. Submit the project SCMP to program management and SCCB for approval. Place the approved project SCMP under configuration control.

3.1.1g Output

1. A project SCMP
2. Identified Tasks

3.1.1h Exit Criteria

Approval of the SCMP and subsequent updates throughout the product's life cycle satisfy the exit criteria.

3.1.2 Manage Implementation of SCMP (A12)

3.1.2a Purpose

The purpose of this process activity (A12) is to ensure implementation of SCM tasks and DTP in accordance with the project SCMP and to use resources and personnel in accomplishing SCM activities.

3.1.2b Role and Responsibility

The following is responsible for **Manage Implementation of SCMP**:

Role	Responsibility
SCM Manager	Identify, delegate, and monitor the SCM tasks.
	Create, implement, and maintain DTP.
	Manage SCM resources and personnel.

3.1.2c Entry Criteria

An approved SCMP exists.

3.1.2d Control

The controls for **Manage Implementation of SCMP** are listed below.

1. The project SCMP states the required tasks to be performed by the SCM organization.
2. The DTP identifies the areas that require documented step-by-step procedures.

3.1.2e Input

Inputs to this activity are listed below.

1. Resources
2. Defined Personnel
3. Audit Reports
4. Review Reports
5. SCM Deficiency Reports
6. Identified Tasks
7. Defined Resources
8. Personnel
9. Trained Personnel

3.1.2f Process Activities

The process activities for **Manage Implementation of Project SCMP** are as follows:

1. Identify the tasks stated in the project SCMP.
2. Determine the DTP required to follow the processes stated in the project SCMP.
3. Define the resources and positions required to implement the project SCMP.
4. Provide resolution of SCM deficiency reports.

3.1.2g Output

Outputs from this activity are listed below.

1. Identified Tasks
2. DTP
3. Defined Resources
4. Defined Personnel

3.1.2h Exit Criteria

Retiring a software product satisfies the exit criteria.

3.1.2.1Manage SCM Tasks (A121)

3.1.2.1a Purpose   The purpose of this process activity (A121) is to ensure that the tasks stated in the project SCMP are implemented in a consistent, correct, complete, and compliant manner.

3.1.2.1b Role and Responsibility   The following is responsible for **Manage SCM Tasks:**

Role	Responsibility
SCM Manager	Decompose the tasks stated in the project SCMP into manageable components (e.g., work breakdown structure).
	Monitor the accomplishment of the identified task.
	Review the identified tasks for compliance with the approved project SCMP.

3.1.2.1c Entry Criteria   An approved project SCMP exists.

3.1.2.1d Control   The approved project SCMP provides control.

3.1.2.1e Input   Inputs to this activity are listed below.

1. Resources
2. Defined Personnel
3. Audit Reports
4. Review Reports
5. SCM Deficiency Reports

3.1.2.1f Process Activities   The process activities for **Manage SCM Tasks** are as follows:

1. Clarify the tasks stated in the project SCMP using resources and defined personnel.
2. Maintain the tasks so that all tasks are current and applicable to the product. Updates to the project SCMP, resources, SCM deficiency reports, and audit and review reports may require tasks to be added, modified, or deleted.
3. Ensure that the tasks are accomplished and fulfill the requirements stated in the project SCMP.

3.1.2.1g Output Output from this activity is composed of identified tasks.

3.1.2.1h Exit Criteria Identified tasks that reflect the current project SCMP satisfy the exit criteria.

3.1.2.2 Create and Maintain DTP (A122)

3.1.2.2a Purpose The purpose of this process activity (A122) is to document the procedures that describe how SCM is performed for a project and update the DTP to reflect the current project SCMP.

3.1.2.2b Role and Responsibility The following are responsible for **Create and Maintain DTP:**

Role	Responsibility
SCM Manager	Direct the development of DTP, and oversee the implementation and maintenance of DTP.
	Identify the functions within the software-related groups, e.g., system engineering, software development, system testing, etc., that the SCM organization must interface with to accomplish a task.
Software-Related Groups	Review DTP.
SCM Organization	Create, implement, and maintain DTP.

3.1.2.2c Entry Criteria This project SCMP and the Sample DTP satisfy the entry criteria.

3.1.2.2d Control The controls for **Create and Maintain DTP** are listed below.

1. The project SCMP identifies all the tasks and the high-level processes that require DTP.
2. The Sample DTP is used as a guideline in generating specific DTP.

3.1.2.2e Input Inputs to this activity are listed below.

1. Identified Tasks
2. Defined Personnel.

3. Defined Resources
4. Audit Reports
5. Review Reports
6. SCM Deficiency Reports

3.1.2.2f Process Activities   The process activities for **Create and Maintain DTP** are as follows:

1. Create DTP for processes identified in the project SCMP using resources, personnel, and guidelines found in the sample DTP.
2. Maintain the procedures so that the process is repeatable. Written procedures provide the instructions for performing SCM (configuration identification, configuration control, CSA, and configuration audits and reviews). A change in a process may require the written procedures to change. Inputs to this activity include defined resources, SCM deficiency reports, and audit and review reports. Defined resources are resources that are necessary to perform the procedures. SCM deficiency reports and audit and review reports may cause the procedures to be modified or deleted. The process of managing procedures includes monitoring these procedures to ensure that the process as described in the DTP is being followed. Monitoring of the processes is accomplished through audits of SCM processes and internal SCM reviews.

3.1.2.2g Output   Output of this activity is the accomplishment of written DTP.

3.1.2.2h Exit Criteria   Written DTP and subsequent updates throughout the product's life cycle satisfy the exit criteria.

3.1.2.3 Manage Resources and Personnel to Perform SCM (A123)

3.1.2.3a Purpose   The purpose of this process activity (A123) is to use appropriate resources and personnel to accomplish the SCM task(s) in accordance with the project SCMP and DTP.

3.1.2.3b Role and Responsibility   The following is responsible for **Manage Resources and Personnel to Perform SCM**.

Role	Responsibility
SCM Manager	Identify and manage the resources and personnel needed to accomplish tasks identified in the project SCMP.

3.1.2.3c Entry Criteria   DTP satisfy the entry criteria.

3.1.2.3d Control   The controls for **Manage Resources and Personnel to Perform SCM** are listed below.

1. The project SCMP states the required tasks to be performed by the SCM organization.
2. The DTP provide step-by-step guidance for personnel required to complete tasks using given resources.
3. Resources define the budget and schedule constraints placed upon SCM.

3.1.2.3e Input   Inputs to this activity are listed below.

1. Resources
2. Personnel
3. Audit Reports
4. Review Reports
5. Trained Personnel
6. SCM Deficiency Reports

3.1.2.3f Process Activities   The process activities for **Manage Resources and Personnel to Perform SCM** are as follows:

1. Identify, define, and direct the resources (i.e., SCM tools, allocated funds, tasking priorities to meet schedules) and personnel (both prior to and after training) needed to follow processes described in the project SCMP. SCM deficiency reports and audit and review reports are inputs that may require the SCM Manager to re-identify resources, personnel, and training needed to support the processes and/or DTP.

3.1.2.3g Output   Outputs of this activity are listed below.

1. Defined Resources
2. Defined Personnel

3.1.2.3h Exit Criteria The exit criteria for this process activity are defined resources and defined personnel necessary to support the SCMP and DTP.

3.1.3 Provide SCM Training (A13)

3.1.3a Purpose

The purpose of this process activity (A13) is to train the SCM organization and software-related groups on processes as described in the project SCMP, DTP, and SCM tools to accomplish tasks stated in the project SCMP.

3.1.3b Role and Responsibility

The following is responsible for **Provide SCM Training**:

Role	Responsibility
SCM Manager	Identify, establish, coordinate, and maintain training as required to ensure effective performance of SCM activity by the SCM organization and software-related groups.

3.1.3c Entry Criteria

DTP satisfy the entry criteria.

3.1.3d Control

The control for **Provide SCM Training** is listed below.

1. DTP provide detailed information on the activities, personnel, SCM tools, skills, and knowledge required to complete a given task. This information can be used to determine training requirements.

3.1.3e Input

Inputs to this activity are listed below.

1. Defined Resources
2. Defined Personnel

3.1.3f Process Activities

The process activity for **Provide SCM Training** is to use defined personnel and resources to produce personnel trained in SCM processes as described in the project SCMP, DTP, and SCM tools. Defined personnel include both those providing training and those receiving the training.

3.1.3g Output

The output of this activity is trained personnel.

3.1.3h Exit Criteria

Trained personnel satisfy the exit criteria.

3.2 Perform SCM (A2)

3.2a Purpose

The purpose of this process activity (A2) is to apply configuration identification, control, status accounting, and audits and reviews throughout the life cycle of a product in order to ensure the integrity of the software release and associated documentation.

3.2b Role and Responsibility

The following is responsible for **Perform SCM**:

Role	Responsibility
SCM Organization	Perform configuration identification, control, status accounting, and internal SCM reviews.
	Assist in performing the configuration audit(s).
	Assist in the independent audit of SCM activities.

3.2c Entry Criteria

The SCM Manager has identified and trained personnel and current DTP exist.

3.2d Control

The current DTP provide control of this activity.

3.2e Input

Inputs to this activity are listed below.

1. CSCI
2. Technical Data
3. CRs
4. Defined Resources
5. Trained Personnel

6. Audit Reports
7. Review Reports
8. CSCI Requests
9. Technical Data Requests
10. Identified Technical Data
11. SCCB Decisions
12. Identified CR
13. Identified CSCI
14. CSA Request
15. Controlled CR
16. Controlled Technical Data
17. Controlled CSCI
18. CSA Reports
19. Project SCMP
20. DTP

3.2f Process Activities

The process activities for **Perform SCM** are as follows:

1. Take receipt of and assign tracking identifiers to the CSCI and its related technical data.
2. Control changes to the CSCI and its technical data through the use of CRs and board decisions (e.g., CCB, SCCB, Software Configuration Review Board [SCRB], and Operational Advisory Group [OAG]).
3. Provide status information and technical data to management and related organizations.
4. Participate in the auditing of software products to ensure correct, complete, consistent, and compliant products.
5. Perform internal review of SCM activities.

3.2g Output

Outputs from this activity are listed below.

1. Identified CR
2. Identified CSCI
3. Identified Technical Data
4. SCM Deficiency Report
5. Controlled CR
6. Controlled Technical Data
7. Controlled CSCI

8. CSA Reports
9. Audit Reports
10. Review Reports
11. Software Release

3.2h Exit Criteria

Retiring a software product satisfies the exit criteria.

3.2.1 Perform Configuration Identification (A21)

3.2.1a Purpose

The purpose of this process activity (A21) is to issue unique identifiers to each CSCI and related technical data and assign tracking numbers to CRs so that they may be tracked through each baseline release. Throughout the following sections, any reference to CSCI includes Software Units.

3.2.1b Role and Responsibility

The following are responsible for **Perform Configuration Identification**:

Role	Responsibility
SCM Manager	Oversee the establishment of the configuration management libraries.
SCM Organization	Issue the configuration identifier to the CSCI and related technical data. Verify that the correct project identifier has been used. Identify and assign a tracking number to the CR.
	Establish the CM libraries.
SCCB	Support the project manager recommending approval or disapproval of proposed engineering changes to a CSCI's current approved configuration and its documentation.

3.2.1c Entry Criteria

CSCI, technical data, or CRs have been submitted to the SCM organization.

3.2.1d Control

Control is provided by the DTP for configuration identification.

3.2.1e Input

Inputs to this activity are listed below.

1. CSCI
2. Technical Data
3. CRs
4. Defined Resources
5. Trained Personnel
6. Audit Reports
7. Review Reports

3.2.1f Process Activities

The process activities for **Perform Configuration Identification** are as follows:

1. Assign a unique identifier to project CSCIs and technical data that includes identification of the associated baseline.
2. Verify project identification for CSCIs and technical data.
3. Establish and oversee the establishment of CM libraries.
4. Assign tracking numbers to CRs.
5. Report any deficiency against this activity using the SCM deficiency report.

3.2.1g Output

Outputs from this activity are listed below.

1. Identified CR(s)
2. Identified CSCI
3. Identified Technical Data
4. SCM Deficiency Reports

3.2.1h Exit Criteria

Each CSCI and associated documentation have been formally identified. All required data has been collected, recorded, processed, and maintained for producing CSA reports. The CM libraries have been established.

3.2.2 Perform Configuration Control (A22)

3.2.2a Purpose

The purpose of this process activity (A22) is to maintain the integrity of the product's technical data and CSCI throughout its life cycle.

3.2.2b Role and Responsibility

The following are responsible for providing **Perform Configuration Control**:

Role	Responsibility
SCM Manager	Manage expeditious processing of proposed changes against approved baselines.
	Manage processing of authorized changes into approved baselines.
SCM Organization	Prevent incorporation of unauthorized changes into the baselines.
	Ensure integrity of baseline releases (e.g., of executable software, source code).
	Perform library functions of CSCI and technical data.
	Perform the administrative functions to support the software boards (e.g., SCCB, SCRB, OAG).
SCCB	Represent the interests of the project management and all project groups who may be affected by changes to the software baselines.
	Authorize the establishment of software baselines, review and approve the changes, and authorize the creation of software baseline products.

3.2.2c Entry Criteria

One of the following criteria must be met to initiate this activity.

1. Receive the approved functional baseline and any further configuration baselines for the CSCIs.
2. Receive the CSCI and technical data to be placed under library control.
3. Receive the CRs.

3.2.2d Control

The DTP provide control of this activity.

3.2.2e Input

Inputs to this activity are listed below.

1. CSCI Requests
2. Technical Data Requests
3. Identified Technical Data
4. SCCB Decisions
5. Identified CR
6. Defined Resources
7. Identified CSCI
8. Trained Personnel

3.2.2f Process Activities

The process activities for **Perform Configuration Control** are as follows:

1. Receive CSCI and technical data.
2. Place CSCI and technical data in the libraries.
3. Process CSCI and technical data requests.
4. Provide CRs to board members.
5. Provide administrative support to the boards.
6. Deliver software releases from controlled CSCIs and technical data, including associated changes to authorized baselines.
7. Report any deficiencies against this activity using the SCM deficiency report.

3.2.2g Output

Outputs from this activity are listed below.

1. Controlled CR
2. Controlled Technical Data
3. Controlled CSCI
4. SCM Deficiency Report
5. Software Release

3.2.2h Exit Criteria

Retiring a software product satisfies the exit criteria.

3.2.3 Perform Configuration Status Accounting (A23)

3.2.3a Purpose

The purpose of this process activity (A23) is to ensure reporting of accurate identification of each CSCI and associated technical data so that the necessary logistics support elements can be correctly programmed and made available in time to support the CSCI and its technical data. A well-designed and proven CSA will enhance management's capability to identify, produce, inspect, deliver, operate, and maintain CSCIs and associated technical data in a timely, efficient, economical manner.

3.2.3b Role and Responsibility

The following is responsible for **Perform CSA**:

Role	Responsibility
SCM Organization	Maintain and verify the data entered into the CSA system.

3.2.3c Entry Criteria

Entry criteria for this activity is the receipt of information on CSCIs, technical data, board decisions (e.g., CCB, SCCB, SCRB, or OAG), and CRs.

3.2.3d Control

Control of this activity is provided by the DTP.

3.2.3e Input

Inputs to this activity are listed below.

1. CSA Request
2. SCCB Decisions
3. Controlled CR
4. Controlled Technical Data
5. Defined Resources
6. Trained Personnel

3.2.3f Process Activities

The process activities for **Perform CSA** are as follows:

1. Receive CSCI and technical data for entry into the CSA system.
2. Generate CSA reports.
3. Report any deficiencies against this activity using the SCM deficiency report.

3.2.3g Output

Outputs from this activity are listed below.

1. CSA Reports
2. SCM Deficiency Report

3.2.3h Exit Criteria

Retiring a software product satisfies the exit criteria.

3.2.4 Perform Configuration Audits and Reviews (A24)

3.2.4a Purpose

The purposes of this process activity (A24) are to:

1. Report deficiencies in the CSCI and associated technical data found in a configuration audit.
2. Track resolution of those reported deficiencies found in a configuration audit.
3. Report deficiencies in SCM activities or products.
4. Track and provide resolution to deficiencies against SCM activities and products as a part of process improvement efforts.

3.2.4b Role and Responsibility

The following are responsible for **Perform Configuration Audits and Reviews**:

Role	Responsibility
SCM Manager	Provide resolution to reported deficiencies against SCM activities or products as part of process improvement efforts.
SCM Organization	Support the configuration audits (FCA and PCA) of CSCIs and their technical data, including tracking resolution of reported deficiencies.
	Provide the auditing activity or independent auditor (e.g., SQA) with the requested data to perform an audit of SCM activities.
	Perform informal review of SCM tasks and products to ensure conformance of SCM procedures.
SQA or Independent Auditor	Perform configuration audits (FCA and PCA) of CSCI and associated technical data.
	Perform audit of SCM activities.
	Report audit findings.

3.2.4c Entry Criteria

Configuration audits and independent audits of CSCI and associated technical data and SCM activities are scheduled. Informal reviews of SCM activities and products are planned.

3.2.4d Control

The DTP provides control for this activity.

3.2.4e Input

Inputs to this activity are listed below.

1. Controlled CSCI
2. Controlled Technical Data
3. Defined Resources
4. Trained Personnel
5. CSA Reports
6. Project SCMP
7. DTP

3.2.4f Process Activities

The process activities for **Perform Configuration Audits and Reviews** are as follows:

1. Support SQA or independent auditor requests for technical data and for CSCI and associated data.
2. Perform informal reviews of SCM tasks, DTP, and CSA reports.
3. Use DTP to generate or assist in the preparation of audit and review reports.
4. Report deficiencies against this activity using the SCM deficiency report.

3.2.4g Output

Outputs from this activity are listed below.

1. Audit Reports
2. Review Reports
3. SCM Deficiency Report

3.2.4h Exit Criteria

The configuration audit and review is completed, results are documented, and deficiencies have been resolved.

The audit and review of SCM activities and products is completed, results are documented, and deficiencies have been resolved.

Notes

1. Key Practices of the Capability Maturity Model, Version 1.1, February 1993.

REFERENCE

This document is adapted from the Navy's Software Process Definition, http://sepo.spawar.navy.mil/sepo/SCMProc.doc. April 1998.

APPENDIX X1 ACRONYMS AND ABBREVIATIONS

CCB	Configuration Control Board
CM	Configuration Management
CMM	Capability Maturity Model
CRG	Computer Resources Group
CSA	Configuration Status Accounting
CSC	Computer Software Component
CSCI	Computer Software Configuration Item
CSU	Computer Software Unit
DCR	Document Change Request
DoD	Department of Defense
DTP	Desktop Procedure
FCA	Functional Configuration Audit
FCD	Functional Configuration Documentation
NAVAIRSYSCOM	Naval Air Systems Command
NDS	Nondevelopmental Software
OAG	Operational Advisory Group
PCA	Physical Configuration Audit
SCCB	Software Configuration Control Board
SCM	Software Configuration Management
SCMP	Software Configuration Management Plan
SCRB	Software Change Review Board
SEI	Software Engineering Institute
SQA	Software Quality Assurance
SRR	Software Requirements Review
STD	Standard

APPENDIX X2 SOFTWARE CONFIGURATION MANAGEMENT

Briefing Evaluation Check Sheet

Key Practice and Sub-practices	Yes	No	Ex
I. Commitment to Perform			
1. The project follows a written organizational policy for implementing software configuration management (SCM).			
a. Responsibility for SCM for each project is explicitly assigned.			
b. SCM is implemented throughout the project's life cycle.			
c. SCM is implemented for externally deliverable software products, designated internal software work products, and designated support tools used inside the project (e.g., compilers).			
d. The projects establish or have access to a repository for storing configuration items/units and the associated SCM records.			
e. The software baselines and SCM activities are audited on a periodic basis.			
II. Ability to Perform			
1. A board having the authority for managing the project's software baselines (i.e., a software configuration control board — SCCB) exists or is established. The SCCB:			
a. Authorizes the establishment of software baselines and the identification of configuration items/units.			
b. Represents the interests of the project manager and all groups who may be affected by changes to the software baselines.			
c. Reviews and authorizes changes to the software baselines.			
d. Authorizes creation of products from the software baseline library.			
2. A group that is responsible for coordinating and implementing SCM for the project (i.e., the SCM group) exists. The SCM Group coordinates or implements:			
a. Creation and management of the project's software baseline library.			
b. Development, maintenance, and distribution of the SCM plans, standards, and procedures.			

c. The identification of the set of work products to be placed under SCM.				
d. Management of the access to the software baseline library.				
e. Updates of the software baselines.				
f. Creation of products from the software baseline library.				
g. Recording of SCM actions.				
h. Production and distribution of SCM reports.				
3. Adequate resources and funding are provided for performing the SCM activities.				
a. A manager is assigned specific responsibilities for SCM.				
b. Tools to support the SCM activities are made available.				
4. Members of the SCM group are trained in the objectives, procedures, and methods for performing their SCM activities.				
5. Members of the software engineering group and other software-related groups are trained to perform their SCM activities.				
III. Activities Performed				
1. A SCM plan is prepared for each software project according to a documented procedure.				
a. The SCM plan is developed in the early stages of, and in parallel with, the overall project planning.				
b. The SCM plan is reviewed by the affected groups.				
c. The SCM plan is managed and controlled.				

Yes   Evidence exists that this sub-practice is in place and followed in a *formal* manner.

No   There was weak or no evidence that this sub-practice is documented, in place or followed in any manner.

Ex   Indications of exceptionally strong implementation of this sub-practice which could serve as a template for *other* SSA.

Source: CMU/SEI-93-TR-25 (12-72-12-83)

SOFTWARE CONFIGURATION MANAGEMENT

Briefing Evaluation Check Sheet

Key Practice and Sub-practices	Yes	No	Ex
2. A documented and approved SCM plan is used as the basis for performing the SCM activities. The plan covers:			
a. The SCM activities to be performed, the schedule of activities, the assigned responsibilities, and the resources required (including staff, tools, and computer facilities).			
b. The SCM requirements and activities to be performed by the software engineering group and other software software-related groups.			
3. A configuration management library system is established as a repository for the software baselines. The library system:			
a. Supports multiple control levels of SCM.			
b. Provides for the storage and retrieval of configuration items/units.			
c. Provides for the sharing and transfer of configuration items/units between the affected groups and between control levels within the library.			
d. Helps in the use of product standards for configuration items/units.			
e. Provides for the storage and retrieval of archive versions of configuration items/units.			
f. Helps to ensure correct creation of products from the baseline library.			
g. Provides for the storage, update, and retrieval of SCM records.			
h. Supports production of SCM reports.			
i. Provides for the maintenance of the library structure and contents.			
4. The software work products to be placed under configuration management are identified.			
a. The configuration items/units are selected based on documented criteria.			
b. The configuration items/units are assigned unique identifiers.			

c. The characteristics of each configuration item/unit are specified.			
d. The software baselines to which each configuration item/unit belongs are specified.			
e. The point in its development that each configuration item/unit is placed under configuration management is specified.			
f. The person responsible for each configuration item/unit (i.e., the owner, from a configuration management point of view) is identified.			
5. Change requests and problem reports for all configuration items/units are initiated, recorded, reviewed, approved, and tracked according to a documented procedure.			
6. Changes to baselines are controlled according to a documented procedure. This procedure typically specifies that:			
a. Reviews and/or regression tests are performed to ensure that changes have not caused unintended effects on the baseline.			
b. Only configuration items/units that are approved by the SCCB are entered into the software baseline library.			
c. Configuration items/units are checked in and out in a manner that maintains the correctness and integrity of the software baseline library.			
7. Products from the software baseline library are created and their release is controlled according to a documented procedure. This procedure typically specifies that:			
a. The SCCB authorizes the creation of products from the software baseline library.			
b. Products from the software baseline library, for both internal and external use, are built only from configuration items/units in the software baseline library.			

Yes Evidence exists that this sub-practice is in place and followed in a *formal* manner.

No   There was weak or no evidence that this sub-practice is documented, in place or followed in any manner.

Ex   Indications of exceptionally strong implementation of this sub-practice which could serve as a template for other SSA.

Source: CMU/SEI-93-TR-25 (L2-72-L2-83)

SOFTWARE CONFIGURATION MANAGEMENT

Briefing Evaluation Check Sheet

Key Practice and Sub-practices	Yes	No	Ex
8. The status of configuration items/units is recorded according to a documented procedure. This procedure typically specifies that:			
a. The configuration management actions are recorded in sufficient detail so that the content and status of each configuration item/unit are known and previous versions can be recovered.			
b. The current status and history (i.e., changes and other actions) of each configuration item/unit are maintained.			
9. Standard reports documenting the SCM activities and the contents of the software baseline are developed and made available to affected groups and individuals.			
10. Software baseline audits are conducted according to a documented procedure. This procedure typically specifies that:			
a. There is adequate preparation for the audit.			
b. The integrity of software baselines is assessed.			
c. The structure and facilities of the configuration management library.			
d. The completeness and correctness of the software baseline library contents are reviewed.			
e. Compliance with applicable SCM standards and procedures is verified.			
f. The results of the audit are reported to the project software manager.			
g. Action items from the audit are tracked to closure.			
IV. Measurement and Analysis			
1. Measurements are made and used to determine the status of the SCM activities.			
V. Verifying Implementation			
1. The SCM activities are reviewed with senior management on a periodic basis.			

2. The SCM activities are reviewed with the project manager on both a periodic and event-driven basis.			
3. The SCM group periodically audits software baselines to verify that they conform to the documentation that defines them.			
4. The software quality assurance group reviews and/or audits the activities and work products for SCM and reports the results. At a minimum, the reviews and/or audits verify:			
a. Compliance with the SCM standards and procedures by: h the SCM group, h the SCCB, h the software engineering group, and h other software-related groups.			
b. Occurrence of periodic software baseline audits.			
Notes:			

Yes   Evidence exists that this sub-practice is in place and followed in a *formal* manner.

No   There was weak or no evidence that this sub-practice is documented, in place or followed in any manner.

Ex   Indications of exceptionally strong implementation of this sub-practice which could serve as a template for other SSA.

Source: CMU/SEI-93-TR-25 (L2-72-L2-83)

Appendix Y

SUPPLIER CM MARKET ANALYSIS QUESTIONNAIRE

1. Do you have a viable engineering drawing and part numbering system? Explain.
2. What is your method of re-identifying parts when changes are made? How do you relate part number changes to the serial numbers of the deliverable item?
3. How do you manage item modifications?
4. How do you inform your own personnel and customers of changes to your product?
5. Do you currently operate using all or any portions of any recognized CM standard?
6. Do you employ a formal change review process? Do you operate a change control board? A Material Review Board?
7. How do you assure the currency, integrity, and consistency of:
   — Specifications
   — Software
   — Documentation
   — Service Manuals
   — Operating Manuals
8. Do you have a release procedure for documentation? Explain.
9. Do you apply serial numbers and or lot numbers to your products? How are they assigned and marked?
10. By what method do you assure that products delivered to your customers comply with the customers order and specification?
11. What type of communication relative to change activity do you have with your suppliers?
12. Do you ever install refurbished components in your products?

13. If a product line is dropped, when is a customer notified? What options are offered the customer?

14. If a component that is supplied to the customer as a spare part is being changed, how and when is the customer notified?

15. How do you support your products? What options are typically available to the customer?

Index

Note: Italicized pages refer to illustrations and tables